D1600508

2005

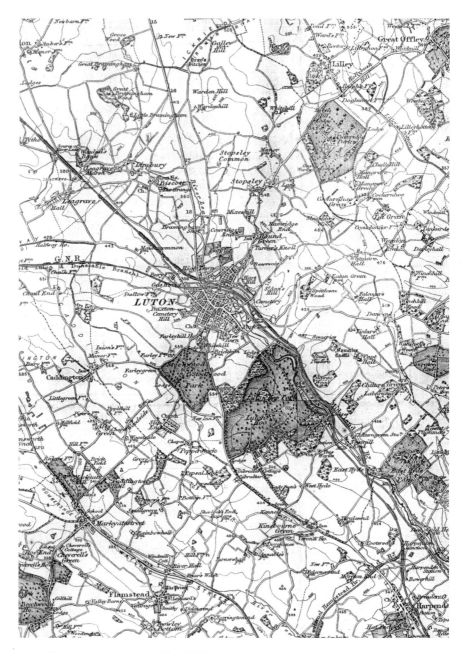

Map of Luton and the hamlets May 1891
Ordnance Survey 1" Bedfordshire
Electrotype taken in 1892
Railways October 1889 [JD]

THE PUBLICATIONS OF THE BEDFORDSHIRE
HISTORICAL RECORD SOCIETY
VOLUME 84

THE EDUCATION AND EMPLOYMENT
OF GIRLS IN LUTON
1874–1924

WIDENING OPPORTUNITIES
AND
LOST FREEDOMS

Anne Allsopp

THE BEDFORDSHIRE HISTORICAL RECORD SOCIETY

THE BOYDELL PRESS

First published 2005

A publication of
Bedfordshire Historical Record Society
published by The Boydell Press
an imprint of Boydell & Brewer Ltd
PO Box 9, Woodbridge, Suffolk IP12 3DF, UK
and of Boydell & Brewer Inc.
668 Mt Hope Avenue, Rochester, NY 14620, USA
website: www.boydellandbrewer.com

ISBN 0 85155 070 3

ISSN 0067–4826

This volume has been published with the
generous help of the Simon Whitbread Trust

Details of previous volumes are available from
Boydell & Brewer Ltd

A CIP catalogue for this book is available
from the British Library

This publication is printed on acid-free paper

Printed in Great Britain by
Cromwell Press, Trowbridge, Wiltshire

Contents

Illustrations

Tables

For my husband,
Basil

Acknowledgements

The choice of subject for this study was triggered by Dr Stephen Bunker who remarked that the education of Luton women had never been the subject of serious research. As I am 'a Luton girl' the idea of filling the gap appealed and this book is based on the subsequent doctoral thesis which I presented at the Institute of Education (University of London) where I was privileged to work with Emeritus Professor Richard Aldrich. I offer him my very sincere thanks for his unfailing kindness and support.

Much of the research was undertaken at Luton Museum and Art Gallery where I received willing help in my search for documents, pictures and other sources of information. I am particularly grateful to Dr Elizabeth Adey, Curatorial Staff, who has helped me with diligence and friendship throughout all the years it has taken me to finish this work. I also thank Mrs Marian Nichols who has an unparalleled knowledge of the hat industry and Mr Chris Grabham who helped to find photographs and put many of the illustrations on disc. Photographs from the Luton Museum Service are acknowledged as (LM) while those which originated with the *Luton News* and are held at the museum are acknowledged as (LM/*LN*).

I have also spent numberless hours at the Bedford and Luton Record and Archive Service where I received the same kind of enthusiastic help from the members of staff. I thank them too.

Luton High School for Girls was a significant part of the educational scene in Luton. Many of the archives remained in the school building, which is now occupied by Denbigh High School. With the permission of the headmistress, Mrs Yasmin Bevan, I was allowed to visit the school on many occasions to access useful documents. I have to thank the members of staff who helped me, most cheerfully and enthusiastically, and I am grateful to the governors of the school who subsequently gave permission for all the archives to be transferred to Luton Museum and Art Gallery for safe-keeping.

Mr A.J. Cook, the former headmaster of Moorlands School, went out of his way to find relevant documents concerning the period under consideration and I do thank him for his time and trouble. Mrs P. Weatherley welcomed me most warmly to St George's School in Harpenden and helped me to look through the old admission books. Sister Monica Coleman, one-time member of staff at St Dominic's Convent School, responded to my enquiries and sent me two histories of the order of nuns which ran the school. Her contribution was invaluable.

Mrs Patricia Gillespie has a complete collection of the *Sheaf* magazines from the Modern School for Girls and she allowed me to copy the editions which related to the years covered in this study. Mr James Dyer has transcribed the Stopsley logbooks and he very kindly allowed me to use them for my chapter on rural schools (Chapter Eight). He also lent me photographs and maps.

Miss Edith Webb, who was a pupil of the secondary school, a student teacher and, later, a headmistress in the town, recorded her reminiscences. She allowed me to read these and also told me much more in lively conversations in her home. Sadly she died before this study was finished. However, I think she knew how much I appreciated her help. Similarly, other ladies have helped me with their memories; I thank Mrs Joyce Browne, Mrs Rosamond Hayward and Mrs Vera Robson.

Being one of a generation which grew up without the help of computers, I frequently came across problems which were beyond my ability to solve. I have to thank family and friends who helped at different times and in different ways, but most of all I am grateful to my son, David, who always came to the rescue when the IT world was collapsing around me.

James Collett-White has edited this volume. He read it very carefully and gave much useful advice. He provided a different perspective, particularly on the relationship between Luton and the county town. I thank him too.

Throughout all these years my husband, Basil, has supported me and believed in me. Without his support the production of this book would have been very much more difficult.

Dr Anne Allsopp
May 2005

Abbreviations

ACP	Associate of the College of Preceptors
ARAM	Associate of the Royal Academy of Music
ARCM	Associate of the Royal College of Music
BCC	Bedfordshire County Council
BEC	Bedfordshire Education Committee
BHG	Beech Hill Girls' School
BHRS	Bedfordshire Historical Record Society
BLARS	Bedfordshire and Luton Archive and Record Service
CMO	County Medical Officer
CRO	County Record Office (now BLARS)
DHS	Denbigh High School
DRG	Denbigh Road Girls' School
FRCO	Fellow of the Royal College of Organists
HGS	Higher Grade School
HMI	His/Her Majesty's Inspector
HRG	Hitchin Road Girls' School
HRGI	Hitchin Road Girls' and Infants' School
HRI	Hitchin Road Infants' School
JD	James Dyer
JP	Justice of the Peace
LEA	Local Education Authority
LEC	Luton Education Committee
LHS	Luton High School for Girls
LL.A	Lady Literate in Arts
LMAG	Luton Museum and Art Gallery
LMS	Luton Modern School
LN	*The Luton News*
LSB	Luton School Board
LTC	Luton Town Council
MO	Medical Officer
NLCS	North London Collegiate School
NRS	Norton Road School
NTS	New Town Street School
P-t.	Pupil-teacher
RBA	Royal Society of British Artists
SMG	St Matthew's Girls' School
TC	Training College
TIC	Technical Instruction Committee
USDL	The Board of the United School District of Luton
VAD	Voluntary Aid Detachment
VD	Volunteer Decoration

Introduction

This book complements two others which have already been published in this series. Volume 78, *Strawopolis* (1999), looked at the transformation of Luton in the middle of the nineteenth century 'from a market town, where hats were made, to principally a manufacturing centre'. Volume 82, *Vauxhall Motors and the Luton Economy, 1900–2002* (2003), explored the life of the town in the twentieth century when the dominant hat industry was replaced by an equally dominant motor industry. This study (Volume 84) has concentrated on the changing role of women against these backgrounds.

The year 1874 was significant as it was the one in which the first Luton School Board was elected. In the same year education became compulsory for the town's children. New schools were built and by 1924 elementary schools were offering a wider and more stimulating style of curriculum. Of particular importance was the opening of a secondary school for girls under the leadership of a dedicated headmistress who brought new vision to the furtherance of higher education for girls. By 1924 the school had established a tradition of excellence and had laid foundations for the future. This book has therefore concentrated on the years between 1874 and 1924.

The focus of this study was originally intended to be the provision of schooling, but it soon became clear that the demands of the traditional hat industry and those of the School Board were closely intertwined. The theme therefore ceased to be education alone but the fascinating relationship between education and the changing patterns of employment for women.

Luton itself is worthy of serious study because its character is in some respects unique. In 1874 political power in the town lay with businessmen, mostly self-made, who ruled over every aspect of urban life and saw that prosperity could be achieved within the hat trade and without academic qualifications. Consequently, before 1874, education, particularly for girls, had not been given high priority. This is reflected in illiteracy rates in Luton, which, in 1856, were 44% opposed to the national average of 35%.

One reason for this was the existence of a domestic industry which dominated children's lives. Women, too, could spend the whole of their working lives in the hat industry and they were undoubtedly central to the prosperity of the town. Whether or not Luton could be described as matriarchal is open to debate. From an economic and numerical point of view, however, and also when women's role within the family is considered, it may well be true to say that Luton was a matriarchal town.

By 1924 the employment scene had changed and the wealth of the town was based on a much wider range of industries. Women were being employed in some capacities in these new industries, usually because they were cheaper to employ than men, but it has to be asked why they chose to do so. The role of women was being transformed from a dominant to a more subsidiary one. Their old freedoms were being lost, but new opportunities eventually brought another kind of freedom. The main theme of this research concerns the working classes, but the lives of the more affluent middle classes are also considered.

By 1924 Luton had also been influenced by the Education Acts of 1870, 1902 and 1918 and by two major wars. The daughters of women who had grown up within the boundaries of the hat industry now accepted the constraints of compulsory education and looked to wider horizons. Commerce and industry offered new opportunities and, for the few, a college education was a possibility.

While it is not the intention to make a detailed study of Bedford, it is nevertheless important at appropriate points to look at the relationship between an independently minded Luton and the more conservative county town whose prosperity was to a large extent based on the success of the endowed Harpur Trust schools. By 1903 Bedfordshire County Council had assumed responsibility for technical, secondary and continuing education, as well as elementary schooling in the hamlets of Luton: Hyde, Leagrave, Limbury-cum-Biscot and Stopsley.

Chapter One looks at Luton's religious, political and economic background and the influences which created the town's independent and distinctive character. It demonstrates how Luton, unlike Bedford, did not have a strong tradition of schooling, but responded conscientiously to external pressures. The importance of the hat trade in Luton is crucial, especially in relation to the economic power of women.

In Chapter Two women's employment is considered from another perspective. Census figures were assessed, *Kelly's Directories* were looked at in an attempt to record developments in private enterprise while newspaper advertisements give an indication of the changing attitudes of employers and employees.

Although the introduction of Sunday schools preceded the date chosen for the start of this research, their contribution to the education of the working classes can never be over-estimated. In Chapter Three a study is made of the way the movement flourished in Luton, with the result that many thousands of children received basic schooling within their folds. Sunday schools also had a considerable influence on the social life of the town throughout the period under consideration.

The School Board era is addressed in Chapter Four. The responses of the School Board and of Luton parents and pupils to such matters as compulsory school attendance, half-time education, Labour Certificates and the teaching of needlework are examined.

Another form of employment, open to intelligent working-class girls who wished to continue their education, was pupil-teaching. Questions are asked as to why girls chose to become teachers rather than follow their peers into the hat trade, which offered a more independent way of life. Chapter Five describes the provision of training within the elementary school system and some case studies have been compiled.

In Chapter Six the increasing involvement of Bedfordshire County Council with the education of children aged over fourteen is examined. This includes technical and evening education and the training of monitors, pupil-teachers and student teachers.

Schooling in the early twentieth century, which was the shared responsibility of Bedfordshire and Luton, is assessed in Chapter Seven. The widening curriculum, education for children with special needs and the ideology of teaching girls to assume a domestic role are considered, particularly in the context of Empire and war. Emphasis is also given to the relationship between education and broader employment opportunities through the work of the Juvenile Employment Agency.

Rural schools, while sharing many of the experiences of urban schools, had their own set of problems, many of them based on their isolation and the fact that they were often considered to have a lower status. Luton and the hamlets are ideally suited to a study of this kind because after 1903 the Bedfordshire Education Committee administered the hamlet schools, while the urban schools remained the responsibility of the Luton Education Committee (LEC). The particular identity of the rural schools is noted in Chapter Eight.

Chapter Nine is concerned with the wide variety of both formal and informal provision, which suited girls' hopes and aspirations, perceived needs, religious beliefs and social expectations.

Chapter Ten is crucial because it focuses on the establishment of secondary education, which was, at least in theory, offered for the first time to children from poorer families. Attitudes towards the secondary school, which was inevitably élitist, are considered and it is interesting to contemplate whether the town and the school lived comfortably together.

The Conclusion demonstrates the extent to which Luton's unique character had changed by 1924. Girls were undoubtedly enjoying an increasing range of educational and employment opportunities, but many of their traditional freedoms and much of their economic independence had diminished.

Chapter One

Luton: *Scientiae et labori detur*[1]

This chapter looks at the character and identity of Luton and notes how the lives of its women changed significantly between 1874 and 1924, particularly with regard to education and employment. To understand the development of education and the widening of employment prospects for girls in Luton it is necessary to look at the background of the town and the surrounding area in the context of the straw hat industry. Luton is in the south of Bedfordshire, about twenty miles from Bedford and by 1874 it had a larger population than any other town in the county. This study does not look at Bedford in detail, but comparisons need to be made between the two towns. Similarities would be hard to find;[2] Luton has been described as a town built on straw whereas Bedford prospered as the result of the endowments of William Harpur.[3] 'Relations between the industrial town and the rural county, dominated by Bedford, were rarely good. Indeed, Luton had long since ceased to feel any common bond with Bedfordshire, whose values, politics and economy were so very different to its own.'[4]

Previous histories of Luton have included the hamlets of East and West Hyde, Leagrave, Limbury-cum-Biscot and Stopsley, and this study has followed the same pattern.[5] From an educational point of view this adds interest, as the hamlets were administered at different times by the Luton and Bedfordshire education authorities. Table 1 provides details of the population growth of Luton, the hamlets and Bedford. The figures for the civil parish of Luton from 1841 to 1891 include the township of Luton and the hamlets of East and West Hyde, Leagrave, Limbury and Stopsley. East and West Hyde were conjoined as the civil parish of Hyde in 1895. Leagrave, Limbury and part of Stopsley were absorbed into Luton Borough in 1928, and the remainder of Stopsley followed in 1933.[6]

---

[1] Translation of the town's motto: 'Due to knowledge and labour.' (*Luton Official Guide 1991*).
[2] S. Bunker, *Strawopolis: Luton Transformed 1840–1876* (BHRS Vol. 78, 1999), pp. 203, 218–221. This lack of affinity still exists.
[3] *Victoria County History: Bedfordshire* (University of London Institute of Historical Research, 1972), p. 149.
[4] S. Bunker and T. Wood, *A Hatful of Talent: The Founding of the University of Luton* (University of Luton Press, 1994), p. 5.
[5] For example, W. Austin, *The History of Luton and Its Hamlets: Being a History of the Old Parish and Manor of Luton in Bedfordshire* (The County Press Newport, 1928).
[6] C.J. Pickford, *Bedfordshire Population Figures 1801–1991* (Bedfordshire County Record Office, 1994), n. 55. Figures for males and females are given in Table 3.

Table 1. Population figures for Luton, the hamlets and Bedford 1841–1931[7]

Parish	1841	1851	1861	1871	1881	1891	1901	1911	1921	1931
Bedford	9,178	11,693	13,413	16,850	19,533	28,023	35,144	39,183	40,242	40,554
Luton civil parish	7,748	12,787	17,821	20,733	26,140	32,401				
Luton township	5,827	10,648	15,329	17,317						
Luton borough						23,960	30,053	36,404	49,978	57,075	68,523
Hyde							557	649	671	636
Leagrave							801	1,270	1,643	
Limbury							377	972	1,534	
Stopsley							787	943	1,140	1,474

The figures in Table 1 indicate that the population of Hyde remained comparatively static, Stopsley grew slowly and steadily. Leagrave's numbers doubled in twenty years but the population of Limbury-cum-Biscot quadrupled in that time. This growth is reflected in the amount of school provision. Hyde did not need a new school, although one was built to replace the old building after the Board took control in 1898, and Stopsley was given new buildings in 1909 and 1912. Schools were built at Leagrave and Limbury in 1875, and in 1913 another larger school, nearer to the town and known as Norton Road, was built for the older children.

The figures given in Table 2 demonstrate that the population of Luton was three times greater in 1911 than it had been in 1871. This is a much greater rise than Bedfordshire which had grown by less than 50%, and Britain where the population growth was slightly more than 50%. Population statistics demonstrate that Luton was a thriving town and played a dominant role in the economy of the county.

Table 2. Population figures (in thousands) for Luton, Bedfordshire and Britain 1841–1931

	1841	1851	1861	1871	1881	1891	1901	1911	1921	1931
Luton[8]	6.0	11.0	15.0	17.0	24.0	30.0	36.0	50.0	57/60.0	69/70.0
Bedfordshire[9]	108.0	124.0	135.0	146.0	149.0	161.0	172.0	195.0	206.0	221.0
Britain[10]	15,914.1	17,927.6	20,066.3	22,712.2	25,974.4	29,002.5	32,527.8	36,070.5	42,749.0	44,795.0

---

[7] Ibid.

[8] Ibid., pp. 24–25. There are two figures for 1921 and 1931, the first for the year concerned and the second for the area of the town as given at the subsequent census. See Figure 3b.

[9] B.R. Mitchell and P. Deane, *Abstract of British Historical Statistics* (Cambridge University Press, 1962), pp. 20 and 22. See Figure 3b.

[10] J. Walvin, *A Child's World: A Social History of English Childhood 1800–1914* (Penguin, 1982), p. 19. See Figure 3a. The 1921 and 1931 figures are taken from *The Oxford History of England 1914–1945*, pp. 164 and 301n.

Hyde, which was influenced by two large estates,[11] lies three miles to the south-east of Luton on the Hertfordshire border. It was, and still is, an agricultural area, detached from the town by the Luton Hoo estate. A railway line from Dunstable to Welwyn via Luton was opened in 1858 and included a station at Hyde. Another line from the Midlands to London via Bedford and Luton was opened in 1868, also with a station at Hyde (Chiltern Green). Access to Luton from Hyde was therefore easy.

Leagrave is about two and a half miles north of Luton near the source of the River Lea, which runs through Luton and Hyde on its way to join the River Thames. In the early years of the twentieth century, Leagrave became known as the 'blockers' seaside'[12] because Luton families used to gather there, especially at Whitsun.[13] A station was built at Leagrave on the Midlands to London line. Limbury-cum-Biscot, to the north of the town, lay between Leagrave and Luton, but, although nearer to Luton than the other hamlets, did not enjoy the same ease of access to the town as they did.

Stopsley covered a wide area on a ridge of the Chiltern Hills, north-west of Luton. Employment in the hamlet was based on agriculture and straw hats, but brick-making was also significant.[14] The railway line did not run through Stopsley but, between 1908 and 1932, Luton had trams, some of which served Round Green which was on the road to Stopsley.[15]

Luton, its Character and Identity

At the beginning of the nineteenth century, Luton was a small market town of about 3,000 inhabitants but, by 1875, it had become 'a thriving industrial centre with a population of over 20,000'.[16] Luton began to flourish above other towns in the area when it became the centre of the straw hat trade, a fact recognized by Sir Robert Peel who claimed that the houses were all built on straw.[17] The name 'Strawopolis' has come to symbolize the strong links which existed between the town and the trade.[18] This was of supreme importance to girls and women, who did most of the work, for it provided them with a large measure of independence, both in time and money.

Commentaries on the history of Luton generally acknowledge that the town is in many respects unusual or even unique. This observation has been endorsed by A. Godfrey who looked at a variety of different towns for his series of Ordnance Survey re-prints. He suggested that Luton's history is quite unlike that of any other

---

[11] Luton Hoo and the Ames family estate.
[12] C.J. Peaple, *The Blockers' Seaside: A Selective History of Leagrave* (Challney Community College, 1980). A 'blocker' shaped the hats on a wooden or metal block.
[13] This was known locally as Leagrave Marsh.
[14] J. Dyer, *The Stopsley Book* (The Book Castle, 1998), pp. 184–187.
[15] C. Brown, *Luton Trams: The Story of a Small System 1908–1932* (Irwell Press, 1999).
[16] J.G. Dony, 'How Luton became a Borough', *Bedfordshire Magazine*, Vol. 15, No. 116 (Spring 1976) p. 135. See maps.
[17] The son of the more famous Sir Robert Peel (1788–1850). This attack on Luton was made in the House of Commons in 1867 by Sir Robert Peel Jnr, MP for Tamworth, during a debate on parliamentary seats. Peel also claimed that the fact 'that there were more women than men in Luton devalued its claim, as in all likelihood the morals of the place would not be that commensurate with the standards expected of a parliamentary constituency'. S. Bunker, *Strawopolis*, p. 226.
[18] S. Bunker, *Strawopolis*, p. 247. Also quoted in the *Drapers' Record 1902*: 'An illustrated description of Luton, the "Strawopolis" of England'.

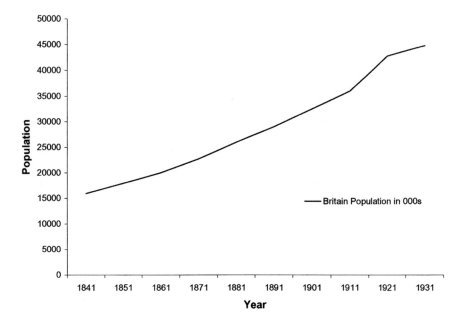

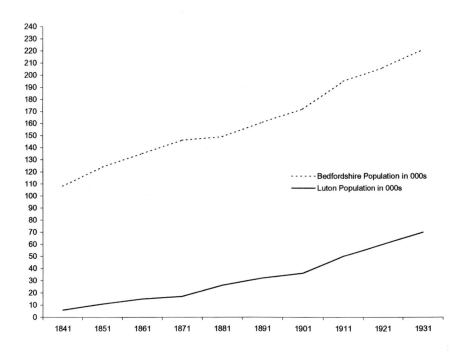

1a & b. Population Graphs of Britain, Bedfordshire and Luton 1841–1931

town.[19] Of particular note were its fiercely independent character and the economic power of its women. Grundy and Titmuss note that there was no leisured class 'for in Luton almost everyone earn[ed] his living'.[20] Economic prosperity, combined with the lack of an established patriarchy, ensured that the character of the town remained highly individualistic.[21]

'Individualistic' may even be an understatement. When Luton was campaigning for its charter, which was awarded in 1876, objectors protested that 'the population of Luton . . . although most industrious and worthy, consisted largely of working men who, from exuberance of spirits or other causes, were not so amenable to control as persons living at Bedford'.[22] This 'exuberance of spirits' may be linked to the fact that Luton had a history of crime associated with drinking.[23] This was demonstrated in 1883 when there was rioting as a protest against a Sabbath parade by the Salvation Army.[24] Austin records how 'the rowdy element, ever on the look-out for occasions on which it can have a free hand, emerged from the slums of the town and endeavoured to suppress the "Army" processions with violence'.[25] Law and order broke down again after the 1895 election when windows were broken throughout the town and many Lutonians had to spend the night in the fields not daring to return.[26] The Riot Act was read twice and forty-six Metropolitan police were sent for. There was more rioting the following evening and reinforcements of mounted police arrived from London. Some people, including several police, were injured, and twelve men were brought before the magistrates.[27]

However, the most significant riot, described as 'the most outstanding event in the history of Luton in the last hundred years',[28] took place in 1919 as a result of great bitterness and resentment over the organization of the official peace celebrations. Worries about unemployment were compounded by the Town Council's plans to ask ex-servicemen to pay for a celebration banquet while council members could attend without charge. There was also considerable bickering over the planning and location of a peace parade. Hostility built up slowly, but became a full-scale riot[29] and this time not only were extra police sent for but the army was forced to intervene.[30] However, they failed to prevent the town hall, which had been opened in 1847, from being burnt and destroyed.[31] The women of the town were not all innocent bystanders; in fact, the chief constable claimed that they 'were as violent as the

[19] A. Godfrey, *Old Ordnance Survey Maps Luton 1922*, The Godfrey Reprinted Edition of 1924. No details were given to justify this claim.
[20] F. Grundy and R.M. Titmuss, *Report on Luton* (Gibbs, Bamforth & Co. Ltd, 1945), p. 21.
[21] S. Bunker, *Strawopolis*, p. 186.
[22] F. Grundy and R.M. Titmuss, *Report on Luton*, p. 21.
[23] S. Bunker, *Strawopolis*, pp. 153–158.
[24] *The Luton and District Year Book and Directory (1908)*, p. 60.
[25] W. Austin, *The History of Luton and Its Hamlets* Vol. 1, p. 199.
[26] J. Dyer and J.G. Dony, *The Story of Luton* (White Crescent Press, 1975), p. 150.
[27] *Luton Year Book (1908)*, p. 61.
[28] J.G. Dony, 'The 1919 Peace Riots in Luton' in P. Bell, ed., *Worthington George Smith and Other Studies* (BHRS Vol. 57, 1978), p. 227.
[29] J. Craddock, *'Where They Burnt the Town Hall Down': Luton, the First World War and the Peace Day Riots of July 1919* (The Book Castle, 1999), p. 93.
[30] Ibid., p. 98.
[31] Ibid., p. 8.

men'.[32] Indeed one woman was among the troublemakers brought before Bedford Assizes and seven appeared at Luton Borough Court.[33] Luton had gained itself a reputation, one consequence being that some seaside landladies, having heard the news, cancelled holiday accommodation bookings which had been made by people living in Luton.[34]

In Luton some administration was in the hands of the Lord of the Manor[35] and the Vestry, but in 1834 the Board of Guardians took over control of the Poor Law and in 1850 a Board of Health, which virtually ran the town, was set up. In 1874 a School Board was elected. However, there was seen to be a need for a more formal system of administration and a charter giving municipal borough status was granted on 26 February 1876.[36] Those who had held office in the Board of Health became officers of the Town Council, so Luton's small-town hierarchy still had control, but in a different capacity.[37] The men who ran the town's industries were members of the Chamber of Commerce, the Town Council and the local Liberal party. They were frequently members of the same religious denomination and were often related to one another by marriage.[38] This small-town atmosphere continued at least until 1945, as Grundy and Titmuss note:

> There is a richness of informal social intercourse, a diversity of small groups pursuing their interests unobtrusively, ample opportunity for discussing the affairs of the town and many an exchange of ideas by chance meetings; for those who are interested in the future of the town still know each other by sight and know where to find each other at most times of the day.[39]

Luton was both individualistic and independent, characteristics which were reflected in its political and religious allegiances. The Established Church had a significant role to play and its power and influence were felt in the field of education. The forceful Vicar of Luton, the Reverend James O'Neill,[40] believed most fervently that Luton schools should come under the Church's protection and patronage. He did not approve of the School Board, but apparently became a member mainly, it would appear, in an attempt to block any ideas which did not agree with his own. The influence of the Church has to be acknowledged, but Luton was predominantly Nonconformist and Liberal. Bunker has pointed out that urban Liberalism, which was committed to free trade and suited 'Luton's entrepreneurs', was the most important political power until after the First World War.[41] However, there was very little sympathy between Luton Liberals and 'Bedfordshire Whigs . . . dominated by the patronage of the Russells'. Luton Liberals had less empathy with

32   Ibid., p. 116.
33   Ibid., Appendix 8.
34   Ibid., Appendix 9.
35   F. Grundy and R.M. Titmuss, *Report on Luton*, p. 21. Links with the manor ended in 1911.
36   J.G. Dony, 'How Luton became a Borough', *Bedfordshire Magazine*, Vol. 15, No. 116 (Spring 1976), pp. 135–139.
37   Ibid., p. 139.
38   S. Bunker, R. Holgate and M. Nichols, *The Changing Face of Luton* (The Book Castle, 1993), p. 59.
39   F. Grundy and R.M. Titmuss, *Report on Luton*, p. 23.
40   K. Rogers, *The Stories and Secrets of Luton's Medieval Jewel* (St Mary's Parochial Church Council, 2000). The Reverend James O'Neill was Vicar of the Parish between 1862 and 1896.
41   S. Bunker, *Strawopolis*, p. 213.

Bedfordshire Liberals than they had with Luton Conservatives.[42] Bunker shows that the links between local commerce and religious outlook – 'good stewardship, hard work, honesty, self-discipline, sobriety, punctuality, plainness – all suited a town the commercial nature of which precisely required these standards of personal conduct. So much of Luton's trade, the purchase of quantities of straw plait for instance, relied upon the above virtues, particularly honesty.'[43]

Grundy and Titmuss note that 'Nonconformity gave a philosophical background to business success and the local control of its organization well suited the temper of the district.'[44] The Quaker family of Brown was important both as an employer and as a provider of education.[45] H. Janes described a Luton around the turn of the century where 'denominational barriers meant little. . . . Non-conformity was then at the height of its power. The Church of England was poor by comparison; the Roman Catholics hardly existed . . . but Methodists, Baptists and Congregationalists were strong.'[46] According to Janes, everybody went to a place of worship.[47] He says that at the beginning of the twentieth century 'optimism was in the air' and there was 'strong religious fervour'. At a mission held by Gipsy Smith, the Christian evangelist, three thousand people were converted.[48]

Luton has been described as an 'Adamless Eden'.[49] This was certainly an exaggeration, but it points to the dominance of working-class women in the town, particularly during the busy season when girls and women moved in from the villages.

Table 3. Population figures for Luton township and municipal borough 1871–1921[50]

	Males	Females	Total
1871	7,349	9,968	17,317
1881	11,654	14,486	26,140
1891	14,504	17,897	32,401
1901	16,424	19,980	36,404
1911	23,522	26,456	49,978
1921	26,734	30,341	57,075

Mr Hunt, the manager of Munt and Brown's, explained that 'it may be taken as a rule that 250 females keep about twenty men employed in blocking &c'.[51] He described the informality of the workplace and noted that over one thousand girls

---

[42] S. Bunker, R. Holgate and M. Nichols, *The Changing Face of Luton*, p. 138. The first South Beds election took place in 1885. *Luton Year Book 1908*, p. 60. Russell is the family name of the Dukes of Bedford.

[43] S. Bunker, *Strawopolis*, p. 137.

[44] F. Grundy and R.M. Titmuss, *Report on Luton*, p. 21.

[45] P.L. Bell, *Belief in Bedfordshire* (Belfry Press, 1986), ch. 9 and pp. 124–125.

[46] From the reminiscences of H. Janes in P.L. Bell, *Belief in Bedfordshire*, p. 135.

[47] H. Janes, 'I Remember, I Remember: Memories of 80 years ago' Part I, *Bedfordshire Magazine* Vol. 12, No. 93 (Summer 1970), p. 184. Janes may have exaggerated, of course.

[48] Ibid., p. 238.

[49] *Mate's Illustrated Guide to Luton 1907* (reprinted by Chantry Press, 1986), p. 6.

[50] Figures based on census returns for 1871 to 1921.

[51] *Evidence upon the Straw Plait and Bonnet Manufacturers* (1864) PP XX11; D. Bushby, *The Bedfordshire Schoolchild Before 1902* (BHRS Vol. 67, 1988), p. 160.

and women would come into the towns to work at the height of the season. The hat industry did employ men for the heavy work, but a far larger proportion of women was earning and this gave the town a reputation as a place 'where the men were kept by the women'.[52] In 1926 the *Daily Express* ran a feature with the subsidiary title, 'Women earn while Men do the Housework'.[53] Bunker notes how easy it was for women to combine their roles: 'in Luton it was thus possible for a woman to stay at home, fulfilling the functions of mother and wife whilst simultaneously exceeding her husband's earnings. As well as the mother, the importance of children to the family-based economy must be stressed.'[54] Certainly the earning power of men and women in Luton bore no resemblance to the idealistic 'family wage' which saw the father bringing in most of the money while his wife worked for a subsidiary wage.[55]

Luton's independent nature has been indicated. 'Throughout its history the plaiting industry was marked by the independence of the plaiters, who were not tied either in the purchase of straw or in the sale of plait.'[56] However, it must be noted here that in the years covered by this book plaiting was not 'an industry carried on in the Town of Luton, but in the hamlets, and in widely scattered rural districts through this and the adjoining Counties'.[57]

While sewing straw hats remained a home industry, women often preferred to work in a hat factory. Even in the factories 'discipline was unknown, workers in the same room coming and going at varying times to suit their own needs. The girls would begin at nine o'clock or even ten o'clock in the morning, working until ten o'clock or midnight, and throughout the night on Friday.'[58] They were accustomed to go to work in nice clothes and 'resented being classed as factory workers who, they imagined, answered the dictates of a factory bell and went to work in clogs and a shawl'.[59] A blockmaker at Vyse's factory said that women work by the piece and go to meals as they please because 'if they do not like one place they can easily go to another',[60] and Bunker notes that Luton possessed 'a middle class who conspicuously were unable to exert any social control through the employment market'.[61] The kind of independence to be found in Luton has been described by Aldrich as

> true independence; not the slothfulness engendered by independent means, nor the dependence demanded of those who were employed as personal servants but the independence of young men and women who were used to

---

[52]   J. Dyer and J.G. Dony, *The Story of Luton*, p. 128. The oral history archive which is being collected at LMAG includes an interview with Violet Vernon who was born in 1911. She recalls earning £15 a week as a machinist when she was 18. After she had a family she earned £10 a week as a designer, but her hours were more convenient. She notes that in the 1930s her salary was five times greater than that of her husband who worked in local government. LMAG is satisfied that these figures are correct.

[53]   Cutting from the *Daily Express*, 13 March 1926 (LMAG).

[54]   S. Bunker, *Strawopolis*, p. 21.

[55]   J. Lewis, ed., *Labour and Love: Women's Experience of Home and Family 1850–1940* (Basil Blackwell, 1986), ch. 4.

[56]   J.G. Dony, *A History of the Straw Hat Industry* (Gibbs Bamforth & Co., 1942), p. 61.

[57]   M/239 Letterbooks of the USDL, 29 May 1891.

[58]   J.G. Dony, *The Straw Hat Industry*, p. 107.

[59]   Ibid., p. 111 (referring to 1868).

[60]   (c. 1862) Quoted in S. Bunker, *Strawopolis*, p. 209.

[61]   Ibid., p. 208.

work and responsibility, and who were ready themselves at an early age . . . to
set up new family and economic units.[62]

This independence of spirit had potential for education. On the negative side, children were tempted to stay away from school when there was money to be made but, on the positive side, people who were minded to attend classes had the time to do so.[63]

Social and philanthropic life

Much of the social life was concentrated on the Church. Sunday schools, adult schools, Pleasant Sunday Afternoons (PSAs) and such-like continued throughout the years of this study, and in the 1920s the Luton Education Committee (LEC) was still allowing children to have days off to attend Sunday school outings. Many people in Luton were committed to the Temperance Movement which, together with the associated Band of Hope, arranged similiar outings.[64] Entries in school logbooks suggest that no opportunity for communal celebration was lost: royal weddings, peace celebrations, floral and agricultural shows, circuses, sales of work and May Day are just a few examples. There was beautiful countryside around the small market town and rail access to some of the beauty spots. On Easter Monday 1906, 20,000 holiday-makers went to Wardown Park, which was fully opened that year.[65] The park also became part of the route taken by the 'Monkey Parade' or 'marriage bureau on legs', a required Sunday evening stroll to be indulged in when the weather was favourable.[66] T.G. Hobbs, who was very well known in the town, was noted for his moralistic lantern shows[67] and organized trips. In 1881 he took 120 people to Snowdonia and in the following years to more and more distant places.[68] The women of Luton did not stay at home; a report, written by a woman, described how those who had travelled to Snowdonia had been caught in torrential rain and a photograph showed the ten ladies wearing 'a grim expression of determination, their heavy long dresses topped by bowlers, deer-stalkers, or feather-trimmed hats'.[69]

The Luton *Year Books* list a variety of clubs and organizations, many of which were open to women.[70] In the *Luton Year Book (1904)* a paragraph is devoted to Miss R.E. Higgins, 'a lady with Liberal views in politics and when she addresses the members of the local Liberal Association her words are given great weight'.[71] Also,

---

[62]   R. Aldrich, 'Elementary Education, Literacy and Child Employment in Mid-Nineteenth Bedfordshire: A Statistical Study', Giovanni Genovesi, ed., *History of Elementary School Teaching and Curriculum* (Bildung und Wissenschaft, 1990). This article was based on a talk given to the BHRS on 24 September 1988.

[63]   J.W. Rowntree and H.B. Binns, *A History of the Adult School Movement* (Headley Brothers, 1903), p. 32. Reprinted by the Department of Adult Education (University of Nottingham, 1985).

[64]   J.E. Davis, 'Luton in Focus: T.G. Hobbs and His Times' Part I, *Bedfordshire Magazine* Vol. 15, No. 117 (Summer 1976), p. 210. Also J. Dyer and J.G. Dony, *The Story of Luton*, pp. 132–133. See Chapter Nine.

[65]   *Luton Year Book (1908)*, p. 64.

[66]   P.C. Vigor, *Memories Are Made of This*, p. 27 (LMAG, 1983). Originally from the *Evening Post-Echo*.

[67]   J.E. Davis, 'T.G. Hobbs and His Times' Part II, p. 236.

[68]   Ibid., p. 237.

[69]   Ibid.

[70]   See also Chapter Nine.

[71]   *The Luton and District Year Book and Almanac (1904)*, p. 99. See Chapter Nine.

2. Sangers' Circus Procession, Market Hill, 1898 [*LN*/LM]

by 1908, the Co-operative Society had been established for twenty-four years and had 1,800 members, representing 1,400 families in the town. A Savings Club and library were open to the society's members and women were 'admitted as members in their own right, and now number over 900'.[72]

The *Luton Year Book (1908)* notes that there were 800 members in the Luton branch of the British Women's Temperance Association, which had been inaugurated in 1892 under the initiative of 'Mrs Eustace of Napier Road with two or three friends'. There was a Friendly Society 'for females only', which met at the Friendly Societies' Hall in Waller Street on the last Monday of each month. The secretary was Miss Olive Howe of Wenlock Street, there were 190 members and the society's funds amounted to £423. There were also Juvenile Societies. The Luton Premier Lodge of the Independent Order of Good Templars names two 'sisters', as female members were called.

The Parish Church is also recorded[73] as having a Women's (the Wenlock) Guild, a Mothers' meeting, a branch of the Mothers' Union, a branch of the Girls' Friendly Society, a Needlework Guild and a Lady-workers' Association.

Listed in the *Luton Year Book (1916)*[74] are Conservative, Liberal and Labour Associations. The League of Young Liberals held meetings 'of an educative nature', consisting of lectures and debates; Miss E. Jaquest of Ashburnham Road was Honorary Secretary of the Primrose League. There was a National Union of Women's Suffrage Society, a Women's Liberal Association and a Women's Unionist Association. There were several religious organizations, brotherhoods (including sisterhoods) and guilds. 'With the idea of assisting the funds of the Children's Home' a Guild of Kindness had been set up (c.1896).[75] It enlisted 'the sympathies of the children, and [had] for its motto, "Live not for yourself alone." A considerable sum of money was raised each year by a sale of work. The Guild [was] managed by a committee of influential ladies.' There was also a Ladies Committee of a local branch of the National Society for the Prevention of Cruelty to Children (NSPCC).

Sports included bowling and chess, while a Dramatic Society, Cage Bird Society, Fine Arts and Crafts Society, Sweet Pea Society, the NSPCC and Royal Society for the Prevention of Cruelty to Animals (RSPCA) are included in the *Luton Year Book (1916)* under 'General Societies'.

There were several clubs listed under the heading 'Club Life in Luton', and 'Places of Entertainment' included picture palaces and the Grand Theatre.[76] The existence of these clubs and organizations ensured that Luton women could find plenty to occupy their free time, if they so wished.

'Women were exercising democratic rights in the Co-operative Movement long before they were given the vote by Parliament', and the first Luton branch of the Women's Co-operative Guild was opened in 1905.[77] Records indicate that women in Luton were glad to use the facilities offered by the Co-operative Society, where the

---

[72] *Luton Year Book (1908)*, p. 40.
[73] Ibid., p. 130.
[74] *Luton Year Book and Directory (1916)*, pp. 63 and 65.
[75] Ibid., p. 53.
[76] *Luton Year Book and Directory (1916)*, pp. 47–53, 63–65 and 71–73.
[77] LMAG 7443, 75th Birthday Souvenir of the Luton Industrial Co-operative Society Ltd 1883–1958 (1958).

dividend in 1888 was 1s in the £ and, the following year, 1s 3d.[78] In 1900 Mrs Sarah Orchard was allowed to withdraw £1 5s 0d from her £1 8s 1d.[79] Miss Perkins, possibly an employee, was 'recommended for convalescent benefit' in 1922[80] and Mrs Duncan from Dunstable was 'recommended for dental benefit up to £2' in 1923.[81] A collective life insurance scheme, set up in 1919,[82] had, by 1923,[83]

> assured all the lives of its purchasing members. Benefits are paid in propor-
> tion to purchases from the Society . . . the Society pays all premiums. In the
> case of married members, 4s in the £ on the average annual purchases is paid
> when the husband dies, and 2s in the £ on the death of the wife. If member is
> unmarried, 5s in the £ . . . is paid to the next-of-kin on death of member.

The *Luton Year Book (1925)*[84] refers to a Guild of Service which was established in 1917. Representatives were sent from a variety of local organizations including the Young Women's Christian Association (YWCA), Girls' Aid Association, Conserva-tive Women and Liberal Women. The General Secretary was Miss E.A. Hockin of Wellington Street, who was also the Secretary of the Luton and District Committee for the Welfare of the Blind. The objectives of the Guild were:

> to provide a friend for all in need of help and advice;
> to secure timely aid for the suffering and needy;
> to bring about, if possible, lasting improvement in the condition of each case,
> by patient study and wise methods of help;
> to prevent overlapping and waste of charitable effort;
> to consider the causes of poverty and bring influence to bear by personal
> effort or through public bodies to lessen or remove such causes.

Several conclusions can be drawn from these Year Book entries. They indicate that a proportion of the female population of Luton, probably from the lower middle classes, concerned themselves with the numerous societies which existed in the town. A larger number, most likely from the working classes, were members of the Co-operative Society and some belonged to Friendly Societies. The fact that women from Luton joined self-help groups suggests that they were responsible members of the community.

Education
In the matter of education, Luton needs to be contrasted with the county town of Bedford. Education was central to the economy of Bedford, which enjoyed the financial benefits of the Harpur Trust, and the Report of the Endowed Schools Commission noted that 'there are but few endowments of this kind in the whole of

---

[78] LMAG 2261, Luton Industrial Co-operative Society Ltd.
[79] BLARS X778/26/7, 19 November 1900.
[80] BLARS X778/26/21, 2 August 1922.
[81] Ibid., 6 March 1923.
[82] LMAG 2261.
[83] *Luton Year Book and Directory (1923)*, p. 18.
[84] *'Luton News' Directory and Year Book of Luton (1925)*, p. 33. (The Guild of Service was still in exis-tence in 1938.)

England to surpass or even equal this'.[85] The Harpur Trust offered a good education to girls in Bedford[86] at a time when Luton did not see the education of either boys or girls as of particular importance.

The Bedford schools flourished and by 1883 the town was 'rapidly becoming the metropolis of education in England'.[87] Bedford began to advertise its most marketable commodity[88] and was much favoured by the class of people who served in the army and colonial service and saw it as a place eminently suited to their children's education and their eventual retirement. The life of an ex-colonial administrator could be a lonely one, but that was not the case in Bedford 'where birds of this feather have flocked together. Paterfamilias has no difficulty about finding kindred spirits to play golf, bridge, or row, or do whatever he has a mind to.'[89] However, boys and girls of Luton left school having received an education that was 'utilitarian and thin'.[90] Their expectations lay in the field of commerce and industry whereas

> 'the Bedford Boy' – and it is rapidly becoming true of the 'Bedford Girl' – is to be found all over the world, in every profession, and in almost every occupation. . . . Many of the pupils go up to the Universities; a great many go into the Army and Navy; a large contingent pass into the legal and medical professions; many join the Indian Civil Service; others go to the Colonies, to the Western States of North America, or to the rapidly developing States of South America . . . and friendships which have begun on the banks of the Ouse are often renewed or continued on the plains and among the hills of India, or in the cattle ranches of California or Brazil.[91]

Unlike Bedford, Luton had no major educational charities. Cornelius Bigland (c. 1679) gave £6 a year for six poor children, Roger Gillingham (1695) gave £10 a year for a schoolmaster, Thomas Long (1756) nominated stock to provide income for a school and John Richards (1731) gave income from property to put boys to school.[92] 'The free school referred to in Long's will, was a school formerly kept in the church, which had no permanent endowment, and was discontinued on the establishment of the national school.'[93] The Bigland, Long and Gillingham trusts were combined on 22 April 1915 and the net income was 'applied in the provision of Secondary School Exhibitions, Technical Exhibitions, University Exhibitions, or Maintenance Allowances, to be awarded to necessitous boys and girls resident in the Borough of Luton, who have for not less than two years at any time attended Public Elementary Schools'.[94] In 1916 the income (£39 14s 8d) provided 'seven free scholarships at the Luton Modern School tenable for seven years'.[95] It is not clear how many girls

---

[85] D. Bushby, *Elementary Education in Bedford: 1868–1903; The Ecclesiastical Census Bedfordshire March 1851* (BHRS Vol. 54, 1975), p. 13.

[86] Ibid., p. 13.

[87] *Daily News*, 31 August 1883, quoted in Ibid., p. 22.

[88] P. Bell, ed., 'Aspects of Anglo-Indian Bedford', *Worthington George Smith and Other Studies* (BHRS Vol. 57, 1978), p. 197.

[89] Ibid., p. 200.

[90] F. Grundy and R.M. Titmuss, *Report on Luton*, p. 21.

[91] P. Bell, ed., *Worthington George Smith and Other Studies*, p. 198.

[92] F. Davis, *Luton Past and Present: Its History and Antiquities* (Stalker, 1874), pp. 108–113.

[93] D. Bushby, *The Bedfordshire Schoolchild*, p. 26.

[94] W. Austin, *The History of Luton and its Hamlets*, vol. 2 pp. 292–293.

[95] *Luton Year Book and Directory (1916)*, p. 73.

received money from the endowments in earlier years but, after the establishment of the secondary school, girls could also be beneficiaries.

According to the *Digest of Returns (1818)* there was one school with a charitable foundation, where 135 boys and 135 girls received schooling. There were three fee-paying schools for boys and three for girls, which taught a total of 255 children. There were also a number of plait schools where the primary aim was to teach children to plait straw for the hat industry. It was thought that 'the poor are abundantly provided with the means of education, and very generally embrace them with much apparent thankfulness'.[96] The *Abstract of Returns (1833)* for Luton and the hamlets note seven daily schools, two day and Sunday Lancasterian schools and six Sunday schools.[97] The National School Inquiry for 1846/1847 recorded a boys' school and an infants' school in Luton, but girls could only receive schooling on Sundays. Biscot and Stopsley had no day schools, but Hyde children could be taught at day and Sunday schools. These schools were supported by 'endowments, subscriptions and payments together with a grant of 40*l* from the National Society'.[98] Significantly, the National School Inquiry also notes that a day school for girls had been tried 'but has not answered, from the nature of the business of this place, viz:- Straw bonnet-making'.[99] Already the effects of employment on education were being felt.[100]

In 1818, Bedfordshire had 6.1% of the population enrolled in Sunday schools. In 1833 the proportion was 15.7%, but by 1851, the county led the whole country with 19.7% of its population attending these schools.[101] In the same year Bedfordshire lagged well behind in day school provision, being fortieth out of forty-two English county units.[102] W.B. Stephens noted in his study of literacy rates that in Bedfordshire, unlike most other counties, 'there is an apparent connection between poor literacy levels in 1866 and relatively high proportions of Sunday-school pupils in 1851 combined with proportions at day school below the national level'. This supports other evidence 'that in these areas the Sunday school was still for many children the main medium of education and one connected with low levels of attainment'.[103]

Stephens has compared literacy rates in provincial England based on the propensity of husbands and wives to sign their names on their marriage certificates.[104] The results showed that Bedfordshire consistently performed very badly[105] and in 1856 the national average of illiteracy was 35% while in Luton it was 44%.[106] It may be that Luton's proximity to London resulted in 'the more enterprising and intelligent

96   *Digest of Returns to Circular Letter from the Select Committee on Education of the Poor (1818).*
97   *The Abstract of Returns: (1833) for the County of Bedford.*
98   *Church-School Inquiry (1846–7).*
99   Ibid.
100   These reports can also be consulted in D. Bushby, *The Bedfordshire Schoolchild.*
101   T.W. Laqueur, *Religion and Respectability: Sunday Schools and Working Class Culture 1780–1850* (Yale University Press, 1976), p. 49.
102   R. Aldrich, 'Elementary Education, Literacy and Child Employment in Mid-Nineteenth Century Bedfordshire', p. 94.
103   W.B. Stephens, *Education, Literacy and Society 1830–1870: The Geography of Diversity in Provincial England* (Manchester University Press, 1987), p. 202.
104   Ibid., p. 3.
105   Ibid., pp. 16 and 191.
106   Ibid., p. 186.

youths' moving to the capital, but probably the most significant factor in this research is the existence of a cottage industry'[107] which employed children who might otherwise have been at school. In 1851 Bedfordshire had the largest percentage (50%) of children aged ten to fourteen employed in domestic industry in any English county[108] and, as late as 1871, 8% of children under ten in Bedfordshire were employed.[109] Stephens says that 'employment patterns are clearly a key to the changing relationships between male and female illiteracy . . . in areas of domestic industry, where a high level of employment for women and girls continued, the relative position of female literacy was depressed'.[110] This had relevance to Luton where the hat industry dominated girls' lives. Other factors which may be significant in the level of girls' literacy in Luton are the female-orientated curriculum[111] and irregular attendance.[112]

Dony has documented the schooling which was available in the town before 1874 and Joyce Roberts has listed the Dame Schools.[113] In 1870, when the Forster Education Act required local authorities to ensure that there were enough school places available, Luton was unwilling to co-operate with the demands of the Education Department. This study will not address in detail the pressures and counter-pressures involved because much has already been written.[114] The most vigorous disagreements concerned the attitudes of the Church and Nonconformists towards education, but there was also resentment of outside interference, disquiet about the introduction of taxation and fear that families would lose the earning potential of their children. The first election to the School Board was held in 1874 and, not surprisingly, those who were elected were men who were already involved in the day-to-day running of the town.

Employment and the local economy

The hat industry[115]

Wheat grown in the area was found to be suitable for plaiting. In earlier days the straws were plaited whole, but finer plait could be made once ways were found to split them. Young children from the labouring and working classes were taught this manual skill from a very early age[116] and were expected to add to the family income as soon as possible. To increase their output many of them were sent to plait schools

---

[107] Ibid., p. 17.
[108] Ibid., p. 168.
[109] Ibid., p. 22.
[110] Ibid., p. 192.
[111] Ibid., p. 18.
[112] Ibid., p. 196.
[113] Quotation from the *Luton Advertiser*, 4 April 1874, in J. Roberts, 'The Luton School Board (1874–1902)' L/LUT 371.01 p. 18; J.G. Dony, *A History of Education in Luton* (LMAG, 1970).
[114] M.A. Marshall, 'Elementary Education in Luton 1809–1874', Typescript essay at LMAG; J.G. Dony, *A History of Education in Luton*, pp. 9–24; S. Bunker, *Strawopolis*, pp. 188–189; V. Evans, 'Education in Luton', Typescript essay at LMAG; J. Day, 'The School Board of the United School District of Luton 1874–1903' at LMAG; J. Roberts, 'Luton School Board (1874–1902)', pp. 79–80; Newspaper reports, posters and pamphlets at LMAG.
[115] The hat industry, though dominant, was seasonal. It was also very susceptible to the fluctuations of the market and to the whims of the straw dealers.
[116] P. Horn, 'Child Workers in the Pillow Lace and Straw Plait Trades of Victorian Buckinghamshire and Bedfordshire', *The Historical Journal* XV11 4 (1974), p. 789.

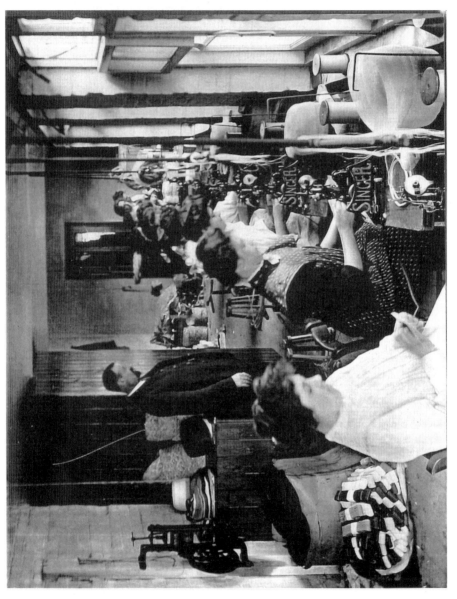

3. Sewing room in an unidentified Luton hat factory c.1907 [*LN*/LM]

4. C.H. Osborne's Dyework & Hat Factory, Melsom Street, 1907–1908 [*LN/LM*]

5. Girls trimming boaters in a Luton hat factory 1911 [LM]

where, in theory, they were given a basic education. In reality, the aim of the school was to ensure that children produced their fair share of plait in a day. 'A child who could not "do its fives", that is, make a simple five-end straw plait, was looked upon as a greater dunce than one who at ten did not know its alphabet.'[117] There was no respite after school hours either, for the children would still be plaiting. 'It was rare to see a girl out of doors without her plait in her hand and working away busily.'[118] Not only girls plaited, so did the boys who were too young to work in the fields and men would plait if there was a need. The town girls once did their fair share of plaiting, but by 1874 the plait was being brought into the town from the hamlets and villages to be sold to dealers, while the town girls and women were busy sewing hats and earning better money.[119]

The 1861 census figures in Table 4 show that 11,476 out of 74,054 females in Bedfordshire were straw plaiters. The figures for 1871 give 20,701 plaiters out of a total of 79,995 females.

Table 4. Female straw plaiters in Bedfordshire 1861 and 1871[120]

	Age of female straw plaiters	1861	1871
Female population		74,054	79,995
Female straw plaiters		11,476	20,701
	5–9	705	837
	10–14	1,888	2,535
	15–19	1,764	3,308
	20–24	1,464	3,281
	25–29	2,075	4,317
	30–34	1,577	2,766
	35–44	1,003	1,925
	45–54	625	1,063
	55–64	308	537
	Over 65	67	132

As Marian Nichols points out, however, these figures do not adequately express how much straw plaiting dominated everyday existence, which was

> intimately bound up with the fluctuating fortunes of the straw plaiting and hat making industries. Its seasonal nature was intensified by the whimsical demands of fashion, but when plait was 'good' everything else was abandoned

---

117   Quoted from *The Hatters Gazette* (1882). M. Nichols, 'Straw Plaiting and the Straw Hat Industry in Britain', *Costume: The Journal of the Costume Society* No. 30 (1996), p. 118. Or this could mean doing five yards; D. Bushby, *The Bedfordshire Schoolchild*, p. 154.
118   D. Bushby, *The Bedfordshire Schoolchild*, p. 152; *Report on Straw Plait and Bonnet Manufacturers* (1864).
119   D. Bushby, *The Bedfordshire Schoolchild*, p. 161.
120   *Census of England and Wales* (1871) *Bedfordshire.*

for it, much to the disapproval of contemporary commentators. . . . No surprise then that everything else was neglected.[121]

In 1856, HMI the Reverend D.J. Stewart noted that 'at Luton and Dunstable, girls are completely absorbed by the straw-bonnet trade, and grow up without any of the instruction which schools would supply'.[122] In the early 1890s, 'the hat trade affected everybody in Luton. One could not escape from it. On the footpath you would meet women with huge white sheets filled with hats which they had machined or trimmed at home.'[123] Lutonians of every social class saw their past, present and future as part of the straw hat business. During the first half of the nineteenth century 'lace-making and straw-plaiting [had] a stranglehold on the lives of Bedfordshire girls'.[124] By the end of the century, however, the straw hat industry had come to dominate the lives of children leaving school rather than children attending school.[125]

It took several years to train a girl to sew bonnets into fashionable styles.[126] Davis recorded that it was the ambition of young girls to leave their cottage homes in order to become sewers in Luton, 'which is considered a condition above that of a plaiter'.[127] This resulted in a migration of girls into Luton during the busy season, 'commencing around October and increasing in intensity from February through to the end of May'.[128]

The introduction of sewing machines in the 1860s was very important to the women in Luton.[129] In many industries the arrival of machinery to do the work which had previously been done by hand forced small manufacturers out of business, but in Luton, as in Colchester,[130] this did not happen. Homeworkers or outdoor hands were able to use machines as well as the factory workers, and 'housewives throughout the town, even the wives of the professional class, would machine in the few weeks that the trade was busy'.[131] It is useful to note here that middle-class ladies in Luton did not have to confine themselves to a purely domestic way of life, as was common in many other towns.

The Royal Commission on the Employment of Women recorded a typical domestic scene. Hats were drying in front of the fire and on the sitting-room tables and chairs. The mistress of the house would probably have sent her washing to be done away from home and the children were likely to be in the care of an older girl. However, 'the supervision, exercised by the mistress, free to leave her machining or finishing at any moment, [was] . . . much greater than would be possible in the case

---

121   M. Nichols, 'Straw Plaiting and the Straw Hat Industry', p. 119.
122   D.W. Bushby, 'Lace, Straw-Plait and Child Employment', *Bedfordshire Magazine* Vol. 17, No. 131 (Winter 1979), pp. 99–100.
123   H. Janes, 'I Remember, I Remember' Part I, p. 182.
124   J. Godber, *History of Bedfordshire* (BCC, 1969), p. 479. Lace-making took place in the north of the county, not in Luton.
125   D. Bushby, 'Lace, Straw-Plait and Child Employment', pp. 100–101.
126   J. Dyer and J.G. Dony, *The Story of Luton*, p. 126.
127   F. Davis, *Luton Past and Present*, p. 25.
128   S. Bunker, *Strawopolis*, p. 12.
129   J.G. Dony, *The Straw Hat Industry*, p. 116.
130   L. Davidoff and B. Westover, ed., *Our Work, Our Lives, Our Words: Women's History and Women's Work* (Macmillan Education, 1986), p. 55.
131   J. Dyer and J.G. Dony, *The Story of Luton*, p. 127.

of a married woman working in a factory'.[132] The points raised in this report indicate that childcare was not a problem for the women of Luton because well-paid work could be undertaken at home where children could be supervised and women had the freedom to adjust their hours to the needs of the family. Logbooks also confirm that older girls were sometimes busy supervising younger children.

The introduction of the 1870 Education Act, which allowed the education authorities to make education in recognized schools compulsory, brought an end to the plait schools, and the straw-plaiting industry itself was doomed when market forces, resulting from the import of Japanese and Chinese plait, changed the whole focus of the trade.[133] There were many who regretted the end of a way of life and attempts were made to keep the skill alive in the schools,[134] but although there was a small demand for English plait until the 1920s and 1930s, most of the skills died out. A Luton Museum project is currently trying to revive 'the techniques . . . used to create a myriad of delightful patterns out of a simple, basic raw material and a minimum of tools'.[135]

Working-class women could work in their own homes as described above or in large factories such as Vyse's. Herbert Janes recalled their factory on Park Square, which was 'a grim, begrimed, red brick building'.[136] The firm moved into new premises, but the grim old building was later used as the first home of the Luton Modern School, a symbol of the progress from hats to wider opportunities. Large businesses would often spring from the humblest beginnings and prosperity could come quickly. Asher John Hucklesby, described as 'Luton's Hat King',[137] began to work in the hat industry at the age of thirteen. He learnt every aspect of the trade and eventually set up in business for himself at the age of twenty-eight. His business flourished and he opened up markets in many parts of the world, including Europe, Canada, New Zealand and Australia. He had hundreds of employees, but no hat factory because he relied on the skill of small hat and bonnet makers to produce hats to his designs. Hucklesby became a prominent member of Luton society; he was elected to the County Council in 1888, became Mayor of Luton five times[138] and was very involved with education in the town. As a member of the Bedfordshire Education Committee (BEC) Hucklesby, together with Rowland Prothero, was an instigator of the new secondary school in Park Square.[139] This school was to open new doors for the girls of Luton and help many of them to see that employment did not begin and end with the hat industry. When Hucklesby died, the Luton Education Committee (LEC) recorded his interest in education and sent condolences to his family hoping that 'the memory of his enthusiasm and energy in good work,

132 *Royal Commission on Labour, The Employment of Women (February 1892)*, p. 30.
133 P. Horn, 'Child Workers in the Pillow Lace and Straw Plait Trades', p. 795.
134 H. Janes, 'I Remember, I Remember' Part I, p. 183; see Chapter Six.
135 M. Nichols, 'Straw Plaiting and the Straw Hat Industry', p. 123.
136 H. Janes, 'I Remember, I Remember' Part I, p. 182.
137 A quotation from the *Daily Mail* in H. Janes, 'I Remember, I Remember' Part II, *Bedfordshire Magazine*, Vol. 12, No. 94 (Autumn 1970), p. 235.
138 B. Benson and J. Dyer, 'Luton's Hat King', *Bedfordshire Magazine* Vol. 26, No. 204 (Spring 1998), pp. 135–140.
139 See Chapter Ten.

whether philanthropic, educational or commercial, may soften the blow of bereavement'.[140]

Another class of business which thrived was that of the 'small masters'. This would be a family concern set up with little outlay and very often run by one of the women. Eric Meadows described how his grandparents, George and Eliza Newbold, set up home in 1881. Their house in Cheapside combined George's business with that of the women in the family: Eliza's sisters made and sold straw hats while orders for coal were taken in the corner of one of the rooms. Meadows remembers his youngest great-aunt who, by 1930, was the only sister still working in the business

> helped by other hands including Billy Russell who blocked the hats . . . sitting by a gas fire in the left-hand room, sewing on headbands or trimmings, always busy, seeing callers and outside workers, the large room cluttered with cardboard boxes and partly finished hats. The other large room on the ground floor was the showroom.[141]

Often, behind what looked like an ordinary house would be a two-storied extension. The lower floor would take the blocking machinery, with the heavy work being done by men, and the sewers and trimmers would work upstairs.[142] This type of small factory was very common until well into the twentieth century. If a business was fortunate enough to produce a successful design, the family could become comparatively wealthy in a few years. These families, although not socially superior from a national point of view, saw themselves as part of the élite in the town and their daughters were often sent not to local elementary schools, but to fee-paying, 'respectable' schools. Luton's hat-making industry was known for its 'adaptability and flexibility'[143] and in the early twentieth century, in an attempt to provide work in the slack season, felt hat-making was introduced. Millinery, which became a side of the business in its own right, and finishing – putting in linings and labels – was done by women in small factory units or at home.

The *Hatters' Gazette*, quoting the *Morning Leader*, described the life of a Luton hat girl. She bore no comparison to the typical factory girl 'with a shawl for headgear'. The Luton girl is 'robust and usually well-fed, her raiment is often fashionable, and she takes a legitimate professional pride in wearing a hat which might be envied in the West End'. A hat girl enjoyed good company at work and her family was 'in quite easy circumstances'. 'On Sundays she pours out of chapel in her hundreds; for the chapel and the Bible-class indeed maintain their hold on her in general, and she is the backbone of the chapel choir. Of all women workers, in fact, she is to be counted among the aristocracy.'[144]

It is not to be wondered at that this independence had its critics. One of the criticisms most often directed at the plait and hat girls was that of immorality. László Gróf has studied evidence from Edlesborough, a village west of Luton, and concluded that 'the vast majority of plaiters were prepared to work hard to gain a

---

[140]   M/226 Minutes of LEC, 14 January 1908.
[141]   E. Meadows, 'A Family Home and Business in Luton', *Bedfordshire Magazine* Vol. 26, No. 207 (Winter 1998), pp. 278–281.
[142]   H. Janes, 'I Remember, I Remember' Part I, p. 183.
[143]   M. Nichols, 'Straw Plaiting and the Straw Hat Industy', p. 123.
[144]   Quoted from the *Morning Leader* in the *Hatters' Gazette*, 1 April 1911, p. 198.

chance of a better life . . . the children of straw were people of moral substance, their legacy one of hard work, our heritage their unique local craft'.[145] In the foreword to Gróf's book Kate Tiller says, 'Mr Gróf also shows how the persistent mythology about the immorality of straw plaiters, rooted in sweeping judgements on smartly dressed young women plaiters made by mainly middle-aged, middle-class, male observers in mid-Victorian times, is not borne out by the evidence.'[146] The girls' smart hats were even discussed at a meeting of the LEC. One member said that the girls were too much associated with millinery but Mrs Carruthers, in defence, said that girls who wore smart hats were 'industrious and liberal-hearted'.[147]

The fact that so many of Luton's hats were exported gave the workers an informal education since they had opportunities to understand life in other countries. H. Janes described how he learnt about the uniting of separate settlements in Australia into one as a result of stamping gold 'tips' or linings for the hats with the words 'The Commonwealth'.[148] Girls showed the same kind of interest. 'Many friendships with those across the seas have been formed in this way, and legend says that it was thus one young lady found a husband'.[149]

New industries

Luton's dependence on the hat industry was at the mercy of market forces. The Chamber of Commerce, which had been founded in 1877,[150] was concerned for its future and, in 1889, made a deliberate decision to address the problem when, together with the Town Council, they set up a New Industries Committee in order to attract new firms. In a publication which listed the attractions of the town, Luton was described as affording 'special advantages for engineering, printing, and other industries in which male labour is more particularly employed'.[151] This was an obvious attempt to remove female dominance from the Luton work scene. It was claimed that Luton could offer an effective railway system, a clean water supply, plenty of cheap and accessible land, good local government, cheap gas and electricity, good housing, good health and education and the opportunity for happy relaxation[152] and had always been a town 'relatively free from the restrictions of trade union organisation'.[153] Another feature listed is 'healthy, pleasant and well-paid occupation for female operatives,' which suggests that, in a town where women had always worked, it was expected that they would continue to do so.[154]

This initiative was successful. Hayward Tyler's (1871) and Laporte Chemicals (1898) were followed by the Co-operative Wholesale Society (CWS) Cocoa and Chocolate factory (1902), British Gelatine Works (1903), Vauxhall Motors (1905),

[145] L.L. Gróf, *Children of Straw* (Barracuda, 1988), p. 112.
[146] Ibid., p. 8.
[147] *The Luton and District Year Book and Almanack (1906)*, p. 100. See notes on Mrs Carruthers in Chapter Four.
[148] H. Janes, 'I Remember, I Remember' Part II, p. 237.
[149] *Hatters' Gazette* 1911, p. 198.
[150] Chamber of Commerce, *Pride and Partnership 1877–1993* (1993).
[151] New Industries Committee, *Luton as An Industrial Centre* (1905), preface.
[152] Ibid. Luton had gas from 1834, clean water from 1870 and electricity from 1896. *Luton Year Book (1908)*, p. 61, states that a £40,000 sewage and storm water scheme was set up in October 1897.
[153] J. Dyer and J.G. Dony, *The Story of Luton*, p. 153.
[154] Luton New Industries Committee, *Luton as An Industrial Centre*, preface.

Commercial Cars (1906), Davis Gas Stove (1907), Kent's (1908) and Skefko (1910).[155] The hat trade continued to be important, however, and, in 1911, nearly 44% of the total workforce and 72% of all employed women were engaged in it.[156] Although women were employed in these new industries,[157] Holden says that the new industries were disadvantageous to them.[158] This was probably because the status that women had been accorded as part of the hat industry began to give way to a subordinate lifestyle where men became earners of a family wage. Holden has produced detailed information concerning the transition of Luton's working force from predominantly female to predominantly male in an earlier volume in this series.[159] It has also been pointed out by Axton that 'by 1914 the dominant position held by the straw plaiting industry had been undermined and was never again to assume such a hold on the townspeople'.[160]

Legislation concerning the employment of women and children was also affecting the traditional way of life.[161] This confused Luton people and so the *Luton Year Book (1908)* published an explanatory article with the approval of Mr Kellett, the Inspector of Factories. In the straw hat trade working hours for women should be from 8a.m. until 8p.m. with 1½ hours for meals, and nobody under eighteen was allowed to work overtime.[162] There were further restrictions and, if any overtime was worked, the necessary forms had to be filled in and returned to the Inspector of Factories. The regulations were there to be obeyed, but in an independent town like Luton workers were able and willing to evade the scrutiny of the inspectors.[163]

Other problems were caused by the traditional independence of spirit enjoyed in the hat industry. 'The unorganized nature of the hat trade, its small units of production, its seasonal nature and lack of regimentation in the work place did not suit the new industries whose modern forms of production needed greater control of their workforce towards large scale organized machine production.'[164] Firms tended to prefer immigrant workers with different attitudes, and women were employed only as unskilled and cheap labour.[165]

Another factor which influenced the employment of Luton women was the outbreak of the First World War. According to Holden, 'the effect was to strengthen the position of the female workforce as they were required in the labour-short economy, and many were attracted away from the hat trade by higher wages and

[155] J. Dyer and J.G. Dony, *The Story of Luton*, pp. 153–154.
[156] L. Holden, 'A History of Vauxhall Motors to 1950: Industry, Development and Local Impact on the Luton Economy' (M.Phil. Thesis, Open University, 1983), p. 226.
[157] For example, in 1906, women were involved in cutting jelly into slices and in packing at the British Gelatine Works. BLARS Z 210, *Souvenir of the Luton Gelatine Works* (1906).
[158] L. Holden, 'A History of Vauxhall Motors to 1950', p. 226.
[159] L. Holden, *Vauxhall Motors and the Luton Economy, 1900–2002* (BHRS Vol. 82, 2003), pp. 137–139 and ch. 7.
[160] C. Axton, 'The Development of Luton 1901–1914', p. 31. The hat industry bolstered the town's economy during difficult times for the engineering industries. Luton remained a relatively prosperous town for most of the twentieth century.
[161] Problems of attendance and half-time education are considered in Chapter Four.
[162] *Luton Year Book (1908)*, pp. 41–43; *Luton Reporter*, 11 October 1907. Dony says that the Provisional Order (1874) was rescinded in 1906 (P.P., 1907, X, p. 299).
[163] J.G. Dony, *The Straw Hat Industry*, pp. 110–113, 129–133.
[164] Ibid., pp. 239–240.
[165] Ibid., p. 255.

regular employment'. However, changes in women's employment during time of war are not as significant as might be supposed because there was always a backlash when men returned home and needed to take up their former employment. Apparently Luton shared the feelings of resentment, which were felt nationally, as articles in *The Luton News* during 1919 and 1920 demonstrated.[166]

Teachers too left their posts during the war, as they were able to earn more money in industry.[167] Women were busy in other capacities; for example, there were the Voluntary Aid Detachment nurses (VADs).[168] Margaret Currie notes that their Joint Commandants were Mrs Nora Durler, wife of a prominent straw manufacturer, and Mrs J.W. Green, from the Green brewing family. VAD nurses were volunteers who needed some form of independence, so it is reasonable to suppose that all the nurses who worked for them had some kind of social standing in the community.[169] These nurses were represented in the Peace Day Procession on 19 July 1919, the day when the Town Hall was burnt down.[170]

The Co-operative Society Cocoa and Chocolate Works (1902)

The Dallow Road site was chosen for the CWS factory because it was in open country, 'at the edge of Luton' with a dry, chalk subsoil and a 'light and clear aspect'. This firm became a major employer of females in the town,[171] with girls and women taking on light work: 'a girl lays a number in a double tray or wire, passes the tray through a bath of melted chocolate so that the thick liquid covers it at every point, runs the tray on and tips out the coated sweets to dry'. It was also considered appropriate that women and girls should put on 'the finishing touches' and pack the chocolates into 'artistic boxes'. This was 'perhaps, the most picturesque, as it is by no means the least important, part of this interesting industry.'[172]

When the factory first opened, with Mr Stafford as manager and Miss Bousfield as instructor,[173] workers came down from the parent company in London. Many of them returned home, but apparently it was not difficult to recruit local workers:[174]

> Straw hat making is a well-paid industry in its season, but thanks to fashion it is so ruinously irregular – day and night work at one time, and then months of idleness – that its average return is no great compensation. The demand for chocolates may be as frivolous as that for millinery, but at any rate it is regular, hence Luton has welcomed its new industry.[175]

The Co-operative News (1903) noted that there were 'over 200 workers, practically all of whom are recruited from the district . . . two-thirds of the employés [sic] are

166   L. Holden, *Vauxhall Motors and the Luton Economy*, p. 143.
167   J. Dyer, *The Story of the Stopsley Schools* (LMAG, 1989) p. 28.
168   'Millennium Memories: A History of Luton and Dunstable', *Luton News/Dunstable Gazette*, 26 January 2000.
169   M.R. Currie, *Hospitals in Luton and Dunstable: An Illustrated History* (Advance Offset, 1982), pp. 63–64.
170   D. Craddock, *Where they Burnt the Town Hall Down*, p. 155. See Chapter Nine.
171   LMAG 103759/380, *Wheatsheaf*, pp. 40–53. No date is given, but comparisons with other accounts suggest that it was in the early days of the factory's life in Luton.
172   LMAG 103759/5, *Co-operative News*, 11 April 1903.
173   LMAG 103759, *Co-operative News*, 18 October 1902, p. 1278.
174   LMAG 103759/6, *Wheatsheaf*.
175   Ibid.

6. CWS Cocoa Works. Band rehearsing for the opening ceremony 1902 [LM]

females, and with their neat blue caps and aprons, [supplied by the CWS] they present a picturesque appearance, while their ruddy cheeks and smiling faces speak of health and contentment'.[176]

The Wheatsheaf recorded that women worked a forty-eight hour week: 8a.m. to 12.30p.m. and 2p.m. to 6.15p.m. on weekdays and 8a.m. to 12.15p.m. on Saturdays. All the weekly employees who had been with the CWS for twelve months 'including the male workers and 60 per cent of the girls – receive annually a couple of weeks' leisure at full wages'.[177]

Vauxhall Motors (1905)

During the years under consideration Vauxhall Motors employed women in the General Office, the Drawing Office, the Cost Office and the Works Office and at the showrooms in London. Female workers were also employed in the lacquering shop and as material handlers.[178] It has also been noted that Miss Olive Amy and Lady Ludlow had shares in the company.[179]

During the First World War 'dilution' took place. This was the technical term for the replacement of skilled workers by unskilled or female workers. In 1914 the machine shop employed four hundred skilled men, but by 1917 this had been reduced to 330 men and women. The firm was obliged to give 'concessions in the form of higher wages, lower hours of work and the granting of premium bonus'.[180]

The hat industry had never been an organized industry 'as far as trade unions were concerned, mainly due to the size of the units, the casual nature of the work, in terms of irregular hours, and the seasonal unemployment which affected the industry in the summer months, and more particularly from November to January'.[181] However, in 1916 the Vauxhall girls went on strike for higher pay and their wages were raised from £1 to 30s a week.[182] Female militancy had arrived, although in a very small way.[183] The following year, there was a dispute

> involving women dilutee workers who were not being paid the same rates as skilled and semi-skilled men who were doing the same jobs. The National Federation of Women Workers were using Vauxhall as a test case because all the women were in the union and the men supported their demand for equal pay, and they wanted to see that the Treasury agreement between the ASE [Amalgamated Society of Engineers] and other unions was carried out . . . The outcome seems to have been favourable to the women.[184]

Vauxhall Motors, which eventually became as significant an employer in Luton as

[176] LMAG 103759/5, pp. 426–427.
[177] LMAG 103759/6.
[178] R. Hart, *The Vauxhall and Bedford Story* (Farnon Books, 1996), p. 63.
[179] Miscellaneous documents from the Vauxhall Archives, Luton.
[180] L. Holden, *Vauxhall Motors*, p. 87.
[181] Ibid., pp. 87–88.
[182] Photograph in *Bedfordshire Magazine* Vol. 9, No. 72 (Spring 1965) p. 326.
[183] J. Burnett, ed., *Useful Toil: The Autobiographies of Working People from the 1820s to the 1920s* (Allen Lane, 1976). The chapter about Rosina Whyatt, who worked in Luton and became a 'committed trade unionist', documents clearly the union negotiations involving the munitions factory and other factories in the town.
[184] L. Holden, *Vauxhall Motors and the Luton Economy*, pp. 100–101.

the hat industry had been, has now closed its car-making factory, although the head-quarters of the firm, Griffin House, is still located in the town.

The Skefko Ball Bearing Company (1910)

According to Holden, women gained 'a foothold in the new industries' in such firms as Skefko (SKF) and Electrolux (established in 1926). This was in unskilled assembly work where their lower wages enabled the firms to cut production costs. Apparently some of the female labour force were happy to work in the hat trade when business was booming and wages were high and then return to assembly work during the slack hat season.[185] In 1912 SKF published a souvenir issue with pictures of women employed in the dining room in 1912, the works surgery in 1914 and the inspection department in 1918.[186]

George Kent Ltd (1908)

An unpublished history of George Kent Ltd[187] gives another insight into the different types of work that women were asked to do. 'While the cloud on the inter-national horizon was becoming more menacing . . . the revolutionary decision was taken to employ female labour' and two forewomen were engaged.[188] Mr A. Hail-stone from Bedford brought with him girls from Bedford High School to form the 'nucleus of a female office staff', even though there were local girls who had been educated to a high standard in the Luton Modern School.[189] This suggests that the usual lack of empathy between Luton and Bedford had surfaced. Towards the end of 1914 the company was asked to undertake the manufacture of a high-explosive fuse,[190] and so began an increasing commitment to munitions, which was to last throughout the war.

The main factory concentrated on fuses while a site at Chaul End, Luton, was opened as a filling factory for fuses, gaines[191] and detonators. Miss Edith Hammond was responsible for the recruitment and welfare of women, who made up about four-fifths of the total employed.[192] Women were also involved in the pressing of TNT and the manufacture of detonators.[193] They became known as 'Kent's canaries' on account of the colour from the TNT which affected their hair and their skin. In July 1916 Violet Golding, who at the age of sixteen worked at putting caps on deto-nators, was leaning over to take one out of the press when it exploded in her hand. She lost the tips of one finger and thumb and had extensive burns. She was recom-mended for the OBE and also received £50 compensation. With some of this she bought a bicycle because prior, to the accident, she had walked to work from Dunstable every day.[194]

185   Ibid., pp. 156–157.
186   SKF, *Inner Ring, The First Fifty Years* Special Issue (1960).
187   LMAG 103426, 'The Story of George Kent Ltd' Part 1 (1955).
188   Ibid., p. 38.
189   Ibid., p. 38.
190   Ibid., p. 39.
191   Tubes attached to fuses.
192   LMAG 103428, p. 40. There is a picture of women working at Kent's in 'Millennium Memories' published by the *Luton News/Dunstable Gazette*, 26 January 2000.
193   Ibid., p. 40.
194   B.E. Escott, *Twentieth Century Women of Courage* (Sutton, 1999), p. 10.

7a & b. Munitions workers at George Kent Ltd [*LN*/LM]

8. Machining grenades, Davis Gas Stove Co. Ltd [LM]

9. Hewlett & Blondeau (Aircraft), Leagrave, 1918 [*LN/LM*]

Girls from the hamlets and villages, who had migrated into Luton to work in the busy hat season, now came to work in munitions. Kent's 'had exhausted the supply of female personnel' and a great many girls came in from the surrounding area. As a result there was a shortage of accommodation in the town. Hostels, the top floors of Luton's largest store, the YMCA and several private houses were rented.[195] Apart from the actual munitions work, there was employment in the canteens 'one for men and a much larger one for women' and in the factory hospital.[196] Holden notes that, in 1916, the women at Chaul End went on strike for better pay and conditions[197] and Dyer and Dony note that 'as there was no hall large enough to accommodate the strikers' meetings they were held on the Town football ground every morning during the ten days that the strike lasted.'[198]

Conclusion

Research has shown that Luton changed in many inter-related ways between 1874 and 1924. A town where education was regarded as strictly utilitarian and where schooling for girls in particular received scant consideration had been required by Acts of Parliament to provide schools for all its children. Luton, which had always valued its independence, also had to submit to the influence of Bedfordshire, which in 1903 was given authority over secondary education and the schooling of children in the hamlets. During the period under consideration, local businessmen had been obliged by market forces to lessen their dependence on the straw hat trade by inviting new industries into the town, industries which did not embrace the freedoms of the traditional way of life.

Whereas working-class women had enjoyed considerable economic strength, they were now being asked to adapt to some extent to a philosophy which saw the father as the earner of a family wage while the wife received a lower or supportive income. Children attending school in the 1920s certainly had a better basic education than their grandparents, but secondary education, which opened up opportunities to succeed in the wider employment market, was by no means available to everyone. Whether life for the women of the town had progressed or not cannot be generalized. For the fortunate, the educated and the more affluent, doors to a wider world had been opened but, for the majority of women new opportunities did not necessarily offer a better way of life and the freedoms of the past still held their attractions.

---

195   LMAG 103428, pp. 40–41.
196   Ibid., p. 41.
197   L. Holden, *Vauxhall Motors and the Luton Economy*, p. 143.
198   J. Dyer and J.G. Dony, *The Story of Luton*, p. 169.

Chapter Two

Further Perspectives Concerning Employment Patterns for Women

This chapter will look at specific information regarding the employment of women. The 1911 and 1921 censuses give detailed figures and these have been compared with national figures and statistics for Bedford. Less exact, but of interest from a social point of view, are details taken from the *Kelly's Directories* for 1890 and 1920. Advertisements in the *Luton News* between 1901 and 1924 indicate general trends and are of value in the assessment of attitudes and expectations. *Year Books* have also provided useful information and it has been possible to make some comparisons concerning wages and salaries.

Observations based on the 1911 and 1921 censuses
The 1911 and 1921 censuses show just how employment for women had diversified since the height of the hat industry and the arrival of the new industries. The number of unemployed females in 1921 also indicates that some women preferred to remain at home after the First World War. Figures for Bedford have been noted because they offer a contrast to the types of employment available for women in Luton.

While the female population of Luton had increased between 1911 and 1921, the number and proportion of women employed fell. In some respects this supports Carol Dyhouse's view that 'the first world war only temporarily increased women's participation in industry, and was followed by a period of intensified social opposition to the employment of married women in industry and professional life'.[1] However, the involvement of women in the new industries seems to have risen, as indicated by the proportion involved with metal, food and chemical production. Significantly, the number of women involved with the hat industry fell from 6,972 (63.5%) in 1911 to 5,992 (59%) in 1921. As women had always worked in the straw industry, there would appear to be no ideological explanation. It is more likely that market forces and the First World War, which had affected export markets, rather than ideology accounted for this drop.[2]

Interesting comparisons can be made between Luton and Bedford. A larger proportion of Bedford's female population was involved in the service industries indicating that the town enjoyed a different social structure, with many families able to employ domestic help. Fewer Bedford ladies worked, although there were significant numbers involved in commercial and public life. By 1921, more Bedford women were working in the food and drink industry, for example at Meltis. It would

---

[1]   C. Dyhouse, *Girls Growing Up in Late Victorian and Edwardian England* (RKP, 1981), p. 150.
[2]   S. Bunker, R. Holgate and M. Nichols, *The Changing Face of Luton* (The Book Castle, 1993), p. 54.

also appear that more of them liked to employ dressmakers whereas Luton women, used to needlework, may have made their own clothes or bought them from local shops. The difference in the numbers of music teachers is also an indication that the cultural side of life was more readily catered for in Bedford.

Table 5. Occupations of girls and women, based on the 1911 Census

Population of Luton: 49,978
Population of Bedford: 39,183

Occupations	National	Bedfordshire	Luton	% of Luton population	Bedford	% of Bedford population
		aged 10 and over				
Local government	50,000	147	23	0.20	22	0.33
Professional	383,000	1,880				
Medical		_673_	_105_	_0.95_	_202_	_3.04_
Teachers		_1,117_	_177_	_1.62_	_315_	_4.74_
Domestic	2,127,000	8,159	1,046	9.52	3,055	45.99
Laundry etc.		1,094	197	1.79	288	4.33
Commercial	157,000	349	80	0.72	146	2.19
Literary, music		258	69	0.62	103	1.55
Transport	38,000					
Agriculture	117,000	333	2	0.02	4	0.06
Metalwork	128,000	126	25	0.22	15	0.22
Wood, furniture		77	7	0.06	50	0.75
Building, brickmaking etc.	47,000					
Chemicals	46,000	50	33	0.30	6	0.09
Leather	32,000	10	3	0.02	2	0.03
Printing etc.	144,000	833	116	1.05	30	0.45
Food & drink	308,000	235	(a) 200	1.82	5	0.07
Food dealers		1,131	315	2.86	281	4.23
Textiles	87,000					
Clothing	825,000					
Textiles and dyeing		_(b) 830_	_31_	_0.28_	_39_	_0.58_
Dealers in dress		_668_	_191_	_1.74_	_260_	_3.91_
Tailoresses		_122_	_7_	_0.06_	_60_	_0.09_
Milliners		_986_	_599_	_5.45_	_182_	_2.74_
Dressmakers		_2,158_	_354_	_3.22_	_801_	_12.05_
Other workers in dress		_(c) 8,412_	_(d) 6,972_	_63.51_	_15_	_0.22_
Total occupied	5,413,000	29,828	10,977		6,642	
Total unoccupied	11,375,000	53,184	10,343		11,984	

(a) Chocolate and cocoa manufacture (CWS Cocoa Works)
(b) Lace manufacture
(c) Straw – plait, hat, bonnet manufacture (including straw hat and straw bonnet manufacture) 8,323
(d) Straw – plait, hat, bonnet manufacture (including straw hat and straw bonnet manufacture) 6,939

Table 6a. Occupations of girls and women, based on the 1921 Census

Population of Luton: 57,075
Population of Bedford: 40,242

Occupation	National	Bedfordshire	Luton	% of Luton population	Bedford	% of Bedford population
	aged 20 and over	aged 12 and over				
Public administration	81,000	238	47	0.46	64	1.04
Professional	441,000	1,923	365	3.62	613	10.01
Midwives		*21*	*5*	*0.05*	*4*	*0.06*
Sick nurses		*404*	*79*	*0.78*	*138*	*2.25*
Teachers		*1,119*	*232*	*2.30*	*295*	*4.81*
Music teachers		*119*	*25*	*0.24*	*54*	*0.88*
Domestic	1,845,000	8,638	1,459	14.50	2,866	46.81
Laundry		*612*	*106*	*1.05*	*149*	*2.43*
Charwomen, office cleaners		396	135	1.34	105	1.71
Commercial	587,000	2,409	727	7.22	778	12.70
Salesmen & shop assistants		*1,763*	*523*	*5.20*	*601*	*9.81*
Clerks, typists		1,626	557	5.53	539	8.80
Transport, communication	72,000	186	47	0.46	61	0.99
Telegraph, telephone		*59*	*19*	*0.18*	*23*	*0.37*
Agriculture	105,000	416	1	0.01	10	0.16
Metal	175,000	335	186	1.84	22	0.36
Chemical processes	35,000	37	31	0.30	–	–
Wood	31,000	94	11	0.11	45	0.73
Leather	33,000	46	18	0.17	4	0.06
Paper, printing	121,000	1,117	202	2.00	104	1.69
Textiles	701,000	176	14	0.14	16	0.26
Clothing	602,000	8,783	5,992	59.58	563	9.19
Tailoresses		*197*	*41*	*0.40*	*52*	*0.84*
Dress and blouse makers		*820*	*145*	*1.44*	*285*	*4.65*
Embroiderers		*48*	*3*	*0.03*	*4*	*0.06*
Milliners		*654*	*415*	*4.12*	*58*	*0.94*
Hatformers &c		*126*	*110*	*1.09*	*–*	*–*
Hat sewers, finishers, trimmers		*5,507*	*4,538*	*45.12*	*1*	*0.01*
Makers of food & drink	123,000	367	81	0.80	165	2.69
Total occupied	5,699,000	27,501	10,057		6,122	
Total unoccupied	11,968,000	59,933	14,360		12,572	

Table 6b. Female population of Luton, employed and unemployed,
in 1911 and 1921

	1911	1921
Total female population in Luton	21,320	24,417
Female population occupied	10,977	10,057
Female population unoccupied	10,343	14,360
Proportion of female population occupied	51%	41%

Table 7. Women's employment in Luton 1890 and 1920,
based on *Kelly's Directories*

	1890	1920	Increase/decrease
Bakers	4	1	–
Beer retailers	2	1	–
Blouse manufacturers		4	+
Boot and shoe dealers		1	+
Butchers	1		–
Clothiers	1		–
Coffee rooms		1	+
Confectionery and pastry cooks	3	19	+
Corset makers		1	+
Costumiers		14	+
Drapers	1	12	+
Dressmakers		21	+
Fancy repositories	2		–
Felt hat manufacturers were listed as businesses and not under individuals			
Florists		1	+
Fruiterers and greengrocers	5	11	+
Furnished apartments	17	5	–
Furniture brokers and dealers		2	+
Grocers and tea dealers	2	10	+
Haberdashers	2		–
Hairdressers		2	+
Hair and scalp specialists		1	+
Ham and beef dealers		1	+
Hardware dealers		4	+
Laundries	5	2	–
Mantle makers	3		–
Masseurs		1	+
Midwives	1	4	+

Milliners		15	+
Milliners and dressmakers	80		−
Mineral water manufacturer		1	+
Newsagents	2	3	+
Nurses		7	+
Ostrich feather cleaners	1	1	=
Outfitters (m)	1		−
Outfitters (f)		1	+
Pork butchers	1		−
Private schools		3	+
Public houses	9	12	+
Saddlers and harness makers	1	1	=
Sausage makers	1		−
Seed merchants	1	1	=
Shopkeepers	32	40	+
Stationers		4	+
Straw finishers	45		−
Straw hat and bonnet manufacturers	65	7	−
Straw hat sewers	5		−
Straw lining and tip manufacturers	2	1	−
Straw machinists	77		−
Straw plait merchant	1		−
Tailors		2	+
Teachers of music		6	+
Temperance hotels		2	+
Tobacconists	3	4	+
Umbrella makers	1		−

Table 7 compares lists in *Kelly's Directory of Bedfordshire, Huntingdonshire and Northants 1890* with those in *Kelly's Directory of Bedfordshire and Huntingdonshire 1920*. The two dates are interesting: in 1890 Luton was beginning to realize that employment opportunities needed to be diversified, while the situation in 1920 was influenced by the ending of the First World War. These observations are less statistically accurate than those from the censuses, but they do allow an insight into Luton's female entrepreneurial class. Some of the occupations listed may describe individual enterprises but others, notably millinery and dressmaking, often involved small partnerships. There are also problems of definition. For example, just what was the job description of a costumier as opposed to that of a dressmaker or a tailor? Figures for milliners are also unclear as they are classed with dressmakers in the 1890 directory but have a separate entry in the 1920 edition.

It is probably true to say that there were other women in Luton who did not choose to have their names included in the directories; the difference in numbers of music teachers noted in the 1921 Census and the *Kelly's Directory* for 1920 probably reflects this. However, although the figures are not precise enough to draw any strong conclusions, some social trends are clear. For instance, it is possible to group women's commercial initiatives under four main headings: food outlets, needlework, retail and services.

Fashion was important, as indicated by the presence of mantle (loose, sleeveless cloaks) makers and ostrich feather cleaners. The hat industry was changing and, according to the lists in Table 7, had, by 1920, ceased to be dependent on straw.

Women were described as 'shopkeepers' and those in the *Kelly's Directories* were shopkeepers in their own right. The indications seem to be that women were involved with selling more attractive commodities, such as confectionery and mineral water, as well as the more basic foodstuffs.

There are also specific mentions of particular kinds of retail outlets, for example florists and newsagents. Interestingly, there were fewer beer retailers noted but more public house landladies and patronesses of temperance hotels. This is in contrast to the figures for 1890 when women in Luton were offering furnished apartments, no doubt to girls who were coming into Luton during the busy hat season.

In 1920, there were fewer private laundresses but this may reflect the presence of commercial laundries in the town. The lists of services provided indicate that the women of Luton were taking an interest in the less basic side of life, for example coffee rooms and hairdressing, and it is clear that learning to play the piano was seen to be an important social grace. The Temperance Movement, which was strong in Luton, is represented.

The increase in the number of nurses and midwives is significant in the national context.[3] Since 1840, there had been individual initiatives to provide trained district nurses, particularly in London and Liverpool.[4] Then, in 1887, Queen Victoria donated the £70,000 given by the Women's Jubilee Offering of Great Britain and Ireland to the furtherance of district nursing on a national scale. This was intended to provide nurses to tend the sick poor in their own homes. The £48,000 collected for Queen Victoria's Diamond Jubilee was also added to the fund, as was the £84,000 donated for her memorial. In 1890 a Rural Nursing Association was established under the initiative of Mrs Elizabeth Malleson and, in 1902, the Midwives Act instigated the setting up of a Central Midwives Board 'to oversee the midwifery profession and to organize relevant qualifying examinations'.[5]

Margaret Currie has studied the provision of public health measures in Bedfordshire between 1904 and 1938[6] and the *Luton Year Book (1908)* supplies information concerning some of the less formal nursing provision in the town.[7] It notes that, amongst the organizations of the Parish Church, were 'the employment of a trained nurse amongst the poor [and] a Working Party for the sick poor in the parish'. Nurse Bush was working as a parish nurse for St Matthew's Church.

There was a Bedfordshire Rural Nursing Association which, according to the

---

3   See also Chapter Six.

4   E.J. Merry and I.D. Irven, *District Nursing* (Baillière Tindall & Cox, 1960), pp. 2–9.

5   P. Horn, *Ladies of the Manor: Wives and Daughters in Country-house Society 1830–1918* (Alan Sutton, 1991), pp. 132–135.

6   M.R. Currie, 'Social Policy and Public Health Measures in Bedfordshire within the National Context 1904–1938' (Ph.D. Thesis, University of Luton, 1998).

7   *The Luton and District Year Book and Directory (1908)*, pp. 129–143.

Duchess of Bedford, was 'now in working order' and it was hoped that before another meeting took place there would be 'village nurses trained and at work in the county'. Courses of instruction had cost the Technical Instruction Committee £160.[8]

Observations based on newspaper advertisements
A random selection[9] of 'Situations Vacant' and 'Situations Wanted' advertisements in the *Luton News* were studied to create a picture of the employment patterns for women between 1901 and 1924. Once again, these observations are not to be taken as mathematically accurate. For example, when a newspaper carried an advertisement for 'machinists', there is no way of knowing how many were required. Confusion can also arise if no indication is given concerning whether the employer is looking for a response from a man or a woman. However, the 'Situations Vacant' and 'Situations Wanted' columns do provide an overview of opportunities and a fascinating 'behind the scenes' insight into the attitudes of potential employers and employees. These observations have been categorized under three main headings: The hat industry, Domestic and Miscellaneous.

The hat industry
Newspaper advertisements give a clear picture of the expectations of women who chose to work in the staple industry. Much of the work was seasonal but 'all the year round' jobs were available. The freedoms of the hat industry were also represented as employers asked for either indoor or outdoor workers.

First came the learners or apprentices (as is noted in Chapter Nine, these were not the formal indentures associated with other industries) and then 'improvers' who were girls who had reached the next level of competence. At the other end of the scale, many advertisements asked for experienced hands or even stated that 'none but the best need apply'.

Machinists were always in demand. There was a variety of different machines, for example 'Lutonia', '10 guinea' or '17 guinea', and employers were often specific about the kind of machining to be undertaken. In 1920, box machinists for straw hats were wanted in London and the deals included such items as 'fine work', 'permanent', 'good wages' and 'meals and season ticket'. Other areas of work in the hat industry included covering wire frames, fancy work, inserting linings (pads), pleating, stiffening and trimming. It seems as though there was some specialization, as advertisements asked for workers in different materials: chiffon, chip, georgette, ribbon, silk, straw, velvet and, as time went on, felt and velour. Increasingly milliners and millinery apprentices were in demand. In 1918, towards the end of the First World War, women were also wanted in the blocking room – traditionally the domain of the men.

For the ambitious there was the opportunity to become a designer or a forewoman, although the two were often linked. One advertisement asked for a forewoman who was capable of managing forty to fifty machines. A forewoman designer who had to be a 'clever designer in both fancy hats and trimmings' was

8   *Luton Reporter*, 17 December 1897.
9   24 January 1901; 1 October 1903; 5 January 1905; 3 January 1907; 12 August 1909; 6 November 1913; 11 May 1916; 3 January 1918; 1 January 1920; 12 October 1922; 22 May 1924.

needed and another was wanted for 'taking charge of [the] trimming department' for a London firm. Another advertisement offered a bonus for a 'forelady and designer'. There were even opportunities to move abroad, as this advertisement indicates: 'required by one of the leading houses in Australia for their Straw Hat Factory, experienced Forewoman; good designer'.

Domestic

Just what kind of people in Luton employed domestic help? Chapter One notes that it was not infrequent for women who sewed hats in their homes to employ girls to take care of the children. Then there was the town's middle-class element, of which this case study is an example.[10] Ruth Trevelyan was the daughter of the Reverend John Trevelyan, a curate at Christ Church who subsequently became the Vicar of St Saviour's. He lived in a 'four-storey house with a kitchen basement and attic accommodation for the maids'. Ruth was born in 1894 and kept a diary, part of which was reproduced in the *Bedfordshire Family History Society Journal*. She had a governess, who was one of the Miss Higgins,[11] before going to boarding school at the age of fourteen. In October 1906 Ruth was taken to her first music lesson with Mr Gostelo [sic], who was the organist at the Parish Church. The following January she wrote about Louise, who was a maid at the vicarage. She also noted that her clothes were made by a Miss Silsby.

Bramingham Villa, later known as Bramingham Shott and then Wardown House, is now the home of the Luton Museum and Art Gallery. Several servants were required for the upkeep of the family who lived there and relevant information has been collected by the Museum Service and produced as an Information Pack.[12] Two other houses which would have needed a full range of servants were Luton Hoo and Stockwood House.

Advertisments in the *Luton News* show that all levels of domestic help were required: between maids (between a skivvy and a parlourmaid), charwomen, cooks and plain cooks, day girls, generals (these could be male or female), kitchenmaids, maids, parlourmaids, 'useful helps', washers and people who could undertake a combination of these tasks. There were other positions which involved looking after children: mother's help, nurse for children, nursery governess, nurse-housekeeper, nursemaid or just 'to look after baby'. Advertisements were frequently placed in the newspaper by registries which were in the business of placing all kinds of domestic help.

Sometimes the physique of the potential employee is indicated with words such as 'active', 'of good appearance', 'strong' and 'tall'. Very frequently it is noted that country girls would be preferred; they were probably seen to be healthy and fit, but there was also the suggestion that they would be less flighty. Experience is sometimes looked for, but on other occasions there are requests for a girl straight from school who would probably be expected to be amenable and teachable.

---

[10] E. Bowlby, 'Ruth's Diary, A Luton Vicarage in Edwardian Times', *Bedfordshire Family History Society Journal* Vol. 13, No. 7 (September 2002), pp. 50–54.
[11] See Chapter One and Chapter Seven.
[12] *Upstairs Downstairs: Wardown House Life in a Victorian Home*, An Information Pack (Luton Museum Education Service, 1999).

However, the matter of character is seen to be more important and indicates employers' expectations very clearly. As befits a town with a strong working class and a background of respectability learnt in the Sunday schools, 'respectable' is a word which appears repeatedly. Cleanliness and honesty were also important. Luton had a strong band of teetotallers and, sure enough, the word 'abstainer' appears, as does 'Christian'. There are phrases such as 'respectable, domesticated, middle-aged woman', 'staid capable woman', 'of kind disposition', 'of good character' and 'superior young girl'. During the period of the First World War 'ineligible' is sometimes used; this is probably to indicate that the potential employee was not likely to be called to the armed services.

It was possible to choose to live at home. There were also situations where girls could live in, which no doubt would have suited girls from country areas. Several advertisements appear for nurse-companions or nurse-housekeepers. This kind of employment must have been valued by unmarried women with no permanent home. A mention of a 'young widow' in one advertisement is a reminder that many women lost their husbands during the First World War and this was a time when women did not have the opportunity to purchase a house in their own right. One Luton headmistress who had worked all her life recalled that she was only able to buy her house because her brother signed the forms on her behalf.

Most of the advertisements offer work in Luton on an hourly, daily or annual basis, but there are also a number of requests from towns and villages around. In 1924 a cook in London could earn £65, while a cook-general in Luton was paid £42. A scullery maid was wanted at Mill Hill School in 1916 and would have been paid £18 to £20. Girls who wanted to travel further afield could have answered this advertisement in 1913: 'Canada wants domestic servants, all classes (female): situations found: full passage money advanced (must be repaid).'

Domestic work was available in commercial establishments and sometimes cleaning was combined with serving in local shops. Work was also available in the kitchens and dining rooms of cafés and hotels. In 1924, a woman was wanted as a waitress in a good class fried fish shop in Wellington Street.

Commercial laundries seem to have taken the place of the independent washerwoman, and laundries in both Luton and nearby towns frequently advertised for workers. Tasks appear to have been specialized: there were 'collar machinists' (in the days of starched collars), 'folding and drying', 'laundresses for hand laundry', 'shirt and finery ironers', packers and sorters. There was also a demand for women to learn and 'work Calender'. This was a type of commercial pressing machine.

Miscellaneous

During this period the opportunities for women to work as clerks and book-keepers widened considerably. The first advertisement in this random sample was found in 1905 when there was a request for an assistant clerk who had passed the 7th standard in arithmetic. After that there were frequent notices in the 'Situations Vacant' for girls to work in offices. In 1907 a young lady was wanted for a 'business house; shorthand and typewriting – Application by letter only, stating qualifications and salary' and in the 'Situations Wanted' a lady from Dunstable desired 'employment for spare hours; would undertake writing or accounts'. In 1924, applicants for a post as shorthand typist were asked to state 'speeds and qualifications'.

During the First World War requests for female clerical help increased as men were enlisted. This was not dilution in the sense that unskilled workers took the place of skilled, for girls also had the required training and experience. In the newspaper for 11 May 1916, there were several requests for clerical workers: one was placed by the Regent Street Dyeworks and asked for a 'Young lady as Shorthand Typist; one with knowledge of French and general office routine preferred. Apply by letter stating experience.' In the same newspaper appeared an advertisement for several lady clerks to work in 'a Government-controlled firm in Luton'. Lady clerks were also wanted to keep the bakery books at Luton Co-operative Society. Women had entered the office world and were there to stay.

Since 1879 the telegraph service had been seen as an acceptable employer of women[13] and this is reflected in this advertisement in 1920: 'Telephone Operator – Young Lady requires situation; used to both exchange and private switchboard working.'

Dressmakers are well represented, but many job opportunities seem to come from commercial departments rather than from individual needlewomen working from home. This trade was also becoming specialized, with apprentices, improvers, coat hands, bodice hands and skirt hands needed. 'Respectable girls' were also wanted in 1918 for light, clean work in the fancy leather export trade. Shop work of all varieties was on offer. Piano teachers gave lessons in mandolin, piano or singing.

The First World War made itself obvious. Girls were wanted for milk rounds and bread deliveries; one bakery wanted a 'respectable woman or ineligible man' to cover its round. Another advertisement asked for a strong woman or girl who was used to horses to work with a horse and cart on deliveries and offered 'exceptionally good wages to capable person'. Girls were learning to drive; there was a request for a 'capable man or girl to drive and take charge of Ford van' and another for a 'competent male or female motor driver'.

As was explained in Chapter One, women and girls were wanted in munitions factories. Also, a rubber works in Harpenden needed strong girls aged over eighteen 'to work both day and night shifts'. They paid the 'Government rate' plus bonus.

Maternity nurses provided a useful service. For example, in 1913 Mrs Minards of Holly Walk thoroughly recommended Nurse Smith of Ivy Road, while Mrs Scott of Alma Street was 'disengaged for June and [the] beginning of July' 1916 and sought work. Another nurse offered to work nights and mornings. These did not claim to be trained midwives, but were probably the kind of lady who lived in the home to look after the mother and baby during the perinatal period. However, in 1922, there was another advertisement from a 'trained maternity nurse' who wanted a case for November or, alternatively, some general nursing.

Unusual advertisements appear. In 1905 a firm in Northampton wanted 'canvassers and collectors' to be paid salary and commission. This may have been to sell the self-help vouchers for clothing clubs which many women in Luton bought, the debt for which was paid off at regular intervals to collectors at the door. The request does not stipulate whether men or women were required, but a similar advertisement in 1920 specifically asked for ladies. In the same issue there was an appeal for a

---

13 L. Holcombe, *Victorian Ladies at Work* (Archon Books, 1973), p. 165.

'lady agent to sell ladies' wear' on behalf of a manufacturer in Nottingham. In 1922, ladies and gentlemen working in factories were 'wanted to form clubs for clothing, drapery etc.'

In 1916, 'smart girls' were needed to 'learn developing, printing etc.' at Arnold's studios in Manchester Street. The wages were 15s a week, rising to £1 after a month. In 1918, girls were wanted for paper bag making. In the same year a lady requested a 'situation as traveller in materials'. Six years later there was a vacancy in a Bedfordshire town for a 'smart all round assistant' (presumably female) who was a good window dresser and stock keeper.

Observations on the wages paid to women in Luton
In Chapter Five some comparisons are made concerning the money to be earned in the hat industry and in teaching. The advertisements which have been considered in this chapter, however, give an idea of the wages paid for other types of employment. Wages in the hat industry appear to be given as weekly amounts, although they could also be calculated on piecework. Domestic work, however, was valued on an annual basis. It would be impossible to draw any firm conclusions from these as the number of advertisements considered is too small. In addition, there seems to be very little reference made to the number of hours that had to be worked.

Table 8. Salary scales for Luton workers 1901–1924

1901	Good plain cook	£20
1903	Between maid	£14
	General plain cooking	£14
1905	Domestic registry offers a variety of jobs	£26–30
1907	Domestic registry offers a variety of jobs	£28/£30
	General	£18
1909	General (probably female)	£18
1913	Cook-general	£20
1916	Hat industry: stitching cantons	10s
	Girls wanted to learn Calender	2s to 8s
	Housemaid	£18
	Scullery maid (Mill Hill School)	£18–20
	Photography: learn, develop and print	15s, increasing to £1 after one month
1918	Box machinist	6s to 12s all the year round work
	General	£24–26
1920	Trimmer	2s 4d, 2s 8d, 2s 9d per dozen
	House-parlourmaid (St Albans)	£35–40
1924	Cook (London)	£65
	General (Luton)	£30
	Cook-general (Luton)	£42
	Parlourmaid (St Albans)	£36

There are some details concerning the wages earned by women in industry during the First World War. For example, Len Holden notes that the highest rate for women working at the Chaul End munitions factory was, at one time, 18s 10d for a fifty-four hour week. These poor wages and conditions were the cause of subsequent industrial disputes. Some archival records remain at the Vauxhall headquarters in Luton where salary rates for office workers during the period 1914 to 1919 have been located. These are detailed in Table 9.

Table 9. Some Vauxhall salary scales for women 1914–1919

General Office:

Miss Underwood	£1 15s 0d in April 1914 to £2 1s 8d in March 1917
Miss Day	£1 2s 6d in April 1914 to £1 11s 10d in May 1917
Miss Sawyer	8s 0d in November 1915 to 15s 0d in May 1917
Miss Gilbert	10s 0d in March 1917 to 12s 6d in May 1917

Drawing Office:

Miss Gilbert	17s 9d in May 1916 to £1 0s 1d in April 1917

Cost Office:

Miss Cherry, Miss Woodhouse, Miss Long	19s 9d in March 1917

Works Office:

Miss Shepherd, Miss Barford, Miss Scrivener	£1 4s 7d in March 1919
Miss Fettes, Miss Blackeby, Miss Coymer	19s 9d in March 1919

Conclusion

Before drawing any conclusions, it is important to note that mere figures do not demonstrate how the character and identity of the indigenous female workforce in Luton had changed. It must not be forgotten that there were women who had come with their families from other areas to live in the town. For example, many of the employees at the Davis Gas Stove Company were from Scotland and their attitude to work was probably quite different from that of women whose relationship with Luton went back for several generations.

This book is concerned with the interaction between employment and education during the period 1874 to 1924. The impact of compulsory education can be seen in the fact that all the advertisements were for girls who had left school. Whereas women in Luton had once had the freedom to spend their lives, as and when they liked, in the hat industry, there were now constraints and these had come to be accepted.

Another important effect of compulsory education combined with the arrival of the new industries was the increase of opportunities for women in clerical posts. These demanded an acceptable standard of literacy and numeracy and there were specific requests, for example a sample of handwriting.

Mechanism did not alter the lives of the hat workers to any great extent, but it does seem to have changed the lives of women who chose to do laundry work. Similarly, there is a suggestion that more dressmaking took place in a business environment rather than in homes. That is not to say that private enterprise had ceased to exist. There were also many different opportunities for workers in retail outlets, which asked for cleaners, counter staff and even managers.

The war years brought both an increased demand for female labour and the arrival of shift work, but the census figures demonstrate that, after the war, there was a revision of labour prospects and opportunities.

Women had more choices. Just what influenced their choice is still a matter of conjecture, but it seems safe to assume that regular work, as opposed to seasonal work, was one attraction. More research would be needed before definite conclusions could be drawn concerning the financial aspects. However, the sheer pleasure of exploring new horizons cannot be discounted.

Chapter Three

Sunday Schools

Growth of the Sunday School Movement

Sunday schools played a significant part in the schooling of children in Luton. Before compulsory education, which came into force in Luton in 1874, Sunday schools were often the only places where children could learn to read and write. Later they became the focus of much of the social life of the town. The schools were so important that they have been considered here, even though some of the material relates to the years that preceded the main focus of this book. Reference has also been made to some other Sunday schools in Bedfordshire in order to present a fuller picture.

Dr Kay Shuttleworth, the first Secretary of the Committee of the Privy Council (precursor of the Ministry of Education), which was set up in 1839 'for the consideration of all matters affecting the education of the people', believed that Sunday schools were the 'root from which sprang our system of day schools'.[1] This belief was shared by Wesleyans in Luton who claimed that their first school was 'the harbinger not only of the fine schools that now are our pride in Chapel Street, Waller Street, and elsewhere but also a great stimulus to the educational movement in general'.[2] It was also said that 'the Sunday School Movement may claim some credit for the splendid Elementary and Secondary Schools of the town'.[3] In order to support this, names are given of men who were active both in Sunday and elementary schools: Mr Henry Blundell,[4] Mr Gustavus Jordan[5] and Mr George Warren, JP, CA.[6]

Robert Raikes of Gloucester, a publisher, has generally been credited with the introduction of Sunday schools although there are in fact records of other schools which existed before 1780, which is when Raikes began to popularize the idea. Raikes, having observed the lawlessness of children running wild on Sundays, believed that by educating the children he might find a way to turn them from crime. 'He saw that in many cases their misdemeanours were the result of ignorance alone,

---

1   F. Booth, *Robert Raikes of Gloucester* (National Christian Education Council, 1980), p. 157.
2   *A Souvenir of a Century of Wesleyan Methodism in the Town of Luton 1808–1908*, p. 5.
3   Ibid.
4   J.G. Dony, *A History of Education in Luton* (LMAG, 1970), p. 25. Mr Blundell was a Wesleyan who was elected to the first School Board in 1874.
5   Ibid., p. 25. Mr Jordan was a Wesleyan who failed in his attempt to become a member of the first School Board.
6   Ibid., p. 44. Mr Warren was Chairman of the School Board 1895–1903, Chairman of the LEC 1903–1914 and Mayor of Luton 1897.

and that if instruction and enlightenment were not provided, many more people would be in the same pitiful state'.[7]

There was also a strong religious dimension to this initiative for it was sincerely believed by Protestants that it was necessary for everyone to read the Bible for the salvation of their souls and that, in order to do, so they obviously had to be taught to read. Whole families would benefit, for children would go home and show their parents a better way of life.[8] For Raikes then, Sunday schools came to represent a power to reform society.

There are references to Sunday schools in Bedfordshire during the decade following the establishment of the Sunday School Movement and, by 1787, schools had been founded in the Bedford area.[9] In Dunstable, five miles west of Luton, the master of the British School, Charles Lamborn, noted the existence of an early school:

> I have endeavoured, but without success, to discover the precise date of the first Sabbath-school. I have been more fortunate as to the devoted individual conducting the same, and what is more interesting, like Robert Raikes the distinguished founder of such institutions, in 1781, was one who never failed in her devotion and attachment to the Church of England. Old Nanny Burton, though at the age of eighty years, still gathered the little urchins together, in her own hired school-room at the back of the premises now occupied by Mr Rush, the brazier.[10]

One of the factors which influenced the number of Sunday schools in any given area was the proportion of Nonconformity. Not surprisingly therefore, the Sunday School Movement became well established in Luton, particularly in the Nonconformist churches.[11] Table 10 shows the proportion of the population of Bedfordshire enrolled in Sunday schools in 1818, 1833 and 1851.

Table 10. Percentage of Bedfordshire population enrolled in Sunday schools 1818, 1833 and 1851

Year	Percentage	
1818	6.1%	Eighth highest in England
1833	15.7%	Joint third
1851	19.7%	First[12]

Also responsible for the popularity of the Sunday schools were the aspirations of many parents from the labouring classes who, according to the *Digest of Returns (1818)*, were apparently 'desirous of having the means of education'. The climate of

---

7   F. Booth, *Robert Raikes of Gloucester*, p. 65.

8   Ibid., pp. 91and 98; BLARS Z 209/73, *The Sunday School Teachers Magazine and Journal of Education* Series 4, Vol. 6 (1855).

9   For more details on Sunday schools see A. Allsopp, 'The Provision, Development and Effects of Sunday Schools in Bedfordshire 1780–1870' (MA Dissertation, 1984).

10   C. Lamborn, *Dunstapelogia* (James Tibbett, 1859), p. 160.

11   A. Allsopp, 'Sunday Schools in Bedfordshire'.

12   T.W. Laqueur, *Religion and Respectability: Sunday Schools and Working Class Culture 1780–1850* (Yale University Press, 1976), p. 49.

opinion therefore seems to have been in favour of education, and the Sunday schools were able to offer some basic schooling at a time when the children were free from the demands of employment. The *Digest of Returns (1818)* do not refer to any Luton Sunday schools, but do observe that 'the poor are abundantly provided with the means of education, and very generally embrace them with much apparent thankfulness'.[13]

The *Abstract of Education Returns: 1833* for Luton and its hamlets gives two day and Sunday Lancasterian schools, one taking eighty-seven boys on weekdays and 105 on Sundays. The other had seventy-eight weekday scholars and 154 Sunday scholars. The Baptists ran three Sunday schools. They taught 223 boys and 311 girls and also had libraries. The other three belonged to the Wesleyan Methodists; one had 109 boys and ninety-nine girls, another (opened in 1825) had thirty-six boys and thirty-four girls. The last (opened in 1831) had twenty boys and fifteen girls.[14]

In 1846–1847 two hundred Luton girls attended school on Sundays, but not on weekdays, and at Biscot thirty-nine boys and twenty-four girls received Sunday tuition. At Stopsley six boys and twelve girls attended school on Sundays, but at Hyde ten boys and twelve girls had schooling on Sundays and weekdays while fourteen boys and sixteen girls went to school only on Sundays.[15]

The *1851 Ecclesiastical Census* also provides numbers of children attending Sunday schools (see Table 11).[16]

Table 11. Attendance at Sunday schools based on the 1851 Ecclesiastical Census

	Morning	*Afternoon*	*Evening*
Stopsley Wesleyan Methodists	40	–	–
Parish Church of St Mary	400	422	130
Old Wesleyan Chapel	200	–	–
Ceylon Baptist Church	200	–	–
Limbury Wesleyan Methodists	–	23	–
Wesleyan Methodists	58	270	–
Ebenezer Baptist (March 1851)	62	–	–
Ebenezer Baptist (November 1851)	69	72	–
High Town Primitive Methodists	178	178	178
Leagrave Wesleyan Methodists	98	99	–
Union Chapel, Castle Street	450	400	–

The Wesleyans had three circuits in Luton and the surrounding villages. Figures for 1884 show that in total there were 4,930 scholars and 863 teachers. Joseph Hawkes made an interesting comment concerning the children from Cockernhoe and Aley Green. It was his 'belief that scores who attended those schools would never have

---

[13] *Digest of Returns to Circular Letter from the Select Committee on the Education of the Poor (1818)*; D. Bushby, *The Bedfordshire Schoolchild Before 1902* (BHRS Vol. 67, 1988).
[14] *Abstract of Returns: (1833) County of Bedford*; transcript in D. Bushby, *The Bedfordshire Schoolchild*.
[15] National Society, *Church-School Inquiry 1846–7*; also in D. Bushby, *The Bedfordshire Schoolchild*.
[16] Figures taken from D. Bushby, *Elementary Education in Bedford 1868–1903; The Ecclesiastical Census Bedfordshire March 1851* (BHRS Vol. 54, 1975).

learned to read at all had it not been for their attendances there'.[17] The circuit schools which are relevant to the areas covered in this book are listed in Table 12.

Table 12. Wesleyan Sunday schools 1884

	Scholars	*Officers and Teachers*
Chapel Street	820	120
Albert Road	199	25
Limbury	36	8
Waller Street	420	65
North Street	240	45
Stopsley	68	16
Round Green	75	18
Leagrave	114	34
Total	1,972	331

The *Luton Year Book (1908)* names some of the Sunday school superintendents.[18] St Paul's, the Congregational Church, Wellington Street Baptist and Waller Street Wesleyan were supervised entirely by men. However, in the Parish Church, the girls' Sunday school was the responsibility of Miss Thomas and the infants' was run by Miss Holyoak. At Christ Church, Miss Bowen was in charge of the girls' and Miss Robinson of the infants'. St Matthew's chose a man, Mr H.E. Cain, for the girls' and a woman, Miss Sewell, for the infants'. The 'respectability' of the Sunday School Movement can be judged by the fact that the superintendents at the Waller Street Wesleyan Church were Alderman G. Warren JP and Alderman L. Giddings JP.

The considerable size and extent of the organization needed to run the schools can be judged by the entry for the Chapel Street Wesleyan Church:[19]

> The officers of the Sunday School are: superintendent, Mr. G.W. Gilder, Myrtle House; assistant superintendents: Mr. M. Godfrey, Mr. W.C. Gillam; musical director, Mr. S. Bennett; treasurer, Mr. A. Barrett; auditors, Mr. H. Arnold and Mr. J. Squires, junr; general secretary, Mr. W.G. Squires; assistant secretaries, Messrs. L.C. Beecroft, H. Fensome and Harold Blows; librarian, Mr. A.H. Blows; assistant librarian, Mr. S. Clarke; representatives to Quarterly Meeting, Messrs. A.J. Bass and T. Ludgate; representatives to Sunday School Union (local branch), Messrs. G.W. Gilder, M. Godfrey and W.C. Gillam.[20]

The 1913 *Year Book* gives specific information and notes that the Luton and District Sunday School Union comprised:

---

[17] J. Hawkes, *The Rise and Progress of the Luton Wesleyan Sunday Schools* (A.J. Giles, 1885), p. 20. These two villages are outside the area covered in this book, but the point is made that Sunday schools were important for the teaching of reading.
[18] *The Luton and District Year Book and Directory (1908)*, pp. 129–141.
[19] Ibid., pp. 135–137.
[20] Ibid., pp. 136–137.

fourteen Free Church Sunday Schools in Luton and seven in the adjacent villages, in which are 5,905 scholars and 671 teachers. There are 2,116 of these scholars in the Band of Hope[21] and 1,904 are members of the international Bible Reading Association. A Teachers' Preparation Class is held in the Wesley Hall every Friday evening during the winter months.[22]

Accommodation

Children were taught wherever space could be found. Sometimes this would be a private home, sometimes rented accommodation and sometimes a corner of the Church building. As time went by, purpose-built schools were established. The schools were financed by individual contributions, subscriptions and, crucially, collections taken at the annual anniversary celebrations.

Hawkes gives examples of schools in Luton. In 1803, a Mrs Neal held a small Baptist Sunday school 'in her own schoolroom'. At the time there was no Wesleyan Sunday school in the town so the Reverend John Crosby Leppington (superintendent from the Bedford circuit) promised the Luton friends that, if they would raise a Sunday school and furnish a room, then he would provide all the necessary books free of charge for one year. The challenge was accepted and the Wesleyans started a school nearby in a cottage in Park Street 'somewhere between the Horseshoes and the Chequers public houses'.[23] In 1812, when the cottage became too cramped, they took over 'a large club-room (an upper room) at the Black Swan Inn'.[24] When, two years later, a new chapel was built in Chapel Street, the school moved into the old chapel. In 1846 'a swarm from the Chapel Street hive' moved into 'the large room in the building in Wellington Street called the Victoria Room'.[25] This was pulled down three years later after the town authorities condemned it as unsafe and the children were moved to another old chapel in Church Street. Around 1865 a school was opened in Albert Road and was held in a 'loft which was far too small' and then 'removed to a room over a baker's shop'.[26] In November 1863 the Waller Street Chapel was opened with a new Sunday school attached.[27]

The Union Chapel, Luton, was also under pressure to increase the amount of room available for the children. First the chapel and schoolroom were enlarged (probably c.1847). It was found necessary 'to carry the new walls down to a depth considerably below the old foundations. Consequently, the floor of the new portion was made eighteen inches lower than that of the old. This new portion was called the Lower Room, and was used exclusively for the girls.' Some time later, the windows were enlarged and ventilators were cut through into the chapel 'in spite of which the atmosphere is often most oppressive when the gas has been lighted a little while'.[28] In 1863, the Union Baptists in Luton advertised for plans for a new school, offering £10 for the successful ones. A Mr Pearson provided the most suitable plans but the local Board of Health refused to sanction the building, which was to have been on

---

21 Bands of Hope were juvenile departments of the Temperance Movement.
22 *Luton News Almanac (1913)*, p. 52.
23 J. Hawkes, *Rise and Progress*, p. 6.
24 Ibid., p. 9.
25 Ibid., p. 14.
26 Ibid., p. 16.
27 Ibid., p. 15.
28 S. Pride, *History of Union Chapel, Luton* (Jubilee Celebration, 1887), pp. 29–31.

burying ground at the back of the chapel. In 1887 the subject was still being considered and there was 'a bright prospect' of a new schoolroom being built.[29]

It would therefore appear that when schools were founded the administrators were grateful to find any room large enough to hold a group of children. Once schools became firmly established, however, there was often a move to provide permanent, purpose-built accommodation. Nevertheless, the growth in numbers and size of the schools meant that the problem of providing adequate teaching space persisted.

Officers and teachers

At one time the Luton Wesleyan School had a rota of four superintendents. This plan 'led to mutual interest, division of labour, and responsibility', but Hawkes considered the later plan, with two superintendents, to be more efficient. While one superintendent was engaged in the school on a Sunday, the other would be in country places 'to preach, to exhort, or to read a sermon'.[30]

Hawkes tells of the 'worthies who conducted the school, and whose names I hold in great esteem for their work's sake'. The first of these was John Underwood, who was a tailor. His successors included: Mr Boustead, one of John Underwood's workmen and also the first teacher; Mr John Waller, gentry; Mr Thomas Stormer, tailor; and Mr John Higgins, plumber and glazier.[31] Mr Benjamin Bolton[32] and Mr George Strange, linen and woollen draper and silk merchant respectively,[33] were superintendents at the Union Chapel, Luton.[34]

From the early days (1803) women became involved in Sunday school teaching. 'As in the days of our blessed Lord, so then the sisterhood came to the rescue, and Christian young women bravely took part in this great, good, and new enterprise'.[35] These school officials became part of 'an interesting little social circle': Miss Sophia Hawkes [Mrs William Underwood] was a class leader to the end, 'the faithful wife of a local preacher and mother of two local preachers' and her sister, Fanny, was the mother of a local Town Clerk.[36]

At the Union Chapel, both Mr and Mrs Benjamin Bolton became superintendents.[37] Women continued to play an important role: seven leaders of the primary department are named in *The Hill of the Lord*.[38] Around a hundred women attended Miss Rose Foster's senior Bible classes, which, together with the men's, enjoyed 'phenomenal success'.[39] Mr and Mrs Higgins were probably from the same Higgins family which features in Chapters Four, Six, Seven and Ten of this book; Mrs John Higgins, who died in March 1873 aged 73, had been a class leader for many years.[40]

---

29 Ibid., p. 32.
30 J. Hawkes, *Rise and Progress*, p. 11.
31 Ibid., p. 11.
32 S. Pride, *History of Union Chapel*, p. 29.
33 Ibid., p. 31.
34 Ibid., p. 31.
35 J. Hawkes, *Rise and Progress*, p. 6.
36 Mr George Bailey was Town Clerk. *A Souvenir of a Century of Wesleyan Methodism*, p. 5.
37 S. Pride, *History of Union Chapel*, pp. 27–29.
38 R.K. Spedding, *The Hill of the Lord: High Town Primitive Methodist Church 1838–1932* (1933), p. 40.
39 Ibid., p. 43.
40 J. Hawkes, *Rise and Progress*, p. 12.

Once appointed, the Sunday school teachers were expected to set an example to the children, especially in standards of punctuality. They were also in many cases expected to visit the homes of children who did not attend regularly. There is evidence to suggest that the Church of England may have paid some of the teachers, but Nonconformist churches flourished with voluntary labour.

Sunday schools, by their very nature, did not leave substantial records. Registers and minutes of teachers' meetings were almost certainly kept for a while, but they tended to be unofficial and were frequently presumed to be the property of the superintendent of the day. Families probably disposed of them, thinking them to be of no value. Printed booklets, such as the one written by Joseph Hawkes, and others produced for centenary celebrations, are therefore invaluable.

Few lists of teachers remain. The social class of the people who ran the Sunday schools has been a matter of debate among historians, but it seems to be the case that, in Luton, tradespeople were very much involved. Hawkes listed several of the men and women who were active in the Luton Wesleyan Sunday School between 1803 and 1883:[41]

John Tebbet Cawdell	Saddler and Collar Maker
James Dunham	Tailor and Draper
Joseph Wood	Schoolmaster, Lancasterian School
Charles Beecroft	Linen and Woollen Draper
Emma Jordan	Wife of Clergyman
The Reverend Josiah Pearson	
George Hunt	Straw Hat and Bonnet Manufacturer
John Higgins	Painter, Plumber and Glazier
William Webb	Straw Plait Dealer
Henry Blundell	Linen Draper etc.
George Wilcox Gilder	Straw Hat and Bonnet Manufacturer, later Mayor of Luton
William Read	Straw Hat and Bonnet Manufacturer
William Dunham	Tailor
William Garrard	Tailor
George Gardner	Tailor and Draper
William Muggleton	Straw and Tuscan Bonnet Manufacturer[42]

The Sunday school booklets also give the names of several women:

Mrs Kate Conquest
Mrs McLean
Mrs Hilda Hale
Mrs Moore
Miss Winifred Lloyd
Mrs Annie Cook
Mrs Walker
Mrs Benjamin Bolton[43]

41 Ibid., p. 12.
42 Ibid., p. 12.
43 R.K. Spedding, *Hill of the Lord*, p. 40.

Most of these women were married and it is probably safe to assume that they came from the same social class as the men listed earlier.

Life was not at all easy. Hawkes tells of a Brother Goodwin who prayed with great feeling 'Lord, Thou knowest we have need of patience, for, O Lord, Thou knowest the scholars are often very contrary!'[44] Although Sunday schools were, in their early years, committed to teaching children to read, the struggle to do so was lifted when day schooling became compulsory which, in Luton, was in 1874. This 'has relieved Sunday School teachers of the drudgery of secular teaching which was absolutely necessary a while ago'.[45] The schools were then able to concentrate on their spiritual life and expand other interests; music, for example, became popular.[46]

Children

Benefactors, subscribers, administrators and teachers believed, as did Raikes, that a school is better for the children than the streets. This better way of life involved basic literacy, but was also concerned with the spiritual welfare of the children who were to be instructed in the principles of religion. The Lidlington School rules[47] stipulated that teachers should aim to teach the children 'to understand and practise every moral and Christian duty'. The Union Chapel, Luton, was even more specific when it was pleased to report that 'Infidelity and Popery are not gaining over the youth in our provincial town.'[48] At Biggleswade children were taught the necessity of fighting against the 'giants of Untruth, Passion, Pride, Selfishness and Idleness'.[49]

Sunday was a busy day for the children. Schools were autonomous and varied in the way they were run, but it was usual for children to attend Church services as well as Sunday school. They were expected to arrive clean and tidy and at least one school, Woburn, demanded that the children should be vaccinated. Punctuality was important, but school hours were adjusted in winter to allow the children to arrive home early.

Discipline was strict and good behaviour was expected. Hawkes records an occasion when a little girl, who had gone to school with her aunt, became 'wearied and unsettled, and somewhat disturbed the order of the school and at the same time interfered with the equanimity of the superintendent'. This gentleman, in rather strong tones, said 'Take that child out.'[50] Any bad behaviour at Union Chapel, Luton, had to be reported to the superintendent and the offender 'publicly admonished or otherwise dealt with, as may be deemed most desirable'.[51] On the other hand, there were rewards, especially for regular attendance. These were often the gift of a Bible.

E.P. Thompson claims in his book *The Making of the English Working Class* that 'in the years between 1780 and 1832 most English working people came to feel an

[44] J. Hawkes, *Rise and Progress*, p. 20.
[45] Ibid., p. 20.
[46] Ibid., pp. 21–22.
[47] BLARS X 135/73, *Rules of Lidlington Sunday and Free School* (1818). Lidlington is a village near Woburn.
[48] S. Pride, *History of Union Chapel*, p. 30.
[49] BLARS X 350/1, Biggleswade Baptist Church Records from 1788.
[50] J. Hawkes, *Rise and Progress*, p. 9.
[51] S. Pride, *History of Union Chapel*, p. 29.

10. Limbury Baptist Church Sunday School 13 June 1918 [LM]

identity of interests' and developed a way of life that was essentially 'respectable'.[52] The social life of many Luton families, which revolved around the Sunday schools and their self-help groups, frequently reflected this working-class 'respectability'. These ideals have also been discussed in T.W. Laqueur's book *Religion and Respectability*.[53]

The anniversary of the founding of each particular school would be celebrated with outings, games, teas and services. The following description of an anniversary treat refers to the Raikes Centenary Anniversary, which was celebrated throughout the country. Special medals were struck to mark the occasion.

> Sunday School treats were held in Scarborough's meadow, now covered by streets, between Dallow Road and Ashburnham Road. Schools taking part in the combined efforts would meet in Park Square and march to the meadow. During the Centenary of 1880, about 10,000 people assembled and joined in community singing before moving off. . . . Later outings went to Ashridge, Wheathampstead or Totternhoe Knolls. A photograph shows Mr Pratt's shop at Totternhoe: his brake met the train at Stanbridgeford for those who could afford it, while the rest walked, and 'pop' was bought at his shop and taken to the Knolls. In the afternoon, races were followed by tea in Mrs Pratt's orchard – a great day for 1s 6d.[54]

Money collected at the anniversary services was vital to support the schools throughout the year. Hawkes tells of one such occasion when a friend of his, a staunch teetotaller, put a note in the collection plate stating that he could not conscientiously donate anything because some of the money would be spent on beer to give to the children and teachers at the annual treat. Hawkes concludes by remarking that 'there was never any beer supplied after that time'.[55]

We are given to believe that the training received in the Sunday schools had the desired effect. 'We found the room very full of rough, unkempt children, under the care of Mr Scrivener and Mrs Scales. Since that time I have observed some of those children grow to maturity – improved in appearance – and take their places as respectable members of civil and religious society.'[56] Schools were likened to oak trees which shed their acorns and they, in turn, grew into mature oaks. This figure was used to describe how the standards of behaviour learnt in the schools were to be taken out into the wider world. In 1885 Hawkes exhorted Wesleyan children to bear witness to the teaching of the Sunday schools[57] and the High Town School, Luton, was pleased to announce that some of its scholars had gone abroad to be missionaries:[58]

> My dear girls and boys, and young women and young men, let me express my hope that when you leave the Sunday School, to whatever part of the country, or the world you may go, (for in these days of emigration and migration, for

52 E.P. Thompson, *The Making of the English Working Class* (Penguin, 1981), p. 11.
53 T.W. Laqueur, *Religion and Respectability*.
54 J.E. Davis, 'Luton in Focus: T.G. Hobbs and His Times', *Bedfordshire Magazine* Part I, Vol. 15, No. 117 (Summer 1976), pp. 207–212. Hobbs was born c.1852.
55 J. Hawkes, *Rise and Progress*, p. 23.
56 Ibid., p. 17.
57 Ibid., p. 23.
58 R.K. Spedding, *The Hill of the Lord*, p. 43.

which there are so many and great opportunities, you cannot tell where your lot may be cast) – I say then that wheresoever you pitch your tent, be sure to carry with you the principles you have learned in this school. If tempted by the ungodly to stray from the paths of virtue and godliness, remember the words, 'if sinners entice thee consent thou not. If tempted to secret faults remember the text, "Thou God seest me." '[59]

Curriculum

It may seem strange nowadays to realize that there was disagreement about whether or not children should be taught to read at all. One point of view was that children who could read would not be content to 'abide the plough' and would despise their lot in life. Then there was the fear that 'seditious pamphlets, vicious books, and publications against Christianity' would influence the labouring classes. On the other hand there were those who, like Samuel Whitbread, wanted the State to provide schools that could create 'an enlightened peasantry, frugal, industrious, sober, orderly, contented' as a result of learning true Christian values.[60]

In view of this diversity of opinion it is not surprising that there were disagreements amongst those who ran the Sunday schools about exactly what should be taught. Whilst there was general approval of the teaching of reading, particularly from the Bible, there was no general agreement about other subjects such as arithmetic. There is therefore no definitive Sunday school curriculum. Sometimes day and Sunday schooling overlapped, with the same building being used for both, and some Sunday schools ventured into weekday and evening classes on their own account. For example, at High Town the lower and upper schoolrooms were in use as day schools up to the time of the establishment and building of Board schools.[61]

There is a very useful account of the way that teachers in the Wesleyan schools actually taught the children to read:

> Many years ago the lessons were pasted on thin boards about six inches long and three wide, square at the top and rounded off where they were held in the hand, with the alphabet one side and short words on the other. Larger boards were also hung up for the use of the teachers, with advanced lessons on them.[62]

There are also printed reading manuals that dictate teaching methods, some of which were circulated by the Sunday School Unions, which flourished throughout the country. The first exercises are accompanied by a list of the letters of the alphabet, both upper and lower case.

> Exercise 1. All the scholars to look at the board or book, The teacher is to name the first letter, which is to be repeated by the first scholar. The teacher is to name the second letter, which is to be repeated by the second scholar, and so on. The teacher is to name the word (when all its letters have been pronounced) which is to be repeated by the third scholar. To continue in the

---

[59] J. Hawkes, *Rise and Progress*, p. 23.
[60] F. Booth, *Robert Raikes of Gloucester*, pp. 156–157.
[61] R.K. Spedding, *The Hill of the Lord*, p. 40.
[62] J. Hawkes, *Rise and Progress*, p. 20.

same manner round the class throughout the lesson, which is afterwards to be repeated without assistance from the teacher.[63]

In a similar way, children progressed to words and then sentences. The main criterion which distinguished easy words from hard was the length; the complexity of the sounds did not seem to matter and the language used was very forced. Another interesting feature was the moral content of the sentences. After each exercise the teacher was to question the children to make sure that they had understood the meaning of the sentences; learning to read was thus combined with spiritual teaching. Below is a selection of sentences which are to be found in *The First Class Book*.

> Wo be to me!
> O fy, to do so!
> All sin. I sin. You sin.
> The way of sin is the way of wo.
> Wo be to the bad.
> Let me not go in the way of sin.
> Go not in the way of a bad boy.
> Read the Word of God with care.
> It is the best book we can have.
> Try to read it well.
> It can make us wise.

The Sunday Scholar's First Book[64] was written by Mrs Hughes (1828). She had been teaching for some years in Sunday schools and had not been able to find a first book 'calculated at the same time, and in a short compass, to teach the elements of reading and impress strongly upon the youthful mind sentiments of piety towards God, and love to their fellow-creatures; to enforce the necessity of performing our duty in this world, and looking for a recompense in that which is to come'. This book also begins with the alphabet, but then progresses to meaningless syllables: ab eb ib ob ub; ad ed id od ud; af ef if of uf; ba be bi bo by etc. The first words to be taught are one syllable words, then the children progress to two, and so on. Again, no great importance is attached to the difficulty of the construction. For example, the first one syllable words to learn are: 'Love God, for he is good' in which 'love' breaks accepted phonetic rules.

Gadsby's *First Book*[65] aimed to 'impart Instruction to children without teaching them to utter Language which can only properly be used by Believers'. This also progressed from sentences with three-letter words such as 'The eye of God is on you all the day' to sentences with four-letter words such as 'Keep from wine, for it will make your head ache.'

Again, it is interesting to note the moral tone in these exercises. As with much nineteenth-century literature for children, they contain a strong message; children should aspire to lives of gratitude, hard work, honesty, obedience and temperance. Exercises include 'As you have come to school once more, I hope you will all strive

---

[63] *The First Class Book for Reading, Spelling and Catechizing* (Sunday School Union n.d. but almost certainly before 1900).

[64] Mrs Hughes, *The Sunday Scholar's First Book* (David Eaton, 1828).

[65] *Gadsby's Educational Books for Sunday Schools, Families and First Book* (1867).

to learn' and 'These books have been bought for you by kind friends, but we cannot teach you if you will not be taught.' Most of the sentences are directed at boys, but some refer to girls. For example, 'A deaf and dumb girl came to our town. She had no food, and was half dead from cold' and 'That girl is very bold and rude. I must talk to her, for her own good.' Five-letter words come next and, lastly, there are 'Exercises in reading', some of which are in verse:

> The child that lies no one will trust,
> Though he should speak the word that's true;
> And he that tells one lie at first,
> And lies to hide it, makes it two.

It seems to be the case that Sunday school teachers were usually 'amateurs' who were sustained by sincerity and enthusiasm alone, so class management could be a problem. Hawkes told a story about the experience of one woman who was standing in for an absent teacher. She had a class 'of well-educated little girls' and asked them 'from what portion of Scripture they were to take the spelling lesson':

> The girls saw that she was not up to it and a little plot was at once laid, one of the perkiest was deputed to carry it out. Asked from what portion of Scripture they were to take the spelling lesson, the deputy said 'Here' pointing to about ten words of Scripture names. . . . 'The astute little sharpers' pointed to a chapter in which words such as 'Tychichus', 'Eutychus' and 'Dionysius' appeared. The poor teacher 'was rather non-plussed, and the little rogues watched with stealthy glee her apparent embarrassment'.[66]

It was the custom to teach girls and boys separately. There were also infant classes, but the age of admissions and also leaving seems to have varied from school to school. Manuals recommend this structure: Alphabet Class, 1st, 2nd, 3rd, 4th and 5th. There are references in other Bedfordshire schools to a Test Class, Spelling Class, Senior Class, Scripture Class, an Elementary Class and a Primary Class.

Some schools had lending libraries. Unsurprisingly, the books which could be borrowed told tales that set out high moral standards. There were also books on Bible stories, Church history, missionary work, nature, famous lives and prayers. Magazines for teachers and pupils were also available.

One book, *A Basket of Flowers*,[67] is probably typical of many. It describes quite clearly the kind of young girl who was being groomed in the Sunday schools. The heroine was Mary Rode whose piety, innocence, modesty and unfeigned kindness towards all she met 'gave to her beauty a rare and peculiar charm'. In her 'bright little living-room there was never a speck of dust to be seen; the pots and pans in the kitchen shone like new, and the whole house was a pattern of order and cleanliness'. She was taught by her father 'to see and admire in the beauty and manifold charms of flowers the unvarying goodness, wisdom, and omnipotence of God'. Mary was falsely accused of theft, but maintained her honesty throughout all her subsequent difficulties and was eventually rewarded for her integrity.

---

[66] J. Hawkes, *Rise and Progress*, p. 20.
[67] C. von Schmid, *The Basket of Flowers* (Blackie & Son, n.d.), p. 10. This book was in the Woburn Sunday School library catalogue.

Music was a popular subject, for example in the Wesleyan Sunday schools:

Not the least of the advantages of the present day (1885) and one which serves powerfully to add to the love towards the school by scholars and teachers, is the great improvement in singing and music. The liberal use of singing in the Sunday School, always a great attraction, is today more powerful than ever. Good music allied with such excellent poetry as is found in our hymn books, is calculated to fill the soul with aspirations after a higher and diviner life, to supply the soul with religious comfort and happiness, and to excite the hope of joining in the music of heaven.[68]

Hawkes went on to explain how he used to teach music 'upon Mr Waite's system' which

was on the principle of numbers to the scale, commencing every scale with Number 1 for the key note. The class being divided into four sections, the object being to train the class to sing in parts, and to sing in tune and time, to read the music without the aid of an instrument, and to give an impetus to better congregational singing. After this class had lasted through several sessions, it was superseded by the more generally accepted Sol-Fa system.[69]

According to Hawkes the singing at Chapel Street was 'surpassed by few country choirs, congregations, or schools' and goes on to say that the Luton Choral Society, which was inaugurated on 4 December 1866, was mainly a Wesleyan society, but that all the choirs in the town were welcome to join. Among the earliest members were the Reverend Wesley Hurt (tenor) and Mrs Hurt (contralto). The organist of Chapel Street (Mrs Bickerton) led and presided at the piano for several years. The society had made 'the Luton public familiar with the immortal works of Handel, Beethoven, Haydn, Mendelssohn and others'.[70]

Changing perspectives
The schools supplied a focus for the social life of both scholars and teachers and remained an accepted and important part of life in Luton until well into the twentieth century. In July 1880, several schools were given permission to have a holiday for the Raikes Centenary Celebration[71] but, in subsequent years, the Luton Board and the Education Committee showed considerable concern about the lack of attendance on treat days. In some years the Luton Board tried to limit the number of absences by asking the schools to hold their treats during the summer holidays[72] and, in 1894, the Clerk was asked to obtain returns to assess the level of absenteeism.[73] These attempts seem to have been unsuccessful and in January 1897 the superintendents were summoned to a conference with the Luton Board.[74] There were to be no school closures in 1899,[75] but by 1901[76] the Board allowed a maximum of four days of

68 J. Hawkes, *Rise and Progress*, p. 21.
69 Ibid., p. 22.
70 Ibid., p. 21.
71 M/218 Minutes of USDL, 22 June 1880.
72 M/219 Minutes of USDL, 19 June 1883; M/221 Minutes of USDL, 23 April 1895.
73 M/221, 17 July 1894.
74 M/222 Minutes of USDL, 26 January 1897.
75 M/223 Minutes of USDL, 27 June 1899.
76 Ibid., 16 April 1901.

closure 'at such times as will least interfere with the ordinary work of the Day Schools'.[77] Miss Beard gave as one of her reasons for resigning from the school at Hyde in 1912 and moving to a school in Luton[78] that she wanted to take advantage of the opportunity for 'several holidays in the summer time, when School Treats are in vogue'.[79] As late as 1920, schools were closed 'when attendance [was] seriously threatened by Sunday School treats'.[80] It would therefore appear that the influence of the informal Sunday schools was so great in the town that it challenged the authority of the Education Committee. This seems to be an indication that the independent spirit of the people of Luton was still a powerful force.

Hawkes explained how the aims and outlook of the Luton Sunday schools had changed during the nineteenth century:

> The opportunities for usefulness are hereby greatly increased, but not only have you all the extra advantages of plant, machinery and organisation, but you have also an educated youthful population to deal with, ready to your hands, to receive divine truth and religious culture. There is no necessity now as there was within my memory, to teach the rudiments of knowledge, the ABC of secular training.[81]

Conclusion

From the point of view of the men and women who gave their lives in their service, the Sunday schools of Luton were no doubt successful. Hawkes explains how they grew from humble beginnings as an oak grows from an acorn:

> The examples produced for your information and your emulation, show that the work begun by a few humble individuals for the improvement of the young and rising race, begun in weakness, and carried on in faith and perseverance with but limited means, but at the same time with trust in God, has grown, and spread, and multiplied, the acorn has produced the oak, or rather many oaks. The small one has become a mighty host, the units have become hundreds, the tens have become thousands.[82]

Some have viewed Sunday schools as vehicles of indoctrination or exercises in social control. As far as Luton is concerned, the aim was certainly to produce a generation of children steeped in the Christian way of life and with values of cleanliness, punctuality, obedience and industriousness. The people of the town seemed to have been happy with the situation and welcomed the social life that the schools introduced.

Did the Sunday schools contribute significantly to the education of the thousands of children who passed through their doors? They offered a basic schooling which compared favourably with dame schools and plait schools, but which was probably less satisfactory than that which could be received in a good day school. The main advantages of Sunday schools were that they were cheap to run, were almost always free to the children and were also held at times when children were not committed to

---

[77] Ibid., 16 April 1901 and 25 June 1901.
[78] Hyde was managed by the BCC.
[79] SD Hyde 1 Logbook of Hyde School, 1 April 1912.
[80] M/229 Minutes of LEC, 7 June 1920.
[81] J. Hawkes, *Rise and Progress*, p. 20.
[82] Ibid., p. 19.

the demands of agricultural work or home industry. This poses an interesting question, which is so far unanswered. While Joyce Godber notes that child labour was an obstacle to education, 'for many children the only day when they were not at work was Sunday',[83] we are given to understand that children in Luton and the surrounding villages spent all their free time plaiting. Did they plait on Sundays or did religious constraints prevail?

It would be gratifying to be able to say that the provision of Sunday schools contributed to a high rate of literacy in Bedfordshire but unfortunately this was not so, as records show that Bedfordshire had consistently low rates.[84] Sound teaching requires sound teachers and the people of Luton were not known for their high educational standards. Bunker refers to the poor spelling found on notices around the town and the alleged deficiencies on the town's monumental inscriptions.[85] However, the Sunday schools may well have provided opportunities and motivation where none had existed before and as W.B. Stephens has suggested 'it may be that the achievement of these institutions in averting disaster has been under-estimated'.[86] While it is difficult to assess the contribution of the Sunday schools towards the basic education for the children of Luton, there is no doubt that they had a considerable influence on the religious and social life of the town.

[83] J. Godber, *History of Bedfordshire* (BCC, 1969), p. 429.
[84] W.B. Stephens, *Regional Variations in Education During the Industrial Revolution 1780–1870* (University of Leeds, 1973), p. 9.
[85] S. Bunker, *Strawopolis: Luton Transformed 1840–1876* (BHRS Vol.78, 1999), p. 176.
[86] W.B. Stephens, *Regional Variations*, p. 11.

Chapter Four

Education in the Time of the School Board

Before 1870, elementary education in Luton was provided by the National and British Societies and in dame or private adventure (small independent) schools. A few respectable establishments offered higher levels of education, but the market for these was small.[1] However, the passing of the 1870 Forster Education Act forced the town to confront the situation. This Act required local authorities to assess the number of elementary school places available and, if there was a shortfall, to 'fill up the gaps'.

The possibility of an elected body having a say in what local children were taught angered members of Luton churches who firmly believed that education was their responsibility. Dony explains how bad feelings on this subject date back to 1834 when the government offered grants towards the building of new schools. The National and British Societies both wanted a school in Luton, but the number of children to be taught allowed for only one grant and that went to the National Society. 'The die was cast for a dispute that was to disturb the peace of Luton for seventy years.'[2]

Dony, referring to the Forster Act, says that 'it would have been impossible to have drafted any Act of Parliament to give more trouble to [mainly Nonconformist] Luton'. A vestry meeting was called, possibly 'the most disgraceful meeting ever held in the town'.[3] The Church promised to build new schools and to provide a sufficient number of places, thereby warding off government interference. Their opponents, led by the treasurer of the British School, wanted a poll which, it was hoped, would support the establishment of a School Board. Some of the points made against the Board system were that it was a 'leap in the dark', that once you have a Board you cannot get rid of it and that there was already a burden of taxation. There was also a fear that educating children with public money would lead to feeding and clothing them as well.[4]

Arguments for a Board were that it would provide and secure the education of the 'entire population . . . calculated to promote the moral and material well-being of the Working Classes – to fit them for higher spheres of usefulness, to give them a "fair start in life", and to enable them the better to make their way in the world'. The education which it would provide would be 'free from all denominational teach-

---

[1] John Dony has written a useful summary of the situation in Luton at the time: J.G. Dony, *A History of Education in Luton* (LMAG, 1970). Also see Chapter Nine.

[2] Ibid., p. 13.

[3] Ibid., p. 22.

[4] Poster at LMAG: 'Six Reasons Why You Should Not Vote for a School Board in Luton' (25 January 1871).

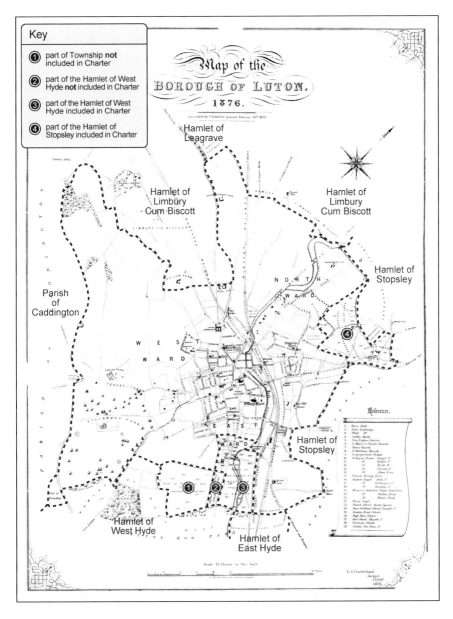

Key

① part of Township **not** included in Charter

② part of the Hamlet of West Hyde **not** included in Charter

③ part of the Hamlet of West Hyde included in Charter

④ part of the Hamlet of Stopsley included in Charter

Map of the
BOROUGH OF LUTON.
1876.

Hamlet of Leagrave

Hamlet of Limbury Cum Biscott

Hamlet of Limbury Cum Biscott

Hamlet of Stopsley

Parish of Caddington

Hamlet of Stopsley

Hamlet of West Hyde

Hamlet of East Hyde

11. Map of the Borough of Luton 1876, E.A. Cumberland [LM]

ing'.[5] The financial burden was dismissed; the working classes are not so 'careless and indifferent about their children's welfare as to be unwilling to pay their share of a small rate to secure for them so great an advantage'. The cost, it was claimed, would be small and 'as education extends, poverty and crime decrease and . . . the poor rate will decrease also'.

No history of Luton in the last quarter of the nineteenth century can be written without reference to the extremely forceful incumbent of the Parish Church, the Vicar of Luton, the Reverend James O'Neill, who was loved by a few for his support of the Church, but hated by many for his aggressive attitude towards other people and other causes. The Reverend James O'Neill made his presence felt in educational circles until his death in 1896. Then, in a letter of sympathy, the Board wrote:

> that the Luton School Board hereby expresses its sincere condolences with the family of the late Reverend James O'Neill BD, for sixteen years a Member of the Board and for six years (1880 – 1886) its Chairman.
>
> A determined opponent of the School Board system, he yet won the respect of his adversaries by his unquestioned powers, his unflinching attitude, and his undeviating consistency. After years of educational controversy, he closed his eyes in peace and amity; and this Board records its tribute of admiration in memory of a long, courageous and devoted life, spent without stint in the service of those interests dearer to him than life itself.[6]

Although the religious content of the disagreement was paramount, there was another powerful argument. This was in connection with the employment of children in the staple industry. Girls in particular were very busy, especially at the height of the Luton hat season. They not only sewed but were also involved with taking and fetching plait and finished hats to and from the manufacturers and the markets. They also cared for siblings while their mothers worked. This was important to the economy of the town and was addressed in the same leaflet:

> As regards the earnings of your children, – when trade is slack, there are too many hands to do the work, and the result is, prices are brought down *so low* that you cannot obtain a fair living. Send the children to school, and then there will be *more work for you to do*, and you will get a *better price* for it. When trade is brisk, and all hands are wanted, the School Board of your own electing would be anxious to study your interests by making such arrangements as would enable you as far as possible to get the benefit of your children's labour.[7]

A poll to consider the advisability of electing a School Board took place on 7 February 1871 and was won by the Church party. However, arguments continued and government pressure stayed firm. On 27 January 1874, the Education Department ordered that there should be an election for a School Board and this took place on 17 February 1874. The Church (Prayer Book Five) supporters had more votes, but the Nonconformists (Bible Five) had more members elected.[8]

5   Poster at LMAG: Frederick Brown, 'The Education Act' (21 January 1871).
6   M/222 Minutes of USDL, 12 January 1897.
7   Poster, 'The Education Act'.
8   J.G. Dony, *A History of Education in Luton;* L.LUT 371.01, J. Roberts, 'Luton School Board 1874–1902' (Dissertation).

This added to the animosity, but the election was allowed to stand. The Reverend James O'Neill was elected, but showed his feelings by his absences and frequent unwillingness to vote throughout the terms of his membership.

The Chairman of the first School Board was William Bigg, a Quaker, who was one of the Bible Five and who, in 1876, became the first Mayor of Luton. The Vice-Chairman, also one of the Bible Five, was Charles Robinson, a straw hat manufacturer. Other Bible Five committee members were the Reverend E.R. Adams, the Vicar of Biscot; Henry Blundell, Wesleyan, who was a leading draper in the town; and Peter Wootton, Baptist, a chemist. Prayer Book Five members elected were John Higgins, a painter; the Reverend James O'Neill; Thomas Sworder, a brewer; and A.P. Welch, another straw hat manufacturer.

There were other towns in Bedfordshire which did not elect a Board until later in the century. One of these, Leighton Buzzard, a market town about ten miles from Luton with schools provided by the Pulford and Bassett endowments, was one of the last in the county to elect a Board, which it did in 1893. It was fiercely resisted, especially by the Quakers.[9] The Forster Act was considered irrelevant in Bedford[10] because the wealth of the Harpur Trust provided schooling for its children. However, by 1897, when the number of children began to outgrow the number of school places, a Board was needed. This was described by the Mayor as a bitter pill to swallow.[11] In contrast to Luton, Leighton Buzzard and Bedford did not need a Board immediately after the 1870 Forster Act because their endowments provided sufficient income and, when school boards were introduced, there was not the same kind of confrontation as had been experienced in Luton. Other parts of the country, however, welcomed the formation of a school board. For example, there seems to have been no resistance in Coventry.[12] Elections there were 'fought on party lines' until 1888 when they had become 'drawn between the non-sectarian and denominational groups'.[13] In Coventry the administration ran smoothly and Board meetings were 'notable for their lack of controversy'.[14]

The Luton School Board met for the first time on 5 March 1874[15] and on 28 April 1874 they passed by-laws which were approved by the Education Department.[16] These acknowledged that the Luton School Board had responsibility for the elementary education of boys and girls. Education was to be compulsory for children between the ages of five and thirteen, unless there was some reasonable excuse. Normally children were obliged to attend school for at least twenty-five hours each school week. However, provision was made for children who were at least ten years old and who had reached the level of education equivalent to Standard V to leave school for work by obtaining a certificate from one of Her

9   M. Stannard, *The Way to School: A History of the Schools of Leighton Buzzard and Linslade* (Leighton Buzzard: Leighton-Linslade and District Museum Project, 1990), p. 41.
10   D.W. Bushby, *Elementary Education in Bedford 1868–1903* (BHRS vol.54, 1975), p. 16.
11   Ibid., p. 66.
12   F.J. Allinson, 'The Coventry School Board 1870–1903: The First Local Education Authority' (MA Dissertation, 1994), p. 54.
13   Ibid., p. 41.
14   Ibid., p. 43.
15   M/216 Minutes of LSB, 5 March 1874.
16   *Committee of Council on Education Report* (*1874–75*) *England and Wales* (HMSO, 1875), Part V of Appendix pp. 16–18.

First and last verses of an Oration given by a scholar from the
Waller Street School at the Congratulatory Dinner held
at the Town Hall on Wednesday, February 21st 1877
to celebrate the success of the Bible Five at the election for
a School Board.

        Those elected on that occasion were:
        Henry Brown JP, Chairman
        Henry Blundell, Vice Chairman
        Revd R. Berry, A.Conisbee, C. Mees, Revd J. O'Neill, T. Sworder,
        Revd J. Tuckwell and P. Wootton
        Clerk, G. Sell

All honour to the Bible Five, to Luton's Rising Star,
Young Henry, the new J.P., who's won the Conqueror's Chair.
Now, list unto the merry sound of music, and the dance,
For Liberty and Right have won; and Falsehood's lost her chance.
And thou, my own, my native Town, proud Luton on the Lea,
Again let rapture light the eyes of all who love to see
The spread of righteousness and truth - the victory of the free,
Labour well paid, - the poor upraised – the fall of tyranny.
Hurrah! Hurrah! For one day's flight has won the chance of war,
And HENRY now sits in the Chair – Our Luton's Rising Star ...

        At first we thought that all was lost, that James had won the crown,
        But soon The Bible Five went up and Catechism down;
        Hurrah! for East, and West, and North, for both sides of the Lea,
        They've lain the tyrant pristhood [sic]down, made lies and falsehood flee,
        Hurrah for Blundell, Berry, Brown, for Wootton, Tuckwell too,
        Ho! Fathers, Mothers, Children dear, bright days in store for you,
        By education you shall rise to honour and renown,
        With Bible truth fixed in your hearts, you'll bless our much loved town.
        All honour to His holy name, from whom all honours are,
        We'll pray for blessings rich and rare on Luton's rising star.

12. The Battle of the Children's Rights, Victory Song of the Bible Five, 1877 [LM]

Majesty's Inspectors. Children aged ten and over who showed that they were 'bene-ficially and necessarily at work' were allowed to attend school for ten hours a week (the half-time system). If parents did not send their children to school they were liable to a fine of not more than five shillings, although those who were too poor to afford the fees could have part or all of the cost remitted. It may seem strange that a town with very little interest in education should make attendance compulsory at the first opportunity and before it was required to do so by law. The answer may be that government funding was dependent on school attendance and Luton wanted that funding. There was no compulsion for children to attend school if there was not one within two miles of their home.

The Luton School Board worked conscientiously to fulfil its duties. The main requirement of the Forster Act was the provision of enough school places and this problem was addressed without delay with regard to both the town and the hamlets.[17] An accepted curriculum had to be offered and annual examinations were to be held by an HMI. The children of Luton would be able to receive a basic elementary education, but at the same time had to give up the freedom and individuality which were characteristic of the town. Managers and teachers were:

> expected to satisfy the inspector that all reasonable care is taken in the ordinary management of the school, to bring up the children in habits of punctuality, of good manners and language, of cleanliness and neatness, and also to impress upon the children the importance of cheerful obedience to duty, of consideration and respect for others, and of honour and truthfulness in word and act.[18]

The members of the Luton School Board had no professional expertise in educational matters, but they had enthusiasm and the will to improve their skills. One way was to correspond with other school boards. They wrote to the Stockport, Manchester and Ipswich Boards to ask 'for information as to the working of the Act in their Districts, and as to the number of Schools, Scholars, Visiting Officers, and the result of increase per cent in the School attendance since the establishment of the Boards'.[19] They also wrote to seven large Boards to 'request them to supply this Board with the amount paid to teachers of their schools . . . and the number of scholars and average attendance'.[20] The Clerk of the London School Board was informed that 'this Board is willing to unite in a joint representation to the Education Department relative to the question of spelling'.[21] At the same meeting it was agreed to send for a copy of 'Gibson's work relative to the keeping of the School Board accounts'. The Birmingham School Board wrote to Luton concerning 'certain clauses in the new Code'.[22] The efforts of the Luton Board were acknowledged by HMI The Reverend C.F. Johnstone who wrote to the Chairman in 1878:

> I have just finished my inspection of the schools in Luton parish for the year 1878 and I have found so much general improvement that I cannot resist writing to you . . . with some congratulations upon the subject. This improvement I feel sure is due in a great measure to the active influence and energy of the School Board.[23]

Letters about half-time attendance and 'the employment of children of school age' were received from the Bradford School Board[24] and Hull wanted to exchange opin-

---

17 M/218 Minutes of LSB, 30 September 1879 and 11 November 1879. The Board was renamed the 'School Board of the United School District of Luton' 11.11.1879. This covered the extra municipal part of the Parish of Luton and the Borough of Luton.
18 *Committee of Council on Education Report (1877–78) England and Wales* (HMSO, 1878), p. 298.
19 M/217 Minutes of LSB, 22 February 1876.
20 Ibid., 28 May 1878.
21 Ibid., 12 December 1876. No particular relevance can be placed on this issue; it appears that School Boards corresponded on a variety of subjects.
22 Ibid., 19 March 1878.
23 LMAG 5/98/36 Letter from C.F. Johnstone.
24 M/221 Minutes of USDL, 14 March 1893 and 19 June 1894.

ions on fees in Higher Grade Schools.[25] It would appear that most major decisions were made after consultation with other boards. In June 1893 the Luton Board decided to join the proposed Association of School Boards and Mr William Drewett, Mrs Emily Carruthers and the Clerk were asked to be representatives at its next meeting.[26] Meetings were attended regularly until the final one in 1903.[27] In 1899, a subscription of 6s was paid for the *School Board Gazette*.[28]

Women in Luton may have had economic power, but they had less political power and lacked the 'social background and social networks' which were available to women in London.[29] Whereas the London School Board had an unusually high proportion of women,[30] Mrs Emily Carruthers, one of the representatives at the 1893 conference, was the only woman to become a member of the Luton School Board, her term being from 1892 to 1895. She was very active in educational circles and really seemed to have had the children's welfare at heart; her voice was sometimes the gentle one when others were looking at practicalities.

Mrs Carruthers was born in Luton and married into the Carruthers family which came from Scotland to set up as hat manufacturers. Her husband was Colonel Andrew Carruthers VD JP, who was Chairman of the Bleachers and Dyers in the local Chamber of Commerce in 1904. In the same year his wife was Honourable Treasurer of the Luton Women's Liberal Association.[31] Mrs Carruthers was elected to the Bedfordshire Education Committee (BEC) and Elementary Sub-Committee, sat on other smaller committees and was a manager and visitor for many Luton schools. In 1916 she resigned and moved to Sidmouth where her husband died the following year. The *Kelly's Directory (1920)* for Luton mentions a Mrs Emily Carruthers living in Downs Road, so it seems likely that she returned to Luton.

The members of the Luton School Board were concerned with any change to government plans concerning education and not infrequently sent letters to state their opinion.[32] They were happy to do this in the belief that Luton had considerable respect in educational circles. For example, the Clerk wrote to a potential applicant for a teaching post that 'The Assistants who have from time to time left the School have had no difficulty in obtaining good appointments as . . . the Board [has] an established reputation amongst larger and more important Boards.' In a similar letter the Clerk claimed that 'Luton Schools have a first-rate representation with the best Education Authorities.'[33]

By the turn of the century attitudes had changed. Children had parents who had been brought up under the rules of compulsory education, fees were no longer

25 Ibid., 5 November 1895.
26 Ibid., 4 July 1893.
27 M/224 Minutes of USDL, 3 March 1903.
28 M/223 Minutes of USDL, 10 January 1899.
29 J. Martin, 'Entering the Public Arena: The Female Members of the London School Board, 1870–1904', *History of Education* Vol. 22, No. 3 (1993), pp. 225–240.
30 P. McCann, ed., *Popular Education and Socialization in the Nineteenth Century* (Methuen, 1977), ch. 9. D. Rubenstein, 'Socialization and the London School Board 1870–1904: aims, methods and public opinion'.
31 *Luton Year Books; Censuses*; J. Dyer and J.G. Dony, *The Story of Luton* (White Crescent Press, 1975), p. 130; Minutes of USDL, BEC and LEC.
32 M/222 Minutes of USDL, 18 May 1897.
33 M/239 Letterbooks of USDL, 11 April 1891 and 15 July 1891.

charged and the Luton School Board was able to congratulate itself on the benefits which education had brought to the town. When Queen Victoria died, the Luton Board sent a letter of sympathy to the Royal Family in which it was pointed out that 'The Board cannot forget that it was during Her glorious reign that the beneficial Acts were passed which concern the education of the young and believe that this and future generations will bless the Monarch who was enabled to grant them such inestimable privileges.'[34]

The following year, when the government threatened to replace the school boards with local education authorities, the Luton Board wrote to the Board of Education outlining the successes of the School Board system and claiming that it had 'more than fulfilled expectations', 'faithfully achieved the purpose of its formation' and 'educated nearly half the children of the Nation to the satisfaction of its Inspectors, the comfort of the Parents, and the gratification of the Country'.[35] After a reluctant start the Luton School Board had fulfilled its obligations conscientiously.

Provision

The Luton School Board had first to provide enough school places for the children of the town and the hamlets. In order to do this constructively, a census was taken, 'such enumeration to be made also in respect of the number of children not attending any School'.[36] In June it was noted that there was to be a census of 'children of school age'.[37] Figures taken from the *Luton Reporter* dated 23 June 1874 show that there were 2,868 children registered at the voluntary and Board schools and that the average attendance was 1,861. The following month a census was taken of children in Stopsley between the ages of three and thirteen.[38] In September the Visiting Officer and the Clerk were asked to report on the number of children paying over 9d per week, the number of children under no tuition, the number of children under alleged tuition and the number of children aged between three and five and between five and thirteen.[39] The Visiting Officer was also asked to provide figures for Biscot, East and West Hyde, Leagrave and Limbury.[40]

The census figures[41] show that 3,593 out of the 4,287 children in the township were alleged to be under tuition, while 694 (just over one sixth) were receiving no tuition. Also, there were more girls than boys in every category included in the census. The number of children paying over ninepence a week for their education was 244 (119 boys and 125 girls), probably in local or out-of-town private schools. The most pressing problems, however, were in the hamlets where provision was far from acceptable. The number of children not being educated was 115 out of 239 in Stopsley and ninety-three out of 149 in Hyde. The situation in Leagrave, Biscot and Limbury was even worse. Out of 110 children in Leagrave, only eighteen were

34 M/223 Minutes of USDL, 28 January 1901.
35 M/224 Minutes of USDL, 7 May 1902.
36 M/216 Minutes of LSB, 19 May 1874; J. Roberts has collated the figures that were published in the *Luton Reporter* in 'The Luton School Board 1874–1902'.
37 M/216 Minutes of LSB, 2 June 1874.
38 Ibid., 21 July 1874.
39 Ibid., 1 September 1874.
40 Ibid., 8 September 1874.
41 Figures taken from J. Roberts, 'The Luton School Board'.

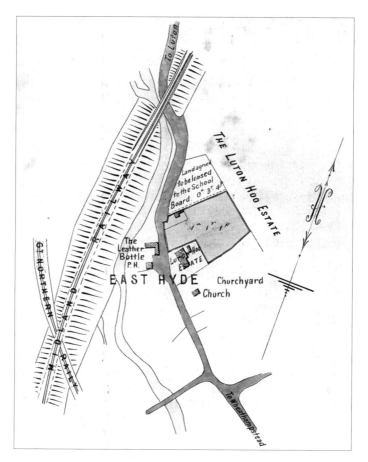

13. Map showing the site of Hyde School, built c.1901 and opened in 1902 [BLARS]

alleged to be under tuition. At Biscot the figures were four out of thirty-eight and in Limbury nine out of fifty-seven. Even before the census figures were published, plans were being made to build a school for Leagrave, Limbury and Biscot.[42] The Luton School Board wanted a joint school for these hamlets, but the Education Department in Whitehall insisted that there should be one in Leagrave and another in Limbury-cum-Biscot. By September 1874, the purchase of land had been approved[43] and the two new schools were opened by the Chairman and members of the School Board in September 1875.

The voluntary bodies were also looking to provide more places[44] although some of their schools were handed to the more affluent Board. At the very first meeting of the Board a letter from Henry Brown, a Quaker, was discussed. He offered to transfer the tenancy of the Old British School, while Mrs Lydia Brown offered to 'negotiate for the transference or letting of the Langley Street Infant School'. The

---

[42] M/216 Minutes of LSB, 24 March 1874 and 28 April 1874.
[43] Ibid., 15 September 1874.
[44] See Chapter Nine.

Board agreed to enter into negotiations.[45] The offer of the Primitive Methodists to let their premises to the Board was also accepted.[46]

The Church was anxious to keep control over as many Luton children as possible and new schools were built, notably St Matthews (1874), Christ Church (1874) and New Town Street (1875). Stopsley was a particular problem because the Church school in the hamlet had been closed between 1871 and 1874. The Clerk wrote to the Vicar 'to ascertain when it was his intention to open the School at Stopsley under a proper certificated Mistress as this Board intended to purchase a site and erect a School at Stopsley, unless the School in question was opened in the course of a short time'.[47] The Board stipulated that 'Stopsley School cannot be recognized by this Board unless a proper certificated Teacher is appointed, the Time Table and Conscience Clause adopted, and the School placed under the inspection of the Education Department.' In 1879 the Stopsley School was taken over by the Board with 'fees [the] same as at Biscot and Leagrave'.[48]

The National School at Hyde continued as a voluntary school for longer, but financial pressures threatened its closure. A letter was received from the Department of Education 'notifying the closing of the present school at East Hyde as from the 30 April next [1898] and requesting the Board to consider what measures should be taken to supply the deficiency of accommodation thus caused'.[49] Terms were agreed for the Board to become temporary tenants.[50] Later a purpose-built Board school was built in Hyde to 'be used as from Monday 5 May [1902]'.[51]

The Luton School Board Minutes show a pattern of entries which developed as the population of the town increased. Problems of overcrowding were investigated and discussed, loans negotiated and new schools built: Waller Street (1876),[52] Chapel Street (1880), Old Bedford Road (1883), Hitchin Road (1883), Surrey Street (1891) and Dunstable Road (1898).[53] All these schools provided an elementary education according to the terms of the government codes, but Waller Street was given special attention in order to equip boys with the commercial skills needed for the prosperity of the hat industry and the new industries which were moving into the town. In 1890 Waller Street was made into a Higher Grade School with a wider curriculum.[54] For example, boys had the opportunity to learn practical chemistry[55] and Pitman's shorthand.[56]

There were plans to open a Higher Grade School for girls. As suggested in Chapter Ten, this was not necessarily because the Luton School Board had become

45 M/216 Minutes of LSB, 5 March 1874 and 17 March 1874. The contribution of the denominational schools is discussed in Chapter Nine.
46 M/216 Minutes of LSB, 24 March 1874.
47 Ibid., 7 July 1874, 22 September 1874 and 29 December 1874; J. Dyer, *The Story of the Stopsley Schools* (LMAG, 1989), pp. 6–7.
48 M/218 Minutes of LSB, 28 October 1879.
49 M/222 Minutes of USDL, 11 January 1898.
50 Ibid., 25 January 1898, 14 February 1898 and 8 March 1898.
51 M/224 Minutes of USDL, 29 April 1902.
52 M/217 Minutes of LSB, 21 November 1876.
53 A complete list of schools with dates can be found in J.G. Dony, *A History of Education in Luton*, pp. 59–61.
54 M/220 Minutes of USDL, 15 October 1889 and 29 October 1889.
55 Ibid., 23 June 1891.
56 Ibid., 21 January 1890.

concerned about girls but because it was a useful alternative to private schools. However, the Education Department did not sanction the school.[57] Later the Board wanted to enlarge the Higher Grade School and offer places to girls,[58] but apparently that plan did not extend beyond the talking stage.[59] There were also attempts to bring girls from the higher grades of the elementary schools together in Langley Street Girls' School. The situation was reviewed regularly, but there were no settled arrangements for girls as there were for boys.[60]

Dony has demonstrated the very direct involvement of Waller Street School in the provision of a generation of local headmasters.[61] The Board, however, was not so concerned with the education of girls[62] and 'changes in headmistresses [do] not reveal the same pattern'.[63] In April 1874 Miss Frances Preedy from Vauxhall was appointed to the High Town Schools.[64] Advertisements were placed in teachers' journals and as a result Eliza Jarman from Eastbourne came to High Town and Ann Simmons from Northampton to Langley Street.[65] Miss Jarman transferred to Chapel Street School in November 1879.[66] Miss Partridge, from East Greenwich, became headmistress of High Town Infants School[67] and, in 1880, Harriet Stickley from Chesterfield took her place.[68] It seems likely that there were not enough local girls to fill these posts because their education had not been sufficiently thorough. This would agree with the findings of HMI the Reverend C.F. Johnstone who wrote that 'the place of women as instructors is an important but it is a subsidiary one'.[69] By 1890, however, Luton heads were being accepted elsewhere. Miss Rachel A. Rhodes was appointed to the Langley Street Girls' School in 1890[70] and the following year left for a post as headmistress of a Girls' Higher Grade School under the Bradford School Board.[71]

The religious dimension

Arguments in Luton between Church and Nonconformist supporters reflected in many ways the deep and involved discussions which were taking place in other parts of the country.[72] Much of the debate focused on what kind of religious education should be given. Children who went to denominational schools could opt out of

---

[57] See Chapter Ten.

[58] M/221 Minutes of USDL, 22 November 1892.

[59] Ibid., 11 April 1893 and 15 February 1895.

[60] M/222 Minutes of USDL, 2 November 1897; M/223 Minutes of USDL, 30 October 1900 and 28 January 1901; M/224 Minutes of USDL, 1 October 1901.

[61] J.G. Dony, *A History of Education in Luton,* pp. 40–41, 46.

[62] Ibid., p. 35.

[63] Ibid., p. 41.

[64] M/216 Minutes of LSB, 28 April 1874.

[65] M/217 Minutes of LSB, 17 October 1876.

[66] M/218 Minutes of USDL, 25 November 1879.

[67] M/217 Minutes of LSB, 19 February 1878.

[68] M/218 Minutes of USDL, 12 October 1880 and 26 October 1880.

[69] Report for the Year 1876 by HMI the Reverend C.F. Johnstone on the schools inspected by him in the counties of Huntingdonshire and Bedfordshire. From *Committee of Council on Education Report (1876–77) England and Wales* (HMSO, 1877), p. 508.

[70] M/220 Minutes of USDL, 4 February 1890.

[71] Ibid., 7 July 1891.

[72] M. Cruickshank, *Church and State in English Education 1870 to the Present Day* (Macmillan, 1963), ch. 3.

doctrinal teaching under the rules of the Conscience Clause.[73] This became a matter of dispute between the Board and the Vicar of Stopsley.[74] However, in rate-aided schools the use of 'catechisms or religious formularies distinctive of any particular denomination' was prohibited.[75] In April 1874, the Reverend E.R. Adams and Mr Peter Wootton (Bible Five) moved that 'in all Schools under the management of this Board the Bible be read and taught on the system adopted and practised by the British and Foreign Bible Society', which meant simple Bible teaching.[76] The proposal was accepted by a vote of five, all members of the Bible Five. The Reverend James O'Neill did not attend the meeting.

A syllabus 'to be adopted in the Schools of the Board' was set out in May 1880.[77] It was agreed that

> the Bible and the fundamental principles of Religion and Morality shall be taught by the Teachers, special regard being had, both in letter and spirit, to the . . . Elementary Education Act 1870 . . . no attempt shall be made to direct attention to attach children to any particular denomination, and that subject thereto the following course of Religious Instructions shall be adopted and carried out.

Work to be done in each Standard was clearly set out. Some parts of the Bible were to be studied for examination and certain chapters had to be learnt by heart. Curwen's *New Child's Own Hymn Book* was to be used in assemblies and set prayers were stipulated. The 'assembly, singing and prayer shall be from 9 to 9.15 and Religious Instruction from 9.15 to 9.45'.[78] Parents were given the opportunity to opt out of religious teaching. For example, in 1880, the headmistress of Hitchin Road Infants' School received a 'message that some of the children were not staying for prayers'.[79] In Church schools the Vicar gave Scripture lessons[80] and visits were made by the Diocesan Inspector.[81] They also had holidays on certain days in the Church calendar: on Ash Wednesday children at St Matthew's assembled at 8.30a.m., the register was closed at 9.00a.m. and then the children went to Church. In the afternoon there was a half holiday.[82]

The London School Board gave the lead in the matter of religious education.[83] However, members of the Luton School Board, while accepting that the London

---

[73] Ibid., p. 24.

[74] M/216 Minutes of LSB, 7 July 1874 and 22 September 1874.

[75] M. Cruickshank, *Church and State*, p. 30. This was the Cowper-Temple Clause.

[76] M/216 Minutes of LSB, 14 April 1874.

[77] M/218 Minutes of USDL, 24 May 1880.

[78] Ibid., 24 May 1880.

[79] L/4/2/54 Logbook of HRGI, 4 March 1878, 8 July 1878–12 July 1878, 30 September 1878–4 October 1878; L/4/2/54 Logbook of Hitchin Road Infants' School, 14 June 1880–18 June 1880. At the beginning of this study Hitchin Road Girls' and Infants' Schools were combined. It is not clear exactly when the schools became separate, but it seems likely that it was c. September 1878.

[80] L/1/2/54 Logbook of St Matthew's Girls' School, 31 May 1886–4 June 1886. St Matthew's School was a Church school and was not administered by the Board. However, some aspects of life in Church schools are important to this chapter. See also Chapter Nine.

[81] LMAG M/211 Logbook of New Town Street School, 12 November 1875. This school was also a Church school. It was transferred from Wellington Street on 18 November 1874.

[82] L/1/2/54 Logbook of St Matthew's Girls' School, 16–20 February 1885.

[83] M. Cruickshank, *Church and State*, p. 43. Members of the London Board had considerable experience in the field of education.

syllabus had 'worked with satisfaction to the Teachers and Parents and Children', were alarmed because some members of the London Board were trying to introduce religious dogma. They were afraid that this would lead to 'an undesirable religious controversy in the country at large, which will do no good to the cause of public education, and may result in a system of secular education pure and simple'. A minute noting their 'deep regret' received the support of two members, while seven voted against it.[84] Religious education in Luton schools was still a subject of debate. In May 1897, the Board wrote to the government concerning proposed amendments to the 1870 Forster Act stating its conviction that 'our whole system of Elementary Education should be National, Free and Unsectarian'.[85] This was a commitment to the Nonconformist stance which claimed that education should be 'free, unsectarian and secular'.[86] Although the matter of the religious curriculum was certainly not settled, the Board and the voluntary schools seem to have worked together in other respects[87] and over the years this co-operation became stronger.[88]

Attendance

The problem of attendance challenged the traditional freedom which Luton people had over their time. The Board had fulfilled its obligation by providing enough school places, but the co-operation of parents had to be encouraged. The matter of attendance was also important from a financial point of view. Board schools were funded by children's fees, the Precept (or special local rate) and government grants which were directly linked to attendance. In order to qualify, a school should have 'met not less than 400 times, in the morning and afternoon, in the course of a year'.[89] On the day of the examination scholars who had 'attended not less than 250 morning or afternoon meetings of the school'[90] could qualify for funding if they passed in reading, writing and arithmetic. Attendance for only 150 sessions was acceptable if the child had permission to attend on a half-time basis or lived two miles or more from the school.[91]

The Luton School Board was anxious to receive full funding and had made attendance compulsory. This attitude of compulsory use of time was foreign to the people of Luton and the Board decided to appoint a Visiting Officer who would 'be required to devote his time in carrying out the Bye Laws relating to compulsory attendance'.[92] His duties were to collect information about local children; make monthly returns concerning those who were absent, irregular or frequently late; warn parents of possible prosecution; and attend Board meetings if necessary.[93] He also had to supervise the denominational schools.[94] Charles Maffey was employed

[84] M/221 Minutes of USDL, 16 May 1893.
[85] M/222 Minutes of USDL, 18 May 1897.
[86] M. Cruickshank, *Church and State*, p. 26.
[87] M/216 Minutes of LSB, 16 June 1874. For example, the Board agreed to pay the fees of children attending denominational schools if their parents were too poor to afford them.
[88] See Chapter Nine.
[89] *Committee of Council on Education Report (1873–74) England and Wales* (HMSO, 1874), p. cxlviii.
[90] Ibid., p. cxlix.
[91] Ibid.
[92] M/216 Minutes of LSB, 19 May 1874 and 2 June 1874.
[93] Ibid., 16 June 1874.
[94] M/211 Logbook of NTS, 13 November 1877.

at a salary of £40 per annum[95] and, in March 1876, Henry William Fetch was appointed as his assistant.[96] When Maffey resigned the following October, Fetch became Visiting Officer in his place. The post also involved liaising with the Inspector of Factories, James Wood, whose duty it was to ensure that children were legally employed.[97]

The problem of non-attendance was one which troubled schools throughout the land, although the reasons may have varied from place to place. One of the concerns in Luton was the inability of some parents to pay the weekly fees, which were initially 2d for children whose parents earned a weekly wage. Parents who were tradesmen and manufacturers 'on their own account' paid 3d for children aged under seven, 4d for children between seven and ten and 6d to 9d for those between ten and thirteen.[98] The problem of nonpayment was obviously worse in the poorer areas. Teachers were sent to collect the fees[99] and parents became troublesome,[100] sometimes keeping children home as a consequence.[101] The collection of fees was a great burden to the headteachers. Miss Stickley at Hitchin Road Infants' School complained about 'the great loss of attendance through School fees . . . I experience great difficulties in collecting the School Fees and find it a great drawback to the regular attendance of the children . . . am 3/11 in arrears.'[102] This problem resolved itself when fees were abolished in September 1891[103] in favour of a government grant:

> It was resolved unanimously That the Fee Grant offered by the Government be and is hereby accepted in the Schools named below; and that from and after Tuesday the 1st day of September 1891 no Fee shall be charged – nor for Books or Stationery – in any of the said Schools; and That it shall be an Instruction to the Clerk to forward a Copy of this Resolution to the Education Department.[104]

The girls in St Matthew's School were given a day's holiday to celebrate the passing of the Free Education Act.[105]

Boys in the Higher Grade School continued to pay fees of 7d a week, this amount to include books and stationery,[106] but in the other schools the burden of fees had been lifted. The removal of school fees was certainly welcome, but there was still a problem for parents because children at school were not contributing to the family income.

Illness was always affecting attendance. The Luton school logbooks continually mention epidemics of the usual childhood complaints. In 1895 the Board requested the adoption of compulsory notification of infectious and contagious diseases and

[95] M/216 Minutes of LSB, 23 June 1874.
[96] M/217 Minutes of LSB, 7 March 1876 and 21 March 1876.
[97] M/216 Minutes of LSB, 9 February 1875.
[98] Ibid., 21 April 1874.
[99] M/211 Logbook of NTS, 1 December 1882.
[100] L/4/2/54 Logbook of HRI, 24 March 1879–28 March 1879.
[101] Ibid., 30 June 1879–4 July 1879 and 13 October 1879–17 October 1879.
[102] Ibid., June 1889–September 1889. Approximately 20p in arrears.
[103] M/211 Logbook of NTS, 1 September 1891.
[104] M/220 Minutes of USDL, 18 August 1891.
[105] L/1/2/54 Logbook of SMG, 31 August 1891.
[106] Ibid.

Please Preserve Carefully for Reference.

TO PARENTS AND GUARDIANS.

INFECTIOUS DISEASES.

(Condensed from Longman's " Manual of School Hygiene," by W. J. ABEL, B.A.,
Clerk of Nottingham School Board.

OCTOBER, 1892.

You are doubtless aware that infectious diseases are frequently spread amongst school children by parents allowing them to attend school when suffering from such diseases, or when residing in an infected house.

The Managers and Teachers cannot think that parents would wilfully send children to school under such circumstances, thereby endangering not only the health but also the lives of other scholars. They therefore invite your most careful attention to the following NOTES, which will, it is hoped, enable you to recognize the more important contagious diseases of children. They would also urge you to do your utmost to assist them in preventing the attendance at school of children who come from infected houses.

You have, we are sure, only to think how *you* would feel towards parents whose carelessness in sending their child to school when not free from infection caused the sickness, or even death, of your own child, in order to make you use every means in your power to prevent such calamity to others.

Should you know of any case where parents *do* endanger the health of other children by their carelessness in these matters, it is clearly your duty at once to inform the Medical Officer of Health of the fact, when it will receive prompt attention. Such information will always be considered as private and confidential if so desired.

The PUBLIC HEALTH ACT provides that any person in charge of a case of infectious disease who :—

(i) *fails to give due notice* of the fact to the Medical Officer of Health ;

(ii) sends, or allows such sufferer (however mild the case may be) to be sent to school, or other public place, until free from infection ; or

(iii) is guilty of other acts tending to spread the disease, SHALL BE LIABLE TO A PENALTY OF FIVE POUNDS.

To be obtained only of E. J. ARNOLD & SON, School Publishers, LEEDS.
Price 1/- per 100 nett; or 9/- per 1,000, with Name of School and Correspondent inserted.
If folded and put into printed envelopes 14/- per 1,000 nett.

14. Circular about infectious diseases, sent to parents and guardians, 1892 [LM]

appointed doctors who were to examine children 'alleged to be unfit to attend'.[107] In 1897 the Clerk was ordered to prepare a circular 'on infectious diseases and personal cleanliness' to be sent to parents.[108] This may well have been based on a pamphlet prepared by the Clerk of the Nottingham School Board[109] which describes the symptoms of the common diseases, the length of absence required and periods of quarantine for anyone who had been in contact with the patient. The particular problems faced by the hamlet schools have been addressed in Chapter Eight.

Children were obliged to help in the home. In New Town Street some of them were 'at home to work and run errands'[110] or 'kept home to help parents . . . Board to make an example'.[111] A boy at Hyde was absent 'to fetch the medicine for his brother who is very ill'[112] and a girl 'has to see to home duties owing to Mrs Tingey having met with an accident'.[113] In High Town a boy of three was admitted because 'an older sister is kept from School occasionally in order to take care of him. The Committee think if Leonard attends School, the sister will also attend better.'[114]

Michael Vyse has studied attendance in Kent.[115] He presents a different picture from that which existed in Luton although illness, caring for children and the demands of the harvests were significant, as they were in Luton. The hop industry involved whole families; women and girls were needed for tying up the hops, as their 'deftness of touch'[116] was important. This is reminiscent of the words of the Earl of Shaftesbury who claimed that when work demands delicacy it passes into the hands of women.[117]

Girls worked at fruit-picking to support jam-making factories and as rag-cutters in the paper mills.[118] However, there are no references in Vyse's study to a female industry which dominated women's and girls' lives in the same way as hats dominated life in Luton.

The straw hat industry was undoubtedly one of the main causes of absenteeism in Luton. Children's earnings had always contributed to the family income and would probably more than compensate for any fines. At New Town Street children were 'kept home to do straw plait' or 'for Straw Work'.[119] The children's 'lack of intelligence' was believed to be because they were 'greatly overworked'.[120] Children from the Hitchin Road School were 'employed at work the whole day though under age'.[121] At St Matthew's School 'attendance [was] poor this week owing to the

[107] M/221 Minutes of USDL, 19 November 1895.
[108] M/222 Minutes of USDL, 23 March 1897.
[109] Pamphlet on Infectious Diseases 1892 from E.J. Arnold, *Manual of School Hygiene*.
[110] M/211 Logbook of NTS, 20 March 1891.
[111] Ibid., 27 May 1891.
[112] SD Hyde 1 Logbook of Hyde School, 1 December 1899.
[113] Ibid., 24 January 1902.
[114] L/4/2/54 Logbook of HRI, 1 May 1896.
[115] M.G. Vyse, 'Elementary Schooling and Working-Class Life in Kent 1862–1902' (MA Dissertation, 1989).
[116] Ibid., p. 28.
[117] Quoted in A.V. John, ed., *Unequal Opportunities: Women's Employment in England 1800–1918* (Basil Blackwell, 1986), p. 15.
[118] M.G. Vyse, 'Elementary Schooling and Working-Class Life in Kent', pp. 29 and 38.
[119] M/211 Logbook of NTS, 4 April 1882, 30 May 1884 and 19 January 1885. This was at a time when, supposedly, town girls did not plait.
[120] Ibid., 11 April 1894.
[121] L/4/2/54 Logbook of HRGI, 11 June 1875.

improvement in the Straw Trade'[122] and, in 1894, 'attendance [was not] so good during the week owing to the prevalence of sickness and the briskness of trade'.[123] In a letter to the Education Department, William Hoyle, the Clerk to the Board, referred to attendance figures for a week in May 1891 'which from the peculiar nature of the Luton trade – so far as the attendance of girls is concerned . . . are of the worst in the year, because of its being the busiest month for the local industry and coming immediately before the great Whitsuntide holiday'.[124]

Children who worked affected the attendance figures and so the Luton Board took part in the half-time system, which had its roots in the Factory Acts. Initially the system was intended to ensure that children who worked in factories had some education[125] and the scheme 'flourished chiefly in the textile areas of Lancashire and Yorkshire'.[126] There, children would be summoned to work by the factory bell and also be expected to be bright enough to concentrate on education for the rest of the day. Luton children who worked half-time were in a much more favourable situation because they probably worked in their own homes. Even if they were not at home they could still have been enjoying the traditional flexibility of the hat industry. The concept of children dividing their time between schooling and employment became an ideological one and arguments were put forward to suggest that the scheme was both efficient and beneficial.[127] However, by the 1880s it was being condemned.[128] It had certainly become a burden to the School Board, the Visiting Officer and the Factory Inspector, who spent time discussing the implementation and enforcement of the system,[129] and also to the schools themselves.

References are made in the early minutes to the numbers of children allowed to attend half-time. Generally there were more girls than boys; for example, in May 1875 there were seventeen girls and three boys.[130] Certificates were given for periods of two or six months. Children who were allowed to work were also obliged to attend school regularly for the required number of sessions. In October 1875, headteachers were told to 'supply the Visiting Officer once a month with a List of all children who do not attend School agreeably to the Half Time Certificates granted by this Board and that such Certificates be granted for the periods ending on the 25 March and the 29 September respectively'.[131] Five hundred certificates were to be printed and 'circulated amongst the Teachers of the Board Schools, such Certificates to be filled up by the Teachers and handed to the Employer when applied for'.[132] The following March, the Clerk wrote to the headteachers to 'request them to forward a List of all children attending their Schools as Half Timers

---

122   L/1/2/54 Logbook of SMG, 1 April 1892–4 April 1892.
123   Ibid., 16 March 1894.
124   M/239 Letterbooks of USDL, 29 May 1891.
125   B. Simon, *Education & the Labour Movement 1870–1920* (Lawrence & Wishart, 1965), pp. 137–142. From 1807, successive governments passed legislation controlling the hours during which children could be employed.
126   Ibid., p. 138.
127   P. McCann, ed., *Popular Education and Socialization in the Nineteenth Century*, ch. 6. H. Silver, 'Ideology and the Factory Child: Attitudes to Half-Time Education'.
128   Ibid., p. 157.
129   M/217 Minutes of LSB, 6 March 1877.
130   M/216 Minutes of LSB, 11 May 1875.
131   Ibid., 19 October 1875.
132   M/217 Minutes of LSB, 16 November 1875.

whose certificates have now expired and showing their attendance during the period of such certificates'. They were forbidden to accept a child as a half-timer without this certificate from the Board.[133]

The certificates were numbered and details, including dates of birth,[134] were kept in a certificate book.[135] In June 1877, it was decided to divide the number of half-timers in each school 'into two groups as equal as possible and that the groups alternate attendance morning and afternoon weekly'.[136] HMI the Reverend C.F. Johnstone was consulted 'especially as to the desirability of increasing the Standard before issuing Half Time certificates'.[137]

The half-time system continued, especially in textile areas, well into the twentieth century, although the numbers of children taking part had decreased by the 1890s.[138] However, for other Boards, such as Coventry, the half-time system does not seem to have been a problem.[139] The Luton Board had made provision for half-time schooling but, by 1893, the practice seems to have declined for they responded to a letter from the Bradford School Board 'on Half-Time Attendance under the Factory and Workshop Act'[140] by noting that 'this Board . . . has so few half-timers in its schools as to make it undesirable to forward its own Copy of the said Memorial'. However, a letter was sent to the local MP, Mr S.H. Whitbread, asking him to support the Bradford Memorial.[141] The reduction in numbers attending on a half-time basis conforms with figures for the rest of the country.[142] Aldrich notes that there were only forty-three half-timers in Bedfordshire Schools in 1896.[143] These figures included children employed in the lace industry.[144]

The Board organized the system, but the schools had the problem of working with it. A number of half-time girls were admitted to St Matthews Girls' School in 1874, several of whom 'were between nine and twelve years old and had not been to school for some [time] and could scarcely read'.[145] The following August, the Factory Inspector 'took a list of those girls who attended badly as half-timers'.[146] The headmistress made a rule that 'except where there were two sisters the half timers should always come in the morning'[147] and the timetable was adapted to suit these girls. Sewing was taken 'from half past eleven until half past twelve on account of the half-timers'[148] and singing from 11.45a.m. to 12.15p.m. for the same

133 Ibid., 21 March 1876.
134 Ibid., 29 May 1877.
135 Ibid., 12 December 1876.
136 Ibid., 15 June 1877.
137 M/219 Minutes of USDL, 22 May 1883.
138 B. Simon, *Education and the Labour Movement*, p. 290.
139 F.J. Allinson, 'The Coventry School Board 1870–1903', ch. 6.1.
140 M/221 Minutes of USDL, 14 March 1893.
141 Ibid., 28 March 1893.
142 B. Simon, *Education and the Labour Movement*, p. 290.
143 R. Aldrich, 'Elementary Education, Literacy and Child Employment in Mid-Nineteenth Century Bedfordshire: A Statistical Study', *History of Elementary School Teaching and Curriculum* (Bildung und Wissenschaft, 1990) p. 98.
144 D.W. Bushby, 'Half-timers at Marston', *Bedfordshire Magazine* Vol. 14, No. 112 (Spring 1975) pp. 340–344.
145 L/1/2/54 Logbook of SMG, 21 April 1874.
146 Ibid., 27 August 1875.
147 Ibid., 26 November 1875.
148 Ibid., 11 February 1876.

reason.[149] In November there were sixty such girls.[150] Annie Impey, who was registered at Old Bedford Road School as a half-timer, only attended school sixteen times in ten weeks. The Clerk wrote: 'I can see no possible way out of it other than that of writing to the Factory Inspector whose course would probably be to summon the parent of the child and also the person who has illegally employed her without Certificate of Attendance at School.'[151]

Children aged ten or over could apply for the Labour Certificate, which allowed them to leave school early so long as they had a prospect of work.[152] Government rules stipulated that in order to obtain this certificate it was necessary to pass an examination given by an HMI or to have attended for at least 250 sessions each year for the previous five years.[153] A certificate received for attendance alone was known as the Dunce's Certificate.[154] In 1893, the national minimum age for leaving was raised to eleven.[155] Details concerning the issue of Labour Certificates began to appear in the minutes of the United School District of Luton (USDL) and, in 1895, it was noted that HMI Mr E.N. Wix had set the date for the examination which would qualify children 'for total exemption from School attendance'.[156] In 1898 the Board received support from the Education Department to raise the 'Standard of Exemption' from Standard V to VI[157] and the following year notification of this was given 'to every Scholar now working in Standard VI which is the Standard of total exemption from attendance at School'.[158] The exam was advertised in the local press and the 'Schedules' had to be returned to the HMI one week before the examination.[159] There was provision for children employed in agriculture to leave school at eleven, but the Luton Board sought and obtained permission to omit this clause from their by-laws.[160]

In 1898 the results of the Labour examination were recorded in the USDL Minutes. These results which may or may not have been typical, are shown in Table 13 but the girls certainly performed better on this occasion.[161]

The types of employment taken up by the children of Luton (not specifically those receiving a Labour Certificate) in 1897/1898 are listed in Table 14.[162]

149 Ibid., 24 March 1876.
150 Ibid., 10 November 1876.
151 M/239 Letterbooks of USDL, 15 June 1891.
152 *Committee of Council Report (1874–75)*, pp. 16–18. By-laws of the Luton School Board 1874.
153 This was raised to 350 attendances in 1900.
154 B. Simon, *Education and the Labour Movement*, p. 138.
155 Ibid., p. 290.
156 M/221 Minutes of USDL, 12 March 1895.
157 M/222 Minutes of USDL, 14 June 1898; M/223 Minutes of USDL, 13 December 1898.
158 M/224 Minutes of USDL, 12 February 1901 and 15 April 1902.
159 M/223 Minutes of USDL, 5 March 1901.
160 M/224 Minutes of USDL, 16 September 1902 and 30 September 1902.
161 M/222 Minutes of USDL, 15 November 1898.
162 Figures from *Minutes of Committee of Council on Education* P.P. 1897–98 LXXV quoted in B. Parish, 'School Attendance in Rural Bedfordshire and Luton 1870–1903' (Dissertation, 1977).

Table 13. Labour Certificate results 1898

	Boys	Girls
Number who took the exam	161	152
Passed	125	135
Failed in one subject	29	15
Failed in two subjects	7	1
Failed in three subjects	–	1
Failed in reading	10	2
Failed in writing	5	5
Failed in arithmetic	28	13

Table 14. Types of employment taken up by children in Luton 1897–1898

	Boys	Girls
Farm and garden work	11	–
Building	3	–
Woodwork	22	–
Metal trades	1	–
Clothing	74 (inc. 66 in straw trade)	154 (inc. 137 in straw trade)
Printing	7	–
Clerical	29	–
Shops	25	5
Transport	40	–
Newsboy and hawker	3	–
Teacher	4	8
Miscellaneous	10	–
Domestic service	–	34
Box-making	–	1

The parent of any child who did not keep to the attendance by-laws was threatened with 'proceedings'; names and steps taken were noted in the Luton School Board Minutes. Parents were first sent A notices.[163] Those who ignored A notices were sent B notices and asked to attend a meeting of the Board to 'give their reasons for nonobservance of the notices'. A small committee would 'hear the statement of the persons who will attend and give such advice and assistance as may be expedient'.[164] After this, legal proceedings could be taken.[165] Sometimes the case was

---

163 M/218 Minutes of LSB, 21 January 1879.
164 M/218 Minutes of USDL, 2 March 1880.
165 M/217 Minutes of LSB, 20 March 1877.

withdrawn, but parents could be fined up to five shillings.[166] However, in cases of hardship the fees were remitted.[167]

It may often have been the case that parents wanted their children at home for some kind of employment, but there were also children who chose to stay away from school. Parents of these truants could be brought before the Board 'that they might be informed as to the powers of this Board relative to sending their children to an Industrial School and further that such persons be requested to bring their Truant children to the meeting so that they may be warned as to their future conduct'.[168] Several Industrial Schools are mentioned in the minutes, but the one most often used was at Walthamstow. Girls were not exempt; in 1882, a father was told to send his daughter to school or she would be sent to an Industrial School.[169] The following year the threat was repeated.[170]

Punctuality was also important because a late arrival would mean that the child did not have a mark in the register and fewer marks could affect the annual grant. Registers had to be kept meticulously because any inaccuracies could, in theory, be taken as an attempt to secure undeserved funding. The Visiting Officer was 'authorized to check registers . . . at the end of each quarter'[171] and the 1887 Report of St Matthew's Girls' School stipulated quite clearly that 'there must be no erasures in the Registers'.[172] Children who were late were punished, sometimes 'with favourable results'.[173] The mother of a little girl at Hitchin Road Infants' School asked the headmistress to discipline her because 'she had played truant several times during the week'.[174] Lateness was a problem at St Matthew's Girls' School. There the headmistress tried marking the register early, which 'greatly diminished the number of late girls'.[175] Later she complained that 'one real drawback to good work in this school is the number of late girls. An account has been kept . . . number has been reduced from 64 to 33.'[176] She tried writing the names and time of arrival of girls in a book which was to be sent to the next managers' meeting.[177] Latecomers at Hyde were kept in at playtime[178] and, at the High Town Girls' and Infants' School, the children were taught a song called 'Lateness for School' to encourage a culture of good and punctual attendance.[179]

However, the emphasis began to change to incentive. In 1893, the Board adopted 'the principles of giving Rewards in classes to Scholars who have made the highest

166   Ibid., 1 May 1877.
167   M/218 Minutes of LSB, 7 January 1879.
168   Ibid., 22 June 1880. Home Office Industrial Schools were set up under government legislation from 1857 to 1933 but were run by private individuals, religious groups and school boards. Earlier industrial schools were independent and run by local people for children in their own community to find them simple work.
169   M/218 Minutes of USDL, 23 March 1882.
170   M/219 Minutes of USDL, 13 March 1883.
171   Ibid., 26 February 1884.
172   L/1/2/54 Logbook of SMG, HMI Report 1887.
173   L/4/2/54 Logbook of HRGI, 15 March 1878.
174   L/4/2/54 Logbook of HRI, 27 June 1884.
175   L/1/2/54 Logbook of SMG, 16 January 1893 and 30 January 1893.
176   Ibid., 17 January 1896.
177   Ibid., 20 January 1896.
178   SD Hyde 1 Logbook of Hyde School, 10 October 1902.
179   L/4/2/54 Logbook of HRGI, 5 March 1875.

number of attendances during the year, and have also passed the standard in which they are presented'.[180] At first, books and certificates were given 'to the scholars who have been most regular in attendance and diligent in their studies'.[181] In July £50 was allocated for prizes 'for 12½ % of the Scholars in each Class; Attendance, Conduct and Progress to be taken into account'. The prizes were valued at 8d for infants of five and under and up to 7s 6d for scholars from Standard VII.[182] There were certificates for children 'who shall make or shall have made not less than 93% of attendances during the school year, due allowance being made for absence consequent upon sickness'.[183] In 1902, a plan to give silver and bronze medals as an alternative to books was introduced.[184] Inscribed were 'Board of Luton arms enclosed in garter bearing inscription Luton School Board, the reverse bearing Never absent, never late with date enclosed in plain garter'.[185] Children in Standard VI or over could earn a silver medal if they had fulfilled the conditions for two successive years and a silver medal with a gold centre for four years.[186]

The Clerk to the Board wrote a short history of the education movement in Luton[187] in which he said that 'as time went on the attendance at the elementary schools became more and more satisfactory. For some time now Bedfordshire has occupied the highest position in the country in the matter of excellence of attendances, and Luton certainly does not fall behind any other part of the county.'[188] Detailed studies of attendance figures in Luton by Parish support this.[189]

Curriculum and ethos of the Board schools
At the beginning of the Board era children followed a curriculum which consisted mainly of subjects which would earn grants: reading, writing and arithmetic.[190] Schools were also examined in music, discipline and organization.[191] By 1878 Standards II to VI could also be examined in geography, history and grammar.[192] However, attitudes changed and subjects were added so that, by 1903, the curriculum had broadened. Children's well-being, individuality and interests were taken into account. In Old Bedford Road Girls' School geography, singing and cookery were introduced in the 1880s, drawing and swimming in the 1890s and history in 1900. Other girls' schools had similar curriculum changes.[193]

One example of the interest in the individual child was the introduction of kindergarten techniques into infant schools,[194] which was no doubt encouraged by

180   M/221 Minutes of USDL, 6 June 1893.
181   Ibid., 9 April 1895.
182   Ibid., 23 July 1895.
183   Ibid., 3 December 1895.
184   M/224 Minutes of USDL, 14 October 1902.
185   Ibid., 25 November 1902 (Medal in LMAG). There is such a medal at LMAG.
186   Ibid., 9 December 1902.
187   *The Luton and District Year Book and Almanack (1906)*, pp. 129–133.
188   Ibid., p. 133.
189   LMAG 130, 1953. B. Parish, 'School Attendance in Rural Bedfordshire and Luton 1870–1903'; 'Luton Schools Logbooks. General History and Logbooks of Individual Schools'.
190   *Committee of Council Report (1873–74)*, p. cl.
191   M/211 Logbook of NTS, HMI Report 1876.
192   *Committee of Council Report (1877–78)*, p. 301.
193   BLARS 130/Luton, 'General History and Logbooks of Individual Schools'. The Letterbooks of the Board have entries concerning materials requisitioned.
194   *Committee of Council on Education Report (1898–99) England and Wales* (HMSO, 1899), p. 698.

15. Children celebrating the Coronation of Edward VII in 1902. Photograph taken at Chiltern Road School in nearby Dunstable [LM]

the existence of a Froebel College in Bedford.[195] The headmistress at Hitchin Road Infants' School, Harriet Stickley, began to introduce kindergarten ideas soon after she was appointed.[196] Her school was:

a model of what an infant school should be. The work is in every respect excellent, and the admirable training and order and bright happy tone of the children make the work of inspection a real pleasure. The real welfare of the little ones entrusted to her care is evidently the first thought of the headmistress and her staff, who one and all deserve the highest praise.[197]

An aspect of the kindergarten system which linked well with Luton schools was plaiting, which the Bedfordshire Technical Education Committee tried to introduce in 1894.[198] Another example of the widening curriculum was the emphasis on Object Lessons. These were intended to help 'the scholar to acquire knowledge by observation and experiment . . . no instruction is properly so-called unless an Object is presented to the learner so that the addition to his knowledge may be made through the senses'.[199] Lists of Object Lessons were shown to the HMI for approval.

Girls could follow the same basic curriculum as boys, but there were significant differences namely needlework and, later, domestic economy. Attar says that needlework has always been the 'most difficult for girls to escape from entirely. It has the longest history as part of the school curriculum, and was taught in every type of establishment which purported to educate girls.'[200] She goes on to say that 'it occupied a great deal of girls' time, at very little expense . . . while boys were taught more advanced mathematics, a foreign language or other subjects which were denied to girls'.[201] Another point of view was that needlework was used 'to teach girls docility' and 'keep them well behaved and quiet'.[202]

After the passing of the 1870 Education Act, the Education Department issued regular Codes which dictated how schools should be run. Under the 1874 Code, girls in day schools were taught plain needlework and cutting out as part of the ordinary course of instruction.[203] This meant that schools presented girls in Luton with sewing lessons focused on domesticity while at home their lives were given to needlework skills which were relevant to the hat industry. Sadler notes that 'the basis of all women's trades is needlework, of which they learn the principles more or less thoroughly in their school work and at home'.[204] Since most girls in Luton already spent a large proportion of their lives with needles in their hands, the insistence that they should spend many more hours sewing in the classroom seems to

---

195 R. Smart, *On Others' Shoulders: An Illustrated History of the Polhill & Lansdowne Colleges now De Montfort University Bedford* (De Montfort University, 1994), ch. 1 and ch. 2. F. Froebel (1782–1852) introduced a style of education for young children based on observation and free expression.

196 L/4/2/54 Logbook of HRGI, 10 November 1882.

197 Ibid., HMI Report November 1892.

198 M/221 Minutes of USDL, 11 September 1894.

199 *Committee of Council Report 1898–99*, p. 703.

200 D. Attar, *Wasting Girls' Time, The History and Politics of Home Economics* (London: Virago, 1990), p. 38.

201 Ibid., p. 38.

202 Ibid., p.,39.

203 *Committee of Council Report 1873–74*, p. cxlviii.

204 M.E. Sadler, *Continuation Schools in England and Wales and Elsewhere* (Manchester University Press, 1908), p. 411.

> ### *Needle Drill*
>
> *One – up my needle must go,*
> *Two – now my cotton I show,*
> *Three – I hold it close to the eye,*
> *Four – to thread it now I must try.*
> *The eye is small but the thread will go through,*
> *I must be patient and so must you*
> *Or we shall never learn to sew*
> *And that will be a pity you know.*
>
> *Now, show who has done*
> *What – only begun?*
> *Pull out the thread and begin again at `One`.*

16. Needle Drill

support the views of Attar that home economics has a 'case to answer' and caused 'general educational harm'.[205]

Attar also points out that the teaching of domestic economy, which became compulsory in 1878, was considered by some to be 'inseparable from [girls'] moral and religious duty'.[206] In 1884, a committee (made up of men) was set up by the Luton Board to enquire about the cost of teaching cookery,[207] and plans were eventually approved.[208] The first cookery school was set up in Langley Street School[209] and another was built at Dunstable Road several years later.[210] Girls from the other schools were allocated times to attend these schools.[211] Domestic economy was also taken as a class lesson at St Matthew's Girls' School which, being a Church school, needed permission to use the Board's facilities.[212] They were taught domestic economy during the week as a class subject and had cookery lessons on Saturday

---

[205] D. Attar, *Wasting Girls' Time,* p. 2. No evidence has been found to indicate the feelings of girls or parents.
[206] Ibid., p. 25.
[207] M/219 Minutes of USDL, 3 June 1884.
[208] Ibid., 21 April 1885.
[209] Ibid., 2 December 1884 and 10 March 1885; M/221 Minutes of USDL, 4 July 1893.
[210] M/223 Minutes of USDL, 24 January 1899 and 5 March 1901.
[211] L/1/2/54 Logbook of SMG, 10 January 1890.
[212] M/222 Minutes of USDL, 1 November 1898.

mornings.[213] In 1890 a cookery instructress, Miss Jowett, was appointed;[214] Miss Parker replaced her in 1891 as both cookery and laundry mistress.[215]

Schooling was very formal. Children had to pay careful attention to the teacher and the teacher was expected to hold the attention of the class. One teacher was 'lively in her manner' and managed to interest the children[216] but, in the same school, the head commented on a reading lesson where the children were inattentive, 'many of them making no effort to keep the place. I have called the Teacher's attention to this grave fault.'[217] Fidgeting was frowned upon.[218] Teaching was to be 'thorough and systematic'.[219] The ethos in Luton schools agrees with the ideas of Davin who argued that education was aiming to 'form a new generation of parents (and especially mothers) whose children would not be wild, but dependent and amenable';[220] in other words, schools were seen as agents of social control. She describes how girls' reading material helped to establish this ideal. Fulfilment and content were to come through 'keeping one's place and doing one's duty'. A girl should learn to become a 'good tidy wife' and cultivate 'patience, humility, modesty, obedience, unselfishness, punctuality, tidiness'.[221] Even though women in Luton were a valued part of the local economy, the perspective offered was, as Davin perceived, 'entirely domestic'.[222]

The character of the people of Luton was not normally one of obedience or compliance but, as has already been noted, the government codes insisted that children should be taught punctuality, good manners, cleanliness, respect for others, honour and truthfulness.[223] Discipline was sometimes a problem, for example in New Town Street School where the HMI reported 'weak school, discipline and instruction unsatisfactory'.[224] Not only the children were obliged to conform; logbooks frequently note that the teachers were 'punctual and attentive to their duties'.[225]

Drill was traditionally taught with discipline in mind. Other considerations were the health of the children and the military needs of the nation.[226] Alan Penn considered whether the boards were targeted by militarists[227] and concluded that 'any military drill provided for children of school age would have to be accommodated elsewhere than in the curriculum of the nation's elementary schools'.[228] Lack of any

213 L/1/2/54 Logbook of SMG, 19 October and 13 November 1894.
214 M/220 Minutes of USDL, 28 October 1890.
215 Ibid., 22 December 1891; M/221 Minutes of USDL, 8 October 1895.
216 L/4/2/54 Logbook of HRI, 13 September 1895.
217 Ibid., 26 April 1895.
218 M/211 Logbook of NTS, 18 June 1891 and 24 April 1903.
219 L/1/2/54 Logbbook of SMG, HMI Report November 1888.
220 A. Davin, ' "Mind That You Do As You Are Told" Reading books for Board School Girls, 1870–1902', *Feminist Review* 3 (1979), p. 90.
221 Ibid., p. 91.
222 Ibid., p. 95.
223 *Committee of Council Report (1877–78)*, p. 298.
224 M/211 Logbook of NTS, HMI Report November 1876.
225 L/4/2/54 Logbook of HRGI, 16 November 1883.
226 P. McCann, ed., *Popular Education and Socialization in the Nineteenth Century*, ch. 7. J.S. Hurt, 'Drill Discipline and the Elementary School Ethos'.
227 A. Penn, *Targeting Schools: Drill, Militarism and Imperialism for Boys, Girls & Mixed* (Woburn Press, 1999).
228 Ibid., pp. 160–161.

evidence regarding the military targeting of schools in Luton seems to support Penn's views. A manual by Norman states that 'a moderate amount of drill brightens up and polishes the children of the working-classes wonderfully. It teaches habits of order, regularity, silence, obedience, neatness, attention, steadiness, and method.'[229] This observation mainly had boys in mind but girls were not excluded[230] and for many years drill was the only form of physical education in the schools. The logbook of Hitchin Road Infants' School notes flag drill, dumb bell drill, hand drill, musical drill[231] and 'hand and foot drills'.[232] Visitors were often treated to demonstrations of drill, recitation and singing and[233] the ability to play for musical drill could be essential for a teacher.[234]

The Board took advantage of opportunities to instil accepted standards. It ruled that:

> being convinced of the injury resulting from the early habit of smoking and taking intoxicating drinks directs that it be an instruction to the Head Teachers of the Board Schools to give occasional or periodic lessons on the mischievous effects and danger to health attending the practice of these pernicious habits and that a copy of Dr Richardson's Intemperance Lesson Book be bought for each School for the use of the Head Teacher.[235]

Children were given moral instruction[236] and taught orderly habits.[237] They could be sent home if they were not clean[238] and received 'training in good habits'.[239] The Head Constable came to reprimand them for chalking on walls[240] and the headteachers of the Hitchin Road Schools were asked to stop the children throwing stones.[241] In 1877 the Board joined the Penny Bank savings scheme to advocate thrift[242] and, in 1899, one hundred slides were hired for magic lantern shows on history, geography and the 'Life and Duties of Citizens'.[243] Luton may have had a reputation for not being amenable to authority, but children in the last quarter of the nineteenth century were being trained to accept discipline and conformity.

Evening schools

Evening schools of various types could earn grants for the three Rs[244] and early Board minutes indicate that there were evening schools in the hamlets. Purvis confirms that they were a feature of rural schools, especially those where the

---

229 F.M. Norman, *The Schoolmaster's Drill Assistant* (Bemrose and Sons, 1875), preface.
230 Ibid., pp. 52–54.
231 L/4/2/54 Logbook of HRGI, 19 October 1888, 29 February 1889, 3 April 1890 and 3 October 1890.
232 Ibid., 14 September 1894.
233 Ibid., 4 July 1890.
234 M/239 Letterbooks of USDL, 11 April 1891.
235 M/218 Minutes of LSB, 1 April 1879.
236 L/4/2/54 Logbooks of HRGI, 6 July 1883.
237 75/67–1 Logbook of HRG, 9 October 1901.
238 L/4/2/54 Logbook of HRG, 16 September 1881; 75/67–1 Logbook of HRG, 3 March 1902 and 13 February 1903.
239 L/4/2/54 Logbook of HRGI, 19 February 1897.
240 Ibid., 3 July 1885.
241 M/220 Minutes of USDL, 14 April 1891.
242 M/217 Minutes of LSB, 16 October 1877.
243 M/223 Minutes of USDL, 19 September 1899.
244 *Committee of Council Report (1873–74)*, p. cl.

National Society was influential, for in these schools extra-curricular activities 'were reckoned to be part of a teacher's responsibility to the community'.[245] Maria Stride was appointed as an assistant teacher at Leagrave 'with a prospect of remuneration for her services at Night School'.[246] A 'night school' at Biscot was approved at the same time. The following year the master of the night school at Biscot was paid 'subject to his paying the expenses of such night school, this Board agreeing to sell Books and Material at cost price'.[247] In 1889, the headteacher of the Stopsley School was 'granted use of Reading Books, Slates etc for the purposes of a night School'[248] and, in 1895, he was given permission to hold classes in elementary science and general subjects.[249]

There are fewer references to evening classes in Luton in the earlier minutes of the Board but, in 1890, a committee was set up to oversee the 'extension of Evening Class Tuition'[250] in Luton and, in the mid-1890s, it was decided to offer evening continuation schools for both sexes, to be 'conducted under the management of the Board for instruction in the higher Standards of ordinary elementary education as set forth in . . . the Evening Continuation Schools Code 1895'. The Finance Committee was 'instructed to take all necessary steps for their immediate formation and future management, including the appointment and payment of teachers and the provision of rooms, appliances and materials'.[251]

Classes under Miss Morrison were to be held in the Old Bedford Road School on two evenings a week and Miss Steward was to be in charge at Langley Street. Miss Parker ran the evening cookery classes at Waller Street.[252] The following year, classes for girls were again offered at Old Bedford Road School together with prizes 'for Regularity of Attendance coupled with Progress and Good Conduct'.[253] Care had to be taken concerning registration, no doubt to check on the finances.[254] In 1897 Old Bedford Road was combined with Langley Street for cookery. Prizes were to be given for domestic economy, needlework (including cutting out) and composition. Langley Street also offered classes in botany.[255] Prizes were to be given for the making of bread, cakes and pies and the provision of a family meal within a set budget.[256] Similar classes were held in subsequent years.[257] In November 1900, boys' classes were discontinued on account of the small numbers but girls' classes continued.[258]

In 1897 and 1898 there were incentive schemes involving the issue of special coupons and book prizes were offered.[259] Classes were open to anyone who was

245   J. Purvis, *A History of Women's Education in England* (Open University, 1991), p. 52.
246   M/216 Minutes of LSB, 2 November 1875.
247   M/217 Minutes of LSB, 11 January 1876.
248   M/218 Minutes of USDL, 23 November 1880.
249   M/221 Minutes of USDL, 22 October 1895.
250   M/220 Minutes of USDL, 2 September 1890 and 16 September 1890.
251   M/221 Minutes of USDL, 10 September 1895.
252   Ibid., 24 September 1895.
253   M/222 Minutes of USDL, 8 September 1896.
254   M/221 Minutes of USDL, 14 January 1896.
255   M/222 Minutes of USDL, 9 February 1897.
256   Ibid., 21 September 1897.
257   Ibid., 23 August 1898; M/223 Minutes of USDL, 18 September 1900.
258   M/223 Minutes of USDL, 13 November 1900.
259   M/222 Minutes of USDL, 7 September 1897. The coupons were presumably to be presented to local tradesmen.

BEDFORDSHIRE COUNTY COUNCIL.

Luton Cookery Classes.

COTTAGE COOKERY.

MONDAY EVENINGS, 7 TO 9.

Lesson 1 —
Lentil Soup.
Apple Dumplings.
Pancakes.
Rock Buns.

Lesson 2 —
Boiling Root Vegetables.
Yorkshire Pudding.
Treacle Posset.
Paris Buns.

Lesson 3 —
Pea Soup.
Onion Sauce.
Railway Pudding.
Yeast Buns.

Lesson 4 —
Hashed Beef or Mutton.
Currant Dumplings.
Barley Water.
Scones.

Lesson 5 —
Baked Plaice.
Cornish Pasties.
Gruel.
Gingerbread Pudding.

Lesson 6 —
Vegetable Soup.
Apple Tart.
Cottage Pie.
Plum Cake.

Lesson 7 —
Irish Stew.
Mashed Potatoes.
Roly Poly Pudding.
Bread.

Lesson 8 —
Mutton Patties.
Milk Pudding.
Beef Tea.
Seed Cakes.

Lesson 9 —
German Soup.
Fig Pudding.
Arrowroot.
Baked Custard.

Lesson 10 —
Boiled Fish.
Parsley Sauce.
Jam Tarts.
Hasty Pudding.

Lesson 11 —
Mutton Broth.
Bread Pudding.
Boiled Cabbage.
Stewed Fruit.

Lesson 12 —
White Soup.
Fish Pie.
Boiled Fruit Pudding.
Porridge.

PLAIN COOKERY.

WEDNESDAY EVENINGS, 7 TO 9.

Lesson 1 —
Fried Codfish.
Stewed Rabbit.
Victoria Buns.
Macaroni Cheese.

Lesson 2 —
Fish Soup.
Minced Meat and Mashed Potatoes.
Milk Rolls.

Lesson 3 —
Lobster Balls.
Beefsteak Pie.
Lemon Cheese Mixture.
Tea Cakes.

Lesson 4 —
Potato Soup.
Rough Puff Pastry.
Sausage Rolls.
Lemon Cheesecakes.

Lesson 5 —
Roast Pork.
Apple Sauce.
Dough Nuts.
Cornflour Cakes.

Lesson 6 —
Carrot Soup.
Rissoles.
Macaroni Pudding.
Queen Cakes.

Lesson 7 —
Boiled Fowl.
White Sauce.
Fried Rice Balls.
Boiled Custard.

Lesson 8 —
Palestine Soup.
Boiled Haddock.
Egg Sauce.
Victoria Pastry.

Lesson 9 —
Fish Cakes.
Stewed Steak.
Semolina Pudding.
Shrewsbury Biscuits.

Lesson 10 —
Filleted Plaice.
Anchovy Sauce.
Curried Meat.
Boiled Rice.

Lesson 11 — INVALID COOKERY.
Fish for an Invalid.
Beef Tea.
Sponge Cakes.
Invalid Custard.

Lesson 12 —
Rabbit Pie.
Fried Sole.
Milk Blancmange.
Gooseberry Fool.

INSTRUCTRESS - - MISS M. PARKER.

(INSTRUCTRESS UNDER LUTON SCHOOL BOARD).

17. Menus for the BCC Cookery Classes taken by Miss Parker [LM]

exempt from attendance at day school and fees could be returned to students who had a good attendance record.[260] An arrangement was made in 1899 for coupons to be redeemable from local tradesmen to the amount of the whole, three-fourths and one-half respectively for percentage of attendance of ninety, seventy-five and sixty of the number of times open.[261] Classes could be discontinued if less than ten students turned up on three successive nights.[262]

In the 1890s girls in Luton were being encouraged to take advantage of further education in evening classes but, apart from the emphasis on domestic subjects and a mention of botany, the Board minutes do not give any definite idea about the curriculum provided. However, girls who had left the elementary schools were being given the opportunity to extend their education if they were so inclined.

Conclusion

The traditional patriarchy in Luton, which mainly represented the business classes, had not previously concerned itself to any large degree with education but responded to the challenges of the 1870 Forster Act, which demanded that elementary education should be made available to all the children in the town and the hamlets. Although the School Board started life reluctantly, it sought to acquire the necessary expertise and served the town conscientiously, working to provide sufficient schools, offer a widening curriculum and address the problems of attendance and child employment. Education remained utilitarian, however, and there was very little vision, especially with regard to the education of girls. During the time of the Board, working-class parents had two main choices for the education of their children: denominational schools and Board schools. The religious dimension, which probably influenced their decisions, remained an important feature in the life of the town but in time the managers of both groups of schools worked more harmoniously together.

The effect of compulsory schooling changed girls' lives fundamentally because they had to accept restrictions over their time and consequently their ability to work in the traditional industry. Compromises were made with the widespread acceptance of half-time schooling and the issuing of Labour Certificates. The matter of attendance occupied a considerable amount of time and energy on the part of the officers of the Board and the teachers but, by the time the Board ceased to exist, a generation had grown up to accept the idea of compulsory schooling.

In the early days of the Board the curriculum was restrained by the demands of the government codes, but these were relaxed and a wider curriculum could be offered. Boys were offered a different curriculum, for example the standard of tuition in arithmetic was higher and a Higher Grade School was opened to prepare boys for commercial roles in the town. However, the curriculum in girls' schools was heavily biased towards domestic subjects, especially needlework, which was seen to be an accepted part of a girl's role and duty in life. Children were beginning to be regarded as individuals and this can be seen particularly in the infant departments where the welfare of the little ones was respected. Although the Luton Board did not

---

260 M/223 Minutes of USDL, 19 September 1899 and 3 October 1899.
261 Ibid., 5 September 1899.
262 Ibid.

enjoy the kudos of the London School Board, there were similarities in the way their schools developed. As Rubenstein notes, schools had become happier places.[263]

Before 1874, girls had enjoyed considerable freedoms but, during the time of the Board, there were constraints in the form of compulsory schooling and social control. Between 1874 and 1903 their horizons were changing from freedom to regulation, from hats to homes, from independence to control. On the other hand, their educational prospects were improving but it would not be until the involvement of the BEC in 1903, that girls would realistically be able to consider any higher form of education.

---

[263] P. McCann, *Popular Education and Socialization in the Nineteenth Century*, ch. 9 pp. 253–264.

Chapter Five

Teaching: An Alternative Occupation

In 1874, employment prospects for girls in Luton were based firmly in the straw industry and for the vast majority of the female population the ability to sew hats was all that was needed to secure an adequate income and maintain a family life. Another significant option, which was open to intelligent girls, was to become a pupil-teacher. It was probably not an easy choice when the enormous freedom which girls and women in the hat industry enjoyed was taken into account.[1] Girls who entered teaching did not enjoy these freedoms for they had strict timetables and were under the control of the managers of their schools, according to the rules of their indentures.[2] Hat girls had the freedom to work at home or to move from one factory to another but, with a few exceptions, they needed to stay in or around Luton to make a living. Teachers could, and did, move to other schools in the area and also to schools in other districts. School holidays may also have been an attraction, although the hat girls had their own holidays during the slack season.

Women in the hat industry socialized with each other, especially in shared work-rooms, but teachers enjoyed a more exclusive social life, often in connection with professional associations. That teachers enjoyed each other's company cannot be denied and 'teaching families' were significant in the town.[3] There is evidence to show that teachers had money to spend on foreign holidays[4] and there were other advantages such as pension rights and tied accommodation. It is not easy to compare incomes because of the different types of salary scale, but it is true to say that experienced teachers did earn more than the average wage in the hat industry. In 1864 it was estimated that few women in the hat trade earned less than 10s a week and many would earn twice that amount.[5] By 1876, adult hat sewers would be earning about 15s a week.[6] Figures for the years 1890 to 1892 and 1917 to 1920 are more specific (see Tables 15a and 15b). Salaries of teachers are given as annual amounts while those of the hat workers are weekly, hourly or piece rate, thus indicating a difference in perceived status.

---

[1] See Chapter One.
[2] M/229 Minutes of LEC, 16 June 1914. By 1914, teachers were no longer required to take on any duties apart from those connected with the work of their school.
[3] There are many names that appear frequently; the Misses Rankin are good examples.
[4] SD Hyde 1 Logbook of Hyde School, 9 September 1912.
[5] J.G. Dony, A *History of the Straw Hat Industry* (Gibbs, Bamforth & Co., 1942), p. 109.
[6] P.P. XXX p. 159, quoted in Ibid., p. 109n.

Table 15a. Female teachers' salaries 1892 v. salaries in the hat industry 1890

Teachers' salaries 1892 (per annum)[7]		*Hats 1890 (per week)*[8]	
Pupil-teachers	£12–18	Forewomen	25s 7d
Assistants	£40–50	Hand sewers	17s 3d
Certificated	£55–70	Machine sewers	23s 8d
Infants' heads	£80–105	Trimmers	19s 1d
Girls' heads	£100–125	Other (time)	21s 2d
		Other (piece)	14s 1d

Table 15b. Female teachers' salaries 1917 v. salaries in the hat industry 1920

Teachers' salaries 1917 (per annum)[9]		*Hats 1920 (per hour)*[10]	
Certificated	£95–140	After a period of four	
Uncertificated	£65–75	years as learners:	
Supplementary	£40–50	Time rate	7d/hr
Monitresses	£10–20	Piece rate	8d/hr
Student	£12 10s–17 10s		

Opportunities to continue with their own studies must have appealed to some girls and others probably chose to teach from a sense of vocation. However, it seems likely that one of the main considerations which made girls decide to become teachers or, perhaps, made their parents decide that they should, was the question of status. This was nevertheless lower than that of the daughters of hat factory owners who were considered to be above the elementary system.

When the Luton School Board (LSB) was formed it inherited the pupil-teacher training system which had been established in 1846.[11] Elementary school scholars with acknowledged ability were given the opportunity to improve their own education while at the same time acquiring teaching skills under the guidance of the headteacher. The system had its limitations, as HMI the Reverend C.F. Johnstone indicated in his General Report on the Counties of Bedfordshire and Huntingdonshire for the year 1876. The remedy for these appeared 'to lie in the development of a higher class of teachers'.[12] The Luton Board conformed to the directives in the Education Department Codes and supervised the training of teachers conscientiously until the Bedfordshire County Council (BCC) took over this responsibility. Research into teaching in Luton will therefore have to be addressed not only in this chapter but also in Chapter Six, which looks at provision by the BCC for the education of children aged over fourteen.

[7]   M/221 Minutes of USDL, 22 November 1892.
[8]   Figures taken from Report of Factory Inspectors for 1890 (1890–1891) P.P. XIX p. 19. Quoted in J.G. Dony, *A History of the Straw Hat Industry*, p. 136.
[9]   E/Sub M 0/4/8 Minutes of BCC Elementary Education Sub-Committee, 12 October 1917.
[10] LM 1319 J.G. Dony, 'Notes on the Labour Conditions in the Luton Hat Industry', p. 18.
[11] *Minutes of the Committee of Council on Education*, 25 August 1846 and 21 September 1846 (HMSO, 1846).
[12] *Committee of Council on Education Report 1876–1877 England and Wales* (HMSO, 1877), p. 506.

Monitors

According to the 1874 Code no pupil-teacher could be apprenticed before the age of thirteen,[13] but girls below that age could become monitors.[14] In 1877 there was a scarcity of girls 'willing to give themselves to the work',[15] even though the Board had asked masters and mistresses 'to suggest names of suitable persons'.[16] Some girls already had classroom experience, for example, Sarah Cain who at the age of eleven 'began to assist in teaching previous to being a monitor'.[17] Others became monitors on a half-time basis.[18]

Lance Jones suggested that parents made decisions on behalf of their daughters.[19] Whether or not this was so, parents were certainly involved. At Hitchin Road School 'a person came with her daughter who has been recommended as a monitor'[20] and the Board minutes note requests for daughters 'to be employed as monitresses'.[21] At Hyde the headmistress was glad of her 'little daughter's help'.[22]

Monitors were taken on trial or probation. Lillie Gray was appointed by the Board as a monitor on a week's trial. She seems to have been in charge of 'over 50 babies' and the headmistress had 'to go into classrooms several times as they were more than monitor could manage' [sic].[23] Elizabeth Barford was 'appointed monitor for a month on trial' in 1882,[24] but girls appointed by the Board in 1890 were given three months to prove their suitability, during which time they would be paid 10s 10d per month.[25] Monitors could be moved from school to school. For example, Miss Vesey was 'transferred to Caddington School as they had no Assistant Teacher there and a Moniter [sic] would do to assist under present numbers'.[26] Monitors were required to respond to any need. At Hyde the monitress and a girl from Standard VI took the Infants' class 'during Miss Stone's absence'.[27] Amelia Pedley came to Hitchin Road Girls' School on trial and 'taught the words of two school songs'.[28]

Monitresses from the voluntary schools sometimes transferred to the Board,[29] but Florence Hills was forced to go against this trend after she appealed for more pay, which the Board viewed as a resignation. Florence asked her headmistress for permission to stay on until the next Board meeting when she intended to send 'an

13 *Committee of Council on Education Report 1873–1874 England and Wales* (HMSO, 1874), p. clv; *Committee of Council on Education Report 1877–1878 England and Wales* (HMSO, 1878), p. 306. The New Code (1878) noted age fourteen instead of thirteen.
14 Ibid. (1878), p. 306.
15 L/4/2/54 Logbook of HRGI, 11 May 1877. The Girls' and the Infants' Departments of Hitchin Road School were separated c.1878. However, entries continued to be made in the same logbook.
16 M/216 Minutes of LSB, 2 June 1874.
17 L/1/2/54 Logbook of SMG, 7 February 1874.
18 M/219 Minutes of USDL, 10 February 1885.
19 L. Jones, *The Training of Teachers in England and Wales* (Oxford University Press, 1924), p. 45.
20 L/4/2/54 Logbook of HRGI, 19 May 1874.
21 M/220 Minutes of USDL, 11 November 1890.
22 SD Hyde 1 Hyde Logbook, 1 July 1901.
23 L/4/2/54 Logbook of HRGI, 13–17 May 1878.
24 Ibid., 3 March 1882.
25 M/220 Minutes of USDL, 23 December 1890.
26 SD Hyde 1 Hyde Logbook, 2 November 1903.
27 Ibid., 3 January 1905 and 6 January 1905.
28 L/4/2/54 Logbook of HRGI, 1 June 1874.
29 M/211 Logbook of NTS, 27 November 1891 and 29 May 1897.

application to stay on',[30] but it seems that the Board would accept no challenge and reported 'resignation of Florence Hills'.[31] In October she 'brought back the lesson books belonging to the Board'[32] and transferred to the neighbouring voluntary school.[33]

Monitresses were under the discipline of the headteacher. As well as helping in the classroom, they had to work hard at their own studies. The headmistress who supervised Elizabeth Barford noted that 'she had not prepared her lessons two evenings this week'.[34] She 'was not able to study as much as I should like', would not 'be suitable for a Candidate'[35] and had to be reproved 'for carelessness in her lessons'.[36] In 1896, the School Board was still advertising for monitors 'under the age of 13 years and 6 months'. They had to have passed the test examination and 'give fair promise of becoming successful teachers'. It was agreed

> that the clerk shall draft a Form of Application to be sent in by each Candidate, which shall contain Particulars as to Age, Qualifications, School now or lately attended, and an Undertaking on the part of the Parent or Guardian as to continuance of the Applicant in the Board's service (if accepted by the Board) and the supply of the necessary Text-books to be used at the Central Classes together with References to the Head teacher of the school attended by the Applicant.[37]

Pupil-teachers

Elizabeth Squires started as a pupil-teacher in Langley St Infants' School after being 'presented as a Candidate last September'.[38] This is typical of the way girls began their teaching careers. The Education Department issued strict guidelines, regularly up-dated, concerning their training and employment.[39] They had to be vaccinated,[40] in possession of a medical certificate, able to read with fluency, ease and expression, understand English Grammar, work accurately the four rules of number, have a knowledge of the geography of the British Isles, be proficient in drawing and able 'to teach a class to the satisfaction of Her Majesty's inspector'.[41] Also required was 'a certificate from managers that the moral character of the candidates and of their homes justifies an expectation that the instruction and training of the school will be seconded by their own efforts and the example of their parents'.[42]

---

[30] L/4/2/54 Logbook of HRGI, 24–28 June and 1–5 July 1878.

[31] M/217 Minutes of LSB, 25 June 1878.

[32] L/4/2/54 Logbook of HRGI, 14 –18 October 1878.

[33] L/1/2/54 Logbook of SMG, 25 October 1878.

[34] L/4/2/54 Logbook of HRGI, 17 March 1882.

[35] Ibid., 12 May 1882. A monitor who had successfully applied to become a pupil-teacher became a candidate. Elizabeth Barford was accepted as a pupil-teacher.

[36] Ibid., 9 June 1882 and 15 September 1882.

[37] M/222 Minutes of USDL, 22 September 1896.

[38] L/4/2/54 Logbook of HRGI, 20 January 1882.

[39] For example, changes to the age when pupil-teachers began work and to their length of service.

[40] M/220 Minutes of USDL, 5 January 1892.

[41] *Committee of Council on Education Report 1873–74 England and Wales* (HMSO, 1874), pp. clx and clxi.

[42] Ibid., p.clx.

For five years, later reduced to four,[43] pupil-teachers were apprenticed to the school managers and entered into a life which was described as either 'the best way of securing a supply of trained teachers' or 'the cheapest and the very worst possible system of supply'.[44] Certainly they were dependent on the competence and benevolence of the headteacher who was responsible for their training[45] and who was paid accordingly. Each year an HMI would assess the school, and the pupil-teacher's results would affect the grant for the following year.[46] Pupil-teachers were answerable to the School Board[47] or, in the case of National schools, to the Vicar.[48] At the end of their training they would be expected to sit for the Queen's scholarship. Permission had to be given[49] and study time was allowed.[50] The standard of competence required was high, as these questions from a mental arithmetic examination show:

51739 x 99
800 articles at 19s 10½d each
5 cwt at 4½d per lb
Number of guineas in £257
Greatest Common Measure of 885, 1239
Interest for 1 year on £197 16s 3d at 4% per annum[51]

At the end of their engagement, pupil-teachers were free to choose their own employment. They could become assistants in elementary schools, apply for a course at a training college or become 'provisionally certificated for immediate service in charge of small schools'.[52]

The headteacher taught the pupil-teachers at times which suited both parties: Lessons could be early in the morning,[53] during the dinner break[54] or after the younger children had left.[55] The headmistress of Hitchin Road School noted:

– Excused their work on Wednesday to enable them to go out to tea.[56]
– Had Pupil-teacher three hours extra for her needlework.[57]
– Mr Shackleton informed the Pupil-teachers that in future their lessons would

---

43 M/211 Logbook of NTS, 13 June 1898; R.W. Rich, *The Training of Teachers in England & Wales during the Nineteenth Century* (Chivers, 1972), p. 191.
44 *Report of the Royal Commission on the Elementary Education Acts* [The Cross Report] 1888.
45 H. Chapman, *Village Schooldays and Beyond, From Pupil to Teacher 1906–1923* (The Book Castle, 1996).
46 L/4/2/54 Logbook of HRGI, 4 February 1881.
47 Ibid., 27 May 1881.
48 L/1/1/54 Logbook of SMG, 12 September 1883. See Chapter Nine.
49 M/239 Letterbooks of USDL, 27 April 1891.
50 M/211 Logbook of NTS, 21 April 1899.
51 T.W. Piper, *Mental Arithmetic for Pupil Teachers and Students in Training Colleges* (Philip & Son, 1887), pp. 82–84. Government examination paper for Females, Christmas 1876. The Preface confirms that this was mental arithmetic as we know it.
52 *Committee of Council on Education Report 1877–78 England and Wales* (HMSO, 1878). p. 307.
53 L/4/2/54 Logbook of HRGI, 25 April 1879–27 April 1879.
54 Ibid., 4 February 1881.
55 Ibid., 6 September 1880–10 September 1880.
56 Ibid., 6 January 1879–10 January 1879.
57 Ibid., 17 June 1878–21 June 1878.

VI CALCULATIONS OF COST.

1. TO FIND THE COST OF A DOZEN:

For every penny in the price per article reckon a shilling, and for fractions of a penny fractions of a shilling.

Calculate by this the cost of 72, 108, &c.

2. OF A SCORE:

For every shilling in the price per article reckon a pound, and for fractions of a shilling fractions of a pound.

3. OF 48:

I. RULE—Call the farthings shillings.

This rule may be applied to such numbers as 432, 384, and 528, where the number of dozens is large.

II. *Exercises*—Find similar rules for 240, 52, 960, &c.; and notice the cases of 239, 241, 959, 961, &c.

4. OF 100:

Take as many pence and twice as many shillings as there are farthings in the price of one article.

5. OF 365:

I. RULE—For every penny in the price of one reckon as many sovereigns, as many half-sovereigns, and five times as many pence.

II. *Exercises*—Consider the reason of this, and find a rule for 366, 372, &c.

6. OF 252:

Reckon the pence as guineas.

---

7. OF 313:

Reckon a pound, a crown, a shilling, and a penny for every penny in the price of one.

8. TO FIND THE COST OF ANY NUMBER OF ARTICLES AT 6s. 8d. AND OTHER ALIQUOT PARTS OF A POUND:

I. RULE—Multiply the number of articles by the fraction which expresses the relation which the price per article bears to £1.

Thus, for 6s. 8d. we take $\frac{1}{3}$ of the number of articles, and we have the price in pounds.

II. *Exercises*—Find rules for 4s., 1s. 8d., 1s. 4d., 1s. 3d., &c.
Also for 13s. 4d., 15s., 18s. 4d., &c.
Also for £1, 1s. 4d., £1, 3s. 9d., &c.

9. AT 4s. 2d. :

Which $= £\frac{5}{24} = £\frac{10}{48}$:—Annex a cypher and divide by 48.

AT 6s. 3d. :

Which $= £\frac{5}{16} = £\frac{10}{32}$ — " " 32

AT 16s. 8d. :

Which $= £\frac{5}{6} = £\frac{10}{12}$: " " " 12.

AT £1, 13s. 4d. :

Which $= £\frac{5}{3} = £\frac{10}{6}$ — " " " 6.

AT £16, 13s. 4d. :

Which $= £16\frac{2}{3} = £\frac{50}{3} = £\frac{100}{6}$:—Annex two cyphers and divide by 6.

AT £62, 10s. :

Add three cyphers and divide by 16.

AT 12s. 6d. :

Add a cypher and divide by 16.

AT 8s. 4d. :

Add a cypher and divide by 24.

Find rules for reckoning at 3s. 9d., 2s. 8d., &c.

18. From T.W. Piper, *Mental Arithmetic for Pupil Teachers*, 1887

be 5–6 pm. Also that they would be required to be at school at 8.45 am and 1.20 pm to get ready apparatus for the day's lesson.[58]
– P.T. Lessons – routine changed to give more time for private study before the examination.[59]

Pupil-teachers were not allowed to teach for more than twenty-five hours per week.[60] During this time they were expected to discipline the children well and were also disciplined themselves. For example, S. Dring was reproved 'for noise and disorder' in her class[61] and also for slapping children[62] and it was considered worthy of a note in the logbook that Emily Woods 'showed her temper'.[63] The pupil-teacher system was criticized because trainee teachers became socially isolated: they had left their peers behind but were not accepted in higher social circles.[64] It also appears that they found it difficult to form friendships across age barriers. This attitude was reflected when S. Dring was 'reproved for her familiarity with Emily Algar and others'.[65] Whoever Emily Algar might have been, the criticism seems to confirm that girls 'existed at that blurred intersection between childhood and adulthood'.[66]

Pupil-teachers had to give Criticism lessons; observations and comments were recorded in a Criticism book as demanded by the Code.[67] Louisa Dickens 'came to school with [hers] unprepared after having had a week to get it up in, her only excuse being that she had forgotten it'.[68] They also studied a variety of subjects. Those required by the Code were examined by HMI and the success or otherwise of each pupil-teacher was noted in the school logbook. Girls were also encouraged to study subjects which were not required by the Code. For example, three pupil-teachers from St Matthew's Girls' School attended art classes for freehand and model[69] and others from Board schools were preparing for practical music examinations.[70] The Religious Tract Society offered prizes for examination successes in religious knowledge.[71]

In 1892 the Luton School Board introduced a scheme for central classes at Waller Street for the instruction of pupil-teachers and monitors. However, headmistresses were still to be responsible for teaching drawing, needlework and domestic economy to their own staff.[72] Teaching boy and girl pupil-teachers together caused

[58] L/1/2/54 Logbook of SMG, 12 February 1897.
[59] Ibid., 11 September 1874.
[60] M/211 Logbook of NTS HMI Report 1894.
[61] L/4/2/54 Logbook of HRGI, 28 January 1881.
[62] Ibid., 5 July 1880–9 July 1880.
[63] M/211 Logbook of NTS, 25 September 1891.
[64] F. Thompson, *Lark Rise to Candleford* (Penguin, 1988), p. 196.
[65] L/4/2/54 Logbook of HRGI, 26 May 1879.
[66] W. Robinson, 'Pupil Teacher: Construction, Conflict and Control 1860–1910', *Cambridge Journal of Education* Vol. 27, No. 3 (November 1997), p. 371; P. Laslett, *The World We Have Lost* (Methuen, 1983) p. 256. Laslett thinks that elementary teachers were obliged to model 'themselves upon their betters'.
[67] M/211 Logbook of NTS, HMI Report November 1900.
[68] Ibid., 30 March 1897.
[69] L/1/2/54 Logbook of SMG, 27 September 1897.
[70] M/239 Letterbooks of USDL, 16 September 1892.
[71] M/223 Minutes of USDL, 24 January 1899.
[72] L/4/2/54 Logbook of HRGI, 13 May 1892.

By self-respect is not implied self-satisfaction or pride – very far from it. It implies having such a respect for yourself as will enable you to be a pattern to those you have to teach – a regard for yourself in your position that shall help you to conduct yourself with lady-like or gentlemanly deportment; to be always the essence of cleanliness and neatness in your habits and dress; and above doing anything that might lower you in the estimation of your scholars or their parents, such as being bribed into favouritism by presents of trifling value. If you have sufficient regard or respect for yourself, you will be able to rise above anything mean. Try, therefore, to cultivate a self-respect that shall make you genuine, well behaved, clean, neatly dressed, and above doing anything of which you would afterwards feel ashamed.

After all these remarks as to your conduct *in* school, this little book would seem almost incomplete without a few words of advice as to your conduct out of school. You will have to study after school hours. If you mean to make your way in your profession, don't allow anything to interfere with your studies. You must have *some* recreation, but take care that it is of the right kind. Be careful in the selection of your friends. Be careful how you spend your spare time, and where you spend it. Don't waste your time in reading what is commonly called `trash`, in the form of various penny papers of questionable repute. Don't spend your evenings in parading the streets up to a late hour at night; and never go to any place of amusement where you would be ashamed to be seen. Set a high value upon your character; and if you wish to become truly great, endeavour first to become truly good.

19. From W.T. Greenup, *Friendly Advice for Pupil Teachers*, c.1877

anxiety in some circles[73] but, although the Luton Centre was mixed, no problems have been noted in the minutes of the Board. Schemes of instruction and timetables at the Luton Centre were prepared by local headmasters.[74] This relieved the burden on other headteachers in the town, but may also have been a considerable relief to some of the girls. Before 1892, Rose Parsons, a pupil-teacher at the Hitchin Road

[73] W. Robinson, 'Pupil Teachers: The Achilles Heel of Higher Grade Girls' Schools 1882–1904', *History of Education* Vol. 22, No. 3 (1993), pp. 367–368.
[74] M/221 Minutes of USDL, 24 April 1894.

School, was frequently reprimanded for careless work but, in February 1893, was presented 'with a prize for good work done at the Centre Class'.[75] It is reasonable to suppose that a change of teacher had some effect.

In 1897 the central classes were established on a more formal basis as a Pupil-teacher Centre.[76] T.E. Margerison MA was appointed as headmaster of the pupil-teachers' central day classes with a salary of £125 rising by £10 to £175.[77] In May 1899 J.H. Hargreaves MA took over with a salary of £170.[78] When the pupil-teachers were at central classes, there could be a staffing shortage in their school[79] so attendance was often staggered.[80] Heads were sometimes unco-operative and students were not always conscientious. Margerison asked the Board to deal with pupil-teachers who were absent 'without due excuse and notification' and circulars were sent to headteachers 'requesting them to see that all Pupils attending the said Classes are not hindered by being kept in their respective Schools'.[81] Quarterly examinations were held[82] and there were incentives in the form of prizes.[83] Parents were asked to co-operate by giving 'information as to the time devoted for preparation of lessons for the Central Classes'.[84]

Considerable debate took place before the passing of the 1902 Education Act concerning the desirability of educating pupil-teachers in secondary schools or in pupil-teacher centres. Those who admired the pupil-teacher centres claimed that there was no proof that the secondary schools were better,[85] but the centres certainly had their shortcomings, as Wendy Robinson explains:

> The chief defect of the pupil-teacher centres was said to be the gathering together of young people who came directly from the elementary school and who would return to the elementary school, and whose experience was there-fore far too narrow. The culture and tone of the centres was compared unfa-vourably with that of the secondary school and centres were accused of having no corporate life or concern with the recreation and physical training of their students.[86]

No information has been found to indicate whether or not the Luton Centre conformed to this model, but the character of the town suggests that little effort would have been made to develop the cultural awareness of the town's pupil-teachers. Attitudes to schooling had always been utilitarian and it was prob-ably not until the opening of the BCC day secondary school that the education of pupil-teachers in Luton began to take on another dimension.

Ex-pupil-teachers were valued as assistant teachers because of their experience

75 L/4/2/54 Logbook of HRGI, 3 February 1893.
76 M/222 Minutes of USDL, 5 October 1897 and 19 October 1897.
77 Ibid., 16 November 1897 and 30 November 1897.
78 M/223 Minutes of USDL, 30 May 1899.
79 75/6–1 Logbook of HRG, 15 January 1904 and 8 January 1906.
80 L/4/2/54 Logbook of HRGI, 7 January 1898.
81 M/222 Minutes of USDL, 20 September 1898.
82 M/211 Letterbooks of NTS, 22 February 1897; M/222 Minutes of USDL, 19 April 1898.
83 Ibid., 15 November 1898.
84 Ibid., 30 September 1902.
85 W. Robinson, 'In Search of a "Plain Tale": Rediscovering the Champions of the Pupil-teacher Centres 1900–1910', *History of Education* Vol. 28, No. 1 (1999), p. 66.
86 Ibid., p. 61.

in a classroom situation and posts were advertised, for example in *The School-master*.[87] The following letter, written by the Clerk to the Board, explains the quali-fications that would be expected and also demonstrates that the Luton Board considered itself to be a commendable employer:

Dear Madam

The Luton Board seek an Ex PT Assistant for an Infant School which has been built about 8 years, has always earned the 'highest possible' Grant, and is considered one of the best in the district.

The Applicant must be able to play accompaniment for Musical Drill and be able successfully to manage large classes.

A Salary of £40 is paid in equal monthly instalments.

The Assistants who have from time to time left the School have had no difficulty in obtaining good appointments as the School and the Board have an established reputation amongst larger and more important Boards.

Should you wish to become an Applicant I shall be glad to hear from you at once, with particulars of past work. Also state age and height,[88] and, if possible, enclose a photographic portrait of yourself which shall be duly returned.[89]

Training colleges

Pupil-teachers who passed a qualifying examination[90] could proceed to a training college if they were able to secure a place[91] and study to become trained teachers. In the early years covered in this book, training colleges were denominational and for boarders,[92] but by 1924 others, including day training centres, had been established by local authorities and universities. A private college for training kindergarten teachers was opened in Bedford in 1882. Miss Amy Walmsley, who was its principal from 1895 until 1927, was a very active and influential member of several BCC Education Committees.[93] She went with Mr Prothero and the Director of Education to a conference in Cambridge to discuss 'the desirability of establishing an Institute for the Training of Teachers'.[94] Luton sent two representatives to a similar conference the following year.[95] In 1905, the Bedfordshire Education Committee expressed its willingness to consider the joint establishment of a Training College for Women in East Anglia[96] and, in 1908, the BEC was 'prepared to recommend the Council to take ten places' in the proposed college.[97] Another conference took place in 1920,[98]

87   M/217 Minutes of LSB, 6 March 1877.
88   M/239 Letterbooks of USDL, 29 April 1891. Height was equated with the ability to discipline.
89   M/239 Letterbooks of USDL, 11 April 1891.
90   The Queen's Scholarship. By 1920 the Oxford Senior Local Examination was substituted for the Preliminary Examination for the Certificate. L. Jones, *The Training of Teachers*, p. 396; EM5 Minutes of BEC, 24 October 1913.
91   L. Jones, *The Training of Teachers*, p. 206.
92   *Committee of Council on Education Report 1877–78 England and Wales*, pp. 308–309.
93   R. Smart, *On Others' Shoulders: An Illustrated History of the Polhill & Lansdowne Colleges now De Montfort University Bedford* (De Montfort University, 1994), pp. 42 and 129.
94   EM1 Minutes of BEC, 23 October 1903.
95   M/226 Minutes of LEC, 16 February 1904.
96   EM1 Minutes of BEC, 19 April 1905.
97   EM3 Minutes of BEC, 17 July 1908.
98   M/229 Minutes of LEC, 13 April 1920.

but it is not clear what decisions were made. Setting up a training college was a major responsibility and, in 1923, a letter was received from the Association of Education Committees concerning the 'serious condition in which local Education Authorities who have established Training Colleges find themselves'.[99]

The minutes record some details about the processes involved in applying for a place at a training college. Two girls were reported to have been successful in the King's Scholarship, one in the Second Class and one, Rubie Rosson, in the First.[100] The question of funding was important and as Rubie Rosson, who was to go to St Gabriel's TC, had passed in the First Class she would have received the necessary financial backing. Girls who lived in South Bedfordshire may have had some support from charities such as the Chew's Foundation[101] and, by 1908, the Bedford-shire Education Committee (BEC) was providing scholarships.[102]

The Letterbooks of the Board record some of the procedures connected with college application. Emily Brightman passed the examination, 'but not high enough to qualify for admission to College'.[103] She was required to 'take Scripture'[104] and had to go to her intended college in Oxford in order to be examined in music.[105] They also noted that Marion West had gone to the training college at Exeter.[106] Students in training needed to observe schools at work and, in 1901, the Board gave permission for 'a student in the Lincoln Training College to visit any of the Schools of the Board during working hours'.[107] Students usually stayed at a training college for two years but, in 1902, the Luton Board inserted 'an additional line in the Scale of Salaries, having reference to Teachers who have had but one year's College train-ing'.[108]

The minutes of the Board reveal details about the early careers of some of its teachers. In 1874 Jane Tuffnell, aged twenty-one and 'late a Student in the Derby Lichfield Diocesan Training School', was appointed as head of one of the voluntary schools.[109] When she resigned in 1877 it was noted that she 'will shortly receive her certificate' and that she is a 'certificated teacher of the First Division'. Her successor was Mary Banks from the same college.[110] Another teacher whose training was recorded was E. Rands who was at Norwich TC between 1891 and 1892; she was selected as headteacher at New Town Street School in 1898.[111] The Board also supplied a testimonial for Annie Preston, a student at Tottenham TC, whom they had previously employed as an assistant teacher.[112]

The debate concerning the efficiency of teachers who learn their skills in the

---

[99]   Ibid., 13 March 1923.
[100] M/224 Minutes of USDL, 18 March 1902.
[101] J. Dyer, *The Story of the Stopsley Schools* (LMAG, 1989), p. 15.
[102] EM3 Minutes of BEC, 17 July 1908.
[103] M/239 Letterbooks of USDL, 6 May 1892.
[104] Ibid., 18 June 1892.
[105] Ibid., 22 June 1892.
[106] Ibid., 1 October 1901.
[107] M/224 Minutes of USDL, 10 December 1901.
[108] Ibid., 22 July 1902.
[109] L/1/2/54 Logbook of SMG, 19 January 1874.
[110] Ibid., HMI Report January 1877 and 29 March 1877.
[111] M/211 Logbook of NTS, 24 January 1898.
[112] M/220 Minutes of USDL, 2 September 1890.

classroom as opposed to those who train in an academic institution is not a new one. Lance Jones's wise observation was that 'experience is no substitute for professional training of the right kind, nor is professional training an adequate substitute for experience. The two are complementary; both are necessary.'[113] The Luton Education Committee (LEC) considered their relative values in 1912 when there was a general shortage of certificated and uncertificated teachers but a surplus of college-trained teachers. The LEC did not feel 'that these teachers have had sufficient experience to justify their appointment at the rate of salary usually paid to a trained teacher' so after careful consideration the Committee resolved to recommend:

> that when it has been found impossible to fill a vacancy for a Certificated [Untrained] or Uncertificated Teacher by the appointment of a Teacher of these grades, a Trained Teacher should be appointed, such Teacher to receive the commencing salary usually paid to a Certificated [Untrained] Teacher.
> After a year's satisfactory service, the Staffing Committee are to report as to the desirability of placing a teacher so appointed upon the scale applicable to Trained Teachers.[114]

Details concerning the staff from three Luton schools between 1913 and 1924 show that there was still a high proportion of unqualified and untrained teachers.

Table 16. Number of qualified and unqualified teachers 1913 and 1924[115]

	Trained and certificated	Certificated	Uncertificated	Other
Beech Hill Girls' School:				
1914	2	1	3	1
	1 with BA			
1916	2		3	
	1 with BA			
1918	2		4	
1919	2		4	
1920	2		3	
Norton Road Mixed School:				
1913	1 (male)	2 (1 male, 1 female)	2 (female)	1 student teacher (male)

113 L. Jones, *The Training of Teachers*, p. 207.
114 M/228 Minutes of LEC, 10 September 1912.
115 Logbooks of Beech Hill Girls School, Norton Road School and Denbigh Road Girls School.

Denbigh Road Girls'
School:

1921	1	3
1922	1	4
1924	1	3
	1 with BA	

Assistant teachers

When listing the staff at the various schools it was the normal practice to name the headteacher, then assistant teachers and lastly pupil- or student teachers. The category of 'assistant teachers' included teachers with a wide range of qualifications. There were ex-pupil-teachers who had passed the Queen's scholarship examination and were counted as uncertificated teachers. Then there were teachers who had studied for the teachers' certificate and who were presented as certificated teachers. Those who had been to a training college were described as trained and certificated. There was also a class of teachers who were both unqualified and untrained. In 1875 they had been termed assistants, under the 1890 Code they were classed as Article 68s and after 1902 they were described as supplementary teachers.[116] There were very few regulations to control the employment of supplementary teachers.

Becoming certificated

Many acting teachers studied for their certificates while they were working. Luton school logbooks and minute books[117] continually refer to study classes for certificates, study leave and time away from school to sit for the examination.[118] The 1874 Code stipulated that, in order to obtain certificates, teachers must be examined and undergo probation by actual service in school. The examinations were held annually and there was a different syllabus for male and female candidates.[119] The ideology which saw girls in a domestic role also affected the training of teachers; needlework and domestic economy were part of their curriculum and the second year syllabus included 'the work of a needlewoman in various branches applicable to the family of a working man'.[120] This requirement conforms with the belief that girls were relative people.

Those who entered for the examination had to have had at least one year in training schools under inspection or, if from an elementary school, to have completed an engagement as pupil-teacher satisfactorily, obtained a favourable report from an inspector or served as an assistant for at least six months in schools under certificated teachers. If the candidate was successful in the examination she had to pass a period of probation.[121] However, over the years many certificates were issued without examination.[122]

---

116 L. Jones, *The Training of Teachers*, pp. 215–216.
117 M/222 Minutes of USDL, 22 September 1896.
118 M/211 Logbook of NTS, 3 December 1883 and 10 December 1883; M/220 Minutes of USDL, 26 November 1889.
119 *Committee of Council on Education Report 1873–74 England and Wales*, p. clii.
120 Ibid., p. cxc.
121 Ibid., p. cliii.
122 A. Tropp, *The School Teacher* (Heinemann, 1957), p. 114; R.W. Rich, *The Training of Teachers*, p. 191.

Students who received a second-class certificate could be up-graded to first class after ten years 'by good service only', while teachers with third-class certificates were not allowed to be in charge of pupil-teachers.[123] Certificates could be 'recalled, suspended, or reduced' at any time if the managers were unable to state that the teacher's 'character, conduct, and attention to duty' had been satisfactory or if the inspectors could not confirm that the school was 'efficient in organisation, discipline, and instruction'.[124] After a probationary period a teacher earned a 'parchment certificate'.[125] Harriet Stickley, the respected head at Hitchin Road Infants' School, was recorded in the 1887 HMI Report as 'Certificated Teacher Second Class' but, the following year, she had been up-graded to a first-class certificate. On the other hand Florence Rankin, who was a member of her staff, had her second-class certificate down-graded.[126]

Headteachers

Advertisements for headships were placed in magazines such as *The School Board Chronicle* and *The School Master*. Applicants were asked to state salary expected, age and qualifications and to enclose recent testimonials.[127] In 1876 Eliza Jarman from Eastbourne, Sussex, was appointed to the High Town Schools at £80 per annum and Anne Simmons became headmistress at Langley Street with a salary of £50 per annum.[128] Miss Simmons resigned in October 1880 and, as Mrs Drewett, requested the return of two original testimonials in June 1885.[129] In 1892 the Board selected three applicants for the post of headmistress of the Surrey Street Schools 'and that they be communicated with in the order in which they are now placed.' The teachers were to be interviewed 'if possible at work in their own Schools'.[130] In 1915 five applicants out of forty-one were short-listed for a headship; none was a serving Luton teacher.[131]

One headmistress, Jane Craig, committed some misdemeanour[132] and was dismissed. This resulted in the other headteachers rallying to her support. A memorial from the Luton Headteachers' Association was sent asking the Board to reconsider and a deputation from the parents of the school and the ratepayers of Luton also spoke in her favour.[133] The Board treated the memorial with less than full consideration stating that 'the names of the oldest and best teachers in the Board's service were missing'.

Miss Craig was 'ready to express regret for any incident for which she may have been responsible, arising out of her dismissal by the Board which may have given offence to Members of the Board' and the 'oldest and best' teachers added their names to another appeal on her behalf. The National Union of Teachers (NUT) also

123 *Committee of Council on Education Report 1873–74*, p. cliii.
124 Ibid., p. cliv.
125 L. Jones, *The Training of Teachers*, p. 183; M/223 Minutes of USDL, 27 November 1900.
126 L/4/2/54 Logbook of HRGI Reports 1887, 1888, 1893 and 1896.
127 M/217 Minutes of LSB, 3 October 1876.
128 Ibid., 17 October 1876. The Hitchin Road schools were at High Town.
129 M/219 Minutes of USDL, 2 June 1885.
130 M/220 Minutes of USDL, 19 July 1892.
131 M/229 Minutes of LEC, 20 July 1915.
132 This seems to have been a criticism of the Board.
133 M/221 Minutes of USDL, 27 February 1894.

sent a petition 'on behalf of Miss Craig'. The Board was 'glad to notice its expression of sympathy for one of its Members in difficulties' but would not reconsider its decision. Their only concession was to allow Miss Craig to apply for a post as first assistant when a vacancy arose at any of its schools.[134] She was given a temporary appointment at her own school with a considerable loss of salary,[135] but resigned the following July.[136] This incident again indicates that the Board was anxious to maintain its authority. It also demonstrates that the headteachers in Luton were prepared to unite in a professional capacity.[137]

Headmistresses were responsible for the running of their schools according to government regulations. They had to ensure that the children made good progress and, until c.1890, their salaries would depend on their success. When there was a shortage of staff their teaching burdens were increased and they frequently had to deal with angry parents. There was clerical work and, in times of hardship, there were children to be fed. Concerts and exhibitions were organized and, by the early 1900s, more and more out-of-school activities to be supported.

Applications for the headship of Surrey Street Girls' School

Some application forms for the headship of Surrey Street Girls' School in February 1899 have been found;[138] none of the applicants was from Luton. The forms were sent for the attention of Mr William Hoyle, Clerk to the Board. Reports were to be on a separate sheet and testimonials had to be verbatim, not extracts only. No more than three were required, 'the most recent being preferred'. The applicants had similar backgrounds: pupil-teaching, Queen's scholarship, training college and additional certificates such as drawing and tonic sol-fa. Here are some extracts:

Beatrice Sage (b. 30 August 1876) was from Banbury where she had a post at the British School. She had been a pupil-teacher in Bath and had passed the Queen's scholarship, second class, in 1894. She then went to St Mary's Hall, a training college at Cheltenham (1895–1897), where she gained a second-class certificate for each year of study. She had qualifications in drawing (freehand and model, geometry and blackboard) and an Intermediate Certificate in tonic sol-fa.

Mrs Theresa Ramskill (b. 4 September 1863) was a widow from Barnsley and had similar qualifications as well as cookery and dressmaking certificates. She was a serving headteacher. Annie Abraham (b. 3 June 1860) had been a pupil-teacher in Manchester, had trained in Warrington and was working as an assistant teacher in Kentish Town. She held certificates in physiology, hygiene and Swedish drill. Louisa Constance Rhead (b. 5 July 1860) from London had been a headmistress since 1884 and offered French. Miss Annie Moore (b. 7 Sept 1874) from Sheffield was able to play the piano.

Amy Moore (b.16 July 1858) had studied at Stockwell Training College and was the head at Malden British School. She could offer advanced piano playing, botany

134   Ibid., 13 March 1894.
135   Ibid., 10 April 1894.
136   Ibid., 3 July 1894.
137   M/221 Minutes of USDL, 22 November 1892. There was also a Bedfordshire Headteachers' Association.
138   These were loose papers found in a Minute Book at LMAG.

and physiology and had a certificate from the County Council Instruction Committee for microscopical botany. Louisa Sutton (b. 4 October 1857) had gained a first-class certificate at the Home and Colonial Training College. Amongst other things she was qualified in advanced science animal physiology. Mrs Georgina See (b. 8 December 1863) had not been to a training college, but was headmistress at a Hampshire school. She had previously worked at the same school, but left when she married. Having been widowed, she returned there. She was able to teach tonic sol-fa and also the old notation.

Ethel Buller (b. 19 June 1871) had been to Salisbury Diocesan Training College and was a headmistress from Bexley in Kent. She was able to offer advanced science, 1st class advanced agriculture, 1st class in history and education and honours in English literature at the examination for Lady Literate in Arts (LL.A). Elizabeth Waring (b. 23 September 1870) was, at the time, 'out of situation'. She numbered among her qualifications 'Swedish drill, kindergarten and hand and eye training certificates'. Mary Cockburn (b. 3 March 1866) had trained at Durham College of Science and was a matriculation student from Durham University. She had studied advanced science, physiography and hygiene, advanced French and elementary Latin and German.

Sara Lawman (b. 17 December 1863) from Nottingham had been a pupil-teacher for an extra year and had a fifth year's PT Certificate instead of a Queen's scholarship and also a qualification in agricultural geology (Cambridge Syndicate), calisthenics and musical drill. She had held three headships, but had resigned on account of her mother's illness. Mary Rhodes (b. 8 January 1867) from Bradford had not been a pupil-teacher, but had passed the Queen's scholarship examination. She had also studied hygiene and animal physiology. Ella Hart (b. 29 October 1865) trained at Swansea, had worked at a Higher Grade school and was, at the time of application, headmistress of a girls' school in Devon. Elizabeth Hill (b. 3 February, presumably 1863) from Birmingham had a certificate for the theory of music from Trinity College and was also qualified to teach domestic economy.

Katherine Bryant (b. 25 July 1870) had followed the normal route of a pupil-teacher, Queen's scholarship and training college. She had held two headships and had passed geography and geology in the LL.A examinations. She wrote to Mr Hoyle:

> I beg to enclose Form of Application for the Surrey Rd.[139] Board School, duly filled in, also verbatim copies of the three last Day School Reports and of three Testimonials. I have other Testimonials equally as good.
> If necessary any of the following gentlemen may be referred to:–
> 1. A:J: Swinburne Esq: H:M:I: Snape Wickham Mkt, Suffolk,
> 2. The Rev: T: Archbold, Burgate, Suffolk (Late Principal Training College, Norwich)
> 3. The Rev: E: S: Finch, Vicarage, Laxfield, Framlingham, Suffolk.
>   I am, Sir,
>   Yours respectfully
>   K: M: Bryant

---

[139] Correspondence in the *Luton News* during 2004 has confirmed that there was some confusion between Surrey Street and Surrey Road.

Miss Bessie Belbin's application was also accompanied by a letter. Both the form and the letter are reproduced here:

Miss Bessie Belbin
Post Office,
Napton
Rugby
d.o.b. 29.6.1862 (age 36)
Pupil-teacher at Heeley, Sheffield Board
Queen's Scholarship 1st Class 1883
Training College: Whitelands, Chelsea 1884–85
First Year 1st Class, Second Year 1st
Present Appointment Head, Locum Tenency [sic] at Napton
Previous Appointments
       Head, Long Newnton Tetbury
       Head, Stanway, Glos
       Sheffield Board Schools 1880–93 omitting 2 yrs at College
Qualifications:
       Drawing: D
       Music: College Certificate for theory, Old Notation and Tonic
       Advanced Sciences: Agriculture – top of College list, Sol-fa
       College of Preceptors and Local Cambridge

In addition to the information I have given on the form I beg to state I was educated at the Day School Company's High School, Sheffield where I was prepared for the examinations I passed and also for the Matriculation although I did not enter having become an elementary teacher by the June of 1880 the time for examination.

I was p.t. for two years only and was then transferred to the Higher Grade Bd School as an ex p.t. for 1½ years and then entered Whitelands where my studies in Mathematics and Languages [were] continued. Previous to my College training I had earned a Science Cert. in Magnetism and Electricity 1st Elem.

On leaving my alma mater awarded me Excellent in Cookery, Hygiene, Needlework and Drill (Military and Swedish. Mme Austerberg's system).

I was one of the six girls who obtained Excellent for the lesson given before the students and College staff and was afterwards on that account chosen to give a lesson before the Bishop, the Diocesan Inspector and the Governing body of Whitelands.

All my testimonials (with the exception of Crooksmoor) I only obtained in November and December 1989 never having required any until this year. In my last school where I only stayed one year, the district being too enervating for me, I prepared the p.t.s for examination and they passed with success.

Needlework is one of my special qualifications and I helped Miss Cleghorn at the pupil teachers' centre classes in that subject.

I am fond of teaching and if I should be fortunate enough to enter your service, I should do my best to gain your approval.
Believe me, Gentlemen
Yours sincerely, Bessie Belbin

These applications paint a picture of a very well educated group of teachers, but none of them was successful. It has to be wondered exactly what else the successful candidate had to offer. She was Miss Edith Stampe who took over from Miss Johnson and was appointed at a salary of £100 per year.

Qualifications

Teachers with particular interests or ambitions had opportunities to take a variety of examinations, some of which entitled them to an increase of salary on a yearly basis (see Table 17).

Table 17. Teachers' further qualifications with salary increments 1903[140]

Salary increment	Qualification
£10	Art Master's Certificate
	Inter BA or B.Sc.
£5	Art Class Teacher's Certificate
	Preliminary BA or B.Sc.
£2.10s	Elementary Drawing Certificate
	Honours in any Advanced Science under the Board of Education
£2	1st Class Advanced Science
	Advanced Certificate under the Tonic Sol-fa College
£1	1st Class in any Art Subject under the Board of Education
	1st Class King's Scholarship
	2nd Class Advanced Science
	1st Class Advanced Science (having previously received a Bonus for a Second Class in the same subject)
	Intermediate Certificate under the Tonic Sol-fa College (having previously received a Bonus for the Intermediate Certificate)
10s	2nd Class in any Art Subject under the Board of Education

The College of Preceptors

The College of Preceptors, which was founded in 1846, aimed to raise the standards and standing of the teaching profession at a time when schoolteachers were receiving a considerable amount of criticism.[141] One of its aims was to provide 'some proof of qualification, both as to the amount of knowledge and the art of conveying it to others'.[142] Awards from the College of Preceptors were especially valuable to women and teachers in private schools. There are records of teachers in Luton taking the examination,[143] but although these qualifications would no doubt

---

[140] M/224 Minutes of USDL, 9 June 1903. These awards were not automatic but were to be considered in the light of the teacher's length of service and general efficiency.

[141] R. Aldrich, *School and Society in Victorian Britain, Joseph Payne and the New World of Education* (Garland, 1995), p. 96.

[142] Ibid., p. 97.

[143] M/222 Minutes of USDL, 14 December 1897; SD Hyde 1 Logbook of Hyde School, 6 December 1898; 75/6–1 Logbook of HRG, 29 August 1904.

have brought more status there was no automatic financial reward.[144] The Board seems to have considered its own examinations to be more relevant. Miss Wingrave had certificates from the College of Preceptors and the Cambridge Examination Board and was allowed to have a trial as a monitor 'with a view to passing the Queen's scholarship Examination so soon as may be'. But in all cases 'persons seeking the office of Monitor under this Board shall pass the Board's preliminary examination before appointment'.[145]

Music

There were regulations concerning the teaching of music in the government codes. Two basic methods were used to teach theory: notation and tonic sol-fa. Notation involved learning the notes as they were set out on the bass and treble clefs. Tonic sol-fa used charts with doh, ray, me, etc., for children to sight-read. This system was popular in Board schools and was therefore 'looked down upon' by respectable society.[146] Teachers were proud to put this qualification on their application forms and it earned a salary increase. The Board agreed to raise Miss L. Sear's salary 'by the payment of [her] Railway Fare (Season ticket between Luton and Leagrave) as soon as she shall have obtained a Certificate from the Tonic Sol-fa College'.[147]

Art

Leave of absence to sit the exams of the Department of Science and Art was allowed[148] and their certificates brought salary increases.[149] In 1891 the Board became a centre for the teacher's examinations in blackboard drawing in connection with the 'D' Certificate[150] and was used for the October examinations in blackboard drawing and light and shade.[151] In May 1892, in the Science and Art examinations for the season, six art and eleven science subjects were taken. Of the 122 art and 237 science papers that were 'worked', over one hundred were by teachers employed in the elementary schools within the Borough of Luton.[152]

Professional associations

The National Union of Elementary Teachers was founded in 1870, and in 1889 it became the NUT. Its aims were:

Control of entrance to the profession and teachers' registration.
The recruitment of teachers to the Inspectorate.
The gaining of a right of appeal.
Superannuation.
The revision of the educational code.
The gaining of the security of tenure.

[144] M/224 Minutes of USDL, 1 October 1901.
[145] M/223 Minutes of USDL, 14 November 1899.
[146] P.A. Scholes, *The Oxford Companion to Music* (Oxford University Press, 1972), p. 1029.
[147] M/220 Minutes of USDL, 21 January 1890.
[148] L/4/2/54 Logbook of HRGI, 16 September 1887.
[149] See Chapter Six.
[150] M/220 Minutes of USDL, 28 April 1891 and 21 July 1891.
[151] Ibid., 15 September 1891.
[152] Ibid., 24 May 1892. There is a certificate at LMAG.

Freedom from compulsory extraneous duties.
Adequate salaries.
Freedom from 'obnoxious interference'.[153]

Women were active in the union from its early days[154] and it became apparent that 'there were some issues upon which women could speak with particular authority'.[155] These included infants' schools, kindergartens and domestic subjects. The NUT played a significant part in the lives of Luton teachers and communications from the central office and local groups were sent when there was felt to be a need. Letters or deputations were received concerning half-time schooling,[156] commercial subjects,[157] scholarships for students attending elementary schools,[158] salaries[159] and complaints against teachers.[160] Of particular interest to women teachers was a 'communication from the Secretary of the National Union of Teachers, having reference to differences in salaries paid to Infant Head-mistresses as compared with Girls' Mistresses'. This was remitted to be dealt with by the 'Staffing Committee'.[161]

Salaries

Table 18. Salary scales paid by the School Board to teachers 1896 and 1898[162]

	28th January 1896	*8th March 1898 (changes)*
Headmasters:		
Higher Grade	£200 x £5 to £250	
Ordinary	£150 x £5 to £175	
Headmistresses:		
Girls	£100 x £4 to £125	
Infants	£80 x £4 to £105	
Assistants:		
Male trained	£70 x £4 to £95	£80 x £4 to £105
Female trained	£60 x £3 to £85	£70 x £4 to £90
Male certificated	£65 x £3 to £85	£70 x £4 to £90
Female certificated	£55 x £3 to £70	£60 x £3 to £75
Female assistants in boys' schools	£5 a year extra	

153 Quoted in A. Tropp, *The School Teacher*, p. 113.
154 T.R. Phillips, 'The National Union of Elementary Teachers 1870–1882' (M.Phil, Thesis, 1991), p. 130.
155 Ibid., p.132.
156 M/221 Minutes of USDL, 26 March 1895.
157 M/222 Minutes of USDL, 25 January 1898.
158 Ibid., 20 September 1898.
159 M/229 Minutes of LEC, 10 July 1917 and 21 August 1917.
160 E/Sub M 0/4/8 Minutes of BCC Elementary Education Sub-Committee, 23 April 1920.
161 M/223 Minutes of USDL, 12 December 1899.
162 M/221 Minutes of USDL, 28 January 1896; M/222 Minutes of USDL, 8 March 1898. Salary scales were noted regularly. 'x' indicates increments.

Male ex p-ts	£50 x £2 10s to £65	£50 x £3 to £65
Female ex p-ts	£40 x £2 10s to £55	£45 x £2 10s to £60
Article 68	£25 x £2 10s to £40	£30 x £2 10s to £50
Boy p-ts	£14, £16, £18, £20	£12, £14, £16, £18
Girl p-ts	£12, £14, £16, £18	£10, £12, £14, £16
Monitors, male and female		10s per calendar month
Higher grade assistants	£10 in excess of ordinary scale	
– first assistant		may rise to £125
– second assistant		may rise to £115
Head assistants	£5 a year extra	
– in higher grade	£15 extra + £10 excess	

In the early years of this study, salaries were negotiated on an individual basis. Teachers would be appointed at a certain salary and would then have to ask for a rise. If it was forthcoming they would write a letter of thanks. One of the first recorded salary scales in the minutes of the LSB was: 'Miss Jane Douglas – £50 plus house and coals'.[163] The following year she was given an extra £5 a year as a person 'attending during the teaching of Female Pupil Teachers at the Langley Street Board School'.[164] By 1876, salaries were listed in the quarterly accounts.[165] The highest was £12 10s 0d (for a teacher) and the lowest 5s (possibly for a monitress). In 1889 it appears that salaries were paid monthly.[166] Headteachers' salaries were made up of separate items. For example, Eliza Partridge at Hitchin Road Infants' Department was to receive £70 per annum, one fourth examination and presentation grant, one half pupil-teachers' grant and £3 for each pupil-teacher. Anne Simmons from Langley Street Girls' School received the same allowances, but £80 rather than £70. Eliza Jarman of High Town Girls' School was paid the same amount as Anne Simmons, but was promised that her salary would not be less that £100 per annum. All these agreements were subject to three months' notice on either side.[167]

Changes in the government codes alarmed local headmistresses. Harriet Stickley of Hitchin Road Infants School wrote to ask the Board to guarantee her a minimum salary of £100.[168] The Board replied that, as 'her average salary of late years has exceeded that amount . . . there was little probability of its being less in the future'. They 'recommended that should such occasion arise the Board should consider her case favourably'.[169] In 1890 the minutes note that

> in consequence of changes in the 'Code' now before the House, by which it would seem that the Merit Grant may be abolished, the Board shall and do guarantee to Miss Raffles and Miss Stickley each and severally the sum of £110 for the year ending 30th September 1890 should the Salary earned by

[163] M/216 Minutes of LSB, 31 March 1874.
[164] Ibid., 16 March 1875.
[165] M/217 Minutes of LSB, 21 March 1876.
[166] M/220 Minutes of USDL, 16 July 1889.
[167] M/218 Minutes of LSB, 4 March 1879.
[168] M/220 Minutes of USDL, 25 June 1889.
[169] Ibid., 9 July 1889.

the said Miss Raffles or Miss Stickley fall short of that amount. And that the said increased Stipend shall be so paid to the said Teachers so long as they – being in the service of this Board – continue to earn the maximum Grant possible to be earned.[170]

As early as 1878, the LSB had made extensive enquiries about rates of pay granted by other boards.[171] In 1892 they introduced a 'Scheme for Fixed Salary in accordance with the recommendation of the General Committee'.[172] Other considerations were included in teachers' salaries. The headmistress at East Hyde was to be paid £85 per annum 'together with House, fuel and lighting'.[173] The cost of travel was often allowed for teachers in rural schools. Mrs Karolina Leaver, the next headmistress at East Hyde, was paid £70 per annum 'together with the cost of a Railway Season ticket between Luton and Harpenden.'[174] Bonuses were given for good reports; when a school was marked 'Excellent' the headteacher had his or her salary increased 'by the sum of Five pounds for the month of January next ensuing the receipt of the report upon such School'.[175] Teachers who ran schools in the absence of the head were rewarded,[176] long service was acknowledged[177] and 'extra services' earned recognition.[178] On the other hand, the wife of the headmaster at Stopsley was expected 'to teach sewing and the Infants free of Salary'.[179]

Every salary scale for teachers between 1874 and 1924 gives lower rates of pay for women than men. This differentiation conformed to attitudes which saw women in a subsidiary role. In theory a man had more responsibilities than a woman although that argument could hardly be used in the case of pupil-teachers, student teachers, bachelors or widows. This point is an interesting one as far as Luton is concerned because working-class women in the hat industry were not seen to be in a subsidiary role.

Case studies

Edith Wing was probably the daughter of George Wing, a bootmaker, who lived at 24 Bute Street.[180] The 1881 census shows that two of her sisters were involved with the family business, one as a boot machinist and another as shop assistant. Edith was ten at the time, which suits the dates given below. She was appointed as monitress at the High Town Infants' School in January 1884 and was accepted as a candidate in the following May. In January of the following year she was apprenticed as a pupil-teacher according to the requirements of the Government Code (Article 83). The report of the HMI at the end of the year says that she passed well. She was given leave to take examinations, one of them being for drawing. In his report for 1888 the HMI notes that 'E.K. Wing has passed fairly but should attend to History and

170 Ibid., 1 April 1890.
171 M/217 Minutes of LSB, 28 May 1878.
172 M/220 Minutes of USDL, 10 May 1892.
173 M/222 Minutes of USDL, 1 November 1898.
174 M/223 Minutes of USDL, 2 October 1900.
175 M/219 Minutes of USDL, 18 December 1883.
176 M/222 Minutes of USDL, 3 November 1896.
177 M/224 Minutes of USDL, 4 February 1903.
178 M/227 Minutes of LEC, 21 September 1909.
179 M/218 Minutes of LSB, 12 October 1879.
180 1881 Census of England and Wales (Bedfordshire).

Needlework at examination. She should be informed that she is now qualified under both Articles 50 and 52.' She left school at the end of the year to go to college and in January 1891 was applying for a headship. Edith must have been in her early 20s, but it was by no means unusual for young women to take on such responsibilities as soon as they had become certificated or trained. The Luton School Board wrote her this testimonial:

> Miss E.K. Wing was a p-t in the Hitchin Road Infant School of the Board, but, being successful in obtaining a good position on the Queen's scholarship List, entered the Saffron Walden Training College in January 1889.
> She possesses high qualifications as a Teacher and her two years College training will undoubtedly have helped to fit her for the post of headmistress.
> She maintains excellent discipline without apparent effort, is painstaking and persevering, and has been accustomed to large classes in a school which has for many years been awarded the 'Excellent' Merit Grant.[181]

Sarah Ann Edwards' teaching career did not run smoothly. In April 1877 she started work at the New Town Street School, a Church school in a very poor area. A reading of the logbook reveals frequent changes of teachers and headteachers and numerous complaints about the difficulties involved in keeping discipline. Sometimes she was sent out to enquire about children who were ill or to collect school fees. Her term of apprenticeship ended in September 1882, she passed the certificate examination (in the third division) in March 1884 and in 1886 she resigned. She had survived for nine years in spite of enormous difficulties.[182]

Rose Ashley Parsons[183] began to work at the Hitchin Road Infants' School as a monitress on a month's trial in September 1888 and was accepted as a pupil-teacher in November 1889. Her headmistress appears to have had high standards. In February 1891 she complained about Rose's home lessons: she 'has again brought her lessons to me very imperfectly prepared. I have warned her several times that I should make an entry about it and I think it right to do so this time.' The next month she 'talked to her very seriously about the matter showing what the consequence would be if she continued to neglect her lessons. She begged me to forgive her, and promised to take more pains in the future.' Rose began to attend the central classes and in January 1893 earned herself a prize (a book or books to the value of 10s 6d) for 'regularity of attendance and quality of work'. In the following September she and the other pupil-teachers were examined in singing, needlework (garments and specimens), reading and recitation at the Pupil-teacher Centre. She passed the Queen's scholarship examination in the second class and began to teach as an assistant at Surrey Street Infants' School with a salary of £40. She then studied for the teaching certificate. In the period between the leaving of the headmistress of Langley Street Infants' School and the appointment of a new one, Rose was transferred to look after the school, for which she was paid an extra £2 2s 0d, and by

---

181 Information about Miss Wing was collected from references in the Hitchin Road Infants' School Logbooks, the Minutes of the School Board and the Letterbooks of the Board.
182 M/211 Selections from the Logbook of NTS.
183 *Census of England and Wales (1881) Bedfordshire.* Rose may have been the daughter of George, a coachman, who lived at 6 Dumfries Street. Her age was given as ten.

January 1900 she was earning £67 per annum. In July 1903 the Board awarded her a special increment 'under the clause for lengthened service', which brought her salary up to £75–80 per annum.[184]

The testimonial given to <u>Florence Rankin</u> in 1898, when she left to marry, notes her career and also gives an insight into what the Board regarded as admirable qualities for a teacher to possess:

> Miss Florence Rankin has been in the service of this Board for a period of twelve years, having successively been Pupil-teacher, Ex Pupil-teacher and certificated assistant. In every respect she has given entire satisfaction, and she now leaves at her own request and to the great regret of the Board and of her co-workers on the staff. She has worked in an Infant department during the whole period, and is fully qualified to take charge of any Infant school.
> During the late illness of the headmistress Miss Rankin was responsible for the conduct of the Hitchin Road School with an average attendance of 250, and dealt with the same in the most satisfactory manner, keeping all busily employed, and maintaining admirable discipline. Her methods are good, her teaching and illustrations of the most modern type, her control of her class perfect, whilst she is gentle and ladylike in demeanour, punctual, obliging and conscientious.[185]

Conclusion

Teaching was accorded a little more status than hat-making and was often chosen by girls who achieved good results in the elementary schools. Very little evidence has been found to indicate what class of family was represented, although it appears that the father of Edith Wing was happy to see his daughters working in both the family bootmaking business and in teaching. There is also evidence to show that teaching ran in families and it may have been, as Marsden suggests, that career advancement was helped by family and Church connections.[186] The type of girl chosen or maybe specifically trained to work in the elementary schools is revealed by testimonials. Conscientiousness and the ability to keep order in the classroom were essential. Miss Rankin was also commended for being gentle and ladylike, punctual and obliging. These are no doubt the ideals which were expected to be passed on to the girls and reflect the ideology of girls as wives and mothers.

During the years under consideration in this study, teaching became more professional in the sense that training was offered in a more structured way and extra qualifications were not only possible but also encouraged. However, the opportunity to gain a place in a teacher training college was in most cases related to the ability of the family to pay the fees. During these years teaching became less constrained by rules and regulations, organized salary scales were introduced and a fuller curriculum could be offered. Many teachers were working in new buildings, which were cleaner and healthier. Teachers also enjoyed more freedom outside the immediate

---

[184]   Various notes from the Logbook of Hitchin Road School and Minutes of USDL.
[185]   M/240 Letterbooks of USDL, 9 July 1898.
[186]   W.E. Marsden, *An Anglo-Welsh Teaching Dynasty: The Adams Family from the 1840s to the 1930s* (Woburn Press, 1997), p. 268.

school environment[187] and often became involved with professional organizations where they were able to share their time with other teachers.[188]

Women in the hat industry were able to earn good money and had economic power. Women teachers were in a subsidiary role and earned considerably less than men, while headmistresses of infants' schools were paid less than the headmistreses of girls' schools. Teachers were seen as agents of social control and were expected to pass on gender-specific values and ideals which saw women's primary role to be that of a homemaker.[189] During the last quarter of the nineteenth century, life in Luton was changing. However, teaching continued to offer employment opportunities that were attractive to girls with intelligence and ability.

---

[187] Formerly teachers were required to accept other responsibilities, such as playing the organ in Church or taking a Sunday school class.

[188] This insular lifestyle was apparent well into the twentieth century.

[189] See N. Bruce, 'Gender and Class: Langley Street Girls' Elementary School, Luton 1890–1922' (MA Dissertation, 1990).

Chapter Six

Teacher Training and the Education
of Students Aged Over Fourteen
Under Bedfordshire County Council

Luton had control over elementary education, but Bedfordshire County Council (BCC) was given responsibility for some other types of provision. The first of these was the setting up of technical training according to the requirements of the Technical Instruction Act of 1889. Some of these classes for women were connected with the straw hat industry, but others were decidedly domestic. They did, however, provide added opportunities for girls in the town to extend their horizons if they so wished.

The Balfour Education Act of 1902 compelled the Bedfordshire Education Committee (BEC) to make provision for the education of children over fourteen and resulted in the setting up of a day secondary school in Luton. Chapter Ten concentrates on this school, which played an important part in the development of girls' education in Luton. Responsibility for the training of teachers was also transferred to the BEC and the pupil-teacher system was superseded by the appointment of student teachers. This change was not without its critics since the number of trainee teachers would be limited, all student teachers being required to have attended the secondary school. Training was provided for unqualified teachers who wished to become certificated and professional development was offered to serving teachers. These schemes were open to girls in Luton but no longer were opportunities relatively equal; education was becoming more selective.

Technical education

Towards the end of the nineteenth century there were concerns that England was falling behind some European countries in technical subjects and the Samuelson Commission (1882–1884) was asked to address the problem. As a result the Technical Instruction Act was passed in 1889. This gave county councils power to establish Technical Instruction Committees and raise a penny rate (one penny in the pound of rateable value) which could be used to pay for technical or manual instruction. The following year the Local Taxation (Customs and Excise) Act allowed money from the increased duty on beer and spirits to be spent by these committees. This became known as 'whisky money'. Under the terms of this act teaching a trade was not allowed, but teaching 'the principles of a trade' was permitted.[1] Alderman Harris, Chairman of the County Council's Committee for Technical Education, said

---

[1] 'Technical Education for Bedfordshire Proposed Grants to Luton and the Straw Plaiting', *Hatters' Gazette*, 1 August 1891, p. 415.

that his committee understood that 'the money is to be expended in technical education, and by that we understand doing what is possible through schools and otherwise to promote the fitness of the people for their particular industries (whatever
those may be)'.[2] Grant money was to be administered by the Science and Art
Department.

Classes were advertised in post offices and other public places.[3] Technical
instruction could be given to 'any persons (other than those exempted by the Act)
whether they [were] engaged in trade or otherwise'[4] and the committee was 'power-
less to refuse teachers, bleachers or others',[5] but classes were not open to 'scholars
under instruction in the obligatory or standard subjects at Elementary schools'
although some of these young people did manage to find their way in.[6] It has
already been noted in Chapter One that people had freedom over their time. With
this in mind it was frequently pointed out that the best time to hold technical classes
was in the slack season.[7] In September 1896 the Luton Ladies asked for a further
course in dressmaking, 'now being a dull time in the Straw trade people would be
better able to attend'.[8]

The ladies referred to were members of the Ladies Committee. There were to be
ladies in each electoral division 'to co-operate with your Committee in all matters
connected with Technical Instruction of the female population'. They were to undertake 'the supervisory management of all branches of female technical instruction
which may from time to time be organized . . . and report'.[9] Table 19 lists members
of the Luton Ladies Committee.

Table 19. Luton Ladies Technical Instruction Committee 1894[10]

Name	Address
Mrs A. Carruthers	The Bury, Luton
Mrs Geo. Carruthers	
Mrs Hugh Cumberland	Crawley Green Road, Luton
Miss Higgins	Wellington Street, Luton
Mrs Hucklesby	
Miss Jennings	25 Upper George Street, Luton
Mrs D. Thomson	Park Square, Luton

Co-opted:
Mrs J. Wright
Mrs Wiseman
Mrs W.H. Brown

---

2   Ibid.
3   E/Sub M 0/11/1 Minutes of TIC, 22 April 1892.
4   E/Sub M 0/11/2 Minutes of TIC, 23 July 1895.
5   Ibid., 23 July 1895.
6   E/Sub M 0/11/1 Minutes of TIC, 15 July 1892; E/Sub M 0/11/2 Minutes of TIC, 23 July 1895.
7   Ibid., 23 July 1895.
8   Ibid., 3 October 1896.
9   E/Sub M 0/11/2 Minutes of TIC, 13 April 1894.
10 Ibid. Mrs Carruthers and Miss Higgins were involved in education. Mrs Hucklesby was probably the
wife of the straw manufacturer and Mayor. Mrs Brown was from the leading Quaker family.

The Ladies Committees met together at least twice a year.[11] We can be sure that some of the ladies were committed to furthering the education of girls and women, since their names appear in other contexts, but theirs was also a social life as this minute reveals: 'Ladies Congress: I am desired by the Duke of Bedford to say that His Grace would be glad to pay the deficit on the luncheon account £1 5s 4d if you think he might be allowed to do so.' His offer was accepted.[12]

A large proportion of the whisky money given to Luton was used to teach subjects which had a direct connection with the straw hat industry. When the committee was discussing the teaching of chemistry in Bedford they noted that 'seeing that Bedford (unlike Luton) does not call for any special line of instruction in this subject, it would be well for this Class [Bedford] to be conducted under the Regulations of the Science and Art Department'.[13] Here is an evidence of the difference between the education provided for people in Luton and in Bedford; Bedford boys could learn the principles of chemistry, but Luton boys were to be limited to its relevance to hats. Luton needed a 'teacher of design, especially in colour, and . . . a teacher of chemistry as applied to dyeing'.[14] They found Mr R.B. Brown of Leicester, an 'expert on dyeing and a competent instructor'.[15] When Luton asked for instruction in the 'principles of applied mechanics, especially as regards the construction of the sewing machine',[16] the committee said that a teacher would need to be sought outside Luton, 'as he should have a scientific knowledge of machinery in general, and not a mere elementary acquaintance with the Science applied simply to the sewing machine and nothing else'.[17] Luton apparently did not have such a man.

Evening classes were still held in elementary schools. The BEC offered to furnish the planned laboratory at the Waller Street Higher Grade School (HGS) and offered grants on condition that there were evening classes open to boys from Luton and Dunstable. When the Luton Technical Instruction Committee (TIC) was also asked to find premises, they rented a house where they 'fitted and furnished two large rooms for class instruction'.[18] It seems likely that this house was the King Street Technical School which was referred to in the School Board Minutes.[19]

One important focus of technical education for girls was straw plaiting. This was not to be the basic plaiting of years gone by because foreign imports were threatening an end to that trade. The committee envisaged a higher standard of plait, which would be able to hold its own against plait from abroad.[20] Experienced straw plait workers were needed 'to move about the districts and teach the art [sic] to Elementary school teachers' who would then pass on what they had learnt to the

11 E/Sub M 0/11/2 Minutes of TIC, 15 April 1894.
12 Ibid., 22 January 1897.
13 E/Sub M 0/11/1 Minutes of TIC, 15 July 1892.
14 Ibid., 24 July 1891.
15 Ibid., 15 July 1892.
16 *Hatters' Gazette*, 1 August 1891, p. 415.
17 E/Sub M 0/11/1 Minutes of TIC, 15 July 1892.
18 Ibid.
19 M/221 Minutes of USDL, 24 April 1894. There is also a note referring to the rent of 11 King Street. E/Sub M 0/11/2 Minutes of TIC, 22 January 1897.
20 *Hatter's Gazette*, 1 August 1891, p. 416.

children.[21] Classes were sometimes held exclusively for teachers.[22] The boards and managers of the elementary schools were to be asked to introduce plaiting into infant schools as a kindergarten subject. Scholarships were offered to those who attended the plaiting instruction classes for attendance, proficiency, success in 'actual Tuition of School Children' and creation of new designs.[23] This was taken seriously; when Miss Aldridge of Westoning was to come for interview with the Luton School Board she was asked to bring her testimonials and, if she was an expert plaiter, specimens of her work.[24]

The two plait teachers who were selected to teach in Luton and the villages were Mrs Elizabeth Bachelor and Miss Ellen Sophie Bachelor, presumably mother and daughter. Later, other daughters of Mrs Bachelor were appointed. Plaiting materials were purchased from Joseph Bachelor,[25] straw plait merchant of 41 Cheapside, Luton,[26] who appears to have been the husband of Elizabeth. The instruction in plaiting went well. 'No fewer than 53 teachers have been under instruction (and more in the villages). The instructresses showed great skill in teaching and in working out 'new and ingenious patterns – many of them of great perplexity . . . mistresses are very quick to pick up the art'. The Luton School Board co-operated by introducing the subject into every infants' and girls' school under its control:

> Already some of the teachers had been taking up the subject in odd times, and were anxious to do more. By its present action the Board not only encourages such teachers to proceed but *requires* them to do so; and it is to be hoped that the Managers of Voluntary Schools in Luton as well as the whole surrounding district will follow the same course.[27]

The principles of plaiting could be taught, but 'any instruction which goes beyond teaching the principles involved, or in which practice is extended with a view to give the manual dexterity of a workman is contrary to the Act'.[28] The Department of Science and Art could not sanction the working of sewing machines as a separate subject, but it could be included under straw plaiting.[29] In July 1892 it was suggested that classes for the principle of machine construction should be established in Luton during the dull season. 'Sewing machines and blocking machines should be taken in [sic] pieces and re-fitted and adjusted by the Teacher and afterwards by Members of the Class'. There were to be no prizes, as 'efficiency would ensure an almost immediate recompense in the way of certain employment'.[30] In 1895 an independent class 'of the utmost importance' was formed 'to teach Students the thorough and practical working of a Straw Hat sewing machine'.[31]

In 1893 the organizing secretary was allowed £30 to enable him 'to visit the

21 E/Sub M 0/11/1 Minutes of TIC, 24 July 1891.
22 E/Sub M 0/11/2 Minutes of TIC, 29 June 1893.
23 E/Sub M 0/11/1 Minutes of TIC, 15 July 1892.
24 M/239 Letterbooks of USDL, 9 June 1891.
25 *Kelly's Bedfordshire Directory (1894).*
26 E/Sub M 0/11/2 Minutes of TIC, 16 June 1894.
27 E/Sub M 0/11/1 Minutes of TIC, 21 October 1892.
28 E/Sub M 0/11/2 Minutes of TIC, 15 December 1893.
29 Ibid., 15 December 1893.
30 E/Sub M 0/11/1 Minutes of TIC, 15 July 1892.
31 E/Sub M 0/11/2 Minutes of TIC, 23 July 1895.

Continent for the purpose of acquainting himself with the system under which the Plaiting Industry in Switzerland is carried on, and also with the system upon which Technical Institutions and Schools in Belgium, Wurtemburg, and other places, are conducted'.[32] In 1895 the committee wanted 'to engage the services of a foreign Instructress in Plaiting' in place of one of the local teachers.[33] However, no evidence has been found to suggest that such a teacher was appointed.

Cookery was also to be taught and it was proposed to obtain the services of certificated teachers of cookery.[34] Again, the instruction was aimed at teachers who would, it was hoped, be encouraged to 'qualify themselves to teach and then include instruction in the subject in their school teaching' so that 'a knowledge of economical and palatable cookery may be diffused through the whole population'.[35] Permission was given by the Luton School Board for the use of their school of cookery where instruction could be given to 'the inhabitants of that town and some adjacent villages'.[36] The committee negotiated with the National Training School of Cookery 'with a view to their recognizing the training already given to the Schoolmistresses during the Summer Course as counting toward the necessary training for the teachers' certificate'.[37]

Miss Rotheram was appointed to teach cookery, laundry and cutting-out.[38] In January 1899 she wrote to the committee complaining about having to take an extra class on Friday and listing her commitments. She said that she had been running cookery schools in Luton for seven years and had 'always found the work a great pleasure'. There were 'always night classes throughout the term' and, on top of that, she had, during the last term, given up her Saturdays and 'trained the School Mistresses quite alone'. The matter was referred to a sub-committee.[39] In the following May, Miss Rotheram entered into a major disagreement with the committee concerning a deficit in her cookery accounts. She considered her losses to be remarkably small and would only be able to reduce them if 'it is made compulsory that pupils buy their dishes which they do not do, unless they choose'.[40]

Another subject offered to girls was 'domestic arts', which included needlework, cutting-out, dress-cutting and nursing.[41] There were classes in dressmaking and the use of the domestic sewing machine. In December 1893, Miss Lily Bone[42] had a class which was attended by 'girls who are far in excess of the number of machines provided for their instruction'. It was suggested that the number of girls admitted at any one time should be limited and that the length of time that they spent in the class should be 'fixed at about 10 or 12 weeks so as to give room for others'.[43] In 1895 it

32 E/Sub M 0/11/1 Minutes of TIC 10 March 1893.
33 E/Sub M 0/11/2 Minutes of TIC, 23 July 1895.
34 E/Sub M 0/11/1 Minutes of TIC, 24 July 1891.
35 Ibid., 10 October 1891.
36 Ibid., 10 October 1891 and 22 January 1892.
37 E/Sub M 0/11/2 Minutes of TIC, 23 September 1893.
38 Ibid., 13 April 1893, 1 February 1896 and 23 July 1896.
39 E/Sub M 0/11/3 Minutes of TIC, 20 January 1899.
40 Ibid., 6 May 1899.
41 E/Sub M 0/11/1 Minutes of TIC, 13 January 1893.
42 See *The Luton and District Year Book and Almanack (1905)*, p. 98. Also, *The Luton and District Year Book and Directory (1908)*, p. 109.
43 E/Sub M 0/11/2 Minutes of TIC, 15 December 1893.

was planned to hold a class for 'cutting-out and making up of garments'. The classes were to be 'carried on as thoroughly, economically and as much for the general benefit and welfare of the community'. The committee was fully convinced that they were 'thoroughly aware of the wants and requirements of the important local industry of this Borough'.[44] Laundry work was also taught.[45]

Other classes for women and girls concerned their health and that of their families. In 1893, the committee wanted a 'lady-lecturer of mature age, wide practical experience in nursing and especially of intimate acquaintance with the special and difficult conditions of home-life among the poor'.[46] In 1897, four scholarships of £30 each were offered to women between the ages of twenty-five and forty years 'residing in the County of Bedford who are willing to attend a six months course of instruction in nursing at a Training Home or Hospital, to be selected by the Beds Rural Nursing Association'.[47] In 1899, eight lectures in health were to be given by Mrs Clare Goslett.[48] Some of these lectures may have been given in Bedford, but Luton women could travel there by rail with comparative ease.[49]

There were plans to build a school for the study of technical subjects in Luton. In 1901, George Sell, Luton Town Clerk, replied to the committee in Bedford to say that 'in the event of the BCC undertaking to make financial provision for the erection of a Secondary Science and Commercial School in this Town, this Council is prepared to provide a site'.[50] The Luton Chamber of Commerce wrote to the Bedfordshire Technical Institute Committee, the Luton Town Council and the local Technical Institute Committee to say that they would offer such an institution 'their hearty support'.[51] However, the Board of Education had their own plans concerning secondary education and these made it inadvisable to proceed with any local schemes.[52]

With the passing of the 1902 Education Act, the Luton Technical Education Committee ceased to exist.[53] The BEC made plans to open a Technical Institution as part of the new secondary school in Park Square, with T.A.E. Sanderson as head of both departments. Members of his staff taught in both day and evening schools. The evening classes are listed in Table 20.

Some assumptions can be made about whether these classes were attended by women and girls. The department of domestic knowledge and 'structure and working of trade sewing machines' were certainly intended for the female population. Art had been popular with girls in Luton and 'blackboard drawing' was probably attended by women teachers. As the teachers of French and German were women, it can be supposed that some of their students might also have been women, particularly those who were involved with the export of hats. Botany was also acceptable for women.

---

44 Ibid., 23 July 1895.
45 E/Sub M 0/11/1 Minutes of TIC, 10 October 1891; E/Sub M 0/11/3 Minutes of TIC, 20 July 1900.
46 E/ Sub M 0/11/1 Minutes of TIC, 23 February 1893.
47 E/Sub M 0/11/3 Minutes of TIC, 22 October 1897.
48 Ibid., 21 July 1899.
49 Ibid., 22 October 1897.
50 Ibid., 26 April 1901.
51 Ibid.
52 E/Sub M 0/11/3 Minutes of TIC, 19 July 1901.
53 SGM 31/1 1 July 1904.

Table 20. Evening classes offered at the Luton Technical Institution
and Secondary School 1905[54]

Department of Science:
    Chemistry, physics   Mr Edmunds and Mr Hoblyn
    Mathematics   Mr Hutchinson
    Botany   Mr Edmunds and Miss Moylan
    Human physiology   Mr Edmunds
    Hygiene, physiography   Mr Hoblyn

Department of Engineering:
    Machine construction and drawing,
    steam, applied mechanics,
    practical geometry   Mr Hutchinson

Department of the Building Trades:
    Building construction,
    builders' quantities
    carpentry and joinery
    manual training (woodwork)   Mr Otter
    Structure and working of trade,
    sewing machines   Miss Bone

Department of Commerce:
    Book-keeping, shorthand,
    geography   Mr Bygott

Department of Language and Literature:
    French, German   Mr Llewellyn
    English   Miss Gardner
    Advanced literature   Mr Edmunds
    English history   Miss Gardner

Department of Domestic Knowledge:
    Dressmaking, needlework   Miss Finlinson
    Millinery   Miss Moylan

Department of Art:
    Light and shade and design,
    freehand, model,
    blackboard drawing,
    geometrical drawing, perspective   Mr May

The next prospectus which has been located is for 1937–1938 when the subjects were similar to those offered in 1908: building, commercial, engineering, matriculation, bakery, confectionery and women's classes. Unsurprisingly there were women teachers for the women's classes, but the only other female member of staff was Mrs G. Berridge in the commercial department.[55] Very little seems to have changed in

---

[54] *Luton Year Book (1905)*, pp. 98–101.
[55] Luton Central Library L.LUT 378, *Prospectus of the Luton Technical College 1937–8*. Mrs Gladys Berridge also ran Berridge's Commercial School, which 'taught shorthand, typing, business management and accountancy' to hundreds of local girls. When it closed in the late 1950s Mrs Berridge accepted a lectureship at what was then Luton Technical College. 'She was a well known and respected member of staff, still teaching until she was over 70.'

the years since the Luton Technical Institution was founded, which accords with the view that the period between 1900 and 1945 was not a time of progress in the field of technical education.[56] It also agrees with information supplied by women who left school even after the time of this study. They all say that they had to use their own initiative to obtain a commercial education in private establishments.[57]

Teacher training
Monitresses, pupil-teachers and student teachers
When the Education Act of 1902 gave the BCC responsibility for providing suitable education for children within the county who were over fourteen years of age, the Education Committee (BEC) lost no time in setting up a combined secondary school and technical institution in Luton. Bedfordshire was also responsible for the training of teachers and, although, in 1903, most aspects of the pupil-teacher system were still in place, changes were about to be made.

Monitresses
Monitresses continued to be employed, but their roles changed and, by 1924, their route into teaching had become a direct one. This was particularly important when there was a shortage of teachers and potential teachers.[58] In 1905, the Bedfordshire Education Committee established a system of examinations which 'all Monitors and Monitresses under 18 years of age' were 'required to sit'.[59] The following list notes the examinations which were taken by monitors. Some monitors did not take the examination.

One had taken the Preliminary Certificate Examination.
One had taken the Oxford Senior Local Examination.
One was preparing for the Preliminary Certificate Examination.
One was preparing for the Oxford Senior Local Examination.
One was preparing for the Cambridge Senior Local Examination.
One had taken the Preliminary Certificate Examination.[60]

The ages of monitors ranged from fourteen years and one month to twenty-one years and two months. Marks for Maud Woollard from Stopsley and Dorothy Osborne from Leagrave are recorded, but top place went to a girl from Riseley. There was a possible total of two hundred marks: fifty each for arithmetic and English, forty each for geography and history and twenty for reading.[61] Table 21 lists subjects that were examined and the marks gained.

---

[56] K. Evans, *The Development and Structure of the English Education System* (Hodder & Stoughton, 1975), p. 220.
[57] Conversations with Mrs Vera Robson and Mrs Rosamond Hayward. The situation regarding commercial education is unclear. In 1915 and 1916, letters were received from the government asking the BEC about the steps that were being taken to train women for clerical and commercial employment to replace men who were joining the forces. EM6 Minutes of BEC, 26 November 1915 and 25 February 1916.
[58] EM7 Minutes of BEC, 13 July 1917.
[59] EM1 Minutes of BEC, 20 October 1905.
[60] EM4 Minutes of BEC, 26 May 1911.
[61] Ibid.

Table 21. Monitresses' examination results

Name	Dorothy Osborne	Maud Woollard
School	Leagrave	Stopsley
Age	18 years, 11 months	19 years, 2 months
Length of service	5 years, 1 month	5 years
Arithmetic (out of 50)	30	33
English (out of 50)	36	43
Geography (out of 40)	29	33
History (out of 40)	23	31
Reading (out of 20)	15	19
Total	133	159
%	66	79

A scheme of scholarships was set up; five were to be offered each year to monitors over the age of sixteen who showed the necessary proficiency. They consisted of 'free tuition for 2 years at the Saturday Classes for the Preliminary Certificate Examination, together with the necessary books, and an annual allowance of £2 towards the cost of travelling'.[62] Under this scheme, monitresses in the county were carefully supervised. In 1913, managers were 'requested to inform the Education Committee whether they consider it desirable to dispense with the services of . . . monitresses who state that it is not their intention to become qualified Teachers'.[63] Those with unsatisfactory marks were told to improve or leave.[64] Monitors who won scholarships could sit for the Preliminary Certificate Examination[65] and, if successful, could become uncertificated teachers. In 1922 it was pointed out that:

> in view of the altered circumstances with regard to the entrance to the Teaching Profession considerable economies can be effected in the appointment of Monitors and Monitresses and that it be recommended to the Education Committee that as a rule the appointment of Monitors and Monitresses be made only once a year after the result of a careful examination.[66]

Case study
Florence Maud Bazley was born on 11 March 1890 and was educated at Dunstable Road School. Her father was a Post Office clerk and, in 1904, the family is noted as living at 60 Crawley Road. In March of that year William Hoyle, Clerk to the LEC, wrote to Mr Bazley to say that his daughter had permission to go to Chapel Street Infant School as a monitor on probation, but without pay. Mr Hoyle also said that Florence could attend the central classes for monitors (presumably at the Pupil Teacher Centre).

---

[62] Ibid., 19 January 1912.
[63] E/Sub M 0/4/5 Minutes of BCC Elementary Education Sub-Committee, 9 May 1913.
[64] E/Sub M 0/4/7 Minutes of BCC Elementary Education Sub-Committee, 21 July 1916.
[65] Photographs of a letter (1923) telling Constance Sanders that she had won a Scholarship for Monitresses and of her Preliminary Examination Certificate can be seen in B. Fraser-Newstead, *Bedfordshire Yesteryears Volume 1: The Family, Childhood and Schooldays* (Book Castle, 1993), pp. 116 and 125.
[66] E/Sub M 0/4/8 Minutes of BCC Elementary Education Sub-Committee, 9 June 1922.

On 19 September 1904, Florence was admitted to the new Luton Secondary School (admission number 57) where she stayed until July 1906. We can assume that she followed the monitors' route into teaching because references to her are found in later LEC Minutes. Between April 1921 and April 1923, her salary scale went up from £230–240 to £258–272. During the Second World War she was teaching at Denbigh Road Junior School.

Pupil-teachers

The situation regarding the training of pupil-teachers is not at all clear. There were specific guidelines which dictated that the system was to be superseded by the appointment of student teachers, but pupil-teachers continue to be mentioned throughout the years of this study and attempts were made to revive the system. The BEC resolved that of the forty pupil-teacher scholarships offered annually, ten were to be from the Borough of Bedford and ten from the Borough of Luton. There were to be pupil-teacher centres in Bedford and Luton, 'both to be continued in the manner in which the Luton centre is at present conducted'.[67] Bedford may have had academic institutions, but it did not have as much expertise in running a school board or a pupil-teacher centre. 'Not more than 40 Pupil-teachers be elected and articled for two years as from 1st August 1905, after which no Pupil-teacher shall be articled who shall not have passed under the new scheme for training such teachers.'[68]

The Board of Education refused to sanction the continuation of the Pupil-teacher Centre at Bedford because of the 'unsatisfactory nature of the buildings' and 'the inconvenient break in education caused by the transference of boys and girls intending to be teachers from the Secondary Schools to the Pupil-teacher Centre'.[69] The BEC urged the Board to give its 'approval for the continuation of the existing PT Centres at Bedford and Luton until the 31st July 1908, until which date the [BCC] Education Committee cannot see their way to bringing into operation their scheme for the training of Pupil Teachers at recognised Secondary Schools'.[70] The way was prepared for the replacement of the pupil-teacher system by student teachers.[71] It was planned to close the centres and accommodate the pupil-teachers at the new Luton secondary school[72] or the Bedford Modern schools.[73]

Pupil-teachers were recruited from the elementary schools and any girl with the necessary qualifications could be accepted. Student teachers, however, were to come from the secondary schools and this meant that the number of potential teachers was limited to those whose parents could afford the fees or who had qualified for a free place. The conclusion of a sub-committee, appointed in 1914 to consider the supply of teachers for elementary schools, was that the secondary schools were unable to produce enough teachers and suggested the return of

---

67 EM1 Minutes of BEC, 22 April 1904.
68 Ibid.
69 EM5 Minutes of BEC, 9 July 1914.
70 EM2 Minutes of BEC, 20 July 1906.
71 Ibid., 24 May 1907. The training of student teachers is discussed in the following section.
72 Ibid., 19 October 1906.
73 Ibid. 18 January 1907.

'external Pupil Teacher Centres with preparatory classes',[74] which would offer twenty pupil-teacher scholarships each year.[75] The Board of Education agreed,[76] but would not commit itself to support the plan indefinitely. One of the conditions was that 'The Head Mistress and permanent members of the staff should be women, in view of the fact that the great majority of the pupils attending the Centre will be girls'.[77]

Pupil-teachers were to be not less than fourteen and no more than sixteen years of age and have reports from their headteacher stating that they were of good character. The parent or guardian should confirm that they had 'an honest intention to become a Teacher in a public Elementary School'. Detailed plans were formalized. However, the Minutes of the BEC in November 1915 stated that 'the County Council did not approve the establishment of a Pupil Teacher Training Centre'[78] and these plans were apparently shelved.

Members of the LEC were not happy to let the matter rest. The Clerk to the County Council wrote to them in a letter dated 17 April 1918 stating that 'in view of the Education Bill now before Parliament, the time was not opportune for the establishment of a Pupil Teacher Centre at Luton'.[79] The following year the Luton and Bedfordshire committees held a conference on the subject.[80] The Board of Education suggested that 'in the event of a Pupil Teacher Centre being established in the Borough (of Luton) it should be in connection with a Central Elementary School'.[81] Plans were agreed the following year,[82] but again no further action appears to have been taken.

Salary scales do not show any provision for pupil-teachers between 1910 and 1918. However, later regulations indicate that the scheme could be revived 'if certain reason is shown'.[83] Evidence seems to suggest that the pupil-teacher system no longer existed. However, when Constance Robinson recalled her teaching career she said that she left school at fourteen (c.1923) and

> took the Pupil-teacher examination at the Town Hall in Bedford and having passed this, went on to attend Queens Park School on Saturdays for instruction in my specialist subjects, – whilst teaching. This continued for three years and was followed by a final examination which lasted for one week. I passed with Honours in music and arithmetic and so became an 'uncertificated teacher'.[84]

Although the pupil-teacher system theoretically gave way to the student teacher scheme it would appear that girls were still able to become pupil-teachers until well into the twentieth century, although pupil-teaching was certainly no longer as easy an option as it had been in the nineteenth century.

[74] EM5 Minutes of BEC, 9 July 1914.
[75] Ibid. From a copy of a letter from the Board of Education.
[76] Ibid.
[77] Ibid.
[78] EM6 Minutes of BEC, 26 November 1915.
[79] M/229 Minutes of LEC, 14 May 1918.
[80] Ibid., 18 November 1919.
[81] Ibid., 13 January 1920.
[82] Ibid., 11 May 1920.
[83] L. Jones, *The Training of Teachers in England and Wales* (Oxford University Press, 1924), p. 57.
[84] B. Fraser-Newstead, *Bedfordshire's Yesteryears Volume 1*, p. 124.

Student teachers

In May 1907 the BEC decided that the scheme for the training of pupil-teachers was to 'be revised to conform with the New Regulations of the Board of Education',[85] which placed more emphasis on the scholars' own education in a secondary school. This plan received criticism because it 'extended the education of intending teachers whilst at the same time lengthening the time in which they were unable to earn a wage'. Another criticism was that most working-class children would be excluded from the teaching profession.[86]

The new scheme involved the provision of bursaries, which gave financial support for girls with an interest in teaching as a career and allowed them to study for an extra year at the secondary school. After the year's bursary, they were, under certain conditions, accepted as student teachers. The LEC was obliged to co-operate with this and appointed one boy and eleven girl student teachers. The difference suggests that boys may have been looking for newer opportunities in local industry and commerce.

> Bursars. Appointment of Student Teachers at a salary of £25 for males and £20 for females, such appointments to date from August 1 1908, and to be conditional upon the said persons passing a qualifying examination before that date.
> That the County Council 'Mistress of Method' be granted facilities for visiting the Student Teachers at their several schools, with a view to assisting in the practical training.
> Honoraria. The offer of the BCC to pay the Head Teacher the sum of £2.10.0 for supervision of each of the Student Teachers was accepted.[87]

Miss M. Gardiner LL.A was chosen as Mistress of Method at a salary of £250 plus her railway fare and other out-of-pocket disbursements. She was required to supervise student teachers in Bedfordshire, Bedford and Luton and 'to give preliminary instruction (generally by Lectures on Saturdays, at Bedford) in the theory of Education to Student Teachers'. Visits were to be made to elementary schools which participated in the scheme so that practical help and advice could be given. Classes and courses were to be arranged in preparation for 'the Preliminary Certificate or Certificate Examinations of the Board of Education, or any other Course of Instruction for Teachers which the Education Committee may deem it necessary to establish'.

Miss Gardiner also had to 'organize, supervise and take an active part in Holiday Courses of Instruction for Teachers' and to 'undertake such work in connection with the Training of Teachers or in Allied branches of Higher Education or such other duties in connection with the work of the Education Committee as may be required'.[88]

The headteacher of the Luton Pupil-teacher Centre, Mr Hargreaves, was asked to

[85] EM2 Minutes of BEC, 24 May 1907.
[86] W. Robinson,'In Search of a "Plain Tale": Rediscovering the Champions of the Pupil-teacher Centres 1900–1910', *History of Education* Vol. 28, No.1 (1999) p. 70.
[87] M/227 Minutes of LEC, 30 June 1908.
[88] EM3 Minutes of BEC, 29 May 1908.

stay for a year to assist, but resigned without completing the year.[89] Miss Gardiner's appointment was terminated in 1910[90] and Miss Amy Walmsley from the Bedford Kindergarten College undertook the work. The following year the sub-committee thanked Miss Walmsley 'for the time and pains which she has expended upon training the Student Teachers as well as upon visiting the Schools to which they are attached . . . [and] desire that the arrangements may be continued next year'.[91]

In April 1909, Dr W.J. Butcher was paid £5 5 0 his annual fee for medically examining candidates for scholarships and bursaries. Pupil-teachers who had been appointed in 1907 and were qualified by age and examination were 'appointed to Student Teacherships for one year from 1 August 1909'. Others, who were not qualified by age to become student teachers but were qualified to become bursars, were awarded bursaries for one year from 1 August 1909. The rest of the pupil-teachers, appointed in July 1907, had their scholarships extended for one year from 1 July 1909, 'subject to satisfactory reports being received from the Head Teachers of their respective Schools'.[92]

The BEC supervised the training of student teachers, but the LEC had to assist by providing elementary schools where the girls could do their training. The Board of Education only recognized schools for this purpose if the headteacher was considered capable of training young teachers.[93] Girls from the Luton Modern School (LMS) were sent to their selected school for a month's trial[94] and, if considered suitable, received a bursary and returned the following year,[95] sharing their time between the school, where they received supervised classroom training, and studies in Bedford.[96] Good schools made sure that the trainees had a varied experience.[97] In 1917, the BEC complained that the numbers of bursars had fallen[98] and, in 1919, resolved to post 'to every Parish Council for public display' information about the bursary scheme.[99] When student teachers had completed their year of training they could either be retained on the same staff or they could be directed to another school.[100] They were then accepted under the rules of the Board of Education as uncertificated teachers and the way was also open for them to attend a training college or become certificated.

Case study

Hilda Puddephatt was born in December 1891. Her father was a straw hat manufacturer (wholesale proprietor) and they lived at 51 Princess Street. She attended Chapel Street Infants School and then the new school in Dunstable Road. Between

[89]   Ibid., 29 May 1908, 12 June 1908 and 27 November 1908.
[90]   Ibid., 22 April 1910.
[91]   Ibid., 14 July 1911.
[92]   Ibid., 23 April 1909.
[93]   Ibid., 15 July 1910.
[94]   LMAG Logbook of DRG, 1 September 1922 and 29 September 1922.
[95]   Ibid., 27 August 1923.
[96]   EM6 Minutes of BEC, 20 April 1916; 1997/35/2 Logbook of NRS, 17 November 1914.
[97]   75/67–1 Logbook of HRG, 4 September 1908 and 2 October 1908.
[98]   EM7 Minutes of BEC, 13 July 1917.
[99]   Ibid., 20 June 1919.
[100] 75/67–1 Logbook of HRG, 29 July 1909 and 30 August 1909; information supplied by Miss Edith Webb.

the ages of twelve and seventeen she went to the LMS, the last year as a bursar. At the LMS she took the Cambridge Junior Local Examination in July 1907 and the Senior Cambridge Local in July 1909. She trained as a student teacher at the Church school in Buxton Road with a salary of £20. Once a week she travelled to Bedford for 'method and that sort of thing'. The Mistress of Method came once a month to hear her Criticism lesson. The first of these lessons was on an orange and the criticism she received was 'you forgot to mention the pungent smell'. Details of salaries in the LEC minutes show that between September 1909 and October 1920 her salary scale rose from £40 to £170.[101]

It is interesting to note that Hilda Puddephatt's father was a straw manufacturer and, earlier in the nineteenth century, would probably have been expected to send his daughter to a private school. However, Hilda went to local elementary schools and the new secondary school. This demonstrates that the elementary schools and the BEC secondary school had been accepted by some, if not all, of Luton's middle classes.

Supplementary teachers

By 1924, the rules which dictated the employment of supplementary teachers, mainly female, which Tropp referred to as 'this flood of cheap, untrained labour',[102] were that the local authority should obtain a medical certificate and provide professional instruction.[103] In 1904, the BCC Elementary Schools Committee recommended that a sub-committee should be appointed 'to determine in each case in consultation with the Director of Education the class in which applicants under Article 68, if appointed, shall be placed'.[104] Subsequently arrangements were made whereby supplementary teachers in Bedfordshire were to be offered training. Miss Walmsley was asked to organize training for between twenty and twenty-five supplementary teachers at the Kindergarten College during the session 1905–1906, at a cost not exceeding £80 for the year, and provision was made for them to take the King's scholarship or equivalent examinations.[105]

Government plans to disqualify supplementary teachers[106] concerned the Elementary Sub-committee which, in 1914, requested the government to postpone this disqualification on account of the shortage of uncertificated teachers and the possible shortage of certificated teachers. Copies of this request were sent to the Prime Minister, the President of the Board of Education and the Members of Parliament for the County.[107] Provision continued to be made to improve the skills of supplementary teachers, for example by allowing them to visit other schools.[108]

Chapter Five looked at some of the reasons why Luton girls chose to teach rather

---

[101] Details from BLARS: various Minutes concerning bursars; 1997/23/1 Admissions Registers of the Luton Modern School; Minutes of LEC concerning salaries; B. Fraser-Newstead, *Bedfordshire's Yesteryears Volume 1*, pp. 118–124.

[102] A. Tropp, *The School Teachers* (Heinemann, 1957), p. 117.

[103] L. Jones, *The Training of Teachers*, p. 216.

[104] E/Sub M 0/4/1 Minutes of BCC Elementary Education Sub-Committee, 27 May 1904. At that time supplementary teachers were known as Article 68s.

[105] EM1 Minutes of BEC, 19 April 1905.

[106] A. Tropp, *The School Teachers*, pp. 187–188.

[107] E/Sub M 0/4/5 Minutes of BCC Elementary Education Sub-Committee, 21 February 1913.

[108] E/Sub M 0/4/8 Minutes of BCC Elementary Education Sub-Committee, 21 May 1920.

than enter the hat industry. One of the possible reasons was that teaching was considered to be slightly higher on the social scale. Perhaps even a post as a supplementary teacher, with its much lower salary, was viewed in the same way. In the salary scales for 1917 listed in Table 22, no mention is made of male supplementary teachers. This accords with the idea that women were expected to follow a subsidiary role.

Becoming certificated

Many uncertificated teachers studied to become certificated. This involved attending classes or sometimes taking a correspondence course. In 1923 the LEC responded to the Board of Education Circular 1296, which stated that the examination for acting teachers, which had been announced for 1923, would not be held. The LEC explained that it had always been their policy to encourage teachers to become certificated and so improve their general status. The Board replied that 'in view of representations made to the Board, the acting teachers' certificate will be held in November 1924'. It would appear that the examination did, in fact, continue for a little longer.[109] Miss Edith Webb, who trained as a student teacher, started at Surrey Street Girls' School in September 1924. She wrote that her

> title as a teacher at Surrey St was 'uncertificated' but soon after starting there it was announced that the external examination for full qualification would be held for one extra year only. So began a correspondence course[110] over the next two years. This meant study and school work every evening and Saturday mornings leaving Saturday afternoon and Sunday free. The examination which lasted a week was taken at Watford and covered twelve subjects. Fortunately I passed with a distinction in History. So I became what one person described as 'Certified' and my salary leapt up 50% from £8 to £12 a month.

The ending of the scheme to allow teachers to study for certificates while working must have made a considerable difference to their career opportunities. Professional categories were 'trained and certificated' or 'uncertificated' and funding would need to be found to progress from one to the other.

In-service training

In accordance with government requirements, in-service training was offered to serving teachers. Classes at the Froebel Kindergarten College were held during Whitsun holidays; thirty scholarships (value of tuition fee £1 11s 6d) were available for elementary teachers who entered their names for this course.[111] The Director of Education submitted a scheme for the instruction of teachers in modern methods for teaching children to read.[112] Classes were also provided for teachers wishing to prepare for the certificate examination of the Board of Education and there were courses of lectures on the Montessori system.[113] A Miss Newman, who had studied under Maria Montessori in Rome, held four classes about her methods and an

---

[109] M/229 Minutes of LEC, 13 February 1923 and 17 April 1923.
[110] L. Jones, *The Training of Teachers*, p. 199; information supplied by Miss Edith Webb.
[111] EM8 Minutes of BEC, 24 October 1919 and 23 April 1915.
[112] EM5 Minutes of BEC, 24 April 1914.
[113] EM7 Minutes of BEC, 19 October 1917.

average of about one hundred teachers from all parts of the county attended. On intervening Saturdays teachers met to discuss points raised and brought up questions to be asked at the next meeting. The LEC wished to put on similar courses if at least fifty teachers were willing to attend.

Nature Study classes were held.[114] Gardening was considered important and classes 'on practical lines' were to be offered to both men and women.[115] Inspectors were expected to pass on their knowledge of modern ideas and HMI Mr J.F. Leaf gave a lecture on the teaching of English.[116] The Director of Education was authorized to spend up to £10 to make arrangements to meet headteachers 'in order to give them an opportunity of discussing with him questions which arise in connection with the Curriculum'.[117]

Academic qualifications

Bedfordshire was contributing to a higher class of teacher, as envisaged by HMI the Reverend C.F. Johnstone, but many successes were due to the personal initiative of the teachers themselves. Several women teachers studied for the LL.A (Lady Literate in Arts).[118] Sadler noted that the St Andrews LL.A was very much easier to obtain than the London BA because it required 'far less force and concentration . . . but [offered] a better, a more intelligent, course of study to the teacher, and the number of women who work for it is rapidly increasing'.[119] University College, Reading, also offered a Diploma of Associate in Letters.[120] Miss Gardiner, who was appointed Mistress of Method to supervise student teachers, had obtained the LL.A qualification.[121] The headmistress of Hitchin Road Girls' School took examinations in 1911 and 1912, and in 1914 entered her name in the logbook as Fanny Wright LL.A.[122] The Education Committee increased her salary from £135 to £140, presumably to acknowledge her success.[123]

No leave of absence has been noted for women in elementary schools to take university degrees, but Margaretta John BA was listed as a member of staff at Beech Hill Girls' School in 1914.[124] Miss Beatrice U. Bone at the Luton Pupil-teacher Centre was successful 'in obtaining a place in the First Class at the recent Examination for Matriculation in connection with the University of London'.[125] Gertrude Jones received a Higher Froebel Certificate in 1917.[126] It may be that she studied for this at the Bedford Kindergarten College with which the County Council had strong links. Women teachers were becoming more academic and more professional in their outlook.

114 EM3 Minutes of BEC, 22 January 1909.
115 EM7 Minutes of BEC, 23 November 1917.
116 M/229 Minutes of LEC, 20 June 1922.
117 E/Sub M 0/4/2 Minutes of BCC Elementary Education Sub-Committee, 28 July 1905.
118 C. Dyhouse, *No Distinction of Sex? Women in British Universities 1870–1939* (UCL Press, 1995), p. 12.
119 M.E. Sadler, *Continuation Schools in England and Elsewhere* (Manchester University Press, 1908), p. 143.
120 L. Jones, *The Training of Teachers*, p. 397.
121 EM3 Minutes of BEC, 29 May 1908.
122 75/67–1 Logbook of HRG 24 May 1911, 24 May 1912 and 5 October 1914.
123 M/228 Minutes of LEC, 7 October 1913.
124 LMAG Logbook of BHG, November 1914.
125 M/223 Minutes of USDL, 23 July 1901.
126 M/229 Minutes of LEC, 13 March 1917.

Needlework

Needlework was regarded as extremely important and girls were expected to be proficient in the subject. Miss Stone (Article 68 at Hyde) was 'granted a week's leave of absence' in 1904 'in order to take Lessons in cutting out, so as to obtain a Diploma in Dressmaking'.[127] In 1905 she 'received her Diploma in Tailor dressmaking'[128] and later that year was referred to as 'a student at Luton Technical School' where she probably did her training.[129] In 1906 she obtained a '1st Class Diploma in "Plain Needlework"' and, as she was 'especially gifted in this Subject' well deserved the honour.[130] She 'gained her first Class Diploma (London) in the "Art of Dressmaking"' in 1907.[131] The LEC paid assistant teachers who were responsible for the teaching of needlework an extra £10 a year provided that they 'obtain within two years from appointment a certificate of proficiency in Needlework issued by an examining body recognised by this Authority'.[132] Diplomas from 'The London Institute for the Advancement of Plain Needlework' were acceptable.[133] The extra £10 (compared with the possible £5 for an LL.A.) indicates the perceived importance of needlework in the curriculum of girls' schools.

Music

Karolina Leaver, headmistress at Hyde, was granted leave to attend a music examination. She was successful in obtaining a 'Diploma of Associate Victoria College of Music' and was entitled to wear a cap and gown and to write the letters AVCM after her name.[134] The following October she was successful in the Licentiate Examination[135] and in 1907 the 'Diploma of Fellowship'.[136] In 1894 Fanny Lake was allowed to take a Trinity College Examination.[137] There is no indication that these qualifications brought an increase in salary as a certificate for teaching tonic sol-fa had done.

Physical education

Miss Stansfeld, the pioneer principal of Bedford Physical Training College, arranged courses. In 1910 the headmistress at Hyde School was one of the chosen candidates for a Saturday Morris dancing class.[138] She also attended instruction on drill and, although she does not say whether or not she passed the examination, she could not speak too highly of the classes; 'not one of we teachers would willingly miss our drill and that speaks for itself. One picks up ideas unconscientiously [sic] in manner, voice, act etc. not forgetting errors one needs to correct.'[139] As indicated

---

127 SD Hyde 1 Logbook of Hyde School, 10 October 1904.
128 Ibid., 3 January 1905.
129 Ibid., 18 October 1905.
130 Ibid., 8 October 1906.
131 Ibid., 26 February 1907.
132 M/227 Minutes of LEC, 12 April 1910.
133 Ibid., 13 March 1917.
134 SD Hyde 1 Logbook of Hyde School, 12 April 1906.
135 Ibid., 25 October 1906.
136 Ibid., 18 April 1907.
137 M/221 Minutes of USDL, 3 July 1894. (Trinity College of Music in London opened in 1872.)
138 SD Hyde 1 Logbook of Hyde School, 17 January 1910.
139 Ibid., 10 July 1911, 12 February 1912 and 28 March 1912.

in Chapter Seven the curricula of girls' schools was becoming less regimented and girls' health and physical needs were being considered.

Professional associations

Considering the independent character of people in Luton, it is not surprising that the National Union of Teachers (NUT) remained very active. Sir Frederick Mander (1883–1964), who was educated at the Higher Grade School in Luton, became President of the NUT in 1927 and General Secretary from 1931 to 1947. He was the Chairman of the BCC between 1952 and 1962.[140] There were also local members of the National Federation of Women Teachers who disagreed strongly with 'that portion of the Departmental Committee's report which recommends that women be paid at a lower rate than men'.[141] They suggested improvements for old buildings,[142] asked for eurhythmics classes[143] and ran folk dancing groups.[144] Other associations are mentioned: the National Union of Assistant Teachers, Luton Teachers' Association, Teachers of Bedfordshire, Buckinghamshire and Hertfordshire, Association of Elementary Teachers and the National Federation of Class Teachers and Luton teachers enjoyed social evenings together.[145] Teachers wanted a voice on the BEC and, in 1903, wrote to the Clerk of the BCC to notify them of this resolution made by the Central Council of the Beds County Teachers:

> That, whilst regretting that the County Council could not see its way to grant direct representation of teachers upon the new Education Committee, we are pleased to note that a pledge has been given to the Board of Education that teachers shall have facilities for placing their views before such Committee.[146]

Married women

Jane Miller describes how a 'marriage bar' was often used as a means of controlling teachers' lives and cutting down the cost of teacher training.[147] Married women were virtually excluded from the teaching profession between the two world wars, but the practice was formally ended by the 1944 Education Act.

The subject concerned both the Luton and Bedfordshire authorities, but many decisions seem to have been made on an ad hoc basis. There are notes of teachers in Luton leaving to marry[148] and of others continuing to teach after marriage,[149] while the minute books and logbooks list many married women as members of staff. Nationally it had been acceptable for married teachers to work but, in Luton, women in the hat industry also continued to work throughout their married lives. No

---

[140] R. Aldrich and P. Gordon, *Dictionary of British Educationists* (Woburn Press, 1989).

[141] M/229 Minutes of LEC, 12 March 1918.

[142] Ibid., 14 May 1918.

[143] Ibid., 10 December 1918.

[144] Ibid., 11 September 1923.

[145] M/224 Minutes of USDL, 25 November 1902.

[146] E/Sub M 0/4/1 Minutes of the BCC Elementary Education Sub-Committee, 12 June 1903.

[147] J. Miller, *School for Women* (Virago, 1996), pp. 49 and 58.

[148] L/4/2/54 Logbook of HRGI, 1 July 1898.

[149] LMAG Logbook of DRG, 19 December 1922.

conflict of duty was perceived. While married women in the hat industry continued to work, things began to change for teachers when the marriage bar took effect.

In 1898, the Luton School Board replied to a letter from the London Board concerning the employment of married teachers to the effect that they had 'no experience warranting them to express any decided opinion thereon'.[150] Eight years later the LEC were not so sure when they were asked to approve the appointment of Mrs Henrietta Kate Fletcher as headmistress of Queen Square Infants' School with a salary of £100 per annum. The LEC, 'having in view the desirability of not appointing Married Women, considered the matter at full length'. They agreed to appoint Mrs Fletcher, but an amendment was carried to the effect that the managers should look for a single woman instead.[151] At the next Board meeting the appointment of Miss Annie Fairbank Wilson was confirmed. Her salary was to be £80 per annum.

The BEC allowed maternity leave. A married woman teacher had to give not less than two months notice of the probable date of her confinement and 'to absent herself from School for a period of not less than 4 weeks before such date and to remain absent for a period of not less than 4 weeks after confinement'. During her absence she was to be paid half her salary for a period not exceeding ten weeks.[152] In 1912 they decided that they would not make rules concerning the employment of married women, but that each case should be decided on its merits.[153] In 1919, Luton gave £40 bonuses to 'married men and widows supporting children' as compared with £30 to 'all other teachers'.[154] In 1923, one committee member proposed that women's employment should be automatically discontinued if they married.[155] There was no seconder and it was recorded that no action should be taken in the case of married women teachers already in the committee's employ, but 'that in future appointments preference be given to unmarried applicants, other qualifications being equal'.

Oral evidence held at the Luton Museum and Art Gallery (LMAG)[156] demonstrates that women in the hat industry were still earning good money, sometimes much more than their husbands, but were not expected to give up their careers. Teachers, on the other hand, were being asked to do so. No relevant information has been found, but it would be interesting to note whether any women left teaching to take up work in the hat industry.

---

[150]   M/222 Minutes of USDL, 9 August 1898. The Luton Board did employ married women, for example Mrs Leaver at Hyde.

[151]   M/226 Minutes of LEC, 25 September 1906.

[152]   EM2 Minutes of BEC, 8 June 1906.

[153]   EM4 Minutes of BEC, 19 January 1912.

[154]   M/229 Minutes of LEC, 12 September 1919.

[155]   Ibid., 13 March 1923.

[156]   LMAG recorded conversations about employment in Luton as a millennium project.

Salaries

Table 22. Salary scales for teachers under the BCC in 1917[157]

Qualification	Average attendance	Men	Women
Headteachers:			
Grade I	Up to 80		£100–150
Grade II	81–150	£140–190	£120–165
Grade III	151–200	£160–215	£130–180
Grade IV	210–250	£180–240	£140–200
Grade V	251+	£200–275	£160–225
Uncertificated		£80–90	£80–90
Assistant teachers:			
Certificated collegiate		£105–170	£95–140
Certificated non-collegiate		£100–170	£90–140
Uncertificated		£70–80	£65–75
Supplementary		£40–55	
Student teacher			
First six months		£15	£12 10s
Second six months*		£20	£17 10s
Monitresses			
First year			£10
Second year			£12 10s
Third year			£15
Fourth year			£20

* Subject to reports of excellence in work and conduct and practical skill in teaching by the superintendent of student teachers of elementary schools.

In the case of illness, the Bedfordshire Elementary Education Sub-Committee discussed and noted different circumstances in detail.[158] Minnie Long was not paid after the first three weeks of her illness,[159] but Lily Sharp was treated with more consideration. She had been absent from school since 25 January 1915 suffering from diphtheria, which was, in the opinion of the Medical Officer, 'probably contracted in the course of [her] work'. Because of the circumstances she was to be paid full salary during her absence, 'the payment, however, not to be deemed as an admission or acknowledgement of liability'.[160] A National Insurance Act was passed in 1911 which affected teachers' salaries and contributions. The amount of benefit paid under the act was to be 'deducted from the amount paid under the Scale in respect of sickness, and that the Scale of Teachers' salaries be altered accordingly'.[161]

Salaries continued to be raised over the years, but the First World War brought significant changes. Serving teachers in Bedfordshire were given bonuses to help

[157] EM7 Minutes of BEC, 19 October 1917. Calculations were based on the average number of attendances made by pupils.
[158] E.g., E/Sub M 0/4/6 Minutes of BCC Elementary Education Sub-Committee, 25 September 1914.
[159] M/226 Minutes of LEC, 17 December 1907.
[160] M/229 Minutes of LEC, 13 April 1915.
[161] E/Sub M 0/4/5 Minutes of BCC Elementary Sub-Committee, 6 December 1912.

with the higher cost of living,[162] while Luton gave an increase of 5% for the period of the war.[163] Bedfordshire and Luton discontinued the bonus schemes in 1917 in favour of increased salary scales.[164] During the First World War, higher salaries in other occupations tempted some women teachers away from the classroom.[165] After the war, in a time of considerable economic hardship, Sir Eric Geddes headed a committee which recommended cuts in expenditure and teachers were obliged to accept lower salaries. Bedfordshire asked for 'an abatement of 5% on the gross salary of each individual teacher'[166] and Luton 'that salaries should be subject to a percentage deduction, and that this applies particularly to Women teachers'.[167]

Another economy under the 'Geddes Axe' concerned pensions; these had been offered to teachers on a variety of terms for many years, sometimes involving contributions and sometimes not. The LEC was of the opinion that 'teachers' super-annuation should be upon a contributory basis and that the provision of a lump sum upon retirement in addition to a yearly allowance should be discontinued'.[168] Bedfordshire drew the attention of Members of Parliament to 'the inadvisability of any additional burden being thrown upon ratepayers by placing a portion of the cost of the superannuation of teachers upon LEAs, and that they be requested to intimate to the Minister of Education their opposition to any such proposal'.[169]

Local authorities had progressed from assessing salaries on an individual basis and had established recognized salary scales but, in 1921, plans for a national scale were introduced at the recommendation of the Burnham Committee.[170] Luton was afraid that the scale was 'higher than the country can afford in its financial stress'[171] and Bedfordshire wondered whether it was 'possible to pay salaries less than the Burnham Scale to teachers in small schools'.[172] However, national scales had come to stay, at least for the forseeable future.

Conclusion

The first involvement of the BCC in the education of children in Luton came as a result of the Technical Instruction Act 1889. The different perceptions of Bedford and Luton soon became clear, for technical classes in Luton were mainly directed towards the skills needed in the hat industry while more general subjects were taught in Bedford. The wider vision which Bedford had in the context of an academic education did not extend to technical education; little was offered to girls apart from a domestic role or plaiting skills, which were already out-of-date.

Bedfordshire was required by the government to supervise the training of teachers in the county. The concept of teacher training changed in tandem with the availability of secondary education. Under the pupil-teacher system any girl from

---

162 E/Sub M 0/4/7 Minutes of BCC Elementary Sub-Committee, 24 November 1916.
163 M/229 Minutes of LEC, 12 September 1916 and 10 October 1916.
164 EM7 Minutes of BEC, 19 October 1917; M/229 Minutes of LEC, 28 June 1917.
165 J. Dyer, *The Story of Stopsley Schools* (LMAG, 1989), p. 28.
166 E/Sub M 0/4/9 Minutes of the BCC Elementary Sub-Committee, 19 January 1923.
167 M/229 Minutes of LEC, 21 February 1922.
168 Ibid.
169 EM9 Minutes of BEC, 16 March 1923.
170 L. Jones, *The Training of Teachers*, Appendix C pp. 437–441.
171 M/229 Minutes of LEC, 21 February 1922.
172 E/Sub M 0/4/9 Minutes of BCC Elementary Education Sub-Committee, 9 June 1922.

the elementary schools could, in theory, train as a teacher, but the new student teacher training programme selected girls only from the secondary schools. This meant that future teachers would receive a better all-round education themselves, but it also began to close the doors to girls from the elementary system. It could also mean that the social background of teachers changed, for many of the girls in the secondary schools came from homes where parents could afford the fees. Teacher training therefore became more selective. Opportunities for acting teachers to become certificated were closing and the financial problems associated with a college training became more significant.

The large underclass of supplementary teachers, mainly women, were probably employed for economic reasons. According to the 1917 salary scale, there were no male supplementary teachers for they would no doubt have seen it as a dead-end job. For women, however, it was considered appropriate to work in a subsidiary role. There was also a change in status for married women teachers who had previously been accepted. Financial restraints and ideology which saw women in a domestic role began to confine them to the home, while married women in the hat industry continued to be employed.

Bedfordshire provided efficient in-service training in which they were helped by the personal initiative of two pioneer women, Miss Walmsley and Miss Stansfeld, who ran the Froebel and Physical Training establishments in Bedford and who contributed considerably to the professional expertise of teachers throughout the county. The personal initiative of teachers themselves has to be acknowledged for they found ways to add to their professional development with university degrees and certificates in music, needlework and art. As befitted the spirit of the age, needlework qualifications were given the highest monetary reward. By 1924, secondary education and continued training, together with personal initiative and enthusiasm, had helped to produce the 'higher class of teacher' which HMI the Reverend C.F. Johnstone envisaged in 1877.[173]

---

[173] *Committee of Council on Education Report 1876–77 England and Wales* (HMSO, 1877), p. 506.

Chapter Seven

Elementary Education 1903–1924

This chapter looks at the effect which the 1902 Education Act had on the schools and on the lives of girls in Luton. Some of the curriculum changes offered a genuinely wider concept of education, an attempt to shift the emphasis 'from mere instruction to education'[1] and a desire to stimulate children as individuals whose physical and mental needs must be met. Others, however, were based on an ideology which thought of girls primarily as potential wives and mothers and presented a challenge to a town where women had, for many years, been an accepted part of economic life.

External influences were significant: the Boer War activated a concern for the health of the nation, the responsibilities of Empire influenced an ethos of duty and service and the First World War affected the lives of children, particularly with regard to their level of attendance. Another major influence on the working lives of children was the setting up of agencies which gave them advice on their choice of employment. Diana St John, having assessed the experiences of girls educated during this period under the London County Council, identified different approaches to the education of girls. The first of these is that schools came a poor second to the influence of the home. The second approach held that girls' education should be directed towards their future domestic roles. A third, very negative, attitude tended to ignore girls almost completely. The fourth was more positive, however, and saw girls as 'pupils in their own right':

> They were seen not as uneducable drudges, not simply as wives and mothers, not as adjuncts to an educational process designed for boys, but as pupils in their own right with qualities, interests and needs sometimes coinciding with those of boys, at other times quite distinct, but in no way inferior or of less account. [2]

Luton schooling is assessed with these factors in mind.

The 1902 Act
County councils were to be responsible for education, but in Bedfordshire both Bedford and Luton were large enough to be Part III authorities and could therefore control elementary education within their boroughs. As far as Luton was concerned the changes meant that the Luton Education Committee (LEC) supervised the

---

[1] 75/67–1 Logbook of HRG, HMI Report June 1909.
[2] D. St John, 'The Guidance and Influencing of Girls Leaving School at Fourteen' (Ph.D. Thesis, 1989) pp. 264–266.

town's elementary schools while the Bedfordshire Education Committee (BEC) controlled secondary education and also assumed responsibility for the schools in the hamlets. The Appointed Days for the implementation of the 1902 Act were 1 June 1903 for Part II and 30 September for Part III.

The BEC appointed sub-committees[3] to oversee every aspect of education, but it is important in the context of this book to note that they wanted as members some 'women having experience in the education of girls'.[4] The two women selected were Amy Walmsley of Bedford and Rebecca Higgins of Luton. Miss Walmsley became principal of the Bedford Kindergarten College in 1895 and was a powerful influence on education within the county.

Rebecca Higgins[5] was a member of a well-known Luton family and had a real interest in education, as her correspondence with the Clerk to the Board reveals. Her uncle had served on the first Town Council and was a member of the Board of Health, the Board of Guardians and the first School Board. In that capacity he had been one of the 'Prayer Book Five' who wanted to maintain Anglican control over education. In 1881, Rebecca was a governess at Blunham in the household of Salusbury G. Payne, JP for Bedfordshire. She became a member of the BEC, but had to resign in 1906 because of deafness.

There are other references to 'Miss Higgins' in the minute books, but these may refer to one of her sisters, Dorcas or Catherine.[6] In 1885, a Miss Emily Higgins provided illustrations for a book, *Old Luton*, written by Dorcas after she gave a lecture on the subject to the Scientific, Literary and Artistic Club of Luton. One of the Misses Higgins was named as the governess of Ruth Trevelyan, daughter of the Reverend John Trevelyan who was the Curate at the Parish Church and, from 1892, the Vicar of the newly created parish of St Saviour. An entry in Ruth's diary for 9 May 1907 says: 'Miss Higgins brought us a bottleful of fish out of the River Lea.'[7]

Luton also realized that the expertise of women was important and the Preliminary Education Committee appointed one woman 'of special experience in local education matters'.[8] Mrs Emily Carruthers[9] was selected,[10] but subsequent minutes indicate that she and a Miss Higgins worked together frequently and in many capacities within the Luton schools.

The LEC found itself having to provide ever-increasing services for children within the schools and lamented the increased demands on the rates. It 'desired to point out' to the Board of Education that its:

almost ceaseless action . . . in the matter of Schools, Staffing, Medical Inspections and possible continued Medical Treatment, the Provision of meals for

---

[3]   The sub-committee referred to throughout this chapter is the Sub-committee for Elementary Education unless otherwise noted.

[4]   EM1 Minutes of BEC, 8 May 1903.

[5]   Information from minute books, year books, 1881 Census, School Board Letterbooks and also a personal letter from Miss Ivy Higgins.

[6]   *The Luton and District Year Book and Almanack (1906)*, p. 139. Miss Dorcas Higgins was co-opted onto the LEC.

[7]   E. Bowlby, 'Ruth's Diary, A Luton Vicarage in Edwardian Times', *Bedfordshire Family History Society Journal* Vol. 13, No. 7 (September 2002). Also see Chapter Two.

[8]   M/225 Preliminary Education Committee Minutes, 3 March 1903.

[9]   See notes on Mrs Carruthers in Chapter Four.

[10]   M/225 Preliminary Education Committee Minutes, 6 July 1903.

necessitous children of school age, Care of Mentally and Physically Defective children and the reduction of times for repayment of loans for buildings is imposing a serious burden upon Ratepayers which ought to be met by increased and Consolidated Grants from the National Exchequer.[11]

Copies of this letter were sent to the Prime Minister, Chancellor of the Exchequer, President of the Board of Education and local Members of Parliament in the hope that 'these repeated and unsettling innovations and requirements may be modified to a considerable degree'.[12]

Attendance

In 1915, the BEC Sub-committee on School Attendance, which was appointed to address the decline in attendance in the county, noted that Bedfordshire was no longer 'in the forefront as it was years ago' and also that the southern district, which included the hamlets and villages near Luton, was 'always below the other districts'. Measures to be taken were 'tighter controls' and more responsibility for the School Attendance Officers who were to visit schools according to necessity and not on 'a fixed itinerary'.[13]

The reports of the Attendance Officer gave 93.6% for 1904 and 93.1% for 1905. In 1904, 664 children made 100% attendance and the figure for 1905 was 886 (allowing for one day's absence for a Sunday school tea).[14] The figures in Tables 23a and 23b indicate the level of attendance in the urban schools.

Table 23a. Attendance figures for pupils in Luton for the years between 1908 and 1911[15]

	Number on roll	Average attendance	%
June 1908	7,772	7,326	94.4
November 1908	7,719	7,131	93.3
October 1909	7,979	7,409	93.0
September 1910	8,129	7,673	94.4
June 1911	8,039	7,423	92.3

Table 23b. Attendance figures for pupils in Luton in 1910 and 1911[16]

	1910	%	Corresponding week in 1911	%
Number on roll	8,095		8,376	
Admitted during period	28		33	

[11] M/227 Minutes of LEC, 18 May 1909.
[12] Ibid.
[13] Ibid., 26 February 1915.
[14] *The Luton and District Year Book and Almanack (1906)*, p. 139. Attendance figures are also given in Chapter Eight.
[15] M/227 and M/228 Minutes of LEC on the noted dates.
[16] M/228 Minutes of LEC Minutes, 12 December 1911. Any apparent discrepancies can be accounted for as figures represent attendance in different months. Figures were always changing.

Removed	59		73
Average attendance	7,363		7,513
%			
Upper department		92.7	91.2
Lower department		87.4	86.7
Gross		91.0	89.7
Number of children absent the whole week through illness	422	5.0	551	6.0
Ditto second week	433	5.0	608	7.0
Number of visits paid to homes of children absent from school (year)	1,292		1,429
Number of notices served	23		47

The reasons for absence in the urban area were not always the same as those in the rural schools. Illnesses, especially epidemics, still accounted for a large proportion, but the Attendance Officer in Luton reported a variety of other explanations.[17] Many children had been absent for long periods and had been provided with the necessary medical certificates. However, 'it frequently comes to the knowledge of the Officer that children absent from school by Medical order are engaged in carrying straw goods, attending babies, selling newspapers and in various other occupations, but without being in actual employment'.[18] The report of the Attendance Officer for 1905 noted that 162 children in Luton who would otherwise have been unable to attend school were able to do so after they were provided with boots paid for by funds collected by the police.[19]

The First World War brought problems. For example, attendance was seriously affected 'by the absence of children for the purpose of waiting in queues to obtain foodstuffs. Reports from the schools show that this evil is growing and that many of the children, after waiting in a queue during the morning, are totally unfit for school work in the afternoon.'[20] To counter this the local Food Committee was to be asked to consider appealing to butchers to open between 4p.m. and 7p.m. instead of in the morning. Also the Board of Education was asked to use its influence to persuade the Ministry of Food to consider rationing. When this was introduced, teachers 'and some scholars' were involved with preparing the ration books.[21] The work of the Attendance Officer was taken very seriously, prosecutions still took place and girls were sometimes sent to industrial schools.[22] It does appear that attendance was given a high priority throughout the period under consideration, although the figures seem to have fallen rather than improved. There were many causes, but the demands of children's work were significant.

17 Ibid., 14 May 1912.
18 Employment will be looked at later in the chapter.
19 *Luton Year Book (1906)*, p. 139.
20 M/229 Minutes of LEC, 12 February 1918.
21 Ibid., 19 November 1918.
22 Ibid., 8 October 1918.

The health of children

In the early twentieth century there was anxiety about the physical condition of children in the nation's schools after it was found that a large proportion of recruits for the Boer War were unfit.[23] It would be pleasing to think that this concern sprang from a desire to help children, but it seems more likely that the need for a healthy nation to fight a future war or to protect the Empire was the main consideration.[24] Two very significant acts which set the pattern for the involvement of the Local Education Authorities (LEAs) in health care were the Education (Provision of Meals) Act 1906 and the Education (Administrative Provisions) Act 1907. The implementation of these acts was to prove expensive and the LEC expressed its concerns over future costs by passing a resolution which asked the government to repay 'the whole or a just part of the cost to be incurred'.[25]

The establishment and development of these services under the Luton and Bedfordshire LEAs have been described and assessed by Margaret Currie in her thesis on social policy and public health measures.[26] This book does not attempt to duplicate her work, but concentrates on the effect which the new laws had on school organization and curriculum for, while the health authorities were mainly responsible, the schools also felt the burden and complaints were made about the amount of clerical work imposed on the headteachers.[27] Medical supervision of the town schools was the concern of Luton, but the hamlet schools were the responsibility of the Bedfordshire Education Committee (BEC). No attempt has been made to analyze the levels of provision in any detail, but it is fair to say that the same responses can be seen in schools under both Luton and Bedfordshire.

Teachers needed to be told what the scheme involved and so a conference was held at the new secondary school to explain 'what would be required from Teachers, Parents, and Scholars'.[28] The following day the headmistress of Hyde School talked about the proposed arrangements in an object lesson and was 'pleased to see that it was taken in the right spirit and [the children] acknowledged it was for their own good'.[29] Forms were sent out to five mothers[30] and on inspection day the headmistress opened the school early to prepare. Four of the mothers attended the inspections although the routine was somewhat upset when the doctor arrived early on account of difficulties with the trains.[31] Similar entries are made in other logbooks; for example, in 1915 forty-seven girls were examined at Hitchin Road Girls' School and, as a result, three were excluded as unfit for attendance.[32] Sometimes the Medical Officer was called in to investigate particular conditions.[33] He also had

[23] B. Harris, *The Health of the Schoolchild: A History of the School Medical Service in England and Wales* (Open University Press, 1995), pp. 7–8.
[24] Ibid., p. 8. This was the opinion of Sidney Webb.
[25] M/226 Minutes of LEC, 11 February 1908. This was similar to the one that the LEC had received from the Felling Council.
[26] M.R. Currie, 'Social Policy and Public Health Measures in Bedfordshire, within the National Context, 1904–1938' (Ph.D. Thesis, 1998) ch. 3.
[27] E Sub M 0/4/8 Minutes of BCC Elementary Education Sub-committee, 21 November 1919.
[28] SD Hyde 1 Logbook of Hyde School, 18 May 1908. Hyde came under the BEC.
[29] Ibid., 19 May 1908.
[30] Hyde was a small rural school.
[31] SD Hyde 1 Logbook of Hyde School, 3 December 1908 and 7 December 1908.
[32] 75/67–1 Logbook of HRG, 15 February 1915.
[33] SD Hyde 1 Logbook of Hyde School, 2 December 1915.

authority to 'examine the clothing and person of any children in attendance at the local school' and to provide treatment.[34] In the case of long absences, children needed a medical certificate; in 1905, 186 orders 'free of cost to the parents were issued . . . where children have been alleged to be sick'. This arrangement 'had been useful in preventing the spread of infectious and contagious diseases, and also had been the means in a great measure of checking attempts at malingering'.[35]

Supporting lessons were given in the schools; for example, hygiene and care of different parts of the body, was taught at Hyde.[36] The BEC Sub-committee reminded its headteachers that standards of cleanliness had to be maintained in the school buildings as well as being expected of the children. There were to be sufficient washing facilities, lectures for teachers on hygiene, and regulations about the cleanliness of school floors, walls and windows. The memorandum also included remarks on breathing exercises and care of teeth.[37]

Teeth

Dental care was thought to be of the greatest importance.[38] In 1911, the LEC recommended that 'the attention of teachers be directed to the grave dental defects discovered in School children and that they be asked to assist in lessening this evil by continually urging scholars to give attention to regularly cleaning the teeth'.[39] School dentists were engaged[40] and again the co-operation of teachers was expected. In 1915, the Secretary to the LEC was asked to buy 'two gross of Tooth Brushes at 27 shillings per gross, and place the same on sale at the school clinic'.[41] A scheme of instruction in the use of toothbrushes was introduced[42] and reference was made to toothbrush drill.[43]

Eyes

From early in the century there were references in the minutes to children being supplied with spectacles. At first these were to be kept at school[44] even though Mrs Carruthers voted against the decision, probably out of concern for the well-being of the children during out-of-school hours.[45] Seven years later they were still 'only to be used for the purposes of instruction and . . . kept at the school'.[46] Apparently schemes for the provision of spectacles needed the approval of the Board of Education, which seems to have stipulated the amount that could be spent.[47] In 1912, the BEC Sub-committee sought permission to spend up to £10, the cost of each pair not

34 M/227 Minutes of LEC, 20 April 1909.
35 *Luton Year Book (1906)*, p. 139.
36 SD Hyde 1 Logbook of Hyde School, 12 November 1908.
37 E/Sub M 0/4/5 Minutes of BCC Elementary Education Sub-committee, 26 April 1912.
38 E/Sub M 0/4/4 Minutes of BCC Elementary Education Sub-committee, 29 October 1909.
39 M/228 Minutes of LEC, 10 October 1911.
40 M/229 Minutes of LEC, 12 January 1915.
41 Ibid., 14 September 1915.
42 E/Sub M 0/4/8 Minutes of BCC Elementary Education Sub-committee, 22 July 1921.
43 EM8 Minutes of BEC, 21 January 1921.
44 E/Sub M 0/4/1 Minutes of BCC Elementary Education Sub-committee, 27 January 1905.
45 EM1 Minutes of BEC 20, April 1906. This could also affect a girl's work potential.
46 E/Sub M 0/4/5 Minutes of BCC Elementary Education Sub-committee, 23 February 1912.
47 Ibid., 4 April 1912.

to exceed 5s.[48] Gradually the cost of spectacles and repairs was transferred to the parents on a sliding scale, so it can probably be assumed that children were then allowed to take them home.[49]

Physical education

Changes took place in the methods of teaching drill; Swedish drill, which was 'more concerned with developing the body than with creating future soldiers',[50] had super-seded the regimented musical drill, dumb bell drill, fan and flag drill. In 1895, the Education Department stated that no grant would be paid to schools where 'provision is not made for instruction in Swedish or other drill or suitable physical exercises'.[51] Organized games also received government approval in 1900 and, again, in 1906.[52] There were real fears in the medical profession that expecting a girl to join in energetic physical activities would 'jeopardize her future offspring',[53] but Madame Bergman-Osterberg, pioneer teacher of physical education for girls, believed that the body should be trained as carefully as the mind, which was rather a strange philosophy in an age when training girls' minds was also considered to be 'new and precarious'.[54]

Luton was fortunate in being able to take advantage of the expertise of one of Madame Bergman-Osterberg's students, Margaret Stansfeld, who established the Bedford Physical Training College.[55] Courses for teachers in elementary schools were provided at Bedford and Luton and steps were taken to ensure that 'more systematic instruction' in physical instruction was given.[56] The logbook for Hyde School lists different activities: marches of various kinds, dancing steps, games like Blind Man's Buff, skipping, running and Morris dancing. In 1909, a new syllabus was received from the Board of Education[57] and, by 1913, physical education was extending its horizons and annual sports meetings were being held in the town.[58] As Mrs Leaver, the headmistress of Hyde School, attended Miss Stansfeld's courses at Bedford it can be assumed that Miss Stansfeld approved of this kind of activity.

Swimming

St Matthew's Girls' School, a National school, had arranged swimming lessons at the end of the nineteenth century; these were held at the Waller Street Baths,[59] between 4p.m. and 5p.m. during the summer months but the logbooks do not indi-

---

[48]   Ibid., 7 November 1912.

[49]   E/Sub M 0/4/0 Minutes of BCC Elementary Education Sub-committee, 20 December 1918; E/Sub M 0/4/9 Minutes of BCC Elementary Education Sub-committee, 22 September 1922.

[50]   P. McCann, ed., *Popular Education and Socialization* (Methuen, 1977), chapter by D. Rubenstein, 'Socialization and the London School Board 1870–1904', p. 253.

[51]   P.C. McIntosh, *Landmarks in the History of Physical Education* (RKP, 1981), p. 208.

[52]   Ibid., p.209.

[53]   S. Fletcher, *Women First: The Female Tradition in English Physical Education 1880–1980* (The Athlone Press, 1984), p. 26.

[54]   Ibid., p.25.

[55]   R. Smart, *On Others' Shoulders: An Illustrated History of the Polhill & Lansdowne Colleges now De Montfort University Bedford* (De Montfort University, 1994), ch. 3.

[56]   M/227 Minutes of LEC, 23 July 1908; EM3 Minutes of BEC, 20 January 1911.

[57]   M/227 Minutes of LEC, 21 September 1909.

[58]   SD Hyde 1 Logbook of Hyde School, March 1911; M/228 Minutes of LEC, 10 June 1913; 75/67–1 Logbook of HRG, 16 July 1913.

[59]   L/1/2/54 Logbook of SMG, 21 April 1898, 30 September 1898, 20 April 1899 and 27 April 1899.

cate how and on what grounds funding was provided. However, in March 1914, the LEC discussed paying for lessons[60] and, the following month, agreed that swimming should become part of the curriculum in the senior departments of local schools,[61] insisting that only physical unfitness and non-attendance could exempt scholars from these lessons. Children were selected by age, beginning with the eldest, and were to be provided with towels and costumes. The Schools Sports Association supervised the scheme but a teacher, preferably a swimmer, was to be in charge of groups. Definite instruction was to be given and certificates for one, two or four lengths could be earned.[62] The scheme was still running in 1922 when 198 children were reported to have qualified for certificates[63] and, in 1923, thirteen girls from Denbigh Road School passed the test and nine received certificates for twenty or thirty yards.[64]

Meals

Hungry children had concerned the schools long before the passing of the Education (Provision of Meals) Act 1906. In 1890, the headmistress of Hitchin Road Infants School noted that two little girls had come to school without breakfast, 'one of whom cried bitterly'.[65] The following week, the Mayor's wife, Mrs Toyer, brought a hot dinner for the poorest children, and the lady visitors 'were so touched by the poverty of these little ones, that they sent in plentiful supplies of bread and butter'.[66] The remedy then had been in the hands of private philanthropy but the 1906 Act allowed LEAs to associate themselves with any committee which would supply meals and to help that committee if necessary.[67] The BEC decided that it was unnecessary to put the act into force,[68] but, in 1914, they approved of plans to provide cocoa for children.[69] Luton's reaction to the act was to appoint a sub-committee which found a few cases of actual need, but as these were 'being adequately dealt with by private funds' the LEC recommended that no steps should be taken.[70]

In 1917, during wartime shortages, the LEC responded to a circular regarding 'the desirability of making provision for the feeding of school children' by saying that they were of the opinion 'that private funds will be sufficient to cope with the requirements'. Arrangements were made with headteachers concerning possible schemes and costing.[71] In 1918, cocoa and biscuits were 'to be supplied where necessary from voluntary sources'[72] and the local Food Committee was asked to think about establishing communal kitchens if necessary.[73] Feeding centres were set

[60] M/228 Minutes of LEC, 10 March 1914.
[61] Ibid., 7 April 1914.
[62] Ibid.
[63] Ibid., 16 January 1923.
[64] Logbook of DRG, 25 September 1923.
[65] L/4/2/54 Logbook of HRGI, 28 November 1890.
[66] Ibid., 5 December 1890.
[67] B. Harris, *The Health of the Schoolchild*, p. 120.
[68] E/Sub M 0/4/3 Minutes of BCC Elementary Education Sub-committee, 25 September 1908.
[69] E/Sub M 0/4/6 Minutes of BCC Elementary Education Sub-committee, 9 January 1914 and 30 January 1914.
[70] M/227 Minutes of LEC, 15 December 1908.
[71] M/229 Minutes of LEC, 11 December 1917.
[72] Ibid., 15 January 1918.
[73] Ibid., 12 February 1918.

up, for example in the cookery centres, Kent's canteen and the Union Chapel Sunday School. The Davis Gas Stove Co. supplied cocoa, Captain A.J. Mander loaned fifty drinking mugs[74] and, by the end of March 1921, 15,090 meals had been served.[75] The supply of school meals was suspended in the following June.[76]

Educating girls to be wives and mothers

Margaret Currie noted that infant mortality rates were 'the most important indicator of public health in the whole community'.[77] Combined with a falling birth rate they could have catastrophic results because fewer children 'implied a threat to the nation's industrial and military might, and to its imperial supremacy'.[78] Figures for Luton were not good; George Newman,[79] part-time County Medical Officer (CMO) for the BCC from 1900 to 1907, showed that Luton compared unfavourably with other parts of Bedfordshire although boroughs in central London were worse.[80] Currie studied the background to this problem and demonstrated that the main causes were the filthy condition of central parts of Luton and the outdated sewage system.[81] Dirt left lying on the roads encouraged flies, which spread diseases, especially during the summer months.[82] The problem was not helped by the heavy workload of the first health visitor and school nurse.[83] Fingers were also pointed at mothers in Luton who offended 'against every law of hygiene'.[84]

The concerns of the health authorities were reflected in the schools. The problem of infant mortality was addressed by the LEC after it had received a circular on the subject from the Board of Education.[85] The following year they discussed their reactions to the National Conference on Infantile Mortality,[86] which recommended that 'in order to combat the prevalent ignorance resulting in wastage of infant life and injury to the health of many survivors' LEAs should be urged to secure 'to all girls in every grade of school a satisfactory training in domestic and personal hygiene and the duties of womanhood'. At the same meeting it was decided to arrange a lecture for teachers on physical development. The message was taken to the schools, as the logbook of Hitchin Road Girls' School indicates: Nurse Jellie went in to give a practical lesson to the first class on infant management.[87]

During the First World War the problem became more acute. In 1917, a letter was received from the National Baby Week Council asking for the committee's 'co-operation in diffusing knowledge of the best methods of safe-guarding the lives and health of mothers and children'.[88] Headteachers were asked to draw the attention of

74   Ibid., 26 October 1920 and 8 February 1921.
75   Ibid., 8 March 1921.
76   Ibid., 29 May 1922.
77   M.R. Currie, 'Social Policy and Public Health Measures', p. 16.
78   Ibid., p.17.
79   Sir George Newman became Chief Medical Officer at the Board of Education.
80   M.R. Currie, 'Social Policy and Public Health Measures', p. 28.
81   Ibid., p. 42.
82   Ibid., p. 47.
83   Ibid., pp. 54–57.
84   Ibid., p. 21, quoting Henry Kenwood, County Medical Officer of Health for Bedfordshire.
85   M/226 Minutes of LEC, 19 November and 25 November 1907.
86   Ibid., 5 May 1908.
87   75/67–1 Logbook of HRG, 14 January 1913.
88   M/229 Minutes of LEC, 15 May 1917.

their scholars to this request. In the same year there was a conference and an exhibition on the welfare of children.[89] In 1922, the LEC considered a request for lessons on mothercraft, but 'in view of what is already being done in this direction, they do not consider further action necessary'.[90] From these remarks it can be assumed that the teaching of mothercraft to the girls of Luton was a part of the school curriculum during this period. The ideal of women as wives and mothers is also reflected in the curriculum; needlework, as a domestic subject and not a commercial one, was an accepted part of girls' lives, cookery became important and, by 1920, 'thoroughly practical instruction in housewifery, calculated to be really useful to girls in their future lives', was given.[91]

Feeble-minded

The Egerton Report (1889) established the belief that there were backward or feeble-minded children who should be taught separately from 'ordinary children'.[92] The problem was not a new one and had been discussed by the Luton School Board at the request of two local headmasters.[93] Under Payment by Results these children could affect the grant at the annual inspection, so lists were made of 'exceptions', who apparently were not entered for the examination. At St Matthew's Girls' School a list was drawn up for the managers to verify before girls were recommended 'as exceptions to the consideration of HM Inspector'.[94] The list included girls who were delicate, convalescing, deaf or 'obviously dull'.

In his Report for 1905, Mr H.L. Sell, the Attendance Officer, noted that there were about twenty children in the town 'who [were] mentally and otherwise defective, and [were] consequently unfit to associate with children in the ordinary classes at school. With one or two exceptions they [were] not in attendance at any school or institution, but several would undoubtedly receive benefit if under proper training.'[95] In the same year the BEC replied to the Royal Commission on the Care and Control of the Feeble-Minded saying that they would not send a witness but would be willing to answer questions and give any information so far as it affected the county.[96]

The Elementary Education (Defective and Epileptic Children) Act 1899 allowed local authorities to make provision for special schooling for feeble-minded children and, in 1907, the LEC discussed the advisability of opening such a school.[97] When the pupil-teacher centre became unoccupied, there was a suggestion that those buildings should be used.[98] In 1913, when the Mental Deficiency Act made provi-

---

[89]   75/67–1 Logbook of HRG, 28 February 1917 and 4 July 1917.
[90]   M/229 Minutes of LEC, 14 February 1922.
[91]   Ibid., 7 June 1920. Also St Matthew's Girls' School – see section on Curriculum later in the chapter.
[92]   I. Copeland, *The Making of the Backward Pupil in Education in England 1870–1914* (Woburn Press, 1999), pp. 167–168.
[93]   M/219 Minutes of USDL, 18 November 1884.
[94]   L/1/2/54 Logbook of SMG, 9 April 1888 and 20 August 1889. Report of the Chairman of the Managers, August 1889.
[95]   *Luton Year Book (1906)*, p. 139.
[96]   E/Sub M 0/4/1 Minutes of BCC Elementary Education Sub-committee, 6 January 1905.
[97]   M/226 Minutes of LEC, 19 November 1907.
[98]   M/227 Minutes of LEC, 23 July 1908.

sion compulsory,[99] the BEC asked for Returns about the number of children who needed special education and asked Attendance Officers for information.[100] They also asked parents if they had any objections to their children being sent to a special school or class.[101] Teachers' courses were held[102] and Dr Archibald, the Luton Medical Officer (MO), went to lectures and a course of clinical instruction arranged by the University Extension Board.[103]

The LEC experienced difficulty finding a suitable site for a school,[104] but, by 1920, 'The Briars', a house in Osborne Road, had been identified.[105] It was bought and approved by the Board of Education and an advertisement for a headteacher was placed.[106] Out of three applicants, a certificated teacher, Miss Beatrice A. Eves from Tonbridge, was selected.[107] The school, for no more than forty-five children,[108] was opened in September 1921, scholars being selected by the MO and the headteacher. Transport was considered and a midday meal, possibly charged to the parents, was to be provided.[109] The Board of Education thought that two teachers were sufficient and, although the LEC objected, would not change its mind, even suggesting that the caretaker and his wife might be asked to help 'in the teaching of gardening and cookery'.[110] The caretaker resigned shortly afterwards,[111] possibly as a result of these expectations, and the cookery teacher from Langley Street Cookery School went to Osborne Road for one half day a week.[112] According to Dony, the school served the town until 1960.[113]

The curriculum

Government reports for the early twentieth century indicate the kind of ethos and attitude which was expected in the schools. In 1909 Christ Church School was commended for training the girls in 'habits of order and neatness'[114] and, in 1910, 'the alertness and intelligence' at Chapel Street Infants' School were exceptionally noticeable.[115] By the 1920s, there was a perceptible change from the mechanical

---

[99]   I. Copeland, *The Making of the Backward Pupil*, p. 174. The following year the Elementary Education (Defective and Epileptic Children) Act 1914 ensured that children over seven and adults were dealt with separately.

[100]   E/Sub M 0/4/6 Minutes of BCC Elementary Education Sub-committee, 26 February 1915.

[101]   Ibid., 9 October 1914.

[102]   Ibid., 30 April 1915.

[103]   EM8 Minutes of BEC, 14 May 1920; M/229 Minutes of LEC, 13 April 1920.

[104]   M/229 Minutes of LEC, 11 December 1917.

[105]   Ibid., 5 October 1920.

[106]   Ibid., 6 December 1920 and 20 December 1920.

[107]   Ibid., 10 May 1921 and 6 June 1921.

[108]   Ibid., 11 April 1922 and 16 May 1922.

[109]   Ibid., 12 July 1921.

[110]   Ibid., 20 June 1922.

[111]   Ibid., 13 February 1923.

[112]   Ibid., 8 May 1923.

[113]   J.G. Dony, *A History of Education in Luton* (LMAG, 1970), p. 60. Dony referred to 1922 as the date when the school was opened, but the Minutes of the LEC give 1921. However, as the school closed not long before the book was published (1960), there would have been less likelihood of an error for the closing date.

[114]   M/227 Minutes of LEC, 21 September 1909.

[115]   Ibid., 14th June 1910.

Summary of Scheme of Instruction
for year ending September 30th 1902.

Subject	Class 6	Class 5	Class 4	Class 3	Class 2	Class 1
Reading	Graphic Reader Royal Germ.	Graphic History	Geographical History Science.	Geographical History Science	Geographical History "Lock Well" Henshaw	History Geographical.
Recitation	Grandma's Angel.	The Pond	The Owl Critic	Council of Horses	Excalibur	Excalibur
Writing & Composition	Transcription and Copy Book writing Answering in sentences	Simple sentences from dictation Transcription and Copy book writing Oral formation of simple sentences	Dictation of harder sentences. Copy book and writing Formation of notes. harder sentences both orally and in writing	Dictation Formation both orally and in writing of shorter or those connected sentences on familiar subjects. Copy Books.	Composition as in Class 2 also reproduction of a short story read or told by book children Letter writing	Composition as in Class 2 together with reproduction of a passage read by children especially geography and history
Grammar	As in Sch. I	Sch. I	Sch. I	Parsing & Analysis of a simple sentence	Parsing & Analysis of a simple sentence	As in class 2. Harder sentences
Arithmetic	As in Sch. I	Sch. I	Sch. I	Sch. I	Sch. I	Sch. I
Geography & History			England.	The British Isles	The British Colonies and Dependencies	The British Colonies and Dependencies
		Reproductions of	History Reader	12 Lessons bearing on Geography. Reproductions of History Reader	12 Lessons bearing on Geography. Reproductions of History Reader	
El. Science & Common Things	Thrift	Object Lessons	Object Lessons	Dom. Economy	Domestic Economy	
Singing	As	As in Appendix IV	As in Appendix IV	As Record	Record Instructions.	
Needlework	As in Appendix III to Record Instruction					
Drawing	As under German Code.					
Physical Training	Sch. III of the Code.					

20a. Scheme of work from the logbook of Hitchin Road Girls' School 1902–1903 [LM]

Scheme of Work in outline — 1910–1911.

Subjects	Class VI	Class V	Class IV	Class III	Class II	Class I
English 1. Reading	Various readers including Commonwealth	Continuous Stories & Nature & History Book	Continuous Stories also Poetry, Geography & History	Various continuous stories, also readers bearing on History, Geography and literature taken during the year		
2. Memory lessons	Short poems read and partly learned	Several poems — narrative - imaginative - Pictorial & other stories	Several poems — narrative, Longfellow, Wordsworth, Chaucer etc.	Lessons and selections - Chaucer, Shakspeare, Tennyson	Lessons and selections - Shakspeare, Longfellow, Goldsmith, Wordsworth, Tennyson	
3. Writing	Oral and written formation of simple very familiar topics	Longer accounts on common topics	Essay writing more English, the simple letter writing	Essays including more radical methodical arrangement	Essay - logical & oral work - chiefly on oral - compound continuous	
Arithmetic	Simple rules, dividers & multipliers up to 6	Simple & Compound Rules, dividers and multiples up to 12.	Simple & Compound Rules, dividers and multipliers not exceeding 99	Compound Rules applied to weights and measures.	Fractions, vulgar & decimal methods applied to weights, mensuration	Stocks & averages, mensuration compound about tasks, bills & mensuration
Geography	Elementary notions with reference to everyday life & surroundings	Bedgardenshire England & Wales		The British Isle Europe in outline	Europe in detail	The British Empire
History	Simple Stories from English History.	55 b.c. – 1154.	Bedgardenshire England & Wales	Botany and Physical geography. 1075 – 1603	Course & & Physical 1688 – 1815.	Course on British Economy Circa 55 b.c. –
Elementary Science	A course of lessons on Plant World.					
Brushwork	Simple Brush strokes applied to Nature work and Memory training.			Principles of varnishes Technology & Perspective	More difficult object embracing rules & Perspective	Models and Nature Work.
Drawing	Simple objects and Nature Work. Memory work.			Harder object embracing more detail		
Cutting out	Simple drawing of folding Gumming together.	Cutting out of familiar objects.		Cutting out & simple drawing patterns	& simple useful garments and dressing them	
Needlework	Hemming, running, seaming & Knitting, flannel & thread.	Seaming - Swiss felt, Stitching hem, Cutting plain & hued.	Stitching, Herring bone	Gathering, hatching Herringbone, Marking Tape	Cutting out useful garments drawing after	Index, gussel, patching, feathersstitching
Physical Exercise	Graded for each class as per Scheme in Code.					
Singing	Songs – 3 groups. (I – II & III – IV/V/VI/VII)			Theory – 4 groups. (I – II & lower III – upper III & IV – V–VII)		
Cookery	Wednesday morning and afternoon.					

Scheme of Work (in outline)
1918–1919

Subjects	Class 7	Class 6	Class 5	Class 4	Class 3	Class 2	Class 1
English — 1. Reading	Phonetic system throughout		Various books: Geographical and Historical	in each class — suitably graded. Readers — Continuous Stories — Poetry Books			
2. Memorising Lessons	Reading of short interesting Poems. Memorising some dramatising it. Simple stories otherwise. Song Story. Globe.		Song-Story. Selections. Chaucer Tales — Southey. Longfellow. Dramatising.	Selections from Longfellow. Tennyson. Byron. Cowper.	Lessons and selections from: Shakespeare. Scott. Browning. Rossetti. Shakespeare. Scott. Longfellow. Wordsworth. Whittier. Tennyson. Milton. Longfellow. Goldsmith. Scott etc (etc.) Verse from Milton & other		
3. Writing	A collection of simple sentences on very familiar topics.		Longer accounts and longer sentences on familiar topics. Comprehension on paragraph. Letter-writing	Compositions — more advanced on style. Phrases on paragraphs. Sentences on paragraph.	Compositions as before. Topical sequence of ideas on style. Letter-writing	All prose work. Percentage. Average. Measuring. etc. Bookkeeping. Shorthand	
Arithmetic	Simple division. Simple rules. h.t.u. Compound rules up to 99. Word money simple.	Simple rules h.t.u. and multiply up to 6. Compound rules up to 12. Simple fractions and simple lengths & measures	Simple rules (h.t.u.) Compound rules (owners and word money up to 12. Simple fractions)	Simple and compound rules applied to weights and measures. Easy fractions	Previous work also decimal and vulgar fractions. mensuration. Method of solids	Europe	The World (in outline)
Geography	Simple interesting stories of the children and customs of other lands. Meaning of a map taught mentally		England & India	The British Isles	Europe		
History	Simple stories from English History & from Greece and Rome		55 b.c. – 1485 a.d.	Tudors & Stuarts (broadly)	1688 – 1820 a.d.	1688 – 1820 a.d.	
Elementary Science							
Brushwork	Simple Brushstrokes applied to Italian modification of colour			mostly	Occasional lessons		
Drawing	Expression with pastel — mostly Nature			Work	Models and Nature Work more advanced	Groups of models. Nature work and common objects	
Cutting-out	A course of lessons graded in difficulty embracing folding. Simple measuring, cutting and sticking			Cutting out of patterns and tacking up	garments in paper after previously drafting and disengaging them		
Needlework	Hemming. Running. Overseaming. Seaming. Knitting (plain)	Hemming. Back stitch. Stitching. Hemstitching. Knitting. Plain band	Run and fell seaming stitching tape. Placing, darning and herringboning. Knitting & fell	Gathering—patching in flannel — darning on stocking web. Band of garment. Knitting & Pod of	Various seams & gathers. patching in flannel & calico. Darning & buttonholing	Drawing & planning & cutting out & making buttonholes & patching	
Physical Exercises	Model Course. Dancing. Swimming			for Class I.			
Singing	Songs — 3 Groups — Classes 1, 2, 3 & 4		5 & 6 – 7.		Theory — 4 groups (Classes 1 & 2 — 3 & 4 — 5 and half 6 — half 6 & 7		
Cookery	Tuesdays and Wednesdays						

20c. Scheme of work from the logbook of Hitchin Road Girls' School 1918–1919 [LM]

obedience, which had been expected in 1874, to individual initiative. Beech Hill Infants' School was praised for using new methods 'derived from experiment and observation'. The keynote was 'freedom for self-expression', as a result of which self-consciousness disappeared and the children developed a 'keen and absorbing interest in their work and so [ensured] rapid progress'. The powers of concentration were well developed at St Matthew's Girls' School and the girls at Old Bedford Road School were praised for being alert and self-reliant.[116] Denbigh Road was a new school but had made a good start. The tone was pleasant and the general atmosphere was one of steady application. The girls were 'learning to be self-reliant and to face difficulties' as they arose and there seemed to be 'good ground to expect development on sound lines'.[117]

The specific regulations which had been part of the government codes were discontinued and, in 1905, the first *Handbook of Suggestions for Teachers* was issued. This offered considerable freedom to individual teachers. The Board of Education stated that the only uniformity of practice that it wanted was 'that each teacher should think for himself, and work out for himself such methods of teaching as may use his powers to the best advantage and be best suited to the particular needs and conditions of the school'.[118]

The timetables from Hitchin Road Girls' School between 1902 and 1919 demonstrate how the curriculum changed between those years.[119] The earliest, from 1902, depended heavily on the old government codes. History and geography concentrated on Britain and the Empire while science covered object lessons and domestic economy. The timetable for 1910 to 1911 offered a wide study of literature and indicated the need for 'logical thought'. However, the emphasis on domestic subjects was maintained with domestic economy and hygiene being substituted for history in classes I and II and cutting out, needlework and cookery taking up a considerable amount of time. An extra subject, under elementary science, was 'civics'. By 1918, the arithmetic syllabus had widened and geography included 'the world'. History was studied in all classes and included 'constitutional points' but cutting out, needlework and cookery were still important.

As a tribute to this more enlightened style of teaching it is fitting to acknowledge one teacher whose enthusiasm and vision had a lasting influence on her students. Miss Marguerite E. Middle BA was the daughter of Mr H.C. Middle,[120] headmaster at Park Street (1878), Chapel Street (1878) and Waller Street (1880) which became the only Higher Grade School in Luton and enjoyed considerable kudos. Mr Middle was thought to be a potential head of the secondary school in 1904, but the BCC thought otherwise and appointed from outside the county. No evidence has been found to show which school his daughter, who was born in 1887, attended but she received her teacher training at Stockwell College and, at some stage, worked for a degree. She became a teacher at Denbigh Road Girls' School.

[116]   M/229 Minutes of LEC, 7 June 1920.
[117]   Logbook of DRG, HMI Report September 1922.
[118]   Quotation from the 'Original Prefatory Memorandum', *Handbook of Suggestions for Teachers* (HMSO, 1946), p. 3.
[119]   See illustrations 20a, 20b and 20c.
[120]   Information gleaned from the Logbook of DRG, J.G.Dony, *A History of Education in Luton*, and conversations with Mrs Vera Robson who was taught by Miss Middle c.1930. Dora Middle, Marguerite's sister, was also a graduate.

Mrs Vera Robson explained that Miss Middle loved literature and poetry and believed that 'if you read and read, you will always have a friend, if you have a book'. She demanded beautiful handwriting, was keen to teach citizenship and did her best to persuade her girls to join the League of Nations Union. If she found a spark of interest, nothing was too much trouble. She invited girls to her home to talk about books and plays. Mrs Robson said that she (Vera Robson) was more than just stimulated; she was given a love of literature which has stayed with her throughout her life.

In the more relaxed atmosphere, children were often taken outside the schools. William Hoyle, the Secretary of the LEC, gave the girls at Hitchin Road Girls' School a lesson on London prior to their visit there[121] and, in the same year, 150 girls went to a Palestine Exhibition.[122] In 1917, the second class went to Someries Castle, taking nature study en route,[123] and the third class visited the Parish Church.[124] A visit to St Albans to see the Abbey, Verulam woods and St Michael's took place in 1921.[125] Denbigh Road Girls' School took twenty-five girls to a Pageant of Local History at the Modern School for Girls,[126] fifty-one to a performance of the *Merchant of Venice*[127] and seventeen to a matinee at the theatre.[128] Learning about nature took children into the fields.[129] They may well have taken with them a copy of *The Field Flowers of Bedfordshire*, which Mr James Saunders of Luton had presented to schools in the county.[130] Visits were made to local factories[131] and Luton girls were involved in eisteddfods, which were held at Bedford.[132]

Cookery and needlework

Although the curriculum was widening, domestic subjects remained central to girls' education. The School Board introduced the teaching of cookery in 1885[133] and the minutes from October 1902 provide considerable detail concerning the building of a new cookery centre at the Dunstable Road School.[134] By 1906, cookery instruction was being given in Langley Street School under Miss M. Briggs and at Dunstable Road under Miss M. Parker and Miss M. Wilkinson.[135] Plans to build a centre at Hitchin Road School[136] were approved by the Board of Education with the recommendation, based on a Report by HMI Miss K. Manley, that laundry classes should

121   75/67–1 Logbook of HRG, 30 May 1907.
122   Ibid., 17 November 1907.
123   Ibid., 2 October 1917.
124   Ibid., 9 November 1917.
125   Ibid., 10 June 1921.
126   Logbook of DRG, 4 July 1921.
127   Ibid., 23 June 1921.
128   Ibid., 14 December 1923.
129   75/67–1 Logbook of HRG, 5 March 1919.
130   E/Sub M 0/4/6 Minutes of BCC Elementary Education Sub-committee, 5 June 1914. Mr Saunders presented 275 copies of his book.
131   M/229 Minutes of LEC, 12 June 1917 and 17 June 1919.
132   75/67–1 Logbook of HRG, 27 February 1924; Logbook of DRG 27 February 1924 and 28 February 1924.
133   *Luton Year Book (1906)*, p. 131.
134   M/224 Minutes of USDL, 14 October 1902.
135   *Luton Year Book (1906)*, p. 137.
136   M/227 Minutes of LEC, 2 March 1911.

Feb 9th 1909

Least Common Multiple

The Least Common Multiple of two
or more numbers is the smallest number
which contains them exactly.
In fractions, we often call it the
Least Common Denominator
Mem: c.f Measure Factor or Divisor }
with Multiple Product or Dividend   }
e.g. 24 is the L.C.M. of 3, 4, 6, 8, 12

Ex:- Find the L.C.M. of 6. 10. 15. 16 & 25

$6 = 2 \times 3$
$10 = 2 \times 5$
$15 = 3 \times 5$
$16 = 2 \times 2 \times 2 \times 2$
$25 = 5 \times 5$

$L.C.M. = 2 \times 2 \times 2 \times 2 \times 3 \times 5 \times 5$
$= 1200$

21a, b & c. Fair copies of work done by Lillie Squires, Leagrave
School, 1909–1910 [LM]

be accommodated as well.[137] Presumably they were included, but insufficient evidence has been found to draw any definite conclusions about the importance of this subject in the curricula of girls' schools. In January 1913, classes for groups of eighteen[138] began to be held in the Hitchin Road Centre, also known as Charles St.[139] In 1922, towards the end of the period under consideration, the LEC approved a scheme 'whereby each girl will attend the Cookery Centres on half a day a week during the last year of school attendance'.[140]

Girls from the hamlet schools were not eligible to attend the Luton cookery centres, but the managers of the Caddington Group were told that the BEC would agree to the hire of a room to be used for cookery instruction.[141] This would be open to girls from Leagrave and Limbury. When the new department of these schools opened at Norton Road in 1913, a cookery centre was frequently mentioned[142] and

[137] M/228 Minutes of LEC, 13 February 1912.
[138] Ibid., 4 January 1913.
[139] 75/67–1 Logbook of HRG, 8 January 1913.
[140] M/229 Minutes of LEC, 14 March 1922.
[141] EM1 Minutes of BEC, 22 July 1904; E/Sub M 0/4/1 Minutes of BCC Elementary Education Sub-committee, 12 May 1905; *Luton Year Book (1906)*, p. 141. One of these references is to a room owned by Mr W.T. Lye JP, a Luton businessman who was one of the managers in the Caddington Group.
[142] E.g., 1997/35/2 Logbook of NRS, 16 September 1913.

High St.
Leagrave, Beds.
July 16th 1909

Dear Maud,

I thought you would like to know how I spent our day's holiday. On Wednesday we had a day's holiday from school for Wardown Fête. On Wednesday morning my sister and I had a game at swings. Then I helped mother cook the dinner. After we had had it I got my self ready and uncle took us for a nice drive to Flitwick to see some of our old friends. We went through Chalton, Fankot, Westoning, and Harlington. At last we reached Flitwick, it is a very pretty place, and nearly everybody has got a very pretty garden in front of the house. They were very pleased to see us. We could not stop very long because it had taken us longer to get there than we expected. As we were coming home we went up Harlington Hill. We all had to get out and walk because it was so steep and I picked some very pretty flowers and quakers. Then we came to Sundon and I saw a big pond and the old church. When we got home it was nearly nine o'clock so I had my supper and went to bed.

Your loving friend,
Lillie

High Street
Leagrave, Beds.
Sept. 16th 1909

Dear Maud,

As our holidays are over, I thought you would like to know how I spent them. We broke up on July 29th for five weeks holiday, but we had an extra week's holiday because of the late harvest. On August Monday it was very showery, only clearing up in the evening, when we went for a walk up the Dunstable Road. The next day was our Band of Hope Tea, when we each received a medal. On Wednesday we had a very nice drive to Totternhoe where we climbed to the top of the Knoll. The following Tuesday we went to Hitchin market. When we had had a good look round we had our tea and started home. On the next Wednesday it was our Horticultural Show. On the following Tuesday we went to Leighton Buzzard. The next week we went to Woburn park where we saw a lot of deer, and to Fenny Stratford. As I have no more time I will close.

Your loving friend,
Lillie

21b.

High Street,
Leagrave, Beds.
Dec. 15th 1910

Dear Eva,

Mother has asked me to
invite you to come and spend a few days
with us at Christmas. We shall expect
you on Christmas Eve by the one o'clock
train. On Christmas Eve we shall
decorate our house with ivy, holly
and mistletoe. As Christmas day happens
on Sunday we shall keep it on Monday
when I hope we shall have a very pleasant
and enjoyable time. On Monday we will
go for a very nice walk, and have many games
as Blind-man's buff and The Postman's Knock.
The following day we are going to hold our
Band of Hope tea to which we hope to go. If
it freezes and the ponds bear we will go
sliding and skating, and if there
should happen to be a down-fall of snow
we will go snowballing which I think we
shall enjoy. We are going to have a
week's holiday from school and I hope
during that time we shall be able to
go and visit some of our relatives that live
at Luton and also visit those that live at
Leagrave. During your stay with us we hope to
go for many long and enjoyable walks
together, and if the weather is too wet
and rough to go out we will stay in and
have some enjoyable games. I shall expect a
letter from you telling us how long you
will be able to stay and wether [sic] it will
be convenient for you to stay with us
for Christmas. As I have no more time and
it is nearly post time I will close.

Your loving cousin,
Lillie

21c.

this may well have been in the same hired room. No references to cookery lessons have been found in the Hyde logbook, which is not surprising considering the hamlet's isolated situation. Nor has any evidence been found to indicate that cookery was taught at Stopsley. The shortage of cookery centres in the rural areas of Bedfordshire was commented on by HMI Miss K. Manley who 'orally reported as to the instruction in Cookery given in this County with a view to requesting the Committee to increase the number of Cookery Centres under their control'.[143]

In 1913, Miss Manley made a report on the teaching of needlework in elementary schools in Luton[144] in which she stipulated the amount of time to be spent on lessons and indicated the equipment which should be available in every school. She complained about the numbers of girls being taught together, particularly at Beech Hill School where seventy children from the first two standards and sixty in the third were crowded into a room, seated three to a dual desk; 'there was little room for themselves, still less for their knitting needles'. In one school, knitting cotton was used over and over again. She also noted that in the poorer parts of the town it was often difficult to sell finished work. This concern over the financial side of the subject had previously been brought to the attention of the LEC by the auditor who complained that there was no check on materials used in the schools and asked for 'some method of tracing [them] to ensure that they have been properly and not extravagantly used'.[145]

The Board of Education had issued a syllabus of instruction in 1909.[146] Miss Manley explained that 'one of the most important sections' was mending. 'Every effort should be made to encourage not only mending but altering and adapting garments'; this no doubt would be very useful for girls who were to be wives and mothers. Emphasis on 'too fine stitches' should be avoided and girls should learn to make overalls with casement cloth or serge, with simple decoration, and then proceed to dress skirts or shirt blouses 'of a good cut'.

In 1911, the LEC considered the use of sewing machines in schools and decided that 'a machine would be of great educational value in a school'. Plans were made for an amount of money to be set aside to provide a sewing machine for each school.[147] However, when Miss Manley made her inspection, she found that some headteachers did not 'as yet' realize the advantages of using sewing machines. This seems to be a strange observation considering that most girls would have been familiar with the sewing machines which were used in the hat industry.

In the first quarter of the twentieth century, needlework was still considered to be crucial in the education of girls. This attitude can be clearly seen in an Inspector's Report on St Matthew's Girls' School where it was remarked that 'the requirements of the Girls in their future life are borne in mind and provided for: Needlework appears to be particularly well taught'.[148] It seems to have been taken for granted that the future life of girls would be domestic.

---

[143]   E/Sub M 0/4/3 Minutes of BCC Elementary Education Sub-committee, 11 December 1908.
[144]   M/229 Minutes of LEC, 8 July 1913.
[145]   M/227 Minutes of LEC, 18 May 1909.
[146]   Ibid., 21 September 1909.
[147]   M/228 Minutes of LEC, 12 December 1911.
[148]   Ibid., 11 June 1912.

Measuring levels of achievement

Schools no longer had to conform to the codes which had set recognized levels of achievement. In 1907, the LEC decided to examine all the Standard VI scholars in Luton schools.[149] At first it was thought that HMI Mr J.L. Fishwick would set the questions in four subjects but later it was agreed that the headteachers should prepare papers for their own schools, although the arithmetic papers were to be uniform 'except that girls' and boys' questions shall be dissimilar'.[150] This agrees with Gomersall's observations that an acceptance of lower academic standards for girls was 'entirely natural and appropriate'.[151] The headteachers were also to examine three subjects from their curriculum, the choice to be made from: grammar, composition, geography, history, elementary science, domestic science, algebra and mensuration, needlework and drawing.

The LEC were not happy with the results, especially in girls' arithmetic which were 'particularly uneven'. It was also impossible to make comparisons because the questions varied 'so much in character and degree of difficulty, and the teachers seem to have an unfortunately low standard of examination'. It also appeared that subjects had been 'prepared in the particular direction in which questions have been set'. There were regrets that only a few schools had submitted English and needle-work so these were in future to 'be made compulsory in boys' and girls' schools respectively'. Future examinations should have limited choice and the questions should be uniform.[152]

The following year, the headteachers were interviewed. It was discovered that there was 'a great disparity as to time devoted to the teaching of important subjects' so alterations were made to existing school timetables to ensure that a minimum amount of time was devoted to them.[153] Mr Hargreaves from the Pupil-teacher Centre was to set and mark the 1908 papers.[154] However, these schemes to standardize the performance of Standard VI children do not seem to have been successful and, the following year, it was decided to dispense with the scheme altogether, provided that headteachers submitted a detailed report about each child.[155]

A Joint Advisory Committee was set up to assist 'interchange of views and opinions' between members of the Education Committee and practising teachers.[156] This committee also considered the curriculum to be offered to children in their last year at school. Their observations reflected the view that children were beginning to be seen as individuals: they declared that 'the last year or so . . . is of the greatest importance . . . [the] highest class should be taken by a specially qualified person and worked upon individual lines'. The teacher should study each scholar's ability 'and develop the children accordingly'. These teachers should 'not be hampered by

---

149   M/226 Minutes of LEC, 22 July 1907.
150   Ibid., 24 September 1907.
151   M. Gomersall, *Working-Class Girls in Nineteenth-Century England: Life, Work and Schooling* (MacMillan, 1997), p. 136.
152   M/226 Minutes of LEC, 25 November 1907.
153   Ibid., 14 January 1908.
154   Ibid., 2 June 1908.
155   M/227 Minutes of LEC, 22 June 1909.
156   M/229 Minutes of LEC, 10 February 1920.

restrictions which some (but not all) Inspectors might wish to impose'.[157] No evidence has been found to indicate how this scheme developed.

The influence of the Empire and the First World War

The concept of Empire

Children in the early twentieth century inherited an Age of Empire. Mangan believes that a study of imperial education and its consequences were 'the means by which coloniser and colonised learned their roles . . . in the formative years of child-hood'.[158] The ethos of a country with heavy responsibilities for the well-being of lands across the globe permeated the schools, but minute books and logbooks reveal feelings of duty and service rather than attitudes of arrogant imperialism.

The establishment of an Empire Day was suggested by the Earl of Meath[159] and the date chosen was 24 May, the anniversary of Queen Victoria's birthday.[160] Empire Day was first celebrated in Luton schools in 1908 and instructions were given by both the BEC and LEC concerning the manner in which the day was to be celebrated. Bedfordshire schools were to be told about the geography of the British Empire, 'its nature and extent [and] its subjects – their difference in race and the unity in privilege and responsibility'. Special reference was made to citizenship.[161] The timetable for Luton schools was specific: a religious service was to be followed by the headteacher's observations on responsibility, duty, sympathy and self-sacri-fice. Class instruction was to emphasize privileges and responsibilities, and aspects of citizenship were to be:

> Love and fear God.
> Honour the king.
> Obey the laws.
> Seek to advance the true interests of the Empire.
> Cherish patriotism.
> Regard the rights of others.
> Follow the path of duty.
> Consider duties rather than rights.
> Seek knowledge.
> Practise self-discipline.
> Work for others.
> Consider the poor, suffering and aged.[162]

Communication between this country and the colonies was encouraged. The LEC agreed to a request from the League of Empire for colonial teachers to visit Luton schools[163] and supported 'a scheme of communication between the country and the colonies' by putting local schools in touch with colonial schools.[164] In 1914, Mr

157 Ibid., 6 June 1921.
158 J.A. Mangan, ed., *Education and Imperialism: Four Case Studies* Aspects of Education: 40 (University of Hull, 1989), p. 1.
159 E/Sub M 0/4/1 BCC Elementary Education Sub-committee Minutes, 13 May 1904.
160 E/Sub M 0/4/3 BCC Elementary Education Sub-committee Minutes, 10 January 1908.
161 Ibid.
162 M/227 Minutes of LEC, 16 February 1909.
163 M/226 Minutes of LEC, 24 March 1908.
164 M/227 Minutes of LEC, 13 December 1910.

Freear from Manitoba gave a lesson to the children at Norton Road on Canadian life.[165] These lines of communication no doubt turned a theoretical ideal into a practical one.

The First World War

The First World War disrupted children's lives. The first effects were felt when some schools were vacated for two or three weeks to allow troops to be billeted in the buildings, often leaving disorder behind.[166] Male teachers went to war[167] as did members of the school health service,[168] and refugees appeared in the class-rooms.[169]

On 8 September 1914, the British Government issued a formal invitation to Belgian refugees to receive the hospitality of the British nation[170] and they were publicly hailed and treated as honoured guests. Serbian children also arrived. Many of these 'alien allies' found their way into public elementary schools and it has been estimated that, in 1914, there were 30,000 refugee children in the country. By 1916, there was a Belgian Self Help Society (Société Belge de Luton) in the town, which had been formed 'for the purpose of providing a rallying ground for Refugees, in the Borough and for social intercourse among the members'. The Honourable Presidents were Mrs E. Schefer and M. Buillon, the President was Mon. G. Clottens and the Secretary was Mlle Jeanne Londos from Dallow Road.[171]

Children were encouraged to contribute towards the welfare of the troops by making garments[172] or collecting pennies.[173] The children in Leagrave School were particularly commended because they asked 'that the money which otherwise would be expended in prizes should be invested in the War Loan or devoted to the cost of garments for soldiers and sailors'.[174]

Schools were involved in teaching the townspeople about the way to cope with food shortages. At the end of an open day at Hitchin Road Girls' School, handbooks on *Economy in Cooking* were issued[175] and lectures were given at the Luton cookery schools.[176] Girls visited a Food Economy Exhibition in the Town Hall[177] and at Hyde two roods of playground were offered to the Parish Council 'for the purpose

---

165 1997/35/2 Logbook of NRS, 20 May 1914.
166 EM5 Minutes of BEC, 9 October 1914; 75/67–1 Logbook of HRG, 31 August 1914; 1997/35/2 Logbook of NRS, 7 September 1914.
167 1997/35/2 Logbook of NRS, 25 November 1914.
168 E/Sub M 0/4/6 Minutes of BCC Elementary Education Sub-committee, 7 May 1915.
169 EM6 Minutes of BEC, 24 March 1916. E/Sub M 0/4/6 Minutes of BCC Elementary Education Sub-committee, 7 May 1915, E/Sub M 0/4/7 Minutes of BCC Elementary Education Sub-committee, 2 June 1916; Logbook of NRS, 6 September 1915.
170 K. Storr, 'Belgian Children's Education in Britain in the Great War: Language, Identity and Race Relations', *History of Education Researcher* No. 72 (November 2003), pp. 84–93.
171 *Luton Year Book (1916)*, p. 71.
172 E/Sub M 0/4/6 Minutes of BCC Elementary Education Sub-committee, 9 October 1914; 1997/35/2 Logbook of NRS, 27 November 1914.
173 SD Hyde 2 Logbook of Hyde School, 28 September 1914.
174 E/Sub M 0/4/7 Minutes of BCC Elementary Education Sub-committee, 29 October 1915.
175 75/67–1 Logbook of HRG, 7 October 1915.
176 EM6 Minutes of BEC, 14 July 1916.
177 M/229 Minutes of LEC, 15 May 1917.

of allotments free of charge for the period of the War'.[178] Hours were changed to save lighting and heating and, in 1915, the BEC ordered that no fires were to be made up late in the afternoon.[179] Economies also had to be made in stationery materials[180] and lighting.[181] The Summer Time Act 1916 was introduced to make the best use of daylight. This was considered to be beneficial although there were 'indications that the sleeping hours of the children were in certain districts somewhat curtailed'.[182] Five years later there were still concerns that the younger children were tired in the mornings.[183]

In 1918, the BEC assessed the contribution which the schools from the county had made towards the war effort.[184] As well as considerable financial support they had supplied garments, hospital requirements and sandbags. There had been egg collections, nearly twenty tons of vegetables had been sent to the Fleet and to hospitals, nearly thirty tons of blackberries had been gathered[185] and forty-four tons of chestnuts and eleven tons of waste paper had been collected.[186] One former pupil had received the OBE and another a medal from the Red Cross.

Schools had also helped in canteen work, organization of concerts and food economy and one headmistress took her daily share in farm work by milking cows. In 1916, the Department of Agriculture and Fisheries wrote to the BEC with reference to the training of women in agriculture[187] and, the following year, a scheme was prepared.[188] The Elementary Education Sub-committee replied to a letter from the War Agricultural Committee to say that they were already carrying out suggestions concerning the release of children for agriculture.[189] The BEC seemed to have been more concerned than Luton with agriculture, which is not surprising since Bedfordshire was a rural county.

Juvenile employment

The Attendance Officer for the LEC, Mr H.L. Sell, stated that 321 children over the age of thirteen who had made the required number of attendances were allowed to leave school in 1905. There were also sixty-one children who earned their certificates by passing an examination in Standard VI, making a total of 382 children who left school before the age of fourteen. Mr Sell regretted that 'many of these children, after following employment for a period, [drifted] back to their homes, where they do little or nothing in the way of regular work'. The 321 children mentioned earlier found employment as detailed in Table 24. Figures for 1904 are also given.

---

178 E/Sub M 0/4/8 Minutes of BCC Elementary Education Sub-committee, 8 February 1918.
179 E/Sub M 0/4/7 Minutes of BEC Elementary Education Sub-committee, 29 October 1915.
180 M/229 Minutes of LEC, 16 May 1916.
181 Ibid., 16 November 1915.
182 Ibid., 12 December 1916.
183 M/228 Minutes of LEC, 12 September 1921.
184 EM7 Minutes of BEC, 19 April 1918, Appendix II.
185 Ibid.; E/Sub M 0/4/8 Minutes of BCC Elementary Education Sub-committee, 8 February 1918.
186 M/229 Minutes of LEC, 11 September 1917 and 12 February 1918. In Luton horse chestnuts were gathered for the Ministry of Munitions. The starch could be converted to acetone by a process invented by Chaim Weizmann. R. Mabey, *Flora Britannica* (Sinclair-Stevenson, 1996) p. 264. M/229 Minutes of LEC, 9 July 1918. Fruit stones were gathered; it is not clear for what purpose.
187 EM6 Minutes of BEC, 19 May 1916.
188 EM7 Minutes of BEC, 20 April 1917.
189 E/Sub M 0/4/7 Minutes of BCC Elementary Education Sub-committee, 19 May 1916. It is assumed that this included girls.

Table 24. Juvenile employment in Luton 1904 and 1905[190]

Occupation	1904	1905
In the staple industry	78	54
Errand boy	84	114
Nursemaid	40	75
At the Gelatine Works	10	2
At engineering works	15	14
At dress-making	18	7
Occupied in own home	27	30
Various	18	25
Total	290	321

Table 25. Labour Certificates issued by LEC 1915, 1916 and 1918[191]

	Passed		Failed	
	Boys	Girls	Boys	Girls
December 1915	67	47	22	26
December 1916	36	53	–	–
January 1918	41	49	35	51
July 1918	18	12	40	36

The figures in Table 26 give the number of Labour Certificates issued by the BEC between 1910 and 1914.

Table 26. Labour Certificates issued by BEC 1910–1914[192]

Year	Applications for exemptions	Certificates Granted	Certificates Refused
1910–1911	964	917	47
1911–1912	1,024	962	62
1912–1913	1,048	991	57
1913–1914	1,030	972	58

During the First World War restrictions on the employment of children in Bedford-shire were relaxed because the enlistment of so many local men had caused a shortage of labour. Girls whose mothers were working in agriculture could be employed on domestic duties as long as the School Attendance Officer had been shown a relevant birth certificate.[193] They were to come within the definition

---

[190] *Luton Year Book (1906)*, pp. 139–140.
[191] Figures taken from M/229 Minutes of LEC. The Education Act of 1918 brought an end to the issuing of Labour Certificates.
[192] EM5 Minutes of BEC, 26 February 1915.
[193] E/Sub M 0/4/7 Minutes of BCC Elementary Education Sub-committee, 24 March 1916. The girl

'Employed in Agriculture'.[194] No steps were to be taken against boys or girls over the age of twelve who themselves were 'employed wholly in agriculture to the satisfaction of the School Attendance Sub-Committee'.[195] Joy Heley of Leagrave was allowed to breach the attendance regulations 'provided that she [was] employed on munition work or other work of national importance'[196] and Ivy Heley (possibly her sister) was allowed to work 'provided that she is fully employed by Mrs Weedon of Limbury Road, Leagrave, as domestic help'.[197]

Restrictions appear to have been tightened again after the war. Children of twelve years of age could only leave school in very exceptional circumstances.[198] In 1920, the Elementary Education Sub-committee noted that, under the 1918 Act, 'the provision for total and partial exemption [ceased] to have effect' although Labour Certificates which had already been granted were honoured.[199] No evidence has been found in the LEC minutes to indicate a similar response to the ending of the Labour Certificate scheme.

Traditionally the education of children was linked to their future employment but, in the nineteenth century, education was revolutionized by the 'rise of the schooled society, a process which removed children from the labour market'.[200] The two aspects of education and employment were closely linked, but each came under a separate government department. The Labour Exchanges Act 1909 allowed Juvenile Advisory Services to be set up under the Board of Trade, but these were criticized by educationalists for the 'lack of consideration given to issues of education and training'.[201] In 1910, the President of the Board of Trade assured an 'influential deputation' that

> it was and had always been the intention of the Board to differentiate between the methods of dealing with adult and juvenile applicants for employment. In the latter case the mere bringing together of the employer and the boy or girl was not sufficient. The child needed special help and advice in the choice of employment, and frequently required some supervision during the first years of his or her industrial life. It was their desire, too, that educational influences should be continued throughout this early period of their child's industrial career. At that age a boy or girl must be regarded not as a mere commercial unit, but as a future citizen.[202]

An alternative scheme was presented by the Education (Choice of Employment) Act 1910, which gave the LEAs 'the power to provide information and advice on employment for children up to 17 years of age'.[203] There were therefore two govern-

referred to was from Potton. However, the relaxation of the by-laws applied to elementary schools throughout the county.

194   E/Sub M 0/4/8 Minutes of BCC Elementary Education Sub-committee, 24 May 1918.
195   Ibid., 26 April 1918.
196   Ibid., 25 October 1918.
197   Ibid., 14 February 1919.
198   Ibid., 20 December 1918.
199   E/Sub M 0/4/9 Minutes of BCC Elementary Education Sub-committee, 19 November 1920.
200   R. Aldrich, D. Crook and D. Watson, *Education and Employment: the DfEE and Its Place in History* (Institute of Education University of London, 2000), pp. 1–2.
201   Ibid., p.70.
202   The *Times*, 8 July 1910.
203   R. Aldrich, D. Crook and D. Watson, *Education and Employment*, p. 70.

ment departments offering similar advice, but with a different bias. During the First World War 'these issues were given an urgency by the largely unwelcome expansion in the demand for child labour'.[204]

In 1911, the LEC considered taking steps under the Education (Choice of Employment) Act 1910.[205] However, the BEC had other ideas and said that 'having regard to the general circumstances of the County, it is undesirable to take steps to bring into operation the Education (Choice of Employment) Act 1910 in respect of the County of Bedford'.[206] In 1917, the LEC received a letter from the BCC suggesting that they should 'submit a draft scheme for the appointment of a Juvenile Employment Committee'.[207] Two months later a letter arrived from the Clerk to the BCC, which said that 'it would be preferable to apply to the Board of Trade under the Labour Exchange Act 1909'.[208] The Board of Education entered the argument in favour of the Education (Choice of Employment) Act and the LEC asked the BCC for its comments.[209] They, however, were not to be moved[210] and plans went ahead to set up a Juvenile Advisory Committee under the auspices of the Ministry of Labour.[211]

In 1921 the Luton Advisory Committee was described by the BEC as 'a most capable Committee [which] is thoroughly alive, has excellent officers and is doing a distinctly good work'.[212] The activities of the Bedford Juvenile Advisory Committee, however, were 'somewhat limited owing to the prevalent abnormal conditions but it is probably doing the work as satisfactorily as a Juvenile Employment Committee would'.[213] Schemes of work were arranged for unemployed boys and girls in Bedford and Luton,[214] leaflets were distributed to children leaving school[215] and interviews were held with children about to enter the labour market.[216] No evidence has been found to indicate what kind of advice was given or how effective the system was in helping unemployed children to find employment. However, the importance of the relationship between the two aspects of children's lives, education and employment had been established. Girls were, in theory, given advice on a choice of employment. However, it seems that while a growing number of girls chose commerce, most of them went into the hat industry.

Very little information has been found concerning the work of the Luton Juvenile Advisory Committee in subsequent years. However, the twelfth annual report of the

---

204   Ibid., p. 69.
205   M/228 Minutes of LEC, 21 November 1911.
206   EM4 Minutes of BEC, 18 October 1912.
207   M/229 Minutes of LEC, 13 March 1917, pp. 254–256.
208   Ibid., 15 May 1917.
209   Ibid., 12 June 1917.
210   Ibid., 11 September 1917.
211   Ibid., 12 February 1918 and 12 March 1918. The Ministry of Labour was set up in 1916.
212   EM9 Minutes of BEC, 16 December 1921.
213   Ibid.
214   EM7 Minutes of BEC, 24 January 1919; EM8 Minutes of BEC, 25 April 1919 and 18 March 1921; EM9 Minutes of BEC, 15 July 1921.
215   M/229 Minutes of LEC, 8 April 1919.
216   Ibid., 17 June 1919; 75/67–1 Logbook of HRG, 28 July 1920, 21 July 1922 and 16 March 1923; Logbook of DRG, 11 July 1924.

committee (1938) gives an indication of the kind of work which had been under-taken.[217]

> [The] work of Committee in placing young people in employment continues to increase steadily. The hat trade and motor and general engineering absorbed the largest number of young workers. . . . A fairly regular flow of fresh registrations enabled most of the permanent and progressive vacancies to be filled with little delay . . .
> The report details the vocational guidance work affected by interviews at the schools with children and their parents. Interviews were held three times during the year at all the elementary schools and 1,133 children were seen.
> The increased number of parents attending these interviews is commented upon as a most encouraging feature. Although the work is primarily for voca-tional guidance, no effort is spared to secure in advance suitable vacancies. It is becoming increasingly difficult for employers to estimate in advance their requirements for juvenile labour, but a number have been willing to interview likely boys and girls with a view to creating a waiting list . . .
> Luton Guild of Service again rendered assistance in connection with the industrial supervision and after-care work.

Conclusion

At the beginning of this chapter Diana St John's observations concerning attitudes to girls' education were noted.[218] It would be fair to say that the first of these attitudes (the importance of home influence) represented the schooling of girls in Luton during the nineteenth century, but the second (girls' roles as wives and mothers) became increasingly strong as ideals of domesticity were presented to them. Whether or not girls were ignored as identified in John's third category is difficult to prove, but historically their schooling was not given high status. However, by the 1920s, there were, happily, schools in Luton where girls received a stimulating education which opened doors to a more exciting life. These represented the fourth of the approaches suggested by St John.

Purvis believes that working-class girls in the nineteenth century were 'unlikely to receive the same schooling as their brothers' and questions whether that schooling was relevant to their daily existence,[219] while Gomersall demonstrates how lower academic standards for girls were seen to be acceptable.[220] Davidoff and Westover show how girls were trained to be wives and mothers while boys were educated for their role in the labour market.[221] Throughout the period being discussed in this book, similar conclusions can be drawn regarding the education of girls in Luton which differed significantly from that of boys, particularly with respect to the amount of time spent on domestic subjects.

Dyhouse, quoting Roberts, says that women in Barrow and Lancaster dismissed

217 *Luton News and Bedfordshire Advertiser*, 10 February 1938.
218 D. St John, 'The Guidance and Influencing of Girls', pp. 264–266.
219 J. Purvis, *Hard Lessons: The Lives and Education of Working-Class Women in Nineteenth-Century England* (Polity Press, 1989), pp. 97–98.
220 M. Gomersall, *Working-Class Girls in Nineteenth-Century England*, p. 136.
221 L. Davidoff and B. Westover, *Our Work, Our Lives, Our Words: Women's History and Women's Work* (Macmillan, 1986), p. 2.

their domestic training as a waste of time[222] and Attar supports this belief in her book *Wasting Girls' Time*, claiming that these subjects 'kept girls' education inferior and their expectations low'.[223] There can be no real argument against familiarizing girls – and boys – with the basic facts of health care. Nor is it wrong to teach nutrition and domestic skills. The fault seems to have been in the proportion of time which girls had to devote to domestic skills while other aspects of their future lives were mainly ignored.

Girls' schools in Luton may well have presented a contradictory ideal in a town where women were an accepted part of the work force. However, a description of the schools would not be fair if it concentrated on the negative aspects. The curriculum was widening and girls' interests were being stimulated in many ways, for example by music and literature, and significant numbers of girls set their sights beyond the hat industry. With compulsory education, girls lost traditional freedoms but some of them, for example the students of Miss Middle, were able to appreciate what had been gained.

---

[222] C. Dyhouse, *Girls Growing Up in Late Victorian and Edwardian England* (RKP, 1981), p. 101.
[223] D. Attar, *Wasting Girls' Time, The History and Politics of Home Economics* (Virago, 1990), p. 148.

Chapter Eight

Rural Schools

Schools in the hamlets

In 1895, the Luton School Board was informed by the Education Department and the Bedfordshire County Council (BCC) that the extra-municipal part of the parish of Luton was to be divided into the four rural parishes of Hyde, Leagrave, Limbury-cum-Biscot and Stopsley. 'It is understood from My Lords'[1] letter that no change is proposed relative to the area of the Luton Urban District.'[2] These schools, in what are known as Luton's hamlets, have been a part of the research for this book and, in particular, studies have been made of the logbooks of the Hyde and Stopsley schools.[3] The hamlet schools were under the control of the Luton School Board until 1903 when they became part of the Caddington Group and the responsibility of BEC. Previously, Caddington School, in a village about two miles south of Luton had been managed by the Caddington and Flamstead School Board.

When responsibility was moved to BCC, the Luton Board was asked to nominate four gentlemen

> who might be elected to serve on the Body of Managers of neighbouring Rural Schools in future to be controlled by the said County Council. In discussing the matter it was pointed out that such nominations might be (or had already been) made by the respective Parish Councils, and it was resolved that a communication be addressed to the said Parish Councils suggesting that their several nominations might well include the names of Members of this present Board who had acted as Managers of the Schools concerned whilst under the control of the Board.[4]

Rural schools seem to have been considered separately from urban schools, probably for two main reasons: they were frequently much smaller and were in more isolated locations. Although there were also similarities between the schools, especially with regard to the curriculum to be followed, this chapter will concentrate on the character of rural schools and the specific problems which they faced. In particular, these involved the vagaries of the weather and the resulting difficulties with travel, the demands of agriculture, the shortcomings of school buildings, the pressures on staff and the apparent lack of esteem in which rural schools were held.

The fact that rural schools were considered to be 'different' in some way is indi-

---

[1] The Education Department.
[2] M/216 Minutes of USDL, 10 September 1895.
[3] The original logbooks of Hyde School have been consulted at BLARS. James Dyer has made a particular study of Stopsley School and his transcripts of the originals have been used.
[4] M/224 USDL, 1 September 1903.

cated by the holding of a Rural Education Conference, which was attended by County Councillor Thomas Brigg, Miss Amy Walmsley and the Director of Education.[5] Rural schools were also given their own, separate, exhibition.[6]

When Thomas Tennant, headmaster at Stopsley, resigned in November 1875, he wrote in the logbook 'I feel compelled to say that my successor will find the school in a very backward condition, owing principally to the irregular attendance, as very little attention is paid to this district by the Luton School Board and the small interest taken in education by the people themselves.'[7]

The same kind of differentiation can be observed in the attitude of the School Board when plans to teach French were being considered.[8] Then, when Junior County Scholarships became available for children who wished to attend the secondary schools, it was stipulated that 'candidates from Elementary Schools in Rural Districts shall not be required to compete on equal terms with children from Elementary Schools in Bedford and Luton'.[9] There was also the proposition that teachers in small schools should be paid less than the amount stipulated on the Burnham Scale.[10]

A comparative study

The Chief Medical Officer of the Board of Education chose Bedfordshire village schools in a comparative study with urban schools (1918) because they provided 'typical country schools'.[11] Just how typical children from the Luton hamlets may have been is open to question, but the findings of the report are of interest:

> The country children appeared rosier and in general appearance healthier and superior in general carriage, while visual defects and hardness of hearing were much less common among them. On the other hand, the condition of their teeth was worse to a great and surprising degree. There was little to choose between the state of nutrition of the town and country children, but the latter were markedly freer from septic conditions of the skin, the eyes and the ears. There was, on the other hand, considerably more mouth breathing and a dullness of expression associated with the presence of adenoids and enlarged tonsils amongst the country children; the frequency of enlargement of the thyroid gland amongst the latter was also a circumstance which impressed itself upon our notice.
>
> In regard to nutrition there was no striking difference. The number of children with clean heads was also about the same, but bad cases of verminous heads were more frequent among the girls in country schools, although in regard to conditions of body cleanliness the position was reversed, the condition of the country children being more satisfactory than that of the town children.

5   E/Sub M 0/4/4 Minutes of BCC Elementary Education Sub-Committee, 28 May 1909. It is reasonable to suppose that these conferences were held regularly.
6   E/Sub M 0/4/2 Minutes of BCC Elementary Education Sub-Committee, 4 January 1907. The exhibition was planned for June 1907.
7   Ibid., 30 November 1875.
8   J. Dyer, *The Story of the Stopsley Schools* (LMAG, 1989), p. 14.
9   EM1 Minutes of BEC, 22 April 1904.
10   E/Sub M 0/4/8 Minutes of BCC Elementary Education Sub-Committee, 9 June 1922. See Chapter Seven.
11   EM7 Minutes of BEC, 24 January 1919, Appendix II.

Children from the country suffered far less from visual defects, hearing impairment, discharge of the ears, anaemia, curvature of the spine or flat feet. However, while 60% of London children had sound teeth, the figure for country children was 35.1%. This was attributed to 'the provision of dental aid' in London. Apparently it was rare for a country child to visit a dentist 'except for extraction owing to intolerable toothache'. Similarly, it was difficult for country children to obtain relief from tonsils or adenoids, again due to lack of medical provision.

Buildings

It has to be said that rural schools were not the only ones to be housed in inadequate buildings. However, the logbooks of Hyde and Stopsley schools tell a sorry tale about the state of the old hamlet schools. Replacements were built, however: the National school building in Hyde was replaced in 1902, Stopsley Infant School was built in 1909 and Stopsley Council Mixed School in 1912. The Limbury and Leagrave schools became seriously short of space and the Bedfordshire Education Committee (BEC) was obliged to address the problem. As a result, a new mixed school was opened in 1913 with 222 scholars.[12] This became known as Norton Road School. The two former hamlet schools were retained as infant schools. As Luton grew and the schools were surrounded by new housing, Biscot, Limbury, Leagrave and Stopsley began to lose their rural identity. However, Hyde, which was separated from Luton by the Luton Hoo Estate, remained and still remains essentially rural in character.

The entries in the Hyde logbook for 1899 are typical of the problems faced. The staff and children returned to school after the Christmas holidays to find the room scrubbed and beautifully clean. But, the following day 'it rained so heavily that the water ran down the Class-room steps right across the floor to the opposite end. In my[13] room the rain came through the North window so that the lower division had to move their seats.'[14] Later that month, when the head went round to the boys' offices (toilets) 'it was simply a pool of mud around the door; The rain had washed the mud down and stopped up the drain.'[15] In June the Inspector complained that he could not recommend the 'higher grant for discipline' because of the 'improper condition' of the closets, which required immediate attention,[16] and, on one afternoon in November, the wind blew out one of the windows.[17] The following February, the infants were unable to go into their room as it was swamped, 'the water lying an inch deep round the wall on the South side of the room. The wet poured down the wall of the girls' room; one boy's coat was wet through: He carried it home in his hand.'[18] In 1901, HMI Mr E.N. Wix stated that 'the playground and offices are in a disgraceful condition and the latter are not fit for use'.[19]

The old school in Hyde 'itself [had] a depressing effect on both Teachers and

[12] 1997/35/2 Logbook of NRS, 15 September 1913.
[13] Miss Horton, the headmistress.
[14] SD Hyde 1 Logbook of Hyde School, 9 January 1899.
[15] Ibid., 20 January 1899.
[16] Ibid., Report June 1899.
[17] Ibid., 3 November 1899.
[18] Ibid., 16 February 1900.
[19] Ibid., 20 February 1901.

Scholars'[20] but, in May 1902, the new school was opened and the headmistress, Mrs K. Leaver, noted that she found the premises bright and pleasant 'which must have an effect on the children eventually'.[21]

The state of affairs was much the same at Stopsley. In November 1880, the head, Samuel Deane, 'found the schoolroom completely full of smoke and consequently school was hindered a half hour while fire was put out and school cleared of smoke'.[22] An entry in the logbook for April 1882 notes that 'the turn-about on the school chimney has blown down so as to prevent the smoke escaping from it. The room is filled with smoke if we attempt a fire, or extremely cold if we have none. Thermometer stands at 40°.'[23]

The toilets frequently caused problems: a heavy storm in 1902 'caused the boys' yard to be flooded with sewage from the dumbwell, causing also the lobby to be soaked with sewage – the girls' W.C.s flooded into the other yard causing a horrible stench'[24] and, in 1905, 'during a thunderstorm this evening the boys' yard and lobby were flooded with sewage from the dumbwell, and only great exertion on my [the head, Mr Breed's] part prevented the school room being flooded. I dug a trench along the boys' yard and so drained it.'[25]

On the other hand, there was more space and air in rural areas. During the First World War 'two roods [about half an acre] of playground at Hyde was offered to the Hyde Parish Council for the purpose of allotments free of charge for the period of the War, on the condition that the land is restored in a proper condition at the end of the tenancy'.[26] Also, the children at both Hyde and Stopsley were able to indulge in the joys of gardening when this became popular. The headmistress at Hyde, Mrs Leaver, was dismayed when flowers were plucked at weekends from the school garden. This was 'very annoying for the children as they had taken extra pains'.[27] Mr Breed, the headmaster at Stopsley School, seems to have been very keen on his gardens and noted that the boys took home fine green peas, lettuces, cabbages, turnips and broad beans.[28]

Caretakers were very important for the smooth running of the school. At Hyde, in January 1917, the school had to be closed in the afternoon as there 'were no fires in the School there being no caretaker. The teacher and boys tried to obtain a fire but the wood was too damp.'[29] The Stopsley logbooks frequently make reference to their inadequacies. In May 1880, 'the caretaker neglected her duty this morning, and as a consequence the school was not in proper order all the morning and after-noon'.[30] In the same year it was noted that 'the Caretaker [had] made a practice of coming to light the fires at 8.30 or even 8.40 instead of the time mentioned by the Clerk of the Board. The result of this person coming so late is that the school is

20 Ibid., 18 October 1901.
21 Ibid., 5 May 1902.
22 Stopsley School Logbook, 2 November 1880.
23 Ibid., 27 April 1882.
24 Ibid., July 1902.
25 Ibid., 30 May 1905.
26 E/Sub M 0/4/8 Minutes of BCC Elementary Education Sub-Committee, 8 February 1918.
27 SD Hyde 2 Logbook of Hyde School, 6 June 1913.
28 Stopsley School Logbook, 6 July 1917 and 23 July 1917.
29 SD Hyde 2 Logbook of Hyde School, 8 January 1917.
30 Stopsley School Logbook, 19 May 1880.

generally in a state of confusion, at the time for the assembling of the scholars.'[31] Then, in 1886, 'the Caretaker has refused duty. No water has been supplied for the schoolmaster since November 17th.'[32]

A supportive caretaker made all the difference. The appointment of a new care-taker, Fletcher, at Stopsley in January 1887 prompted the headmaster to say: '[I] am pleased to say he does his work thoroughly well and the place is beginning to wear an orderly and clean aspect.'[33] A later logbook entry stated: 'I have noted the fact that the new caretaker has during this winter never failed to have a good fire in each of the rooms by 9 a.m. This is a pleasant contrast to former years experience.'[34]

The removal of sewage, sometimes the responsibility of the caretakers, was defined as 'scavenging'. In December 1914, the Elementary Sub-Committee of the BEC decided to reduce the following caretakers' salaries because the scavenging work was to be undertaken by the Luton Rural District Council: Arthur Bird (Leagrave) by £5, Robert Ayling (Limbury) by £1 10s. and Leagrave, Norton Road, by £1 15s.[35] The Luton Rural District Council was

> requested to arrange for the scavenging of the Limbury County Infant School to be carried out on Fridays instead of on Wednesdays as hitherto; that the bucket be changed from one convenience to the other in the midweek in order to ensure an even use of such buckets and that the Caretaker be instructed to leave the door of the offices open on Friday nights when the scavenging is performed.[36]

Weather

Observations on the weather take up a lot of space in the logbooks. Sometimes the heat is mentioned, but more often the problems were caused by snow, ice and rain. Hyde remains, even today, in a comparatively isolated situation and, in 1984, when the school closed, former pupils came to record their memories, which frequently related to the weather. One woman said that on cold days her mother used to give her children hot jacket potatoes to hold to keep their hands warm.[37]

Typical comments are: 'deep snow. 5 children came wet – sent home. No-one else came'[38] and 'last week the most unsettled week in my experience whilst in charge of the school. A good attendance considering Self caught in a snow drift, pretty well drenched on my way to Station.'[39] In 1916 there was 'another new heavy fall of snow and roads not fit for children to traverse. If no more children come I feel it will be advisable to close for the rest of the day.'[40] Apparently this was an exceptionally bad month because no children arrived on the 8th and, on the 28th, the children were sent home at 2.30p.m. 'as the sky threatened a storm and only just in time for the

[31] Ibid., 26 November 1880.
[32] Ibid., 22 November 1886.
[33] Ibid., 21 January 1887.
[34] Ibid., 15 March 1906.
[35] E/Sub M 0/4/6 Minutes of BCC Elementary Education Sub-Committee, 1 December 1914.
[36] E/Sub M 0/4/7 Minutes of BCC Elementary Education Sub-Committee, 26 November 1915.
[37] Reminiscences by former pupils collected by A. Allsopp, 1984.
[38] SD Hyde 1 Logbook of Hyde School, 14 February 1900.
[39] Ibid., 2 March 1908.
[40] SD Hyde 2 Logbook of Hyde School, 7 March 1916.

blizzard which raged was the worst known for some years. The following day the children were unable to get to school because of storm damage, fallen trees having blocked the roads.[41]

In January 1917, there were problems with ice. The headteacher, Miss J. Watkins, could not reach the school from her home in St Albans 'owing to the extremely slippery roads due to the severe frost and snow'.[42] Coal was in short supply, no doubt because of the war, and the children were cold. Fires were not only needed to warm the children, but also to dry their clothes: 'it has been necessary to have a fire in the Infant Room to dry wet clothing and boots of scholars'.[43] An entry in the Hyde logbook for 1898 states that the teacher was obliged to collect all the copy books in because of the gloom. 'The children have had to recite because it was too dark to do anything else.'[44]

The headteachers at Stopsley make similar comments. In January 1881 the 'snow [was] as high as the hedge on the Hitchin Road'[45] and, in 1889, the school had to be closed because there was no coal in the place; 'a supply of fuel should have arrived yesterday but the frostiness of the roads prevented it'.[46] Mr Breed noted that

> Mr Cripps, grocer, who is a newcomer to the village, says his little girl has complained bitterly of the cold schoolroom. I am forwarding his letter to the Board. Chilblains on the feet have put about a dozen children on the sick list. My own little girls tell me that to sit and write in the winter-time is most painful – with a temperature of 40°.[47]

Travel

Children and staff in rural schools frequently had long distances to travel and school hours were adapted according to the time of year. In November 1898, the afternoon session at Hyde School was brought forward to 1p.m. and the children were allowed to leave at 3.30p.m. To accommodate this, the lunch hour was shortened[48] and children brought their lunches with them. During the summer it seems to have been normal for children to return home for dinner. This caused problems for William Titmus. The headmaster, James Cooper, spoke to his mother 'about her child's leaving school at twelve and not returning in the afternoon. She promised to give him his dinner with him in future'.[49] Mrs Darby, headmistress at Hyde, was delighted when permission was given for school hours to be altered to 1.15p.m. to 3.30p.m.:

> This is a very agreeable concession as it enables me to get a train to Luton at 3.45 instead of waiting until 5.20, it is also of great benefit to those children who come over 2½ miles to school, allowing them to get home in the winter before it grows quite dark.[50]

41 Ibid., 28 March 1916 and 29 March 1916.
42 Ibid., 22 January 1917.
43 Ibid., 3 August 1917.
44 SD Hyde 1 Logbook of Hyde School, 12 December 1898.
45 Stopsley School Logbook, 19 January 1881.
46 Ibid., 28 November 1889.
47 Ibid., 7 March 1902.
48 SD Hyde 1 Logbook of Hyde School, 29 November 1898.
49 Stopsley School Logbook, 21 March 1882.
50 SD Hyde 2 Logbook of Hyde School, 4 February 1915.

It seems that the staff at Hyde School usually travelled in by train, although Miss Cant used to cycle if the weather was fine.[51] The two railway lines which served the hamlet could have provided an excellent service, apart from the fact that the railway timetable did not always synchronize with the school timetable. Also, there could be delays; on 14 December 1915 the headteacher had to walk to school as there was 'a block on the GN line'.[52] Another headmistress from Hyde, Annie Poole, complained that

> the train service to Chiltern Green has been altered this week. I cannot now get to School by Midland Railway until about 9.15 a.m. unless I catch 7.30 a.m. train from Luton which necessitates my leaving home at 7 a.m. I received permission to arrive at School for 9.15 for this week until I can make other arrangements. It has been very difficult to come at all this week. I have to leave home at 7.50 a.m. take train to Harpenden, wait there for half an hour and then I have been able to make a connection to Chiltern Green Station arriving at Chiltern Green Station at 9 a.m. and School at 9.15 a.m.[53]

Under these conditions she and Elsie Cant, a pupil-teacher, had to walk home or 'wait four hours in the cold for [a] train'.[54]

Messages were relayed to Hyde School by telegram. In 1916 a telegram arrived from the Medical Officer of Health authorizing the closure of the school, apparently on account of an epidemic of measles[55] and, on another occasion, he sent a telegram notifying the school that his intended visit had been cancelled.[56]

The headteachers of Stopsley School did not have to travel because they lived in the school house, but other members of staff had to find their own way to work. There was no train service to Stopsley and no form of public transport was available until 1908 when a tram service to Round Green, on the road to Stopsley, was opened. Again, the set times for afternoon school were of considerable importance and concessions had to be made in wintertime; in 1881 it was noted that 'owing to the days getting shorter, and the fact of some children having to walk over two miles, the school hours during the winter will be from 1.30 to 3.40 p.m.'.[57]

Teachers at Stopsley had to walk to and from school and they found it a considerable burden. In 1886 the assistant had 'three miles of very rough roads and inclement weather to contend with'.[58] Two years later a monitor, Charles Creasey, left to work in a private school 'having obtained what he considers a better post in Luton, and then the long walk morning and evening will be avoided'.[59] During a severe snowstorm Miss Boddy, the sewing and infant mistress, had 'not ventured the journey from Luton'.[60] Then Miss Spark, having been at the school for six weeks, sent in her resignation as she found the walk 'too fatiguing for her'.[61] She agreed to

51 Ibid., 7 July 1917.
52 Ibid., 14 December 1915.
53 Ibid., 4 January 1918.
54 Ibid., 18 January 1918.
55 Ibid., 4 February 1916.
56 Ibid., 13 November 1919.
57 Stopsley School Logbook, 31 October 1881.
58 Ibid., 11 January 1886.
59 Ibid., 11 April 1888.
60 Ibid., 10 March 1891.
61 Ibid., 23 June 1891.

stay until the harvest holiday, which was 'very fortunate as her appointed successor declined to accept the post when made acquainted with the fact that there was a walk of 2½ miles to and from the school'.[62]

A pupil-teacher left because he had to walk 'all the way from Bramingham Shott [Wardown] near Luton; a terrific journey in winter'.[63] In 1900, Miss Pearce, a trained and certificated teacher, made the effort to get to school from Luton in spite of a severe snowstorm which 'covered the roads to a great depth'. When she arrived there were no scholars and the headmaster, Mr Breed, noted that 'after some warm refreshment I advised her to journey at once to Luton and sent the teachers home again and the few boys who were very wet. Temperature 35°.'[64] Cissie Cox was sent to Stopsley from Hitchin Road School, but 'her parents . . . made representations to the Board that the walk from Luton was not a tonic but too much for her frame! And in this fine weather too!'[65]

Although the hamlet schools were very near to Luton by modern standards, they were far enough away to cause all kinds of practical problems. The headteacher at Hyde, Mrs Darby, did not arrive at school until 10.50a.m. on 1 June 1916 because she had stayed in Luton to change the salary cheques. When she arrived she found the Assistant Director of Education waiting for her.[66] Whether or not this was a direct consequence is not noted but, the following week, a letter was received from the managers to say that there would have to be a two-hour dinner break (to accommodate trips to the bank?). This meant that Mrs Darby would have to wait for the 5.30p.m. train home. She found this 'much too long without a proper meal'[67] and in September she resigned.[68] Samuel Deane, the headteacher at Stopsley, had a similar problem. He had been to Luton in the dinner hour to pay fees into the bank and could not get back in time to open school 'at the usual hour.'[69] The same dilemma existed in 1918 when Mr Breed went to fetch the salaries between 10.15a.m. and 10.45a.m. on 2 August, the day the school broke up for the summer holiday. When HMI Mr Dymond visited the following December he advised Mr Breed to keep to the rules by collecting the salaries during his lunch break.[70]

Attendance

The problems of absenteeism seem to have filled the teachers with despair. In 1909, the headmistress at Hyde, Mrs Leaver, commented that 'one seems to have to begin all work over again'.[71] In 1915, a similar remark was made by her successor, Mrs Darby: 'work much hindered as a whole owing to attendance'.[72] Sometimes, as in November 1887, the Attendance Officer was called in: 'Mr Sell visited parents last week and considerable number was called before committee. Result, average has

62 Ibid., 17 July 1891.
63 Ibid., 7 January 1896.
64 Ibid., 14 February 1900 and 15 February 1900.
65 Ibid., 27 September 1900 and 3 October 1900.
66 SD Hyde 2 Logbook of Hyde School, 1 June 1916.
67 Ibid., 15 June 1916.
68 Ibid., 18 September 1916.
69 Stopsley School Logbook, 23 March 1880.
70 Ibid., 11 December 1918.
71 SD Hyde 1 Logbook of Hyde School, 13 September 1909.
72 SD Hyde 2 Logbook of Hyde School, 8 November 1915.

risen from 80.6 last week to 89.1 this week.'[73] Illness was a problem for every school, although Mr Breed's remedy for keeping down measles by 'frequently sending tar fumes among the children whose breath I understand to be the main source of infection' can hardly be recommended.[74] Infection was also used as an excuse by the healthy:

> Measles has spread and the attendance has fallen very low. Visited the absentees and found that quite a number of children were away for no reason whatever. Thus Wm Plummer has been away a fortnight 'because Lizzie Hawkins has been away, and he has as much right to stay away as she has' . . . They have simply taken advantage of the outbreak of measles to take a week or more holiday.[75]

Children in rural areas were always expected to respond to the needs of the agricultural community. The logbooks frequently refer to boys working in the fields, but girls were also involved to some degree. One former pupil described how the girls used to sit on the wagons at harvest time while the horses plodded back from the fields to the farms.[76]

The summer holidays for the urban schools were predictable, but those for the hamlet schools were open to negotiation. In 1888, Mr Shoosmith at Stopsley noted that he was 'still waiting for the commencement of harvest, in order to close school for Holidays. The cold weather of this week has probably caused a delay of five or six days.'[77] The school closed on 31 August. In July 1894, the Luton Board announced that schools within the Borough 'shall close for the usual midsummer holiday on Friday the 27th of July; but that the 'Hamlet' Schools shall all close on some day to be hereafter fixed'.[78] When the timing of the harvest had been assessed, it was announced that 'schools at Leagrave, Biscot and Stopsley do close for the Midsummer Holidays on Friday 10th day of August'.[79]

The harvest holidays were official holidays, but the farmers wanted more. In July 1898, 'boys were absent carting hay, their names being passed to the Board's Attendance Officer'[80] and in September 'many boys [were] in the harvest fields'.[81] The headmistress, Miss Horton, noted that 'the farmers employ the boys whenever they can'.[82] Other field work included 'helping in the two days shooting',[83] possibly on the Luton Hoo Estate, and strawberry picking.[84] However, the main focus was on the cereal harvest. In October 1888, there were 'still a few fields of barley to be gleaned and many have been away on that account'.[85]

Understandably, the farmers were sometimes less than co-operative. 'Notices

73 Stopsley School Logbook, 28 November 1887.
74 Ibid., 7 December 1906.
75 Ibid., 10 March 1892.
76 Reminiscences by former pupils collected by A. Allsopp, 1984.
77 Stopsley School Logbook, 15 August 1888.
78 M/221 Minutes of USDL, 5 July 1894.
79 Ibid., 17 July 1894.
80 SD Hyde 1 Logbook of Hyde School, 14 July 1898.
81 Ibid., 5 September 1898.
82 Ibid., 29 June 1900.
83 Ibid., 18 November 1902.
84 SD Hyde 2 Logbook of Hyde School, 10 July 1914.
85 Stopsley School Logbook, 8 October 1888.

[were] sent to Messrs Shaw and Osborne, farmers, warning them against employing children under age. Lad, William Toyer from the First Standard, has been away five weeks, working on [Mr Osborne's] farm.'[86] Five years later an entry in the logbook states that 'this week the elder boys have had permission to go haymaking, now and then. I have had occasion to write to Mr Allingham, farmer, who has certainly abused the privilege I have granted, but he fell into my rule [of boys coming in the morning] late in the week.'[87] Again, boys took advantage of the situation. 'I [Mr Breed] called on Mr Shaw this morning and found that no boys were working for him, as it was too wet. However, they were not at school all day.'[88] Truancy was far from unusual.[89]

In 1904, children from Hyde School were given a week's extra holiday 'on account of [the] harvest'[90] and boys were given permission in 1924 to help with the late harvest.[91] However, there were other harvests to be gathered: 'the acorns are ripe and whole batches of children stay away for days at a stretch in order to go acorning. What with acorning, gleaning, blackberrying, taking care of babies, or going to Luton, there seems to be abundant excuse in the parents' opinion to be continually keeping the children from school.'[92] The attendance was very bad; 'this is chiefly due to sickness, mostly sore heads and blister pox. One lad, Whittemore has been away for a fortnight through want of boots. Now that work is falling off in Luton, I have a great difficulty in many cases in obtaining the fees.'[93]

The need to pay fees certainly affected attendance, a matter which greatly concerned the headmasters at Stopsley School. When schooling became compulsory, parents lost much of the family income to which their children had contributed while at the same time they were obliged to find money to pay their fees. In cases of severe hardship the Poor Law Guardians helped out.[94] The collection of fees also added to the problems of the headteachers who had to pursue the debts with dogged determination and make sure that the books balanced. Although the logbooks were full of references to fees, it does seem somewhat strange that very little is made about the euphoria which must have been felt when fees were abolished in 1891.

Debts mounted up and, in November 1884, there were arrears because many of the people in Stopsley were 'in a state of semi-starvation'.[95] The headmaster, Mr Johnston, wrote to the Luton School Board about the arrears which he inherited from his predecessor 'and which I desire to be written off the books'. Although there were 'many cases of dire poverty in the village' there were 'many parents who might well pay, who do not do so'.[96]

Mr Johnston was notified that 'the Committee appointed to inquire into arrears

86   Ibid., 8 August 1890.
87   Ibid., 21 June 1895.
88   Ibid., 18 September 1896.
89   Ibid., 14 June 1880.
90   SD Hyde 1 Logbook of Hyde School, 29 July 1904.
91   SD Hyde 2 Logbook of Hyde School, 12 September 1924.
92   Stopsley School Logbook, 14 October 1887.
93   Ibid., 21 October 1887.
94   Ibid., 15 March 1886.
95   Ibid., 10 November 1884.
96   Ibid., 29 January 1886.

of Fees' would sit at the school at 6p.m. on 25 March.[97] Later, 'acting upon the express instructions of School Board Committee', he sent several children home to collect their fees.[98] This action did not always have the desired affect:

Have made a decided stand against the wretched, dilatory way, in which some of the parents . . . pay the School Fees. If allowed they will get 2 or 3 weeks in arrears and then send about half of what they owe, promising to pay the next during the week; a promise which is seldom kept. This week then I have sent a few of them home for their money, and John Blow has not returned. In the majority of cases, however, the parents seeing me to be in earnest have paid up.'[99]

In 1888, there was another lament from the headmaster, Mr Shoosmith:

This ought not to be so, as Harvest Time is just over, and the men have received their wages. The people, however, are very poor, and run into debt to a fearful extent during the winter months. This poverty is indeed the great enemy to the rapid advance of the school. Irregularity arises from it, as any and every opportunity is seized for earning a copper, gleaning, acorning, odd jobs at the farms, etc. Then again during the winter months the distress is dreadful. The children (some at least) are half starved and half clothed, and of course cannot be expected to advance as rapidly as they would do under better circumstances'.[100]

In a letter from the Clerk to the Board to the Education Secretary, it was pointed out that 'Straw Plaiting is not an industry carried on in the Town of Luton, but in the hamlets, and in widely scattered rural districts through this and the adjoining Counties.'[101] The hat trade was seasonal but, when it was brisk, it affected attendance to a considerable extent. For example, 'the attendance of this school is gradually lessening. Can attribute no cause except that this period [Spring] is the most busy time of the year in the hat trade.'[102] In 1891, it was noted that there was 'bad attendance in the Upper Standards, especially among the girls; owing principally to the "busy season" in the straw trade'.[103]

Monday and Thursday were the days when many parents either went to Luton themselves or sent children on their behalf.[104] Arthur Harris was punished 'for being absent from school yesterday afternoon [Monday], it being the Plait Market at Luton, his mother goes there to buy or sell'.[105] At Stopsley 'the attendance is always small on a Monday owing no doubt to numerous errands to Luton on account of staple manufacture'[106] and it was felt that 'the only remedy for the rather irregular attendance lies in the thorough enforcement of the law'.[107] Entertainments kept

[97]   Ibid., 25 March 1886.
[98]   Ibid., 30 March 1886.
[99]   Ibid., 5 December 1890.
[100] Ibid., 20 October 1888.
[101] M/239 Letterbooks of USDL, Letter from Board to the Secretary of the Education Department, 29 May 1891.
[102] Stopsley School Logbook, 21 April 1884.
[103] Ibid., 22 May 1891.
[104] Ibid., 23 January 1882 and 29 January 1885.
[105] Ibid., 10 October 1882.
[106] Ibid., 25 March 1885.
[107] Ibid., 10 March 1885.

children away from school: there was the annual April Fair[108] and in 1886 a circus came to town.[109] The Statute Fair was held every September[110] and in 1891 the school was closed for a bazaar in aid of the Teachers' Orphanage.[111]

Then there were other excuses; one of the strangest was noted by Mr Deane at Stopsley. He told the children that he would not punish any latecomers 'until our clock kept proper time'.[112] Sarah Bunker returned to school after being away for several weeks because her mother had falsely stated that she was thirteen years of age. However, the Attendance Officer, Mr Sell, had checked the register of births and found that she was only twelve.[113] There were also parents who were seen 'to set the Board and its decrees at defiance and that with impunity'.[114]

Attendance figures for the rural schools were lower than those for the urban schools. The examples noted in Table 28 show that Hyde had a higher average attendance than the other hamlet schools in the last quarter of 1914. The figures in Table 27 for Midsummer 1913 indicate that Hyde children were probably busy in the fields.

Table 27. Attendance figures in rural schools Midsummer 1913[115]

	Number on books	Average attendance	%	Number under 5	Summary
Hyde	44	38.5	87.5	5	Sickness during April and May
Leagrave	246	223.0	90.6	–	Closed three weeks for measles
Limbury	161	138.0	85.7	–	Closed four weeks for measles
Stopsley Mixed	133	127.0	95.4	–	Chickenpox in May and June
Stopsley Infant	88	72.5	82.3	12	Chickenpox in May and June

Figures for the quarter ending Christmas 1914 are similar.

Table 28. Attendance figures in rural schools Christmas 1914[116]

	Number on books	Average attendance	%	Number under 5	Summary
Hyde	42	38.8	92.3	–	Sickness in November
Leagrave Mixed	264	235.1	89.0	–	Sickness in November
Leagrave Infant	135	114.0	84.4	20	Sickness in November
Stopsley Mixed	159	138.2	86.9	–	Scarlet fever and mumps
Stopsley Infant	86	74.4	86.5	19	Scarlet fever and mumps

[108] Ibid., 20 April 1884 and 20 April 1885.
[109] Ibid., 1 April 1886.
[110] Ibid., 20 September 1886.
[111] Ibid., 18 March 1891.
[112] Ibid., 19 April 1880.
[113] Ibid., 28 January 1886.
[114] Ibid., 27 May 1887.
[115] EM5 Minutes of BEC, Appendix A, July 1913.
[116] EM5 Minutes of BEC 8 January 1915.

No comparative figures have been found for the earlier years of this research and attitudes to compulsory schooling may well have been changing by 1913 as 'second-generation' children were coming through the system. The Luton School Board had also introduced incentives. For example, Leagrave School, having achieved 100% attending for the week ending 26 October 1900, was granted a whole day's holiday on 5 November.

Staff

It is not possible to generalize about the staff in rural schools. For example, there seems to be a considerable contrast in the attitudes towards the appointment of headteachers at Stopsley School and Hyde School. Mr Shoosmith and Mr Breed, both from the prestigious Waller Street Higher Grade School, were appointed to Stopsley, but Hyde always had headmistresses. One explanation could be that, according to the culture of the age, Stopsley was held in higher esteem. On the other hand, while Stopsley experienced considerable growth in population, Hyde did not. Therefore it seems likely that better qualified or experienced teachers did not wish to work there. Rural schools were usually smaller than urban schools and the salaries of teachers reflected this.[117]

Fred Shoosmith recorded his first impressions of life at Stopsley (1887):

The School Registers are dirty and the entries in them concerning Admission, Birth etc. of children are few and small, and in some of the Registers, these dates are totally absent. More than this, last Quarter's Returns were left uncalculated with one exception, and that one was incorrect. Children's names are entered for the new Quarter who have left the school for a considerable period. . . . More serious than this is the absence of the Schedule for 1886 . . . it is a very serious inconvenience to me, as the 'Standard last passed' has not been entered in the School Registers. . . . The children's knowledge of Grammar and Geography is nil, V Standard boys not knowing what a noun is. . . . A great difficulty I experience in making myself understood by the children arises from their exceedingly limited vocabulary e.g. not a single child in the school knew the difference between Surname and Christian name. . . . I had the greatest difficulty in explaining what I meant by 'the roundness of the earth'. I tried the word 'curve' and still the word not understood . . . the only word known as applied to lines not straight was 'crooked' and a curve was called a 'corner'.[118]

The Board wrote to Miss Carrie Ashton from Bridgwater to say that an assistant was needed for a 'School in a hamlet two and a half miles from the town. It is "Mixed" and under a Master. The Assistant takes Infant and Standard I in a separate Class room and is also responsible for Needlework. The last is very important. Can you undertake it?'[119] The teaching of infants and responsibility for needlework were often linked, but it seems to have been taken for granted that headmasters' wives often fulfilled these roles.[120]

---

117   E/Sub M 0/4/8 Minutes of BCC Elementary Education Sub-Committee, 9 June 1922.
118   Stopsley School Logbook, 14 January 1887.
119   M/239 Letterbooks of USDL, 1 April 1891.
120   Stopsley School Logbook, 15 January 1880 and 7 May 1886.

It has already been pointed out that a teacher's life was rather insular. This is demonstrated by an entry in the Stopsley logbook: 'A lad named William Adams had been on trial this week as monitor. He was found to be unsuitable since he [spoke] broad village patois, and would never have least influence over children, as he is a playmate of theirs.'[121] The School Board minutes record requests for transfers. In April 1893, Miss Christie asked to be transferred from Leagrave to a 'town school'[122] and, in 1903, Miss Breed, Miss Cant and Miss Cowley moved to Luton Schools.[123]

The significance of 1903 was that the hamlet schools were being taken over by BEC while Luton schools were to be supervised by LEC. By working in Luton, pupil-teachers had easy access to the Luton Pupil-teacher Centre. When Miss Beard from Hyde resigned to move to Luton she gave three reasons: to gain experience in a larger infant school, as now she prefers them to older children, to gain a higher salary under the Luton scale and to enjoy several holidays in the summer 'when [Sunday] School Treats are in vogue'. Mrs Leaver, the headmistress, supported her move, which gave 'general regret but for her own interest, it is best'.[124]

The Hyde logbooks give an insight into the loneliness and frustration which was felt by headteachers who were often on their own, struggling with a lack of staff and feelings of detachment and isolation. Mrs Leaver wrote in 1907, 'another year with a new state of affairs – staff out of order – so alone' and 'still single-handed'.[125] Her last entry in the logbook notes that she was preparing to leave everything in order and concludes: 'The Last in the Old School, The First in the New, Often and often the sole one too. Finis.'[126]

Mr Breed, who was headmaster at Stopsley between 1893 and 1925, also felt the burden of trying to cope with inadequate staffing. However, all the accounts of his colourful life suggest that he knew everyone and everyone knew him, no doubt because he lived within the community.

Case studies[127]

Karolina Leaver

Mrs Leaver was born in Paris on 20 March 1861 and came from Oldham. She was a certificated teacher, but had been out of teaching for twelve and a half years when she was appointed as Infant teacher in Stopsley in June 1900. Early the following month, Mr Breed, the headmaster, went 'by chance to the School Board Offices' and was 'informed by Mr Hoyle that the Staffing Committee have recommended that Mrs Leaver be removed from Stopsley to the charge of East Hyde as Head Mistress'. Mr Breed was not best pleased because he was concerned about the welfare of the children at Stopsley. Mrs Leaver was to move at once but the Hyde logbook states

---

121   Stopsley School Logbook, 21 January 1887.
122   M/221 Minutes of USDL, 11 April 1893 and 25 April 1893.
123   Stopsley School Logbook, 5 June 1903; SD Hyde 1 Logbook of Hyde School, 30 September 1903; M/224 Minutes of USDL, 6 July 1903.
124   SD Hyde 2 Logbook of Hyde School, 1 April 1912 and 23 April 1912.
125   SD Hyde 1 Logbook of Hyde School, 1 October 1907 and 18 October 1907.
126   SD Hyde 2 Logbook of Hyde School, 27 November 1914.
127   Information from logbooks, Board minutes, BEC minutes, letterbooks and J. Dyer, *The Story of the Stopsley Schools.*

that she began her work there the following October. Her salary was to be £70 per annum 'together with the cost of a Railway Season ticket between Luton and Harpenden'. In January 1902 her salary scale was £70–75 and, in January 1903 £75–80.

In June 1901, the School Board expressed their sympathy with Mrs Leaver 'whose husband died in South Africa on the 15th ultimo'. This explains something of the sadness which shows through in some of the entries she made in the school logbook. While at Hyde, Mrs Leaver studied to pass music examinations and gained a diploma of the Associate Victoria College of Music.[128]

Two of her daughters helped at the school. Marguerite became a monitress in September 1905, but left to work with the kindergarten class at the private Luton High School. Mrs Leaver frequently mentioned the loneliness of a teacher in her position, but she certainly enjoyed the company of other teachers she met at in-service training courses at the Kindergarten and Physical Education Colleges in Bedford. Travel by train to Bedford from Hyde was very convenient.

The minutes of the LEC note that Mrs Leaver was requested to send in her resignation at the end of the summer holiday in 1914.

Elsie Cant

Elsie Cant came on probation as a monitor to Hyde School in May 1902 and was formally accepted as a pupil-teacher from 1 July 1902. The headmistress, Mrs Leaver, and the principal of the central classes for pupil-teachers were required to give a report concerning her suitability for the job. Mrs Leaver's comments on hearing one of Elsie's first object lessons were that her manner was too abrupt and that she was not 'drawing out from children themselves sufficiently'. Later she received favourable reports. For example, her lessons were 'more painstaking and instructive' and the children were more in sympathy with her.

In 1903, when Hyde School became the responsibility of BEC, Elsie was transferred to Hitchin Road Girls' School in Luton so that she could continue to attend the pupil-teacher centre in Waller Street. She also spent some time at Langley Street Girls' School. Then, although she had never been in charge of an infants' class, she returned to Hyde in May 1912 as infant mistress. Her salary as an unqualified teacher was £45. From May 1918 she was in charge of needlework.

When the headmistress, Annie Poole, resigned at the end of 1918, Elsie Cant took charge of the school until the appointment of Minnie Masters in October 1919. HMI Mr Dymond 'gave [Elsie Cant] great encouragement to do the best [she] could under difficult circumstances'. Eventually, in 1927, she became headmistress in her own right. By this time the school had been reorganized and children over eleven years of age had to move to Luton; the girls went to Langley Street and the boys to Waller Street. The following year one of her pupils, Amy Radford, was a successful candidate in the examination for Luton Modern School and an entry in the logbook claims that some of the credit should go to the school where Amy had been 'well taught'.

As headmistress Miss Cant was required to write in the logbooks and her

---

128   See Chapter Six.

22. Dorothy Thorne (standing) and Miss Mantz at Stopsley School c.1914 [JD]

23. Ethel Toyer, standing beside Mr Breed, Stopsley School c.1918 [JD]

accounts of the difficulties she experienced during the Second World War make fascinating reading.

Dorothy Thorne

Dorothy Thorne was the daughter of the head gardener at Putteridge Bury and was born on 22 November 1899. She started at Stopsley School in November 1911 as a monitress and immediately gained the approval of Mr Breed, the headmaster. He said that 'during the whole of November I have been hampered for want of assistance but by the continual help of Dorothy Thorne I have got on surprisingly well for order and attention to work'. Again, in December 1913, he said 'I am glad to say the work done throughout the school reflects the greatest credit on the intelligent and hearty service done by [amongst others] Dorothy Thorne, monitress.'

In 1915, she was awarded a Monitress Scholarship for two years of tuition, free books and travelling fees of £6 10s 0d per year. She continued to teach at Stopsley at a salary of £10 per annum. After two years studying part-time at Bedford she came out second in the course and was accepted for a special short kindergarten course. In October 1917, she was appointed assistant teacher at Stopsley at £65 per year. She was eighteen at the time.[129]

In September 1917, she sat the Oxford Senior Local Examination, which qualified her to go to a teacher training college. Dorothy Thorne is a good example of a girl who took a different route into teaching when many students were becoming bursars after following a course at a secondary school. In July 1918, Mr Breed paid her another compliment saying 'of the kindly co-operation of Miss Thorne for so many months I cannot speak too highly'.

Miss Thorne left Stopsley School in the summer of 1919 to start a two-year course at Hockerill Teacher Training College in Bishop's Stortford with a grant of £100 from the Chew's Foundation, but came back to Stopsley to teach on a temporary basis during her Christmas and summer holidays. In October 1921, she finished college, coming fourth out of sixty students in the examinations with a 'distinction' in English and 'merit' in botany, needlework, drill and handwork.

Ethel Toyer

Ethel Toyer was born on 13 March 1905 and took up a post as monitress at Stopsley School under Mr C. Breed on 1 May 1919 and was eighth on the monitors' list in July 1920. In 1922, she became a member of staff at Stopsley Infant School under Miss G. Clarke. The following December she took her Preliminary Certificate Examination and passed history with distinction. She worked for a time in Leicester, but eventually became headmistress at Lilley, a village two miles from Stopsley.

Children

Samuel Deane from Stopsley examined the children over seven years of age as soon as he took up the headship in 1879.

---

[129] J. Dyer, *The Story of the Stopsley Schools*, p. 15.

Table 29. Children in Stopsley examined in Reading, Writing and Arithmetic 1879[130]

Reading

Could not read a word of one syllable	32
Could not read a single letter of the alphabet	11
Could read a word of one syllable	8
Could read a word of two syllables	10
Could read a word of three syllables	5
Total	66

Writing

Could not write a mono-syllable	22
Could not form a single letter of the alphabet	22
Could write a word of one syllable	18
Could write a word of two syllables	3
Could write a word of three syllables	1
Total	66

Arithmetic

Could not add 29+42+13	42
Could not make a figure	12
Number of children who worked the above addition sum correctly	12
Total	66

In 1882, James Cooper, the next headmaster, observed that he was still labouring to improve the brainpower of the scholars: 'Their want of intelligence is to be accounted for by many or rather all of them, never having moved beyond the bounds of this and the neighbouring parishes. Not one boy had seen a fishing rod before today.'[131] The lack of interest by both parents and children is a recurring theme in the Hyde and Stopsley logbooks, especially in the early years of this study. The following year Mr Cooper complained that

> all the work of the school suffers from the extreme opposition our work endures from the parents. The attendance is bad and any species of discipline that is exercised brings the parents down to the school, and the noisy and disgraceful manner in which they behave is a real hindrance to our work. The children know the feelings of their friends and take advantage of them. I am often troubled by someone shouting into the school, and calling all manner of disgraceful names both at me and the School Board, and on enquiring the cause of the uproar, I find that this unseemly behaviour is produced by my having punished some child by keeping him in or whipping him, of which act I know nothing until they inform me of it.'[132]

---

[130] Stopsley School Logbook, 10 November 1879.
[131] Ibid., 21 February 1882.
[132] Ibid., 5 October 1883.

The situation at Stopsley appears to have improved.[133] However, very little seems to have changed at Hyde. Mrs Darby, who took up the headship in December 1914, wrote

> Arithmetic deplorable. There is not the slightest attempt at reasoning. Standards I and II just answer at random dividing or multiplying just as they think they will . . . the children seem lazy and indifferent. It will take some time to rouse their interest in their work and make them think for themselves . . . Composition is equally bad . . . the children seem to have few ideas to express on any subject.[134]

Her initial enthusiasm very soon waned, no doubt on account of poor attendance by the children and travelling difficulties for herself, and she resigned in September 1916. Her successor, Jane Watkins, resigned the following May. The next headmistress, Annie Poole, complained, as her predecessors had done, 'I find children possess very little knowledge on even ordinary subjects . . . needlework chaotic.'[135] She resigned at the end of 1918.

There were practical problems. In the early days of this study Stopsley children were often living in extreme poverty.[136] This had a direct influence on the children's attitude to schooling as was demonstrated when free dinners were given to about 120 children in the village; 'the brightening and cheering effect of which has testified to their great need'.[137]

A succession of headteachers was concerned with the lack of cleanliness which they found. Mr Johnston 'had to speak repeatedly to children who [came] with dirty faces and hands'[138] and 'to several of the children respecting dirty habits and uncleanliness'.[139] Mr Breed noted that he was 'just entering on a campaign to eradicate [dirty children's] unfitness for school'.[140] He notified the National Society for the Prevention of Cruelty to Children (NSPCC) when one boy managed to pick twenty-nine lice off his brother's hair and jacket.[141] A mother came to complain after a similar incident and Mr Breed was able to point out that she also had lice crawling over her sleeve.[142]

Curriculum

The basic curriculum in rural schools followed the same pattern as the curriculum in urban schools. Specific information is given in Chapter Four and Chapter Seven. Rural schools were at a disadvantage in some respects, however. For example, it was difficult to provide cookery classes. In 1908, HMI Miss K. Manley 'orally reported as to the instruction in Cookery given in this County with a view to requesting the Committee to increase the number of Cookery Centres under their control'.[143]

---

133   Ibid., 13 November 1918.
134   SD Hyde 2 Logbook of Hyde School, 1 December 1914.
135   Ibid., 27 July 1917.
136   Stopsley School Logbook, 10 November 1884.
137   Ibid., 12 January 1891.
138   Ibid., 26 March 1884.
139   Ibid., 25 February 1885.
140   Ibid., 15 February 1898.
141   Ibid., 12 July 1904.
142   Ibid., 9 December 1912.
143   E/Sub M 0/4/3 Minutes of BCC Elementary Education Sub-Committee, 11 December 1908.

One of the advantages of rural communities was the opportunity to learn from nature. In October 1899 at Hyde, 'a boy brought a live hedge-hog' and 'another boy caught a live mole in the playground'.[144] In 1905, it was noted that the children went on a monthly ramble and saw 'many interesting things' on the way.[145] Mr Breed at Stopsley was also eager to explore the surrounding countryside. As has already been mentioned, rural schools were ideal centres when gardening became popular.

The perceived difference between urban and rural schools is indicated by the financial provision allocated for school libraries. No doubt the size of the schools was a major consideration, but the fact that Hyde is omitted demonstrates that rural children were not treated as equals.

> That where any Boys' or Girls' School belonging to this Board the sum of £1 or more than £1 shall be raised by the Teachers or Scholars of the said School the Board shall allocate an equal sum in accordance with the Table next following the total sum to be expended in the purchase of Books for the said Schools' Libraries.

Table 30. Grants for School Libraries[146]

Town schools	£5 0 0
Higher Grade School	£7 10 0
Leagrave and Stopsley	£2 10 0
Biscot	£2 0 0
NB: Hyde is not mentioned	
Amendment:	
Higher Grade School	£7 10 0
Board Schools within the Borough of Luton	£5 0 0
Leagrave, Biscot and Stopsley	£2 0 0
NB: Again, Hyde is not mentioned	

Evening schools were set up, for example in Stopsley. With the permission of the managers, Thomas Tennant, headmaster, opened a 'night school' for boys 'which was attended by 16 first night and 25 second night'.[147] The following week a girls' 'night school' was opened with an attendance of twenty-one.[148] In 1877, James Brown, another headmaster, 'posted notices for opening on the 3rd December a night school for males and females'.[149] This day turned out to be very wet, but six boys 'of neglected education' attended.[150] The following day was also very wet, but two girls arrived for their classes.[151] The following week's attendance was eleven boys and two girls.[152]

[144] SD Hyde 1 Logbook of Hyde School, 31 October 1899.
[145] Ibid., 6 April 1905.
[146] M/222 Minutes of USDL, 11 February 1896, amended 10 March 1896.
[147] Stopsley School Logbook, 5 March 1875.
[148] Ibid., 12 March 1875.
[149] Ibid., 1 December 1877.
[150] Ibid., 3 December 1877.
[151] Ibid., 4 December 1877.
[152] Ibid., 10 December 1877.

In 1895 Mr Breed started an evening school with twenty-two children, thirteen of whom were 'old school-boys'. They were 'studying agriculture with an addition of Longfellow's poems for reading and writing occasionally'.[153] Mr Breed also wanted to teach French.

> Word building first interested them during reading lessons. For the boys it may be useful if they ever enter Luton warehouses, and it is to me a great experiment towards enticing them to stay longer at school, and above all towards starting an evening class for the whole village for those who have just left the day school.[154]

Apparently the Board disapproved. Whether or not Mr Breed persisted, which would have been consistent with his dogged character, is not clear. Whatever ensued, Mr Breed was not happy to let the matter rest for he later wrote 'Mr King Johnson made a friendly call. He is an old boy, a cowman's son dealing in French wines in his own business. He is my outstanding witness re the teaching of French, vetoed here years ago because "of no use to rurals" '.[155] It does appear that Mr Breed's evening classes were appreciated. He wrote:

> I was much touched this evening by receiving at the lads' Saturday 'social' a very nice umbrella from the scholars who attended the evening school this winter. To think that my rough and ready Stopsley lads could be so kind to me! But I knew they enjoyed the winter evening lessons.[156]

Conclusion

It is not possible to describe a 'typical rural school' as opposed to a 'typical urban school'. Both were bound by government legislation, so the curriculum would have been similar. Nor is there any such thing as a typical rural school, which can be demonstrated by the fact the Hyde School seems consistently to have been accorded less status than the larger Stopsley School. However, there were significant differences between rural and urban schools. For instance, the hamlets were more isolated and this caused considerable problems for both staff and pupils as they struggled, often in snow and ice, to make their way to and from school. Consequently, attendance suffered. Other factors affected attendance, in particular the demands of agriculture. A perusal of the logbooks reflects the frustration of headteachers who had to cope with these problems and also the sense of isolation that they often felt.

It has not been possible to assess the qualifications and experience of all the teachers in the hamlet schools. However, as better-qualified teachers usually applied for posts in larger schools with higher salary scales it is probably safe to make the generalization that the smaller the school, the less qualified the staff. As the population in the hamlets grew, the schools became larger and attitudes towards them changed.

In 1918, Mr Breed believed that 'a new type of child' was attending the schools[157] and, in 1928, Miss Cant recorded that the first child from Hyde had been

153 Ibid., 29 October 1895.
154 Ibid., 19 January 1894.
155 Ibid., 25 January 1921.
156 Ibid., 4 April 1903.
157 Stopsley School Logbook, 13 November 1918.

allocated a place at the Luton Modern School. She said: 'now others in the village are anxious for their children to do likewise. This was an exceptional child of course but she had been well taught here.'[158] The hamlets had said farewell to the poor and struggling rural schools which had existed in the days before the arrival of the School Board.

---

[158] Hyde 2 Logbook of Hyde School, 8 November 1928.

Chapter Nine

Learning and Living[1]

This chapter looks at the choices made by parents who did not wish to educate their daughters in non-denominational schools or who, for social reasons, chose to send their daughters to independent schools. Informal opportunities were also open to women and girls who were prepared to use their own initiatives, attributes which were very much in keeping with the character of people in Luton. Skills learnt in the home were also valuable, especially in the context of the hat industry. The contribution of these informal types of education was significant, but information is limited because very few records were kept. They are discussed here under the heading *Learning and Living*, which Harrison describes as learning 'in terms of social purpose rather than institutional form'.[2]

The first sections outline the provision of the Church and Nonconformists in elementary and Sunday schools. In the early days covered by this study the National Society supported New Town Street (St Paul's), St Matthew's, Queen Square, Stopsley, Church Street and Christ Church schools. The Quakers also provided substantially for the town: the endowed Langley Street School remained until the early days of the Board and independent provision on a small scale has been noted. However, their major contribution was probably the adult schools, which offered a similar kind of self-help to that found in the Sunday schools and appear to have been well supported. According to Dony, the Methodists set up schools in High Town and Chapel Street and also the Crown and Anchor School.[3]

Adult education has been taken to mean not only education for adults but, as has been suggested by Gordon, Aldrich and Dean, as education for people who were not attending school on a formal, regular or full-time basis[4] and for cultural, general, social, community or political interests.[5] Several examples of this type of informal education, springing from personal or group initiatives are to be found. In the early days of the twentieth century, as employment prospects for girls began to widen, there was a need for secretarial training. Many girls with determination and initiative wanted to turn their backs on the local hat industry and move into office work[6]

---

1   This title is taken from J.F.C. Harrison, *Learning and Living 1790–1960: A Study in the History of the English Adult Education Movement* (RKP, 1963).
2   Ibid., p. xi. These two aspects, social purpose and institutional form, cannot easily be separated.
3   J.G. Dony, *A History of Education in Luton* (LMAG, 1970), p. 59.
4   P. Gordon, R. Aldrich and D. Dean, *Education and Policy in England in the Twentieth Century* (The Woburn Press, 1991), p. 212.
5   Ibid., p. 228.
6   According to Mrs Vera Robson, girls in the 1920s and 1930s fell into three main categories: most girls went into the hat industry; those who had been to the secondary school worked in banks, offices, libraries

but it appears that the evening classes held at the local secondary school did not meet this demand and Luton girls learnt their skills in private commercial schools. It is interesting to note that, by 1912, a Miss M.N. Moody was on the Committee of the Luton Shorthand Writers' Association.[7]

Many parents who considered themselves to be above the working classes wanted independent schooling for their daughters. There are records from a number of these young ladies' establishments and in some cases details of ethos and curriculum are given. There were also schools in nearby towns which were made accessible by the railway or provided board. In time, the manufacturing and business classes came to accept that the local day secondary school suited their needs and the independent sector lost out to it. The last section of this chapter will consider these independent schools.

While it has been relatively easy to locate material for the other chapters in this book, evidence concerning the denominational, adult and independent schools has been harder to find because it is in the nature of these independent providers, who were often not answerable to a higher authority, to leave fewer records than Board and Local Authority schools. Some of the National school logbooks are available and those from New Town Street (St Paul's) and St Matthew's Girls' have been examined with a view to assessing the involvement of the local Church and the diocese. The adult schools did keep some records. Much of the evidence concerning the independent schools has been obtained from contemporary advertisements, but Luton year books and almanacs have been invaluable since they often note the current educational situation and the names of schools or private tutors as businesses. There are sometimes longer articles on specific educational themes or about notable individuals.

Denominational schools

Church of England schools

Although Luton was predominantly a Nonconformist town there were also dedicated followers of the Church who resented the non-denominational Board schools and who believed that the provision of schools which taught their doctrines and catechism remained important. The 1870 (Forster) Educational Act allowed this dual system to exist: there 'were to be two types of school, different not only in the spirit of their religious teaching, but different also in their control and management'.[8] The Board schools could demand adequate funding by presenting an account or precept to the town but, although the Church schools received government grants, their resources were more limited. It seemed likely that teachers would move into the Board schools, which were better resourced, but it has not been possible to find evidence from the minutes or logbooks to suggest that this happened. There were cases of monitresses transferring,[9] but no definite trends

and the professions; girls who had done well in the elementary schools and wanted to improve their qualifications were 'on their own' and paid for private secretarial training.

[7]   *Luton News Almanac (1912)*, p. 69.

[8]   M. Cruikshank, *Church and State in English Education 1870 to the Present Day* (Macmillan, 1963), p. 33.

[9]   M/211 Logbook of NTS, 27 November 1891.

24. The National School in Church Street [LM]

have been found. The Church continued to open schools even after the establishment of the Board: St Matthew's in 1874, New Town Street in 1875 and St Mary's Hall in 1885.[10]

From the early days of the Board, all Luton schools received visits from a variety of officials: local managers, visiting officers, factory inspectors and HMI. Church schools, however, were also under the supervision of the local vicar and diocesan inspectors. The formidable Vicar of Luton, James O'Neill, who believed that all schooling should be the responsibility of the Church, was a regular visitor but comments in the logbooks show that he did not always arrive in a sympathetic frame of mind.[11] Clergymen went into the schools to instruct the children according to the tenets of their beliefs. For example, the children of St Matthew's Girls' School were taught Church catechism, liturgy and litany.[12] Classes 'for Holy Scripture' were held[13] and in March 1893 the Reverend A. Webb gave 'a very interesting missionary address'.[14] An annual Diocesan Report on the New Town Street School noted that Walter W. Williams was 'glad that the children are taught the Creed, the Lord's Prayer and the Commandments. This is the Church's rule for the children as soon as they shall be able to learn.'[15]

---

10   A complete list can be found in J.G. Dony, *A History of Education in Luton*, p. 59.
11   M/211 Logbook of NTS 17 June 1891, 6 July 1891 and 14 November 1893.
12   L/1/2/54 Logbook of SMG, 15 October 1882, 12 November 1888 and 21 March 1889.
13   Ibid., 25th November 1892.
14   Ibid., 8 March 1893.
15   M/211 Logbook of NTS, 25 July 1904.

As has been noted in Chapter Four, religious differences caused considerable acrimony. These feelings seem to have mellowed over the years and the two systems began to co-operate, although the religious element in the Church schools remained strong. In 1876, there was 'some discussion concerning the relative efficiency of denominational and Board schools' and the Clerk of the Board was asked to write to the managers of the various denominational schools to request 'that they would supply this Board with copies of the Documents No 17a containing the Inspector's Report upon the last examinations with a view to the same being laid before the Public'.[16] Only one National school, Christ Church, complied.[17] Another 'refused to make a return and no answers [were] obtained from the others'. The Board then asked the Department of Education to supply the necessary information, if it was within their powers.[18] The minutes do not make clear what the outcome was but, the following year, further attempts were made to improve relations. The Board would 'be glad to meet as early as possible the managers of the Denominational Schools to confer upon any question affecting the harmonious working of the different schools'.[19] Conferences were held from time to time and there were hopes that the 'administrative system lately adopted by the School Board shall have full and due effect in securing the regular and orderly attendance of all children in the parish of Luton'.[20]

Co-operation between the schools increased over the years. When the Luton Pupil-teacher Centre was opened, students from the denominational schools were able to attend provided that their costs were paid.[21] Salary scales had varied but, after the Balfour Act, teachers in denominational schools were paid by the local authorities according to their set scales and the differentiation disappeared. The Clerk to the School Board was asked to obtain information from the headteachers of voluntary schools in Luton 'as to their several qualifications; and also obtain particulars from other Boards as to payments made to Teachers under the several Scales in operation with them; and also whether alterations (when made) are retrospective'.[22]

In 1903, the LEC took over responsibility for the running of the non-provided schools and interviewed the managers of New Town Street, Christ Church, Queen Square and St Mary's Hall to consider a scheme to implement the new arrangements.[23] The minutes from these schools were to be made available, any endowments considered,[24] buildings up-graded,[25] and fees abolished.[26] A number of Nonconformist rate-payers were angry that non-provided schools were to receive funding from the rates and rebelled by refusing to pay their dues. Some were prose-

---

16 M/217 Minutes of LSB, 22 February 1876.
17 Ibid., 7 March 1876.
18 Ibid., 21 March 1876.
19 Ibid., 3 April 1877.
20 Ibid., 15 June 1877.
21 M/221 Minutes of USDL, 13 March 1894; M/222 Minutes of USDL, 11 January 1898; M/223 Minutes of USDL, 10 January 1899 and 12 June 1900.
22 M/224 Minutes of USDL, 6 January 1903.
23 M/226 Minutes of LEC, 29 September 1903 and 13 October 1903.
24 Ibid., 8 December 1903.
25 Ibid., 13 October 1903 and 24 November 1903.
26 Ibid., 24 November 1903 and 8 December 1903.

cuted, but there are no records of any Luton people being sent to prison.[27] The LEC received a letter from the Passive Resistance League and the Luton and District Free Church Council asking them to 'cease to provide for the cost of giving religious instruction in non-council schools'. The Education Committee responded by giving notice 'that as and from the first day of November, 1906, no salary will be paid by the Education Authority to any teacher in the said Non-Council Schools for giving denominational teaching therein'.[28]

Quaker schools

The Quaker presence in Luton was significant, with families such as the Greens and Browns often linked by business interests.[29] William Bigg, also a Quaker, became the first Chairman of the School Board and, in 1892, the Board recorded an obituary to Henry Brown who had been a 'zealous worker in the cause of Education and the sincere friend of Teachers'.[30] The Society of Friends had set up a 'British School' in Langley Street in 1836 for children whose parents did not wish them to attend Church schools and, the following year, an evening school for girls was established in the same building.[31] Mr Daniel Brown funded the Infant School in Langley Street and a private school run by Miss Phoebe Drewett (c.1876) has also been noted. It was a mixed school with six boarders where music was one of the subjects taught.[32]

At the first meeting of the School Board on 5 March 1874, a letter was received from Mr Henry Brown Sen. offering to transfer the tenancy of the Langley Street School, known as the Old British School, to the Board. This was to be a complicated transaction because of the legalities involved in dissolving a tontine. Meanwhile the Langley Street Infants' School premises were leased for six months.[33] The British and Foreign School Society was consulted and the Board also sought the approval of HMI Mr Johnstone.[34] In July, the Board negotiated with Mrs Lydia Brown, widow of Daniel, for the purchase of the school house and premises[35] and the school was eventually transferred to the Board.[36]

Adult schools

The Adult School Movement reflected the ideals of the Sunday schools. In their early days both aimed to teach the labouring poor to read the Bible, but changed the emphasis after the 1870 Education Act when school boards had to ensure that all children received a basic education.[37] The adult schools were originally set up by leading Quaker families, but became non-denominational and extended their scope

---

27 J.G. Dony, *A History of Education in Luton*, p. 46; G. Vowles, *A Century of Achievement* (BCC, 2003), p. 32.

28 M/226 Minutes of LEC, 25 September 1906.

29 S. Bunker, *Strawopolis Luton Transformed 1840–1876* (BHRS Vol. 78, 1999), pp. 141–142, 251–252.

30 M/220 Minutes of USDL, 10 May 1892.

31 W. Austin, *History of Luton and Its Hamlets* (The County Press, 1928) Vol. 1, p. 136.

32 J. Lea, 'E.V. Lucas and Luton', *Bedfordshire Magazine* Vol. 15, No. 37 (Summer 1956), p. 204.

33 M/216 Minutes of LSB, 17 March 1874 and 12 May 1874.

34 Ibid., 16 June 1874, 23 June 1874 and 22 September 1874.

35 Ibid., 21 July 1874 and 28 July 1874.

36 Ibid., 13 July 1875.

37 A. Hall, *The Adult School Movement in the Twentieth Century* (University of Nottingham, 1985), p. 21.

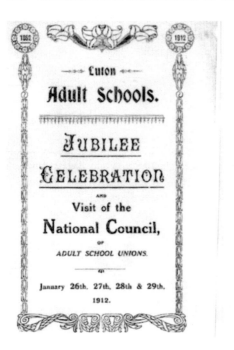

Programme of the Celebrations.

SATURDAY, JANUARY 27th.

Visit to Sir Julius Wernher's Conservatories at Luton Hoo.

To start from Church Street School, at 1.30 p.m., under the direction of Henry Kilby.

DALLOW ROAD "AT HOME"

from 2 to 4.30 p.m.

Music and Games.   ::   Light Refreshments.

Tea and Reception of the National Council

in the Assembly Hall, Church Street, at 5.

Tickets Sixpence, from all School Secretaries.

Followed by a CONFERENCE at 6.30.

SUNDAY, JANUARY 28th.

9.0 a.m.   MEN'S SCHOOLS:

Church Street,
Waller Street,
Bury Park,
Dallow Road.

2.15 p.m.   WOMEN'S SCHOOLS:

Church Street,
Castle Street,
Dallow Road.

(National Councillors will be present at all the above Schools).

Fireside Gatherings

in the Afternoon from 3 to 6.

MASS MEETING

in the ASSEMBLY HALL, at 6.45.

Speakers:

WILLIAM CHARLES BRAITHWAITE, B.A., LL.B.

and others.

At 6.30, SELECTIONS by the MASSED CHOIRS and during the evening.

"An Evening Hymn" (Blumenthal)
"The Peace of God" (Bluebery)
"Moonlight" (Eaton Faning)

COLLECTION.

MONDAY, JANUARY 29th.

6.0 p.m.   PUBLIC TEA in the Assembly Hall.

Admission by Ticket only   Sixpence.

To be followed by a

Great Jubilee Gathering

IN THE PLAIT HALL,

at 7.30.

Chairman:

THE MAYOR OF LUTON,

Alderman H. O. Williams, Esq., J.P.,

accompanied by THE MAYORESS, who will present

CERTIFICATES.

Three Ten Minute Addresses by

EDWARD SMITH, J.P.   EDWIN GILBERT,

President of the Midland Union   Organising Secretary of the N.C.

ROBERT E. GIBBONS,

President of the Somerset Union.

OLD ENGLISH DANCES by the GIRLS' SCHOOL.

SELECTIONS by the MASSED CHOIRS.

Conductor   ·   Mr. Walter Harts.

"Four Jolly Smiths"   "An Evening Hymn"
"Moonlight."

COLLECTION

25. Programme for the Adult Schools Jubilee Celebration 1912 [LM]

to provide a broader education covering historical, political and literary as well as religious topics.[38] The movement later became known as the National Adult School Union[39] and the *Luton Year Book (1908)* described its work in Luton.

> The Luton Friends' Adult School, a purely undenominational effort, is an institution to be proud of, for it possesses both numbers and influence, and it fills a most useful place in the life of the town. Opened in 1862, within the walls of the old National School building at the lower end of Church street, the membership has slowly grown up to a total of more than 900 men and women with branch schools in the Castle-Street Meeting House, and in the Council School premises in Waller-street . . . Since the beginning of June, 1905, Adult Schools for men and others for women have been commenced at Leagrave, Slip End, Dunstable, and Markyate; while at Stopsley and Bury Park (Luton) Adult Schools for men are also actively at work, and filling a long-felt need.[40]

The adult school was probably the most significant contribution by the Society of Friends to the education of people in Luton. Rowntree and Binns[41] refer to Luton as a town 'where people are largely engaged in home industries and have considerable control over their hours of work'. The school opened in 1862 with two adult classes held on Sunday mornings between 9a.m. and 10.15a.m. No scholars under sixteen years of age were accepted.[42] William H. Brown was to be the treasurer and Benjamin Seebohm to be the secretary.[43] The classes were for the instruction of 'young men and women of the more neglected class in Reading, Writing and the Holy Scriptures' who were to be admitted at the discretion of the Superintendent.[44] The first half hour was devoted to learning to read and write and the rest to reading the Bible and Scripture lessons.[45]

The first teachers' meeting was held at the home of Mrs Lydia Brown, 48 Park Street, on 4 July 1862 and it was recorded that thirty-two men and forty-two women had been admitted.[46] At the end of the first year there were forty-nine men and eighty-two women, which shows that the adult school initially appealed to more women.[47] As the numbers increased, the women decided to meet in the afternoons.[48] By 1883, 1968 men and 1,504 women had been admitted[49] and, by 1892, 3,260 men and 2,041 women had been enrolled.[50] At first classes were held on

---

[38] Ibid., ch. 1.
[39] A. Hall, *The Adult School Movement*, p. 208; *Luton Year Book and Directory (1916)*, p. 49: 'The Adult School is non-sectarian in character and includes men and women of all shades of belief.'
[40] *The Luton and District Year Book and Directory (1908)*, pp. 139–140.
[41] J.W. Rowntree and H.B. Binns, *A History of the Adult School Movement* (Reprint: University of Nottingham, 1985), p. 32.
[42] X 563/63 *Jubilee Souvenir of Luton Adult School 1862–1912*, p. 5.
[43] Ibid., p. 7.
[44] Ibid., p. 6.
[45] Ibid., p. 10; A. Hall, *The Adult School Movement*, p. 37. The first half-hour later became a time to discuss a 'wide range of human interest: scientific, social, historical, literary and others'.
[46] X 563/63 Friends Adult School *Jubilee Souvenir*, p. 8.
[47] Ibid., p. 10.
[48] Ibid., p. 11.
[49] Ibid., p. 17.
[50] Ibid., p. 21.

Sundays, but over the years activities took place on other days and clubs were formed, so that the social life began to mirror that of the Sunday schools. There was a savings club,[51] a temperance society[52] and an excursion fund.[53] Perhaps recalling the days when girls liked to listen to stories as they plaited,[54] the ladies in dress-making and knitting classes enjoyed hearing an interesting book read aloud as they sewed.[55]

Table 31. Annual Report of the Friends' first-day adult school[56]

	End of 1903			*End of 1904*		
	M	*F*	*Total*	*M*	*F*	*Total*
Number of teachers	15	5	20	18	5	23
Membership of classes (including teachers)	598	313	911	620	310	930
Average attendance	346	202	548	350	200	550
Admitted since last report	114	68	182	118	77	195
Left since last report	98	77	175	96	80	176
Admitted since 1862	4,728	2,900	7,628	4,846	2,977	7,823

	End of 1922			*End of 1923*		
	M	*F*	*Total*	*M*	*F*	*Total*
Membership of classes (including teachers)	209	249	458	177	230	407
Average attendance	125	145	270	95	141	236
Admitted since last report	10	34	44	16	15	31
Left since last report	55	65	120	48	34	82
Admitted since 1862			10,535			10,566

Membership figures for 1912 were 976, including teachers.[57]

The figures in Table 31 show that women attended the adult schools in considerable numbers. In the early part of the twentieth century more men than women were enrolling but, by the 1920s, numbers were reversed although membership in general was falling. This was in contrast to national figures, which show that there were more male members than female.[58] Although conclusions are hard to draw, the change in proportion between males and females attending these classes may reflect

---

51   Ibid., p. 16.
52   Ibid., p. 17.
53   Ibid., p. 19.
54   'Amongst the Bonnet-Sewers', *The Quiver* (1884), p. 276.
55   X 563/63 Friends Adult School *Jubilee Souvenir*, p. 19.
56   X 563/49. Annual Report of the Friends First-Day Adult School.
57   *Luton News Almanac (1913)*, p. 52.
58   A. Hall, *The Adult School Movement*, p. 213. National figures for 1922–1923 were 28,412 men and 22,349 women.

some aspects of life in the town. With the arrival of new industries the economy was becoming more structured and more men were becoming principal wage-earners. It may therefore be that it was decreased interest by the men rather than new interest by the women which affected these figures.

There were classes for women at Castle Street, Church Street and Bury Park where studies included the life and works of Francis of Assisi, James Russell Lowell and Dr Elizabeth Blackwell. Outings, concerts, socials, visits to summer schools and to the infirmary were organized. The lesson *Handbook* sought to regularize the discussions which became a distinctive feature of the First-Half-Hour[59] after schooling became compulsory. It was used at the Sunday classes in the Dallow Road School for women. The Wednesday classes held there aimed to 'stimulate interest in literature and art'.[60]

Private enterprise and initiative
Information about the different ways in which Luton girls could use their time and energies, other than in formal schooling, is limited. It is clear that women and girls did find ways to occupy their minds although some opportunities would no doubt have been closed to working-class girls. Societies, particularly those run by political parties, are noted in the Luton year books. The meetings of the League of Young Liberals were 'of an educative nature, consisting of lectures and debates'[61] and, as Miss Rebecca Higgins gave talks to the local Liberal Association,[62] it may be safe to assume that some of its members were women. A Mechanics' Institute, which existed between 1845 and c.1882,[63] had a library and reading room and was open to men and women. The charge for full membership was 2s 6d (12½p) and for evening readers 1s 6d (7½p), while women paid 1s (5p). Bunker mentions a Women's Literary Institution which was established in 1859.[64]

A free library was opened in 1883 but the 'supply of books was very meagre'.[65] This opinion concurs with that of the Report on the Employment of Women 1893, which was concerned that 'the so-called library seemed . . . a collection of unreadable and worthless books and therefore the refusal of the managers to lend them out hardly amounts to a grievance'. The report also noted that 'no special provision for the intellectual improvement of young men and women seems to be made in the town'.[66] The number of visitors to the library, presumably in 1899, was 3,856 males and 1,222 females.[67] In 1902, the library carried twenty-one daily, fifty-three

[59] X563/49 Annual Report; 1986/70 *Luton Adult Schools Jubilee Celebration and Visit of the National Council of Adult School Unions*, January 1912. Information about the *Handbook* can be found in A. Hall, *The Adult School Movement*, pp. 98 and 214.
[60] 1986/70. Adult Schools Jubilee Celebration.
[61] *Luton Year Book (1916)*, p. 63.
[62] *Luton and District Year Book and Almanack (1904)*, p. 99. Also see notes on R. Higgins in Chapter Seven.
[63] W. Austin, *The History of Luton and Its Hamlets*, pp. 147 and 199.
[64] S. Bunker, *Strawopolis*, p. 177.
[65] W. Austin, *The History of Luton and Its Hamlets*, p. 199.
[66] *Royal Commission on Labour, The Employment of Women (February 1893)*, p. 31. The societies that have been mentioned were active before or after 1893 when the Commission reported on its findings. There may therefore be no contradiction.
[67] *The Luton Year Book and Almanack (1900)*, p. 45.

weekly and forty-four monthly magazines.[68] A fine new library, funded by Andrew Carnegie, was opened in 1910 and served the town well until it was demolished in 1962.[69]

The Luton branch of the Workers' Educational Association (WEA) was one of the first to be founded in the Eastern District. All the original branches were in 'important urban manufacturing centres with some owing their origins to university extension as centres under the Cambridge Syndicate and others under the aegis of the Oxford Extension Delegacy viz. Luton and Wellingborough'.[70] Later, the Luton branch was described as having 'commendable characteristics'.[71] The *Luton Year Book and Directory (1912)* also saw fit to mention the establishment of the WEA, which was 'helping to develop the University Extension movement by the organiza-tion of Tutorial Classes which give opportunities for continued courses of study and joint co-operation between students and teachers'.[72] The *Luton News Almanac (1912)*[73] states that the WEA met at the Co-operative Hall and also that one of the Vice-presidents was Mrs A. Pilling, so it appears that women were involved from the early days.

Four years later, the *Luton News Almanac (1916)*[74] refers to the WEA as 'a Society of men and women united by the desire to bring within reach of every man and woman the higher education of universities. It is non-sectarian and non-polit-ical, and is composed entirely of democratic organizations.' The entry records that the Luton WEA had 'successfully carried through a four years' course on the Indus-trial History of England, under University Tutorial Class principles' and was begin-ning one on the Modern History of Europe under Mr J.G. Newlove from Ruskin College. Between 1920 and 1921, there was one WEA class, from 1921 to 1923 there were two and, in the following year, there was again just one. These were 'other classes' as opposed to 'tutorial classes'.[75]

Art and music classes

Art and music were seen to be respectable subjects for girls and women. The Luton year books listed piano teachers and there were a number of art classes held under the rules of the Science and Art Department. The art class described below is inter-esting on two counts. It indicates how such classes were run and it also refers to Miss I. Carruthers,[76] probably a member of a prominent family who came to Luton from Scotland. Emily Carruthers, another member of the family, worked hard in the cause of education as a member of the Board and the Education Committees. The woman in question was almost certainly Isabelle Carruthers, who was born in

---

[68] *The Luton and District Year Book and Almanack (1902)*, p. 61.

[69] M/227 Minutes of LEC, 29 September 1910. Children from local schools formed a guard of honour from the railway station to Mill Street for Dr Carnegie when he opened the Carnegie Library.

[70] V. Williams and G. J. White, *Adult Education and Social Purpose: A History of the WEA Eastern District 1913–1988* (WEA Eastern District, 1988), p. 6.

[71] Ibid., p. 40.

[72] *Luton Year Book and Directory(1912)*, p. 41.

[73] *Luton News Almanac (1912)*, p. 69.

[74] *Luton News Almanac (1916)*, p. 80.

[75] V. Williams and G.J. White, *Adult Education and Social Purpose*, p. 39.

[76] *Census of England and Wales (1881) Bedfordshire; Census of England and Wales (1891) Bedford-shire.*

Dunstable. Her father was Thomas Carruthers, an insurance agent from King Street. The 1891 Census refers to her as a 'painter (art teacher)'.

Miss Carruthers corresponded with William Hoyle, Clerk to the Board, concerning the running of her art class. In 1891, she was allowed the use of a room or rooms in the Higher Grade School (HGS)[77] to hold a class each Saturday night from 7p.m. to 9.30p.m. 'until the time of the Art examination in May or June next'. The following March, Hoyle sent her Form 90 (timetable of examinations), Form 264 (instructions), Form 119 for School No. 20 and Form 119 for School No. 20E.[78] Isabelle was to consult with Mr H.C. Middle from the HGS and return the forms as quickly as possible.[79] The form for the Guildford Street School seems to have needed correcting because a science teacher's name should have been entered beside geometry, which was no longer an art subject.[80] The following January, Hoyle sent a letter asking Isabelle to inform her students about the distribution of prizes.[81]

Women learning and living during the First World War

The First World War brought opportunities for women to do voluntary work. Mrs Staddon, wife of the Mayor, was the only woman on the Food Control Committee which came under attack for not being 'representative of the working class majority' and for 'double standards' over the distribution of food.[82] However, the work of the Voluntary Aid Detachment of the Red Cross met with more approval. In 1915, Miss J. Jellie led six classes on home nursing, the average attendance at which was sixty, and Dr Seymour Lloyd took the same number of classes on first aid with an average attendance of 112.[83] Similar courses were held in 1916 and 1918, but the support was not as great.[84]

Convalescent care for repatriated soldiers was given at the Bute Hospital and then at Wardown House.[85] Margaret Currie notes that there was only one qualified nurse, Sister Hobbs, and the rest of the nursing was done by the Voluntary Aid Detachment (VADs) under their Joint Commandants who were 'both wives of influential businessmen'. A hospital for officers at Luton Hoo was also mainly staffed by VADs. Currie notes that there was no record of the conflicts that arose in some hospitals between professional nurses and VADs 'to the contrary, local people still speak of the harmonious atmosphere which prevailed'.[86] The contribution which VADs made towards the war effort was acknowledged when they were represented in the 1919 Peace Procession.[87]

[77] M/239 Letterbooks of USDL, 22 January 1991.
[78] This was possibly the school in Guildford Street.
[79] M/239 Letterbooks of USDL, 12 March 1992.
[80] Ibid., 17 September 1892.
[81] Ibid., 3 January 1893.
[82] D. Craddock, *Where they Burnt the Town Hall Down* (The Book Castle, 1999), pp. 37–38 and 154.
[83] EM6 Minutes of BEC, 16 July 1915.
[84] Ibid., 14 July 1916; EM7 Minutes of BEC, 12 July 1918.
[85] D. Craddock, *Where they Burnt the Town Hall Down*, p. 34.
[86] M. Currie, *Hospitals in Luton and Dunstable: An Illustrated History* (Advance Offset (Hitchin) Ltd, 1982), pp. 63–64.
[87] D. Craddock, *Where they Burnt the Town Hall Down*, p. 155. Land Girls were also represented.

26. VAD nurses at Wardown House September 1918 [LN/LM]

Industry and commerce

Of paramount importance to girls and women were skills in hat-making. These were learnt either at home or in small family businesses.[88] Dony noted that the felt hat-makers of Cheshire belonged to a union, but showed that there would have been serious drawbacks to membership for workers in Luton. Firstly the union catered for men only and secondly 'it was a craft union recognising apprenticeship and a strict line of demarcation between skilled and unskilled operations, points which meant little in Luton'.[89] 'Experience' or, as it is described in Ainley and Rainbird, the 'mastery of a craft'[90] generally took the place of formal apprenticeships. Dony notes that there was a real difference: in Luton pieceworkers could very soon earn 'a wage comparable with that of an experienced worker, and this on a process considered skilled in Cheshire'.[91] These good workers, independently minded Luton women, were not bound by formal agreements and employers tried hard to keep them for they were 'exceedingly difficult to replace'.[92]

Luton Museum has been setting up an Oral History Archive and has evidence from women who had two-year apprenticeships in the 1920s and 1930s. These involved being taught 'everything that was in the factory': fetching and carrying, putting in linings, making bows, machining, millinery and finishing.[93] Some may have been informal apprenticeships, but papers have been found for Lilian Scott who began a formal apprenticeship in 1915.[94] Luton had become an industrial town and it seems likely that the idea of 'apprenticeships', even though they may have been informal, was being accepted.

Women in Luton ran family businesses, having no doubt learnt their skills as they grew up. This was also learning by experience. There were other girls and women from different backgrounds who looked for opportunities to gain commercial expertise in the changing employment situation.

In April 1895, the Luton Chamber of Commerce, on the proposal of one of the members, F.W. Beck, advocated a system of sound commercial training 'based on the one run by the London Chamber of Commerce'.[95] It was expected that most of the work would be undertaken at the HGS.[96] For the first year the Chamber offered to bear all the expenses of the examination and charge no entrance fees. It also provided prizes of £1, £2 and £3 for general proficiency in the first examinations, to be taken in July 1896. There were also to be subject prizes for single subjects. Successes were to be marked by 'joint certificates of the London and Luton Chambers of Commerce'.[97]

---

[88]   J.G. Dony, *A History of the Straw Hat Industry* (Gibbs, Bamforth & Co., 1942), p. 105.

[89]   Ibid., p. 147.

[90]   P. Ainley and H. Rainbird, ed., *Apprenticeship, Towards a New Paradigm of Learning* (Kogan Page, 1999), p. 4.

[91]   J.G. Dony, *A History of the Straw Hat Industry*, p. 177.

[92]   Ibid.

[93]   Luton Museum Oral History Archive: Violet Vernon (started work in 1926) and Doris Green (began in 1930).

[94]   LMAG Archive on working practices in Luton. Articles of Apprenticeship Lilian Scott 25 November 1915: Schedule The Factory and Workshop Act Lilian Scott 29th December 1915.

[95]   *Luton News*, 25 April 1895.

[96]   This suggested that most of the work would be directed at boys.

[97]   *Luton Reporter*, 3 September 1895.

The following May, Miss Bone reported that forty pupils, with five machines between them, had joined her sewing machine class. The average attendance at each class had been six. Since Christmas that number had fallen off 'owing to the pupils getting busy with their different branches of work'.[98] She noted that conduct and progress had been very satisfactory, 'some of the pupils showing great skill and promise to become clever workers'.[99]

Mr F.N. Shearmur, teacher of machine construction, said that he had given instruction to thirty-two of Miss Bone's pupils but regretted 'the absence of two of the principal machines in use in the town (viz.) the hand stitch, for which there is a great demand at the present time'. He hoped that the committee 'could remove this restriction' so that the large number who wished to attend his classes would not be disappointed.[100]

Miss Finlinson taught the 'domestic sewing-machine class (cutting out, etc.)' and reported thirteen students. Each student first cut out the garment in paper and then in material 'after which she puts it together as far as possible with machine. Very few of the students knew anything of the domestic sewing machine, so time had to be devoted to learning the same.' At the end of the course was 'a sort of examination' in which students made up a child's garment to demonstrate what they had learnt. Thirty-one 'persons' joined the commercial book-keeping class; it would be nice to know if any of them were female.[101]

Since these classes under Beck's scheme would have competed with continuation classes run by the School Board and others provided by the Bedfordshire County Council (BCC) Technical Instruction Committee, it is not surprising that they were unsuccessful and were only offered for one year. According to Bunker, the Chamber of Commerce then assumed a promotional role by offering prizes for technical achievements.[102]

Very little information has been found concerning commercial training for girls in Luton although there were opportunities for boys: shorthand lessons were given in the Waller Street Higher Grade School[103] and the evening classes at the secondary school also seem to have been for boys. During the First World War, the government asked the Bedfordshire Education Committe (BEC) to train girls to take the place of boys who had joined the forces but, although steps had apparently been taken, no relevant information has been found.[104] Conversations with women who can remember the early part of the twentieth century indicate that there was a real desire to learn shorthand and typing in order to escape from the hat trade, but the same conversations reveal that the only practical way to achieve this was by using personal initiative and funding.

Relevant to this theme is an interesting comment by Mr David Smith, the local missioner of the industrial Christian Fellowship, which was reported in the local

---

98   The hat season.
99   *Luton Advertiser*, 1 May 1896.
100 Ibid.
101 Ibid.
102 S. Bunker and T. Wood, *A Hatful of Talent: The Founding of the University of Luton* (University of Luton Press, 1994), p. 6.
103 M/220 Minutes of USDL, 9 January 1890 and 21 January 1890.
104 EM6 Minutes of BEC, 26 November 1915 and 25 February 1916.

newspaper. He said: 'I address both men and women in the canteens of our local works, and, of the two, I am inclined to think the young women show the superior intelligence.' He based his opinion on the fact that 'girls continue to study more after leaving school'.[105]

One secretarial school which was popular with Luton girls for many years was 'Berridges' in Collingdon Street, which offered shorthand and typing, and many women speak about their appreciation of the instruction they received there.[106] Another commercial establishment, House and Williams of Manchester Street, advertised regularly in the local newspaper.[107] All kinds of typewriting, duplicating and shorthand work were undertaken and tuition was offered in 'shorthand, type-writing, book-keeping and general office procedure'. Fees were not revealed, but were available on application. Another way for Luton girls to learn commercial skills was by correspondence course. These too were advertised in the local paper:

> Pitman's Shorthand is easy to learn, easy to write and easy to read.
> It holds the world's records for speed and legibility. Taught everywhere.
> Students desiring postal lessons in Shorthand, Book-keeping or other
> commercial subjects should apply for free booklet 'Home Study' which
> gives particulars of 80 Postal Courses.
> Write today to Pitman's School,
> 227, Southampton Row, London WC1[108]

This was a time when there was an evolution in the business world: men who wrote up ledgers were being replaced by women who could type. In Luton, men were still being employed in offices[109] but employment opportunities also existed for girls.[110] The *Luton News* carried advertisements for a female shorthand typist, aged about twenty-three, who had had 'good experience in the Correspondence department of an engineering firm'. Applicants were to write to the paper 'stating age, qualifications and salary expected'.[111] The following week there was an advertisement for a young lady with knowledge of shorthand and typing.[112]

Holden also noted that these were significant years in the development of women's employment.[113] Whereas women had for many years been involved in the management of family hat businesses, men had been dominant in the commercial aspects of industry. By 1923, this was changing and women were entering the commercial market. They wanted office jobs, were prepared to train for them and were being accepted by employers.

---

[105] *Luton News and Bedfordshire Advertiser*, 9 December 1926.
[106] For example, Mrs Joyce Browne, Mrs Vera Robson and Mrs Rosamond Hayward. See Chapter Six.
[107] For example, *Luton News*, 15 February 1923.
[108] For example, *Luton News*, 26 July 1923.
[109] The *Luton News* carries advertisements. See Chapter Two.
[110] Miss Richardson claimed that jobs in the large factories always went to girls who had been to LMS.
[111] *Luton News*, 1 March 1923.
[112] *Luton News*, 8 March 1923.
[113] L.T. Holden, 'A History of Vauxhall Motors to 1950: Industry Development and Local Impact on the Luton Economy' (M.Phil Thesis, 1983), p. 252.

Independent schooling for girls

Before the 1870 Forster Education Act, parents often chose to send children to one of the many small independent schools which were set up in private houses. A list of dame schools open in 1874 and private schools advertising in and after 1886 can be found in Joyce Roberts' unpublished study.[114] The names and addresses of independent schools are also noted in Luton year books. Whereas children of every class might attend these schools, Gardner notes that, by the 1880s, 'the link between the working class and a network of independent schools . . . was severed not only in fact, but also in popular perception'.[115] The idea of a 'private school' became an 'exclusively middle-class educational preserve'.[116] Another reason why these schools became unattractive to working-class families in Luton was their inability under the terms of the 1876 Education Act to issue Labour Certificates.[117]

The schools discussed here were usually chosen by parents who considered themselves to be above the working classes and who looked for schools with a perceived level of respectability. For example, the principal of Luton High School for Girls mentioned that her father was the Reverend W.J. Hutton, which no doubt gave her some social standing,[118] and the Convent claimed to be for the daughters of gentlemen. Advertisements indicate other reasons why parents chose particular schools: Luton High School provided a 'sound education' and Brathay Lodge was 'High-Class' and employed 'qualified and experienced' teachers.[119] Other attractions were location and a broad, balanced curriculum leading to recognized examinations. A kindergarten run on Froebel lines was also an advantage.

It is interesting to note that Miss F.M. Hutton also had formal qualifications. She had had 'a highly successful career as a teacher in various high schools in London and elsewhere and [had] gained, amongst others, the following diplomas and certificates: Associate of the College of Preceptors, Senior Cambridge Local, Senior Trinity College, London (music) [and] Advanced Certificates of the Science and Art Department'.[120]

Some of the schools described themselves as 'high schools'. When Sara Burstall attempted to define a high school[121] she had in mind the larger schools which were 'under some degree of public control'.[122] Nevertheless, as the name was used for smaller private schools, it can be presumed that the proprietors aspired to the same ideals. High schools aimed 'at a liberal education, cultivating the whole nature . . . while they retain[ed] from the older type of girls' schools the tradition of English, modern languages, music and art'.[123] Another point of similarity between Sara

---

114 Report on Dame Schools by the Visiting Officer 1874. J.E. Roberts, 'Luton School Board (1874–1902)' (Dissertation 1982).

115 P. Gardner, *The Lost Elementary Schools of Victorian England: The People's Education* (Croom Helm, 1984), p. 188.

116 Ibid.

117 Ibid., p. 205.

118 *Mate's Illustrated Guide to Luton* (Chantry Press, 1986). First published in 1907.

119 *The Luton and District Year Book and Almanack (1904)*, p. 44.

120 *Luton-Illustrated: A Descriptive Account of Luton* (W.T. Pike & Co., n.d. but c.1899).

121 S. Burstall, *English High Schools for Girls: Their Aims, Organisation and Management* (Longman, Green & Co., 1907).

122 Ibid., p. 1.

123 Ibid., p. 11.

27. St Dominic's Convent School

Burstall's schools and the high schools of Luton was the presence of a kindergarten. Younger children could come with their older sisters for whom it would also be an advantage, as it helped 'to develop their womanly instincts and to check that selfish absorption in [their] own concerns which is one of the failings of the modern schoolgirl'.[124] This ethos demonstrates that girls were expected to assume a domestic role and that following their own pursuits or interests was considered to be unacceptable and selfish.

St Dominic's Convent

It proved difficult to acquire background information about this school, but eventually books were received from France from a former teacher at the school.[125] Until 1920, the Dominicans ran the school,[126] but then the sisters of Sainte-Marie took over. The Congrégation de Sainte-Marie was established by Mère Melthide who left the Jansenist congregation of Sainte Marthe of Port Royal after converting to the Catholic faith.[127] The order had as its particular aims: instruction, education, catechism, youth groups, orphanages, hospitals, hospices, clinics and visits to the poor in their homes. At the beginning of the twentieth century some of the French schools

---

[124]   Ibid., p. 49.
[125]   Sister Monica Coleman sent: *Les Ordres Religieux: La Congrégation des Sœurs de Sainte-Marie* (Letouzey et Ané, 1925); S.M. D'Erceville, *De Port-Royal à Rome Histoire des Soeurs de Sainte-Marie* (La Colombe, 1955); and a pamphlet: *Congrégation de Sainte-Marie*.
[126]   Sister Monica Coleman believes that there was a break in the school at this time.
[127]   Letters from Sister Monica Coleman dated 13 September 1998, 20 September 1998, 8 October 1998 and 9 October 1998; W. Boyd and E.J. King, *The History of Western Education* (A & C Black, 1980), pp. 254–261.

closed[128] and the nuns, who had dedicated their lives to education, looked for new opportunities. 'Heaven seemed to supply the answer'[129] when a request came for a Catholic school to be opened in Dorchester, England. Another was established at Ashford, which transferred to Luton in 1920.[130] A school was also opened in Mexico where the headquarters of the order has been since 1995.[131]

The Convent School in Rothesay Road was advertised in *Mate's Illustrated Guide* (1907) during its early days under the Dominicans. It was described as a 'Boarding School for the daughters of gentlemen'[132] and its advantages were that it was within thirty-five minutes of London,[133] in a healthy situation, 500 feet above sea level with bracing air and was run by sisters who held diplomas for teaching. Little boys could be accepted as boarders. It offered a sound Catholic education with daily mass and benediction in the chapel twice a week. Pupils were prepared for public examinations in England and France and there were special facilities for modern languages. Private lessons were offered in piano, harmonium, singing, drawing, painting, embossed leather, scientific dressmaking and embroidery. This advertisement reveals the kind of curriculum that was thought to be suitable by families who considered themselves to be socially above the elementary system.

Sister Monica Coleman believed that, in 1920, there were only about fifteen children and they probably saw it as a finishing school. By 1924, 'there can't have been many sisters in Luton, but there were two English ones, trained teachers, and a French one, a doctor of music, plus two others, one French and one Irish who assumed the running of the house'. The premises were shared by 'the lady who had bought it for the Congrégation and she lived there with her lady's maid until the sisters had reimbursed the £1,000 she had paid'. Sister Monica thought that the curriculum would have included English language and literature, arithmetic, history, geography, music, drawing and embroidery. In 1928, Barbara Aylott, who was educated at the local authority secondary school, was teaching there.[134] In 1959, as Mrs Andrews, she became town mayor.

Luton High School and Brathay Lodge

This must not be confused with the BCC girls' secondary school that eventually took the same name. In 1895, this school, at Milton House in Dunstable Road,[135] was run by the Misses Gilfillan,[136] who believed the high school system of teaching to be 'the most efficient means of imparting instruction and developing the mental powers'.[137] The proprietors were trained and experienced teachers, holding certificates of London University Matriculation, Cambridge, Oxford, College of Preceptors, South Kensington Science and Art. As Miss Gilfillan had spent considerable

128 S.M. D'Erceville, *De Port-Royal*, pp. 153–154.
129 Ibid., p. 154.
130 Ibid., p. 157.
131 Letter from Sister Monica Coleman.
132 *Mate's Illustrated Guide*, p. 30.
133 As boarders were accepted it is reasonable to believe that not all the pupils came from Luton.
134 *Sheaf* No. 9 (Spring 1928), p. 41.
135 *Illustrated Bedfordshire Its History and Commerce* (Thomas Forman & Sons, 1895), p. 35.
136 Ibid. It was previously run by the Misses Robinson.
137 Ibid.

time on the Continent she could give special attention to the teaching of modern languages and had 'lately adopted the new Gouin conversational method of teaching them'.[138] The teacher in charge of the kindergarten held the full certificates of the Froebel Society, a system that was claimed to be superior to

> every other system of teaching for very young children [and] is now universally acknowledged . . . it is the only system based upon true psychological principles . . . no other system is so well calculated to develop the reasoning faculties of a child, without producing a sense of tedium or straining the mental powers.[139]

The High School used similar advertising to that of St Dominic's Convent. Attention was drawn to the picturesque and healthy situation and the home comforts offered to boarders. The curriculum consisted of English grammar, composition and literature, ancient and modern history, physical and political geography, Latin, French, German, natural science and hygiene, needlework, freehand, landscape and model drawing, painting in oils and water colours, class singing and harmony, music, piano, violin and callisthenics. Pupils were prepared for public examinations and private coaching was available.[140]

The *Luton Year Book (1904)*[141] has an advertisement for Brathay Lodge, a 'High-Class School for Girls', whose principal was Miss Hutton ACP. The music professor was Fred Gostelow ARCM FRCO ARAM, a much respected organist at the Parish Church for many years, and H. Stannard Esq. RBA of Bedford was in charge of painting. The advertisement offered similar advantages to the Convent and High School, but extra items were: the latest improvements in ventilation and heating, asphalt drill and play ground, tennis, hockey, swimming and cycling. In January 1905, 'a gathering took place at the Luton High School to celebrate the amalgamation of that institution with Brathay Lodge School' with Miss Gilfillan being responsible for the combined school.[142]

By 1907, the school was based in Cardiff Road. Miss Gilfillan, a university graduate, was the principal and was assisted by Miss Hutton, daughter of the Reverend W.J. Hutton.[143] The school was recognized by the Board of Education under Regulations 3 and 4. The same advantages of a 'High School' were being advertised and it was claimed that girls could be prepared for public and Froebel examinations and trained for secondary school teaching.[144] In the same year Marguerite Leaver, a monitress at Hyde and daughter of the headmistress, left the school to take up a post at the High School kindergarten. Later that year her mother was allowed leave to

---

138   Ibid, pp. 35–36; F. Gouin, *The Art of Teaching and Studying Languages*, translated by H. Swan and V. Bétis (Philip and Son, 1892). The Gouin method aimed to teach languages in the same way that children learned their mother tongue.
139   *Illustrated Bedfordshire*, p. 36.
140   Ibid.
141   *Luton Year Book (1904)*, p. 44.
142   *The Luton and District Year Book and Almanack (1906)*, p. 90. The school was known as Luton High School. It seems likely that it closed soon after 1907.
143   Probably the former principal of Brathay Lodge.
144   *Mate's Illustrated Guide*, p. 30 and advertisement.

attend the open day at the town hall.[145] By 1908,[146] Mrs Webb was headmistress, assisted by Miss Newlyn LL.A and Miss Litchfield NFU.

Moorlands

While most of the independent schools in Luton have closed, Moorlands School, based at Leagrave Hall, has survived into the twenty-first century. It was run by a succession of private owners but, since 1995, has been administered by a charitable trust (The Filmer Trust) which was set up to purchase the school. The former head-master, Mr A.J. Cook, was very helpful and did his best to find early records. However, the only archives that have been located are two prospectuses (n.d.), regis-ters from 1930 to 1931 and a school magazine written by children between 1933 and 1934.[147]

References in the Luton year books[148] indicate that Miss Costin LL.A was the headmistress in 1906 and had left by 1936, to be succeeded by Miss Iris W. Spencer. It is believed that the school opened in a building opposite the town's moor (hence its name) and moved to 35 King Street where it was to be found in 1906. By 1918, it had transferred to 159 Dunstable Road. The *Luton News* carried regular advertise-ments[149] stating that the school, under Miss Costin, offered 'good all-round educa-tion for girls' with the 'individual capacity of each pupil' being 'carefully studied'. One of the prospectuses found names Miss Costin LL.A as the principal. Even though there is no date, the reference to Miss Costin suggests that the prospectus reflects the character of the school during the early part of the twentieth century.

Qualified and experienced mistresses and specialists helped Miss Costin whose aims were 'to give thorough mental, moral and physical training to pupils from five years of age to matriculation standard, and to encourage and develop any special ability'. Backward children were carefully studied and special attention was 'paid to observation and memory training' and elocution. The kindergarten class was 'made particularly bright and attractive' and the lessons were 'in accordance with the methods of Froebel and Montessori'. Boys were prepared for 'boys' schools' and 'no pupil [had] ever failed in an entrance examination'. There is no indication that this school took boarders.

A register for 1930 has survived. This is strictly speaking outside the scope of this study although it is close enough to be relevant. The addresses indicate the class of parents who sent their children to the school. These were almost certainly above the level of the working classes; one was Dr O'Meara and children came from Someries Farm and Biscot Mill. Many addresses point to roads with comfortable detached houses. Using this slender evidence it can be suggested that during the period under consideration the school prepared boys for other schools, but it had high academic expectations for its girls who stayed there throughout their school lives. Moorlands School survived and therefore must have offered what parents in

[145]   SD Hyde 1 Logbook of Hyde School, 13 September 1907 and 4 December 1907.
[146]   *Luton Year Book (1908)*, p. 171.
[147]   From the archives of Moorlands School.
[148]   Entries under 'Private Schools', *Luton Year Book (1906)*; *Luton Year Books*: 1918, 1923 and 1925; *Luton News Year Book* 1926–1927; *Luton News Directories* 1931 and 1936.
[149]   For example, 15 February 1923.

Luton required. This appeared to be matriculation standard for girls and a high success rate for boys in entrance examinations for further education.

York House

According to Greta Kent,[150] Miss Gilfillan's school was 'where the children of the wealthier people went',[151] but York House was run by less qualified but dedicated teachers and provided for a lower social class. Greta Kent attended the school around the turn of the century. It was kept by Miss Haysmen, but was 'taken over by three charming ladies, Miss Haynes the elder, headmistress, Miss Amy, her sister who did most of the teaching, and Miss Marriott, their niece, who had charge of the infants'.[152] The school was attended by boys and girls, not many of whom were over ten years of age. Greta Kent's description deals mainly with the day-to-day running of the school and not with educational ideals as have been noted in the high schools. However, her recollections serve as useful material for an understanding of the methods used at the time.

The children were given good groundwork, not only in the three Rs but also in singing, painting, drawing and sewing. Spelling was no problem; girls stood in a semi-circle around Miss Amy's desk and the top girl was given a word. If she spelt it correctly, she kept her place. If she did not, then the word was passed around until the girl who spelt it correctly assumed the top place. Reading began with two-letter words and progressed to longer ones. A textbook, Butter's *Etymological Spelling Book and Expositor*, gave information on grammatical structures and origins of words. Poetry was enjoyed,[153] but arithmetic receives only a brief mention as it was obviously not a favourite with Greta Kent. Other traditional subjects were history, geography and map drawing.[154]

In needlework classes some of the girls brought tray-cloths to embroider, but Greta's mother insisted that she learnt to darn by following patterns from a chart on the wall.[155] An older girl would read stories as they worked and this was regarded as a treat.[156] Every day began with a prayer and Christmas was celebrated with traditional songs and decorations.[157] The school was a happy one and Greta paid tribute to 'the kind and patient women who well earned our love and respect'. She did not claim to be an educated woman, but 'at least [she] was shown how to make the most of what was given by those who probably held no acknowledged qualifications, but were so unselfishly inspired'.[158]

The Luton Modern School (LMS) *Sheaf* magazine records that an old girl, Dorothy Gent, became Principal of York House School.[159] One of the pupils, Norah

---

[150] G. Kent, 'Luton from the Wings: Childhood Memories of Edwardian Luton', Luton Libraries, 1976. Greta Kent was the daughter of a musician at the Grand Theatre.
[151] Ibid., p. 11.
[152] Ibid.
[153] Ibid., p. 12.
[154] Ibid.
[155] Ibid., p. 11.
[156] This way of life has been noted with straw plaiters and in the adult schools.
[157] G. Kent, 'Luton from the Wings', p. 12.
[158] Ibid., p. 13.
[159] *Sheaf* No. 9 (Spring 1928), p. 41.

Woodward,[160] was admitted c.1912 and stayed on as a pupil-teacher.[161] She left in 1924 at the age of nineteen and went to do clerical work at Vauxhall Motors Ltd. An advertisement for dancing and deportment classes at York House School, on Tuesday evenings at 8p.m. beginning on October 4 1898, has been located. It does not state whether the lessons were linked to the school or whether the premises were being rented, but it can be assumed that such classes were considered to be an educational asset.[162] York House has not survived, but seems to have been successful in its day because it offered a happy environment and a thorough basic schooling.

Moreton House

Moreton House, Dunstable, which was opened in 1864 by Mrs Bennett, was one of the schools which became popular with Luton's middle classes[163] before moving to Watford as a boarding school in 1925[164] or 1926.[165] The *Illustrated Bedfordshire* (1895) refers to its advantages, which were similar to those of Luton 'high' schools.[166] It was 'situated in a locality noted for its bracing air', was only thirty-three miles from London and enjoyed 'excellent railway communication with all parts of the kingdom'. There were twenty-five boarders between the ages of seven and sixteen and weekly boarders were also accepted. 'Entire charge [was] taken of pupils from abroad.' Magazine articles about the school have been written by Vera Day, a former pupil and daughter of Frank Sharman, headmaster of the Ashton Elementary School. It appears that Mr Sharman was happy to teach the children of Dunstable, but did not think his school suitable for his daughter.[167]

Pupils were prepared for local examinations and, by 1895, there had not been a single failure. Apart from the more academic subjects, freehand and model drawing, painting, class singing, plain and fancy needlework and callisthenics were offered. The kindergarten system was adopted for younger children and it was the aim of the principals, the Misses Herington, 'to combine with the discipline of a school the moral and social advantages of a home, and to make the life of their pupils both cheerful and beneficial'. Interesting comparisons can be made between the curriculum at Moreton House and the neighbouring Ashton Grammar School for boys whose headmaster was L.C.R. Thring. This school offered pure and applied mathematics, Roman and Greek history, practical chemistry and shorthand.[168] Mathematics and chemistry were considered to be suitable for boys, but it is worth noting again that shorthand also fell into that category.[169]

In 1914, Moreton House celebrated its jubilee and the local newspaper reported

---

160   Norah Woodward, b. 29 May 1905. Information supplied by her daughter, Mrs Jean Munn.
161   What exactly this involved is not clear; compare Chapter Six.
162   LMAG Education Box 1.
163   *Dunstable Borough Gazette*, 8 July 1914.
164   V. Day, 'Moretonia', *Bedfordshire Magazine* Vol. 25, No. 196 (Spring 1996), p. 150.
165   P. Bird and B. Carrington, *Dunstable in Camera* (Quotes Ltd, 1992), p. 34; V. Day, 'A Child's World of Two Dunstable Schools', *Bedfordshire Magazine* Vol. 14, No. 110 (Autumn 1974), p. 254.
166   *Illustrated Bedfordshire*, p. 37.
167   It is of course possible that Vera Day went to the elementary school when she was younger.
168   *Illustrated Bedfordshire*, pp. 36–37.
169   See Chapter Ten.

the speeches.[170] The Rector, Canon W.W.C. Baker, referred to the 'sound training both intellectually and morally' and the happy feeling that evidently prevailed between the headmistress, her staff and the pupils and also mentioned that the previous year's successes had included the London Matriculation. Mr C.C.S. Benning, the town clerk, believed that the 'real basis of school life was home life' and complimented the girls on their excellent performance in the sports. The head-master of the boys' school had been asked to say a few words 'on the educational side' and advised the girls that 'it did not matter a little bit what they were being taught as long as they were doing their very best to learn' and that they should 'learn the great lesson of over-coming difficulties'.

Three weeks later the *Dunstable Borough Gazette* reported the speech day of the Ashton Grammar School and how different that was.[171] Lady O'Hagan spoke on the value of science, her admiration for the beautiful laboratories and 'the developments for the teaching of science, which she believed to be so absolutely necessary'.[172] Emphasis was placed on academic achievements although character training was considered important.

Vera Day has written two articles for the *Bedfordshire Magazine* recalling her days at the school during and after the First World War. The fact that she saw three separate 'classes' in the school supports the observations of Joyce Godber who described the boarders in the Harpur Trust schools as 'the élite'.[173] Local girls were probably more highly thought of than the Luton girls.[174] She described how she set off for school in her tussore dress and panama hat:[175]

> Boarders, Dunstable girls and Luton girls were three hard and fast divisions, though of course we all shared the staff, and the separate movable desks, Palgrave's *Golden Treasury* and the motto over the hall door, 'Honour before Honours'. We read Shakespeare and Ruskin, learned French and began *German without Tears*, did needlework sitting round three long dining room tables, and basket work in the garden. . . . Art was a normal lesson and we sat for Mr Ablett's exams, but music was an extra, like dancing and callisthenics . . . eventually a few of us went to the boys' Grammar School to sit in tiered rows in July doing our Junior or Senior Cambridge exams'.[176]

Vera Day recalled the school song which referred to the old girls who were 'working their way up' and new girls who were 'learning to play up, aye and play the game', which revives memories of old schoolgirl stories. Perhaps it is not surprising that a former member of staff was Elinor Brent-Dyer who wrote a series of *Chalet School* stories for girls.[177]

Magazines from Moreton House School between 1914 and 1921 have

170 *Dunstable Borough Gazette*, 8 July 1914.
171 *Dunstable Borough Gazette*, 29 July 1914.
172 Ibid.
173 J. Godber, *The Harpur Trust 1552–1973* (Bedford: The Harpur Trust, 1973), p. 115. This may have been because girls who boarded came from more affluent families.
174 Ibid. Fee-paying girls from Bedford 'came next'.
175 Photograph of girls from the school: *Dunstable in Camera*, pp. 34–35.
176 V. Day, 'A Child's World of Two Dunstable Schools', pp. 252–254.
177 Letter from Mrs Geraldine J. Hogg in *Dunstable Borough Gazette*, November 1998.

survived.[178] Luton girls seemed to have attended in significant numbers during these years for there was a poem entitled 'Lament of the Luton girls', which bemoaned the fact that they had to get up early to catch the 8.40a.m. train, carrying their season tickets, books and lunches. They might have to brave the rain and then struggle home again with their homework. The magazines indicate that, although girls were entered for the Cambridge Local examinations, a great deal of emphasis was placed on the examinations of the Associated Board of the Royal Academy and the Royal College of Music, Trinity College and the Royal Drawing Society.

The magazines also list the kinds of employment which had been found by girls who attended the school. As this period covers much of the First World War, it is not surprising to note that several girls became nurses, both in this country and in France. One was a sister at Guy's, one a matron at Roedean and another girl ran a hostel with twenty girls under her charge. Some ex-pupils went into teaching although not via the route taken by girls from the Luton Secondary School. Enid Whiteley was junior mistress at 'The Elms' Finchley Road and hoped to take up a course at the Kilburn Art School. Irene Lockhart went to train at the Liverpool Physical Training College before becoming a games mistress at Lee on Solent. Kindergarten studies were considered acceptable; Bertha Thorne went to Clapham Training College for kindergarten students to take the Higher Froebel Examination.

Secretarial work was becoming popular and one girl had been to Holborn Hall College for her commercial skills. Places of employment included Barclays Bank and the Education Offices in Luton. However, the hat industry did not altogether lose its hold. Joyce Squires (b.1909), the daughter of Harry Squires, managing director of Welch and Sons, hat importers, would very much have liked to go into agriculture but spent her working life running a hat business of her own.[179]

Transferred allegiance

The admission registers for the LMS note the schools previously attended by pupils (see Table 32).

Table 32. Transfers from private schools to the secondary school[180]

School previously attended	1904	1905 and 1907	1912	1930
Brathay Lodge	1			
High School/Miss Gilfillan's		11		
Miss Kennington's		1		
Sebright (Markyate)		1		
Harpenden		1		
Governess		1	1	
Miss Costin's		1	1	
Convent			1	2

[178] Z 930/1/1–13 Magazines of Moreton House School.
[179] This information was gleaned in a conversation with Mrs Joyce Squires.
[180] 1997/23/1 and 1997/23/3 Admission Registers of LMS. See Chapter Ten. LMAG Admission Registers of Luton High School.

York House	1	
Miss Wright's	3	
Miss Higg's	1	
Moreton House (Dunstable)	1	
Luton Preparatory School		1
Private school in Sweden		1
Moorlands		1
Aberfeldy (Dunstable)		3
Mrs Fletcher (Dunstable)		2
Walton House (Harpenden)		1
Cleveland		1

In the early days of the LMS, parents appeared to be suspicious and preferred to keep their daughters at the older private schools. However, when the credibility of the LMS had been established, more children began to attend and the private schools began to lose pupils. The school that seems to have been most affected was the Luton High School. This is not altogether surprising when considered against the background of the Waller Street HGS for boys, which enjoyed considerable kudos in the town. The Clerk to the Luton Board had written to the Education Department to say that there was a growing demand for a similar school for girls 'by parents above the ordinary labouring class, largely connected with the staple industry as small manufacturers and by others who would gladly pay a ninepenny fee for the educational and social advantages that would accrue'.[181] The day secondary school had, in a sense, answered that request and probably fulfilled everything that this type of Luton parent wanted. However, there were still parents who preferred to pay for private schooling rather than enter their daughters into local authority schools, possibly because they believed them to have a higher social standing.

The Harpur Trust schools
The Taunton Commission (1868) recommended that the Harpur Trust should use some of its funds to establish secondary schooling for girls.[182] Consequently the Bedford High School and adjoining Bedford Modern School opened in 1882.[183] There were no other grammar schools for girls in Bedfordshire and children from all over the county 'even from Luton'[184] attended the Harpur Trust schools.[185] It appears that there was a hierarchy within the schools themselves: boarders were the élite ahead of fee-paying pupils who were ranked higher than pupils with free places; the country children came last.[186] The Modern School appears to have had headmistresses trained in the ways of Frances Mary Buss while the High School was more influenced by the views of Dorothea Beale from Cheltenham Ladies College.

181 LMAG 8969/91 Letterbooks of USDL, 29 May 1891.
182 J. Godber, *The Harpur Trust 1552–1973*, pp. 93 and 110.
183 Ibid., p. 111.
184 This may refer to the distance between the towns, although rail travel between Luton and Bedford was not difficult. It could also reflect the view of Luton held by some of the people in Bedford.
185 Ibid., p. 114.
186 Ibid., p. 115. Similarities have already been noted at Moreton House School.

According to Joyce Godber, rules at the high school were stricter and much emphasis was placed on ladylike behaviour.[187] However, academic excellence became important to the teachers who delighted 'to discover ability in girls who had had few opportunities to foster it and eventually hand them on to the universities'.[188]

Felicity Hunt researched the Harpur Trust schools and described how class had a strong effect on the organization of secondary education.[189] She also discussed the ethos and the changing curriculum to be found in girls' schools. Middle-class girls were expected to become cultured and ladylike,[190] but, after 1902, the Board of Education made continuous attempts to feminize the curriculum and 'by the 1920s, femininity for middle-class girls meant domesticity, just as it did for working-class girls by the 1900s'.[191]

A few names of Luton girls have been found in the registers and reflect the class distinctions of the day. Mary Rhoda Percival from Hart Hill, Luton, was admitted to the Modern School in 1890. Her father, Frank Ellard, had a straw hat manufacturing business in Bute Street.[192] Ettie Flint was the daughter of Joseph Flint of Clifton Villas, Rothesay Road; he also manufactured straw hats at his premises in Upper George Street.[193] Florence Lane was the ward of J.H. Jennings of Upper George Street.[194] Agnes Gladwell lived at John Street, but it is not clear who her father was.[195] A pupil who did not fit the hat-makers' mould was Florence Hooper, the daughter of the Reverend G. D. Hooper, a Baptist Minister who lived in Oakthorpe, Hart Hill.[196]

While the hat manufacturers seemed to have preferred the Modern School, other prosperous businessmen chose the High School. The first register of the Bedford High School names three Luton girls. One was Edith Sworder from Holly House, Luton, whose father, Thomas Sworder, was a brewer and a well-known figure in Luton life.[197] The other two girls named were sisters: Alice and Hilda Blundell of Moulton Lodge, The Crescent. Their father was the owner of a large department store in the town. Alice was entered as a boarder with a Bedford address.[198]

St George's School, Harpenden

This school claimed to be the 'first purpose-established co-educational boarding school in England'. Co-education was 'the cornerstone' of the school and 'children could live [there] in an atmosphere closely related to family life, based on sound

---

[187] Ibid., pp. 111–112.

[188] Ibid., p. 112.

[189] M.F. Hunt, 'Secondary Education for the Middle Class Girl: A Study of Ideology and Educational Practice 1870–1940 with Special Reference to the Harpur Trust Girls' Schools, Bedford' (Ph.D. Thesis, 1984), p. 398.

[190] Ibid.

[191] Ibid., pp. 410 and 413.

[192] 130 BED Girls' Modern School Register Admission No. 516 and *Kelly's Directories*.

[193] Admission No. 536. She left for health reasons and was re-admitted as No. 629 in 1891.

[194] Admission No. 538 1890. No other details.

[195] Admission No. 542 1890. She may have been the daughter of James Gladwell of John Street who was a straw hat manufacturer.

[196] Admission No. 706 1893.

[197] Fac.80 Photocopy of the first register of pupils at Bedford High School. Admission No. 113 d.o.b. 28 July 1865. *Census of England and Wales (1881) Bedfordshire.*

[198] Admission No. 219 d.o.b. 26 July 1870, Admission No. 444 d.o.b. 1 January 1873.

Christian principles'.[199] This was in contrast to the Luton secondary school which was mixed, not because of ideology but expediency. St George's was said to be the choice of 'a number of parents who were unconventional and intellectual'.[200] A few such parents (presumably) were to be found in Luton. Mr H.F. Howard, a mechanical engineer of Hart Hill House, Luton, sent two sons and a daughter to St George's. Henry (b.1899) and Charles (b.1901) were admitted in 1910 and Frances (b.1905) began in 1917. Marjorie Godfrey, daughter of Mr Godfrey, a bleacher and dyer of The Mount, London Road, was admitted in 1916 at the age of twelve. May Hart, daughter of Mr E.J.F. Hart, also a bleacher and dyer of Studley Road, attended from 1922. Two other girls, who were admitted in 1924, were Norah Ford-Smith of Tennyson Road, whose father was the sub-manager of Barclays Bank, and Pauline Jones, daughter of Mr E.G. Jones who lived in Westbourne Gardens but whose occupation is not listed.[201] There is no indication that these children were boarders and, as rail travel would have been easy, there is a possibility that they travelled in daily.

Case Study

Mrs Kathleen (Madge) Milner MBE (b.1889)

Mrs Milner, whose father, William Austin, was a respected Luton solicitor and author, was educated at St Albans High School and attended Heatherleys School of Art (founded in 1845) between 1915 and 1918.[202] The following report from the *Luton News* is important to this study because it illustrates the expectations which governed the lives of middle-class girls. Mrs Milner retired after twenty-eight years service on the Bench at Luton Magistrate's Court. She had been a Councillor, County Councillor and an Alderman and was also said to be 'an artist of excellent quality, designer, traveller, authority on law, and a great believer in Do-it-yourself'. In 1936 she became a Justice of the Peace.[203]

> Daughter of the late Mr William Austin who wrote *The History of Luton and its Hamlets*, Mrs Milner is certain that, had she been born a boy, she would have entered the legal profession.
>
> As she told other magistrates, 'In those days, it wasn't the done thing for a girl to become a solicitor'.
>
> Instead of what might have been a brilliant career at the bar, Mrs Milner became a textile designer and later, still as Miss Austin, worked at George Kent's during the First World War . . .
>
> It was while working at Kent's with some 1000 girls in her charge, that she met Mr Bart Henry Milner, later to become her husband.
>
> They were married in December 1918 and, in March the following year, left for Southern India where her husband became a tea planter. Eighteen months later, they were back in England at the end of a battle against illness.
>
> Then in 1936, Mrs Milner was appointed magistrate. Her already vast knowledge of the law was to be put to good use.

---

199 P. Weatherley, *A History of St George's School, Harpenden* (St George's School, 1982).
200 Ibid., p. 30.
201 Details from admission registers of St George's School. Nos 166, 167, 447, 492, 744, 819 and 820.
202 *Who's Who in Luton* (Pullman Press, 1959).
203 *Luton News*, 23 April 1964.

She became the first woman deputy chairman of the Bench – and almost certainly the only one ever to cycle to court. Her keen interest in the juvenile court led to sitting on the Bench there, until she was 65.

Now, at 75, she is required by law, to retire altogether from the legal field.

A member of the WVS, she is often to be seen washing great mountains of dishes in their kitchen at Park-street.

She founded the first Girl Guide Company in Luton; is a member of the Women's Section of the British Legion, sits on the Board of Governors of all the schools in Luton – and still finds time to potter about in the garden.

Conclusion

Margaret Bryant has shown how London had a 'diverse and quickly responsive market for educational experiments'. She also acknowledged the importance of 'women reformers [who] could meet and exchange ideas and experience and give mutual support and encouragement'.[204] The atmosphere in Luton was very different. Emily Carruthers worked conscientiously in administration and Rebecca Higgins showed an interest in the theories of education, but Luton had to wait until the arrival of Miss H.K. Sheldon, headmistress of the secondary school, before a pioneer in the mould of the London ladies appeared on the scene.

However, the women of Luton were able to learn by a variety of different methods, which made the town distinctive in its own way. In the nineteenth century, the most powerful influence came from the home, which was where traditional hat-making skills were learnt. This informal learning, passed from mother to daughter, had important economic value and was refined by practical experience within the work situation. The Luton hat industry did not provide formal training like that found in the hat-making districts of Cheshire until the 1920s when some limited instruction seems to have been offered.

In Luton, with its distinctive and independent way of life, the values of the wider community were important. The dogmas of the Church were catered for in the National schools, but it was the Sunday School Movement which flourished. Women continued to be involved in their administration before, during and after the period covered by this study. The adult schools, which were established by the Society of Friends and which became non-denominational, followed a similar pattern and were well supported by women who wanted to extend their learning.

Social expectations demanded that some parents should send their daughters to private schools which, in the years covered by this book, were seen to be middle-class establishments. Parents were faced with the choice of deciding which of these schools were suited to their needs. Felicity Hunt noted that gender and class were the organizing principle of education for the middle classes[205] and Walford adds that schooling depended on social class, 'as well as – and perhaps more than – gender'.[206] Fearon classified schools by girls' leaving ages.[207] This information is not available as far as Luton girls were concerned; father's occupation has provided

---

[204] M. Bryant, *The London Experience of Secondary Education* (The Athlone Press, 1986), pp. 311–312.

[205] M.F. Hunt, 'Secondary Education for the Middle Class Girl', p. 398.

[206] G. Walford, ed., *The Private Schooling of Girls Past and Present* (Woburn Press, 1993), p. 9.

[207] M. Bryant, *The London Experience*, p. 323.

the only indication of social class and has suggested that patronage began with the local schools and went upwards through the straw hat manufacturers who supported the 'high' schools. Those of the highest social class, leading members of Luton society, preferred the Harpur Trust schools.

The curriculum in the private schools, with the exception of York House, suggests that the girls were being trained for their social standing in the community. General expectations suggest that this meant ladylike accomplishments which prepared girls to be wives and mothers.[208] Very little evidence has been found regarding any future employment of girls attending private schools, but as far as Luton was concerned an involvement with the hat industry may well have been considered socially acceptable. By the 1920s, most of the private schools seem to have disappeared, probably because the local day secondary schools satisfied local needs. However, there were parents who still chose to send daughters to other towns, particularly Bedford, for a more socially acceptable education.

Personal initiative, a characteristic of Luton, stimulated the women of Luton to follow their interests and to look for a solution to their needs. This was evident when recognized providers failed to offer commercial training in a changing economic environment. Then many women and girls found and paid for what they wanted. They were turning their backs on the traditions of the past in favour of the new industrial age. In this respect they were leaving behind their old identity and becoming more like women in other towns.

---

[208] G. Walford, *The Private Schooling of Girls*, pp. 35–36; C. Dyhouse, *Girls Growing Up in Late Victorian and Edwardian England* (RKP, 1981), p. 58.

Chapter Ten

Secondary Education for Girls

Higher education for girls

Historically the education of girls was considered to be of less importance than the education of boys for 'women were identified with the private domain of the home'.[1] This was believed to be a 'natural division'; women were 'relative rather than autonomous beings' and were 'inferior and subordinate to men'.[2] From about 1845, there grew up a movement which fought for the provision of secondary and higher education for women,[3] but no evidence has been found to suggest that this movement had any support in Luton where education for girls was seen to be unimportant. According to June Purvis one reason for the campaign to educate girls from the middle classes was the large number of 'poorly educated middle-class women [who] had to earn their own living'.[4] This was not significant to Luton in the context of the hat industry.

After 1874, girls in Luton received a basic elementary schooling, but middle-class parents did not see this as appropriate for their daughters. The education which they received has been considered more fully in Chapter Nine, but it is safe to say that most of them were either taught at home or attended private schools. Another route which could be taken by girls who wanted to improve their own education was the pupil-teacher system and this is addressed in Chapter Five. Crucial to this study is the establishment in 1904 of a recognized secondary school which began to take significant numbers of girls from the middle classes as well as capable girls who earned a free place. With the arrival of this school, opportunities for girls began to match those for boys although, in the early days at least, boys still seemed to have received more consideration.

When a separate secondary school for girls was opened in 1919, it was run on similar lines to the North London Collegiate School, the pioneering school run by Frances Mary Buss. She had introduced a wide curriculum and expected high standards from her girls, many of whom received a college education and became headmistresses themselves. In this way a network of similar schools grew up throughout the country. Although this falls outside the years studied in this book it is interesting to note that the London school was evacuated to Luton in September 1939 and

---

1   J. Purvis, *A History of Women's Education in England* (Open University Press, 1991), p. 2.
2   Ibid., pp. 2–3.
3   M. Bryant, *The Unexpected Revolution: A History of the Education of Women and Girls in the Nineteenth Century* (University of London, 1979), ch. 1.
4   J. Purvis, *A History of Women's Education in England*, p. 75.

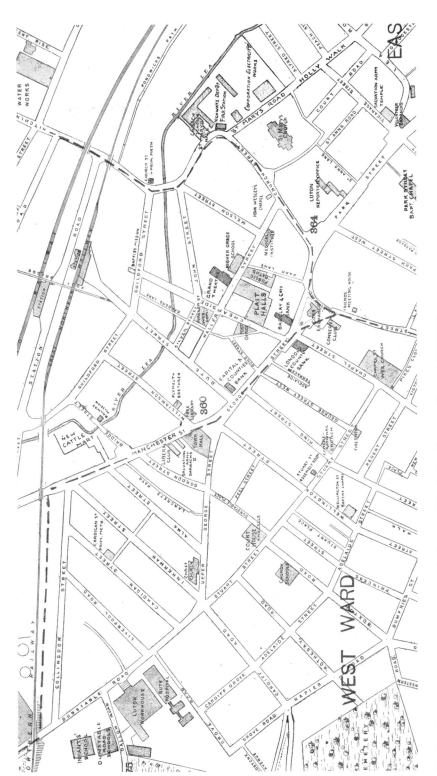

28. Map of Luton presented as a supplement to the *Luton and District Year Book and Almanack* 1904 [LM]

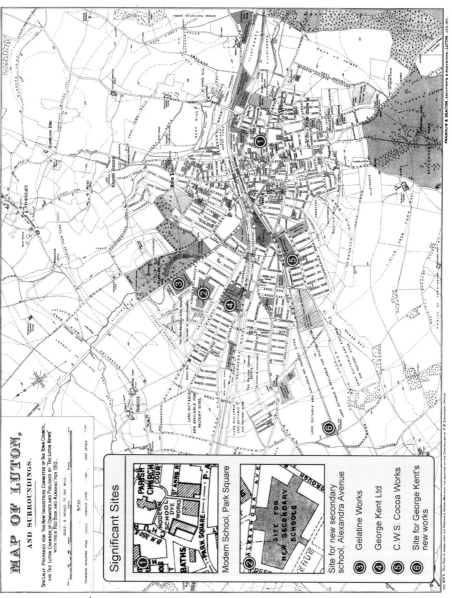

29. Map of Luton based on the Ordnance Survey Map with the sanction of HM Stationery Office 1915 [LM]

shared the school buildings of the Luton High School for Girls before returning to its new premises, known as Canons, soon after Easter 1940.[5]

Luton's attitudes to higher education for girls

The Board schools in Luton did not cater for children of the professional or business classes. According to Dony it was considered better for girls 'to have good manners, some idea of household management and inconsequential conversation than to be educated'.[6] Dony also says that 'The Board, throughout its history, was much more concerned with providing boys with a good education than girls.'[7] However, the value to the town of boys receiving an education which fitted them for commercial life was addressed and a Higher Grade School (HGS), which carried considerable status, was opened at Waller Street.

In 1891, a year before central classes for pupil-teachers were set up, the Luton School Board attempted to establish a Higher Grade School for girls and there were discussions with the Education Department concerning a suitable site. The Clerk to the Board noted 'that an opportunity for the acquisition of a property had been indirectly brought under our notice on terms so favourable as to render it doubtful if such an opportunity might again occur'.[8] The Education Department refused to agree to the plan as it was considered that there were sufficient school places for girls. Whether or not anyone in Luton had been influenced by the strong movement for girls' access to secondary and higher education for women[9] is doubtful. The Board does not appear to have developed a concern for the education of Luton girls in general and it seems more likely that better-off parents, some of whom were paying for girls to travel to Bedford or Dunstable[10] for their education, were interested in an acceptable local school.

The following October, the Clerk wrote to the Education Department again to explain just how suitable the premises were. There was a large house, stables, laundry and garden in a property which had been unoccupied for some time and a purchase price or rent was being negotiated. Mr W. Hoyle added that 'in the judgement of many, well-qualified to form an opinion, it would have been a useful acquisition for a Girls' Higher Grade School and a Laundry School. Beyond this, the Board have no special reason for urging the immediate purchase of the property.'[11] Dony notes that there was an attempt to build up Standards V and VI for girls at the Langley Street School, but this failed 'probably because so few girls reached standard VI and for those who did there was the attraction of becoming pupil-teachers'.[12] The Board, with its lack of concern for academic life, seems to have had no strong inclination to provide a higher form of education for girls in Luton but, in 1902, the government introduced an Education Bill which was to take away respon-

---

5   *The North London Collegiate School 1850–1950: A Hundred Years of Girls' Education* (Oxford University Press, 1950), pp. 184–186.
6   J.G. Dony, *A History of Education in Luton* (LMAG, 1970), p. 42.
7   Ibid., p. 35.
8   M/239 Letterbooks of USDL, 29 May 1891.
9   M. Bryant, *The Unexpected Revolution*, ch. 1.
10 The railway link to Dunstable was opened in 1858 and the one to Bedford and St Albans in 1868.
11 M/239 Letterbooks of USDL, 5 October 1891.
12 J.G. Dony, *A History of Education in Luton*, p. 39. Pupil-teachers are considered in Chapter Five.

30. Park Square c.1906 The building with Georgian-style windows housed the offices of the Luton Secondary School [*LM/LN*]

sibility for such decisions from the Borough and hand it to Bedfordshire County Council (BCC).

Bedfordshire County Council's response to the 1902 Education Act

The BCC Education Committee, which had responsibility for educating children over fourteen years of age in Bedfordshire, included two women 'having experience in the education of Girls',[13] one from Bedford and one from Luton. These were Miss Amy Walmsley, the Principal of the Bedford Kindergarten College, and Miss Rebecca Higgins. The *Luton Year Book (1904)* noted that Miss Higgins 'has taken a deep interest in education, and her appointment on the . . . committee is therefore well deserved'.[14] In May 1905, she resigned because of deafness and her place was taken by Mrs Emily Carruthers who had worked tirelessly under the Luton School Board.[15] Alderman Hucklesby, 'Luton's Hat King',[16] was also on the Education Committee. He was a Liberal, Mayor of Luton on five occasions, a member of the Chamber of Commerce and a J.P. He also belonged to the Congregational Church and the Temperance Movement. From 22 April, he served on the BCC Higher Education Committee with Mr Rowland Prothero, later Lord Ernle.[17] Together they were influential in the establishment of a secondary school in Luton.

The Luton Day Secondary School[18]

The BCC Education Committee lost no time in fulfilling its obligations.[19] In October 1903, representatives from Luton Town Council and the Ashton Trust[20] were each asked to appoint three members to join a Sub-committee of the BCC 'consisting of County Alderman Joseph Miller, County Councillor Charles Bailey Halliley, Mr Frederic [sic] William Conquest, Mr Geoffrey Howard and Mr Rowland Edmund Prothero with a view to considering the desirability of establishing a day secondary School and technical institute in Luton'.[21] The following month it was agreed that scholarships, free places and assisted places would be available[22] and, by January 1904, the committee was ready to discuss funding.[23] It was decided that this would consist of a grant of £3,000 from the BEC, a county loan and a 1d rate to be raised each year by the Luton Town Council (LTC). Six

[13] EM1 Minutes of BEC, 8 May 1903.

[14] *The Luton and District Year Book and Almanack (1904)*, p. 51 and p. 99. See Chapter Six.

[15] Notes about Mrs Carruthers are included in Chapter Four.

[16] B. Benson and J. Dyer, 'Luton's Hat King', *Bedfordshire Magazine* Vol. 26, No. 204 (Spring 1998), p. 135. See Chapter One.

[17] J. Godber, *History of Bedfordshire* (Bedfordshire County Council, 1970), p. 549n; *Webster's Biographical Dictionary* (G. & C. Merriam Co., 1972). R. Prothero (1851–1937) became agent-in-chief to the Duke of Bedford in 1898 and President of the Board of Agriculture from 1916 to 1919. He became the first Baron Ernle but in this book is referred to as Rowland Prothero.

[18] In 1908 the name of the Day Secondary School was changed to Luton Modern School. When the departments separated in 1919 they were known as Luton Modern School for Boys and Luton Modern School for Girls. In 1930 the Girls' School became Luton High School for Girls. The Boys' School became Luton Grammar School for Boys in 1944.

[19] This chapter has been enlarged in A. Allsopp, *Crimson and Gold: The Luton Modern School for Girls and Boys* Volume 2 (The Book Castle, 2004).

[20] The Ashton Foundation maintained schools in Dunstable.

[21] EM1 Minutes of BEC, 23 October 1903.

[22] Ibid., 6 November 1903.

[23] Ibid., 22 January 1904.

governors were to be appointed by BCC, six by LTC and three were to be co-opted. At least one governor was to be a woman (a token presence, but better than nothing). The school was to be established in temporary buildings, ready for opening in 1904.[24]

Local expectations probably favoured the appointment of Mr H.C. Middle, headmaster of Waller Street HGS, or Mr J.H. Hargreaves from the Pupil-teacher Centre as headmaster of the day secondary school. The BEC, however, decided in favour of T.A.E. Sanderson, a Cambridge graduate and 21st wrangler.[25] Sanderson recalled that he was previously on the staff of Bath College, a school run by a private company on public school lines, and 'my decision surprised some of my colleagues, for the new school was to be under a local authority and, moreover, was to be a mixed school. But, in addition to being in charge of the Army class, I was also College Bursar, and therefore able to foresee that before long the company must go into liquidation, as in fact did happen a few years later.'[26]

Sanderson records that he found the post exceedingly trying and had problems with governors who wanted to have their say and children who did not want to keep the rules.[27] One of his greatest difficulties, however, seems to have been the presence of girls. 'One of my greatest reliefs was the opening of the Girls' School – not that the pupils gave any trouble, but I found a male staff far easier to deal with than a mixed one.'[28]

There were plans to name the school the King Edward VII Grammar School, 'but higher authorities would not allow this as it could cause confusion with King Edward VI schools, whose foundation had direct connection with the monarchy'.[29] From 1908, it became Luton Modern School instead; 'Modern' being an indication that classics would not be a significant part of the curriculum.[30]

Felicity Hunt explains that 'class-based organisation of Victorian education is well-known and it is generally accepted that this tradition had a profound effect upon the organisation of secondary education at least until the 1940s'.[31] This tradition could be seen in Bedford with the Harpur Trust[32] whose schools 'reflected the general attitude of the day, when class distinctions were more marked . . . The Grammar and High Schools believed themselves superior to the Modern Schools.'[33] The modern schools also took more country children.[34]

The school was mixed not because of ideology but for practical reasons. Sheila

---

24 Ibid., 22 April 1904.
25 J.G. Dony, *A History of Education in Luton*, p. 47.
26 T.A.E. Sanderson, 'Founding a Grammar School', *Bedfordshire Magazine* Vol. 4, No. 30 (Autumn 1954), p. 237.
27 Ibid., p. 238.
28 Ibid., p. 239.
29 J.G. Dony, *A History of Education in Luton*, p. 47. This school is referred to as Luton Modern School in this chapter.
30 H.C. Barnard, *A History of English Education from 1760* (University of London Press, 1969), pp. 130–131.
31 M.F. Hunt, 'Secondary Education for the Middle Class Girl: A Study of Ideology and Educational Practice 1870–1940 with Special Reference to the Harpur Trust Girls' Schools, Bedford' (Ph.D. Thesis, Newnham College, University of Cambridge, 1984), p. 398.
32 J. Godber, *The Harpur Trust 1552–1973* (White Crescent Press, 1973), pp. 110–116.
33 Ibid., p. 115.
34 Ibid., p. 114.

Fletcher has discussed the merits of single-sex schools and concludes that, in most cases, schools were mixed for matters of economy.[35] William Hoyle, the Clerk to the United School District of Luton (USDL) and later to the Luton Education Committee (LEC), was of the opinion that there were distinct advantages and recorded his views in a letter to Rebecca Higgins. He was unable to recommend a book which gave an unbiased opinion, but passed on his 'considerable experience as Headmaster of large schools in Lancashire with more than 1,000 children'. It was his belief that the sexes should be taught together. Claims which stated that this made girls 'rough and rude' could be counteracted by the effect on boys: 'it softens and refines [them], makes them more courteous and chivalrous and teaches the [gentle?] ones to be brave and self-reliant. Much may be said on both sides and my opinion is in favour of union where the Teachers can and will keep watch.'[36]

Sanderson confirmed that the Luton school was mixed 'not as a matter of principle but of convenience'.[37] He reiterated the point at a speech day in 1919 saying that as there was no such school for either sex, 'a mixed School was provided merely as a matter of expediency, not at all because its founders considered such an arrangement preferable to separate Schools for boys and for girls'.[38] Boys and girls shared the school but used separate entrances[39] and, for at least some of the time, sat at opposite sides of the classroom. At the 1919 speech day, Mr Whitbread, the Chairman, referred to Rowland Prothero as the 'father of this great school'.[40] Prothero claimed to have supplied the school with its badge and its motto and his account is very significant to this study because it brings together attitudes to learning and the influence of the straw industry. The badge consisted of 'three ears of corn loosely bound together'.

> I meant it to connect this new foundation with an ancient monastic establishment in the neighbourhood, which had been conspicuous for keeping alight the lamp of learning during the Dark Ages. In the fine parish church of Luton is the tomb of one of the abbots of the Abbey of St Albans, Abbot John of Wheathampstead. From this monument are taken the ears of corn which were his punning arms. But monastic institutions were unpopular in Luton, and the ears of corn, with their stalks might have been unacceptable, if they had not also represented the material of the straw-plaiting industry on which the commercial prosperity of the town had been founded. The motto links together badge and school, by the reward which awaits the labour alike of sower and teacher. Without a sowing, neither soil nor mind will yield harvest. This is tensely expressed in the Latin motto: 'Ubi semen, ibi messis'.[41]

This dual theme of sowing corn and teaching was continued throughout the life of

35 S. Fletcher, 'Co-education and the Victorian Grammar School', *History of Education* Vol. 11, No. 2 (1982), p. 87–98.
36 M/240 Letterbooks of USDL, 9 November 1896.
37 T.A.E. Sanderson, 'Founding a Grammar School', p. 238.
38 LMAG Box 4 Magazine of LMS 1919, p. 7.
39 In the new building (1908), SGM 31/1 Minutes of LMS, p. 60.
40 LMAG *Old Lutonian*, p. 4.
41 Lord Ernle, *Whippingham to Westminster*. Quoted in the *Old Lutonian* No. 50 (August 1968), p. 17. 'Where the seed is, there shall the harvest be.' Since Prothero wrote this, it has been shown that the arms in the church are not those of Abbot John of Wheathampstead but are in fact those of William of Wallingford, Abbot of St Albans from 1476 to 1492.

the mixed school and, later, the separate schools. At the speech day in 1919, Sanderson referred to 'Examination successes, Athletic distinctions and promising careers' as signs of healthy growth.[42] But 'the real harvest' would grow slowly 'a harvest of good citizens who will always place Public Duty before private interests; of real sportsmen who will always play the game; of men who will swear unto their neighbours and disappoint them not even though it be to their own hindrance'.[43] On 14 September 1904 and with these high ideals, the Luton Modern School opened the doors of an old hat factory in Park Square to forty-seven boys and thirty-eight girls.[44] Table 33 lists the Board of Governors, each to hold office for three years, and Table 34 notes the staff of the school.

Table 33. Board of Governors at Luton Modern School 1904

The Duchess of Bedford
Miss Amy Walmsley (Bedford Kindergarten College)
Mrs Wernher (from Luton Hoo)
Mr R.E. Prothero MVO (Chairman)
Alderman Warren (Vice-chairman)
Messrs W.R. Hawson
Asher J. Hucklesby
W.T. Lye
E. Oakley
A. Oakley
C.H. Osborne
R. Richmond
J.H. Staddon
A. Wilkinson
H.O. Williams[45]

Table 34. Members of staff at Luton Modern School 1904

Job title	Name	Salary
Principal	T.A.E. Sanderson MA	£300 per annum
Senior Assistant	E.W. Edmunds MA B.Sc.	£200 per annum
Assistant	J. Bygott	
Assistant	Miss Clara S. Gardner LL.A	
Assistant	J.B. Hoblyn ARCS	
Assistant	C. Wesley Hutchinson BA	
Assistant	W.E. Llewellyn	
Assistant	Frederic F. May ARCA	
Assistant	Miss R.E. Moylan	
Assistant	W. Otter	

---

[42] LMS Magazine 1919, p. 6.
[43] Ibid.
[44] *Sheaf*, Spring 1931, p. 16. Some *Sheaf* magazines can be seen at LMAG. Figures taken from BCC Minutes and school magazines indicate that there were usually more boys than girls at the schools.
[45] *The Luton and District Year Book and Almanack (1905)*, p. 97.

Miss Stansfeld from the Bedford Physical Training College offered weekly gymnastics classes at £35 per annum.[46] Apart from Mr Edmunds, Mr May and Mr Otter, who had been instructors under the Technical Instruction Committee, the staff appear to have been appointed from out-of-town since none of the names is familiar from the time of the Luton School Board.

The difference between elementary and secondary teachers has been pin-pointed by Summerfield who notes that attendance at a secondary school was a 'sine qua non for secondary school mistresses from about 1900 and acted as a form of class distinction'.[47]

Mr Edmunds subsequently wrote to the governors with a request for a revised salary scale and reminded them of the importance of the school to the life of the town: it was the only institution for higher education and 'makes the highway for any boy[48] who has the ability to proceed to University'. Edmunds claimed that 'the standard of work done at the school was as high, and measured by average was probably higher, than that done at Bedford Modern School'. He went on to ask that the governors should recognize the 'high standard of personal life and character' that was expected of the teachers and that 'the future depended greatly and largely upon the personal character and devotion to duty of the present staff'. Edmunds claimed that, as the next generation of the town would reap the benefit, a salary of £200 would 'not be an exceedingly great reward'.[49]

The *Luton Year Book (1905)* revealed the feelings of Lutonians. It noted that such a school, which provided for children in the south of the county as well as Luton, had been needed for years. 'The desirability of Luton lads receiving a special training for commercial life has been repeatedly urged by the Luton Chamber of Commerce'.[50] An academic curriculum was not mentioned; nor was there any reference to the education of girls. However, the official prospectus[51] claimed that the education offered was for both professional and commercial life and prepared the way for a university and higher technical education and also for prospective teachers. The *Luton Year Book (1905)* also printed a short article beside the calendar for July. This did not set out to make a direct case concerning the value of educating girls, but the fact that it was considered worth publishing suggests that it reflected the views of many in the town. It was entitled *Are College Girls Marrying Girls?* and refers to a 'certain professor of a Western University' who 'declared vigorously that the college-bred girl was wholly worthless as a domestic wife'. It was acknowledged that educated women might well disagree, but then went on to give some statistics which suggest that, although the unnamed professor may not be altogether correct, 'we must confess that [a college education] lessens her chances of matrimony'.[52]

---

46 SGM 31/1 Minutes of LMS, p. 42.
47 P. Summerfield, ed., 'Women, Education and the Professional Labour Market 1900–1950: The Case of the Secondary Schoolmistress', *History of Education Society*, Occasional Publication No. 8 (1987), p. 40.
48 Note that girls are not mentioned.
49 SGM 31/2 Minutes of LMS, October 1913, p. 101. In view of the fact that Edmunds was already receiving this amount, it could be that he is referring to a general salary scale.
50 *Luton Year Book (1905)*, p. 97.
51 Ibid., p. 98; Transcript of Stopsley School Logbooks, 12 September 1904.
52 Ibid. The reasons given are: the involvement of educated girls with the teaching profession and the

Entrance to the school was by examination. In theory every child in the town was able to sit for the examination to qualify for a free place.[53] However, it seems likely that local headteachers were selective about which children were entered and there may have been capable children from poorer families who were not given the opportunity.[54] Fees were £1 10s (£1.50) per term. Monitors who had attended the Pupil-teacher Centre were transferred on half fees.[55] One of these was Nellie Breed, daughter of the headmaster at Stopsley.[56]

The general course covered four years; after the first two, some specialization was allowed. The curriculum covered English, geography, history, French, German, mathematics, higher arithmetic, geometry, chemistry, physics, domestic hygiene, botany, drawing, manual training and needlework, but not Latin. At the end of the course, pupils were permitted to sit for the London University Matriculation Examination or for the Junior Certificate of the London Chamber of Commerce.

In 1906, HMI Miss Crosby and HMI Mr F.W. Westaway inspected the school. They noted that the idea of scholarships was new to Luton, but stated that in their opinion many would be needed 'to ensure the existence of the school'.[57] In 1912, it was noted that free places were given to the first twenty children on the list.[58] In 1913, there were twenty-six.[59] Opportunities were available for Junior County scholarships and County Pupil Teacher scholarships[60] and, by 1918, 'two leaving scholarships to the value of £50' were provided annually by the BCC.[61] Scholarships were also available from the Bigland, Gillingham and Long Foundation.[62]

The concept of a secondary school was new to Luton[63] and one of the greatest problems which Sanderson had to face was the reluctance of some parents to allow their children to stay long enough to take advantage of the education on offer. HMI Mr Westaway and HMI Miss Crosby were insistent about 'the need to fix the idea in the public mind that the School Courses should be prolonged for a period of four years'.[64] Sanderson later complained that the school would not be able to 'perform the functions proper to a Secondary School unless School-life covers a considerable period of years'. Many pupils had been leaving before the age of sixteen. Sanderson also regretted that 'pupils [had] joined too late', but this had been remedied to a certain extent 'by the regulation under which we give preference to those under 13 years of age'. He looked forward to the time when children left school at sixteen or preferably eighteen.[65]

---

fact that 'what are probably her most attractive years, physically, are spent in comparative isolation from the opposite sex'.

53   25% of the number admitted.
54   A. Allsopp, *Crimson and Gold*, ch. 1.
55   SGM 31/1 Minutes of LMS, 9 September 1904, p. 29.
56   1997/23/1 Admissions register Luton Modern School.
57   Ibid., p. 112, 10 October 1906.
58   SGM 31/2 Minutes of LMS, p. 42.
59   Ibid., 1 July 1913, p. 77.
60   SGM 31/1 Minutes of LMS, p. 112.
61   SGM 31/3 Minutes of LMS, p. 59.
62   LMS Magazine 1919, p. 7.
63   A former pupil and member of staff has observed that, in her opinion, the school never sat happily in the town.
64   SGM 31/1 Minutes of LMS, 10 October 1906, p. 112.
65   LMS Magazine 1919, p. 7.

In 1908, the Duke of Bedford opened the school's new building opposite the old site in Park Square. Dony believed that, although there were free places open to all, the character of the school was essentially middle-class.[66] The school 'kept itself aloof from the rest' and kept different hours.[67] It took no part in inter-school activities such as football competitions, athletic meetings and swimming matches. It had some excellent teachers 'Hoblyn for science, Edmunds for English, but equality of education for both sexes meant little so long as Sanderson's idea of education beyond the School Certificate[68] . . . was mathematics, physics, and chemistry and no more'. Dony sums up his criticism by saying that 'if any town needed a wider concept of the purpose of education it was Luton'.[69] The girls of Luton had new opportunities, but the vision found in schools such as the North London Collegiate School was still absent.

In Sanderson's speech, given on 24 March 1919 in the presence of H.A.L. Fisher, President of the Board of Education, he reviewed the progress which had been made since 1904. There had been just under one hundred pupils when the school opened. By May 1908, the numbers had risen to 177 and by 1918 to 411 – a figure which 'strains the accommodation to the utmost'. The figures in Table 35 demonstrate the growth of the mixed school.[70]

Table 35. Number on roll at Luton Modern School 1904–1918

Year	Girls	Boys and Girls
1904	39	85
1905	67	113
1906	61	114
1907	70	146
1908	86	207
1909	88	237
1910	96	243
1911	127	276
1912	136	297
1913	145	334
1914	153	350
1915	148	352
1916	158	381
1917	176	384
1918	181	390

[66] J.G. Dony, A *History of Education in Luton*, p. 49.
[67] Ibid. Wednesday afternoon was a holiday, but there was school on Saturday morning.
[68] This examination replaced the Cambridge Local examination.
[69] J.G. Dony, *A History of Education in Luton*, p. 49.
[70] These were collated by Mrs Iris Bond, one-time secretary of Luton High School for Girls. The apparent discrepancies for 1908 and 1918 are probably the result of figures being recorded at different times in the year.

Sanderson went on the say that the school had been entering children for the Junior and Senior examination but, since 1915, had concentrated on the Senior Examination. Whole forms rather than individuals were being entered for the examinations of the Cambridge Syndicate. Table 36 shows the results up to this time.

Table 36. Results of Cambridge Syndicate Examinations 1915–1919.[71]

– In the Junior, 256 passes, including 17 honours, 3 of which were in the first Class.
– in the Senior, 242 passes, including 75 honours, 16 of which were in the first Class.
– 34 of our pupils have passed the Matriculation Examination of London University, 11 of them being placed in the first Division.
– 4 boys have successfully attempted the Intermediate Examination in Science,
– and one girl the Intermediate examination in Arts of the same University.
– Some years ago one of our boys won a Royal Scholarship for Chemistry at the Imperial College of Science and Technology; and
– later on another boy was awarded a £60 Scholarship for Science at Trinity Hall, Cambridge.

It is certain that the Luton Modern School provided a higher standard of education than had been previously known in Luton but such an education was open to a limited number of the town's children and most of the places were taken by children whose parents could afford the fees. The free places were open to all, but many families were restricted by the cost of the uniform and school life in general.[72] An example of this can be seen in the regular charity collections. Children promised to donate a certain amount each week and those who were only able to offer the minimum felt it keenly when others gave much more.[73] Miss Webb has described her experiences of the Luton Modern School:

> A teacher came to see my father and persuaded him to let me sit and the result was that I joined the school in September 1917. The headmaster was T.A.E. Sanderson and the staff was of rather mixed ability since many of the men were in the forces. However I made good progress in a bright class and was very proud to wear the school uniform including the wide brimmed straw boater. November 11th 1918 was an exciting day when I saw the Town Crier, Charlie Irons, on the top of St Mary's Church tower, ringing his bell and declaring that the Armistice had been signed.[74]

At the 1919 speech day, the President of the Board of Education, H.A.L. Fisher, made observations about education in general and Luton education in particular. In his opinion a good secondary school was one of the best pieces of good fortune which could happen to a town because 'it enriches the life of the town in a thousand and one different ways'. Referring to the plans for a new girls' school he recommended, 'don't stint your imagination'. The new school should be 'planned for posterity . . . beautiful and attractive . . . cathedrals of the mind . . . spare no

[71] LMS Magazine 1919, p. 8.
[72] This has been commented on in many conversations. Girls who attended Luton schools before the 1944 Education Act, frequently mention the fact that their parents could not afford the uniform, which was compulsory, or the means-tested special places.
[73] Information supplied by Miss E. Webb.
[74] Ibid.

expense'. 'The function of education is to make people desire to learn more, it is to quicken curiosity, it is to give an appetite for books, it is to refine taste'. Fisher re-iterated the views of the headmaster concerning children leaving to earn a living without taking full advantage of the secondary education that was theirs and threw out a challenge to the town:

> Well, now what contribution is Luton going to make to this? Are you going to leave it all to be done by Bedford? Have you no ambition, ladies and gentlemen? If I was a citizen of Luton I would not rest until my educational institutions far exceeded those of the rival city.[75]

The Luton Modern School for Girls

The next, very significant contribution which was made for girls was the establishment of a separate school. This was to be on a site on the outskirts of the town in old army huts from Ampthill in Bedfordshire. A headmistress had to be chosen and the choice which was made was a momentous one; nobody who ever had anything to do with Miss Helen K. Sheldon will ever forget her. She was a lady with the vision and steely determination to provide Luton with a school such as it had never seen before – or since.[76] The minutes of the school give the bare details. There were five candidates; three were interviewed: Miss E. Edwards from the Girls' Grammar School in Bradford, Miss F.M. Jackson from the Luton Modern School and Miss Sheldon from King Edward VI Grammar School in Handsworth. It was unanimously resolved 'that Miss H.K. Sheldon be appointed headmistress of the Girls' Modern School in accordance with the terms and conditions contained in the Scheme'. Her salary was to be £400 rising by increments of £50 to £500 per annum.[77]

Miss Sheldon had been educated at the Royal Holloway College (1902–1905)[78] and obtained Oxford Final Honours – School of English Language and Literature.[79] In 1940, she recalled how she had first come to Luton not realizing at the time 'how much I should love this town'[80] and promised that she would try 'to give the town the best gift it could have, a good School'.[81] Sir Frederick Mander responded by saying that 'during her twenty-eight years of service she had made [it] one of the finest in the country'.[82] She never lost her sense of vocation.[83] The head of her co-school, the Grammar School for Boys, paid her this patronizing compliment: 'Mr Webb said that she was not only a great Head Mistress; he was convinced that she would have also made an equally great Headmaster'.[84] In 1945, she was awarded the

---

[75] LMS Magazine 1919, p. 16.

[76] Carol Dyhouse points out that educated women were often described as 'formidable'. C. Dyhouse, *No Distinction of Sex? Women in British Universities 1870–1939* (UCL Press, 1995), p. 156.

[77] SGM 31/4 Minutes of LMS, 25 June 1919.

[78] *Sheaf*, November 1947, p. 4; information from the Royal Holloway College Ref: RHC/AC/200/1.

[79] *Luton Year Book and Directory (1923)*, p. 19. Students were allowed to sit for their chosen examination. C. Bingham, *The History of the Royal Holloway College* (Constable, 1987), pp. 82–83.

[80] *Sheaf*, 1940 p. 5.

[81] *Sheaf*, November 1947, p. 22.

[82] Ibid.

[83] *Sheaf*, July 1945, p. 4.

[84] *Sheaf*, November 1947, p. 19.

31. Helen K. Sheldon, headmistress of Luton Modern School for Girls

OBE.[85] When she retired, Mr J. Burgoyne, former Mayor of Luton and governor for many years said:

> Miss Sheldon came to Luton in 1919, and accepted responsibility for fostering the highest graces of our young womanhood; for giving to our people cultural aspirations beyond and above the provisions of compulsory standards of education; for moulding a reputation – character – and not least, a tradition for the new school-building which came to her control, fresh from the builder's hands.[86]

It was resolved that there would be twelve assistant mistresses in addition to a domestic science mistress, art mistress and a teacher of music. Women teachers from the mixed school were to transfer, apart from Miss Jackson, one of the unsuccessful candidates for the headship, who was allowed to remain with Sanderson.

Table 37. Members of staff at Luton Modern School for Girls 1919[87]

Staff:

Miss B.L. Bracey		
(BA Birmingham)	Geography and History	£170
Miss H.G. Budge		
(ACTC Board of Education, Teacher Artists'		
Certificate, Royal Drawing Society, Bronze		
Medallist Association of Art)	Art	£200

---

[85] *Sheaf,* July 1945, p. 4.
[86] *Sheaf,* November 1947, p. 3. The new building did not materialize until 1930.
[87] SGM 31/4 Minutes of LMS, 7 October 1919.

Miss A. Cooper		
(BA Birmingham)	Mathematics and Latin	£180
Miss M.A. Newton		
(BSc London)	Science	£200
Miss P. Peacey		
(1st class, Board of Education Diploma)	Domestic Science	£150
Miss P.L. Rickards		
(BA Hons in French, London B ès L. Paris)	French and History	£210

Staff transferred from the Mixed School:

Miss V.M. Barnes		
(BA London)		£170
Miss J. Macfarlane		
(Cambridge Higher Local and residence abroad		£220
Miss M.M. Netherwood		
(BA Birmingham)		£170
Miss A.L. Price		
(BA London, Honours in English and French)		£200
Miss C.K. Thomas		
(BA Victoria)		£220

Awaiting appointment:

Miss D.C. Rose	to be appointed	Drill Mistress	£6 per half day per term
Miss Macfarlane	to be considered as	Second Mistress	

To be advertised:

Post of full-time Singing Mistress, capable of assisting in certain ordinary school subject.

One member of staff, Miss Bracey, is interesting. She was brought up on the Cadbury Estate at Bournville, joined the staff in 1919 and, after working for two terms, was appointed to the permanent staff in March 1920. In 1921, she was given leave for one year, without salary, to attend a geography course.[88] Instead she went to Vienna and undertook voluntary work with the Friends War Victims Relief Committee, becoming a 'considerable figure in the Society'.[89] The governors of the Luton Modern School were not pleased with her change of plan and gave her the option of resigning or having her engagement terminated.[90] She chose to resign and stayed in Europe for many years to work and to help refugees. The Society of Friends say that she spent twenty-one years in their international service, 'for 13 of which, she was Directing Secretary of the Friends Committee for Refugees and Aliens, and its predecessor, the German Emergency Committee'. After the Second World War she was appointed to 'head up a small department of the German section of the Foreign Office' and in 1951/1952 held a similar appointment with the American High Commission in Germany. In 1942 she was awarded the OBE.[91]

88 SGM 31/4 Minutes of LMS, 7 October 1919, 23 March 1920, 3 May 1921 and 12 July 1921.
89 Communication from the Religious Society of Friends in Britain, 27 October 1999.
90 SGM/4 Minutes of LMS, 4 October 1921, 6 December 1921 and 17 January 1921.
91 Information supplied by the Library of the Friends House, London: Friends House Library, Box L16, *The Friend*, 1942 p. 12 and 1946 p. 500; *Friends Quarterly*, 1953; *Oxford Times*, November 1985.

The school was officially opened on 30 September 1919 by Mr Cecil Harmsworth, MP for Luton, and the sense of euphoria which was felt at the time has been recalled many times by the girls who were there. Two hundred and nine girls 'all brimful of excitement' gathered together at the Park Square school and then 'at last we were free . . . Mr Harmsworth turned the silver key which was to unlock a treasure trove richer than any of us then imagined'.[92] Twenty-one years later, in an issue of *The Sheaf* which was dedicated to reminiscences, there are articles that speak of the old army huts 'to which one grew unexpectedly attached in spite of their inconveniences'.[93] They became 'an almost legendary Elysium'.[94] Miss Macfarlane, the first senior mistress of the school (1919–1939), recorded her impressions:[95]

> The other day I came across some 'Snaps' that I had taken a long time ago, and in a flash I was back in 'the huts' sitting in an 'outside form-room' with door flung wide open. The song of the lark arose above the practising of German vowel sounds, and as heads bent over exercise books, I could see green grass and a field of waving corn. For the sake of those who do not know what is meant by an 'outside form-room' let me explain briefly the layout of the huts.
>
> A wide corridor led up the centre, with form-rooms opening from it on either side. Through each of these 'inside rooms' you passed into an 'outside room' – much to be desired in summer, but not quite so pleasant in winter, for when the wind blew hard, it seemed to come through every crack in the wooden walls and sometimes even put out the one stove that heated each form-room.
>
> At the top of the corridor was the hall, running across the width of the four classrooms. This, of course, had to be used not only for Prayers, but also for Gym, for singing lessons and in the end for a form-room. As it was the only room in which there was any clear space at all, you can imagine the competition for it for rehearsals when a play was being produced. As the years went by, the roof began to leak rather badly, and what would you damsels of a later age say to doing your School Certificate examination with buckets and pails set about to catch the raindrops as they fell? Perhaps you would prefer the years when the sun blazed down on the corrugated roof, and the floor had to be watered to prevent the temperature from rising up to 100°.
>
> Such was the inside of our school. Now what of the outside? Not a seat anywhere, nowhere to sit except on the steps of the outside form-rooms; no tennis courts, no netball court, and only a rough hockey ground! . . . The netball 'court' was just a cinder patch. . . . Cricket and rounders were played on a piece of waste ground where the houses now stand in Alexandra Avenue. The road up the Avenue, by the way, was not made up for a few years, so you ploughed your way to school through thick mud when it rained, counting yourself lucky if you arrived without losing a shoe or a rubber boot.

92 *Sheaf,* December 1940, p. 2. (Special Twenty-First Birthday Edition.)
93 *Sheaf,* 1940, p. 15.
94 Ibid., p. 11.
95 *Sheaf,* November 1947, pp. 6–7.

The school continued to grow and the cry of insufficient room was a recurring one throughout its life.[96]

Table 38. Number on roll at Luton Modern School for Girls 1919–1924

Year	Number on roll
1919	209
1920	250
1921	301
1922	330
1923	319
1924	309

Miss Sheldon, however,

> allowed no deficiencies of buildings or of equipment to cause a lowering of the high standard set for her school . . . no one who was privileged to share with Miss Sheldon, even in the humblest capacity, the building up of Luton High School and the creation of its fine tradition could fail to be permanently influenced by her meticulous care for detail and her passion for perfection.[97]

This sense of euphoria and commitment to the school is typical of recollections and reminiscences, for the school did develop a tradition and feelings of loyalty. This elation, however, was only shared by a small proportion of Luton girls and could probably be described as élitist when placed against the background of Luton as a whole.

Although girls were admitted at the age of nine, the school's main aim was to provide girls between the ages of ten to eighteen with a 'sound general Education, which shall fit them for the needs of professional and commercial life, and which shall form a step in the passage from the Public Elementary Schools to the Universities or to the Higher Technical Institutions'.[98] Entry by the age of twelve was necessary in order to obtain the full benefit of the education on offer. Parents were continually encouraged to allow their children to remain at school as long as possible[99] and were told that there would be a fine 'not exceeding £5' if a girl was taken from the school before the age of sixteen. Each year there was to be an advertisement in the local newspaper with details of the examination for free places which was open to children who lived in the south of the county[100] and which was held in May or June. The subjects tested were English (spelling, grammar and composition) and arithmetic, special attention being paid to handwriting and general neatness.[101] Fees were £2 a term,[102] rising to £3 the following year.[103]

---

96   See n. 70.
97   *Sheaf,* November 1947, pp. 7–8. The name was changed to Luton High School in 1930.
98   SGM 31/4 Minutes of LMS, 15 July 1919.
99   *Sheaf,* Spring 1924, p. 15.
100 SGM 31/4 Minutes of LMS, 15 July 1919.
101 Ibid., 15 July 1919.
102 Ibid.
103 Ibid., 2 December 1919.

The Preparatory Course, to be commenced at the earliest possible age, included English (reading, grammar, and composition), English history, geography, arithmetic and algebra, practical geometry, nature study or elementary science, drawing, needlework, singing and drill.[104] This was the same as the curriculum for boys except that needlework was substituted for woodwork. The General Course, which began when the girls were eleven and lasted for five years, was English (grammar, composition and literature), history, geography, French, Latin or German, mathematics, theoretical and practical science, drawing, needlework, cookery, singing and drill.[105] It was decided to apply to the Board of Education to add advanced courses in science and mathematics for the boys and modern studies for the girls.[106] At the end of the General Course whole forms were entered for the Cambridge Senior Local Examination.[107]

A homework timetable was supplied each term and girls were expected to state the exact amount of time needed to complete the work.[108] School hours were weekdays between 9a.m. and 12.20p.m. and also from 2p.m. to 3.30p.m. and it was expected that girls would come for organized games on Saturday mornings. The boys, on the other hand, still had to attend each morning from 9a.m. to 12.20p.m. and then from 2p.m. to 4.15p.m. on afternoons except Wednesdays and Saturdays, which were set aside for games. Girls therefore worked fewer hours than the boys, which was in keeping with the ideas of the time.[109]

The ideal of a girls' 'high school', as pioneered by Frances Mary Buss and described by Sara Burstall,[110] was reflected in the ethos of the school in Luton.[111] We can therefore make the links that were described at the beginning of this chapter. Girls and teachers who were educated at the North London Collegiate School took their ideas to other areas and other schools. The spirit of Miss Buss had come to Luton, seventy years after the London school was founded.

Girls at the Luton Modern School were set high standards in everything and very soon successes were being recorded. The first edition of *The Sheaf* in 1924 lists form prizes (for the whole year's work) and subject prizes. Five girls had passed the Cambridge School Certificate with honours and twenty-seven at other levels, some having distinctions and some Equivalent London Matriculation;[112] two girls had passed the London Intermediate Arts Examination; and another two the London Intermediate Science Examination. The first girl from the school to graduate was Vera Stanton with a London BA in German.[113] By 1924, girls were at University

---

104   Ibid., 15 July 1919.
105   Ibid., 15 July 1919.
106   Ibid., 2 December 1919. 'Modern studies' was a one-year course of general studies to be followed after the School Certificate examination. E. Kaye, *A History of Queen's College* (London: Chatto & Windus, 1972), p. 156.
107   Minutes of the LMS, 15 July 1919.
108   It may well have been the case, as it was later, that girls did not answer this question honestly. The homework always took much longer than was claimed.
109   S. Burstall, *English High Schools for Girls: Their aims, Organisation and Management* (Longman, Green & Co., 1907), pp. 94–98.
110   Ibid.
111   This was still apparent in 1943.
112   *Sheaf*, Spring 1924, p. 16.
113   Ibid., pp. 2, 16 and 27.

College, London, and the Royal Holloway College, five girls were at training colleges, one was at the Norland Institute, another was nursing at Queen's Hospital, Birmingham, and eleven girls were taking commercial courses. Six were bursars, another six were teaching in private schools and two had posts at Laporte's Chemical Works. One student was studying singing and music at Trinity College.[114]

News of the progress of girls who had left was regularly recorded in the school magazines and there were many accounts of life in different colleges and universities. More unusual entries were sent by Josephine Juett from the Art Training College at Clapham High School[115] and Marjorie Thorn who was the first girl in the school to choose a career in photography.[116] There is an article which describes the elation felt when it was learnt that Edith Smith had won an Open Scholarship for French to the Royal Holloway College.[117] Girls from Luton who, twenty-five years before, would have had no chance to reap academic success were now given that opportunity. The BCC provided leaving scholarships,[118] but there were also charities to be tapped. Hilda Gregory had a scholarship from the Bigland Foundation,[119] Edith Smith was given money by the Draper's Company and the Chews Foundation[120] and won a State Scholarship[121] and Winifred Ball received a Governors' Exhibition.[122]

The school was divided into houses[123] which were named after famous women. Girls chose the house colours and mottoes and had to choose well because 'they would last as long as the School lasted. It was a great responsibility.'[124] The houses were Boadicea (*non sibi sed patriae*), Grace Darling (*immersabilis*), Elizabeth Fry (*non nobis solum nati sumus*), Helen Keller (*per ardua ad alta*) and Florence Nightingale (*sursum corda*). When the school grew bigger, three more houses were added. There was considerable competition between the houses for stars, gardens and sports and each house had its social occasions and chosen charity.[125] Particular interests were encouraged and societies formed. By 1924 there was a Literary, Historical and Debating Society, an Art Club and a French Club. A choir practised each Tuesday after school, gave concerts and took part in the Bedfordshire Eisteddfod (in which the elementary schools also took part).[126] A National Savings Association began well but, by 1924, enthusiasm had declined. It was lamented that the statistics 'seem to force upon one the sad conclusion that thrift is not a virtue which thrives of itself'.[127]

Charity and service to others were always high on the list of priorities. One thoughtful activity was the annual collection of wild flowers which were sent to

---

114   Ibid., p. 27. Probably Trinity College, London.
115   *Sheaf*, Spring 1926, p. 34.
116   *Sheaf*, Spring 1928, p. 41.
117   *Sheaf*, Summer 1924, p. 8.
118   SGM 31/5 Minutes of LMS, 21 March 1922.
119   SGM 31/4 Minutes of LMS, 2 December 1919.
120   *Sheaf*, Spring 1925, p. 10.
121   Ibid.
122   Ibid.
123   *Sheaf*, 1940, p. 9.
124   Ibid.
125   *Sheaf*, Spring 1924, pp. 3–8.
126   Ibid.
127   Ibid., p 13.

schools in the East End of London 'far from any park or open space'.[128] Visitors came to give talks and outside visits were organized.[129] Altogether there was never a shortage of activities. A prefect system was set up and Old Girls had regular meetings, usually of a social nature.[130] Sports were taken very seriously and, in 1920–1921, an invitation to join the Midlands Netball League was accepted. Games were played against local elementary schools, St Albans High School, Bedford High School, Bedford Modern School, Hitchin Girls' Grammar School, Northampton Girls' School, Kettering High School and Cedars School at Leighton Buzzard. Sports day included competitions between individuals and also between houses.[131]

There was always a great love of literature and drama. The governors allowed Miss Sheldon £100 to build up a school library,[132] but that amount was far from sufficient so the girls were asked to donate a book when they left and many 'responded generously'.[133] It has to be asked how the poorer girls with free places felt about that. Large-scale stage performances took place; a former member of staff recalled that 'for long it was the custom to "get up" something for the annual prize-giving – scenes from *A Midsummer Night's Dream*, from the "Alice" books, and so forth. These efforts were much rehearsed, and polished to an incredible degree.'[134] P.C. Vigor described in an amusing way the culture of literacy which was being instilled into the secondary school girls:

> For instance, against all the odds, I once dated a High School girl, being conditioned for a middle-class life by Miss Helen K. Sheldon, a strict disciplinarian, and after a meeting or two my date repeated these lines of Shelley to me:
> > 'The fountains mingle with the rivers . . .'
> At the time I wondered what she was babbling about: now I marvel at the type of literature then available to well-brought [sic] up young ladies.[135]

It can be seen that, from the very beginning, Luton Modern School for Girls aspired to the highest standards in all aspects of school life. However, over and above all else, Miss Sheldon wanted a tradition to pass down to later generations.[136] In 1924, she asked whether standards were being set high enough and whether the tradition being built had 'the right ingredients':

> First of all, I think we must put that greatest of all virtues 'Charity', or to use the word easier to understand 'Love' . . . And with love let us put its twin-brother unselfishness . . . I just want to mention three others: A cheerful spirit . . . the power of imagination to illumine the dull things . . . and last, but

128 *Sheaf*, Summer 1924, p. 10.
129 *Sheaf*, Spring 19245, pp. 16–20 and Summer 1924, pp. 11–15.
130 *Sheaf*, Summer 1924, pp. 32–35.
131 Ibid., pp. 5–6.
132 *Sheaf*, 1940, p. 5.
133 *Sheaf*, Summer 1924, p. 36.
134 *Sheaf*, November 1947, p. 5.
135 P.C. Vigor, *Memories Are Made of This* (LMAG, 1983), p. 58. Vigor came to Luton when he was aged 12, c.1925. In 1991 he wrote a series of reminiscences for the *Evening Post Echo*, which have been reproduced in his book.
136 This was: 'Our school tradition of honesty, unselfishness and hard work has been worthily gained. Let us pass it on unsoiled.'

by no means least, the power to see the other person's point of view, always a difficult thing, perhaps the most difficult thing of all.[137]

Later, a tradition card with the following ideal was given to every girl to keep in her desk as a reminder of the standards expected of her on a daily basis:

Our school tradition
of
unselfishness,
honesty
and
hard work
has been worthily gained.
Let us pass it on unsoiled.

Admission registers

Admission registers from the mixed school for 1904, 1905–1907 and 1912[138] provide background information concerning the social class of girls who were admitted, the schools they had formerly attended,[139] the length of time they spent at the secondary school and eventual employment prospects. These statistics have been examined in an attempt to establish whether there are any trends in social mobility or significant changes in employment opportunities in the early years of the twentieth century. The figures are by no means complete, but several conclusions can be drawn. These suggest that, during the first year of the school, parents were wary and kept their daughters at the private schools.[140] However, the secondary school seems to have proved its worth and girls began enrolling in the local authority school.[141]

It appears that girls were mainly from the commercial classes; schoolmasters and one physician represent the professional classes. Established family tradesmen, proprietors and managers in industry sent their daughters to the school. Most parents had to pay, although a limited number of girls who passed the required examination were allocated free places. Figures show that some parents were helped financially, but there is no indication about how such decisions were made. Bursars were given financial help to stay at the secondary school before becoming student teachers.[142]

As has been noted, parents were often reluctant to allow their children to stay until the age of sixteen. By 1930,[143] the parents of girls who left school early were said to have broken their agreement and were fined: twenty-two out of the ninety-three from the class of 1930 had to pay, although five others were excused because of financial stress, father's illness or because the girls had permission to help at home.

The early registers from Luton Modern School give very little specific information concerning girls after they left except in the case of student teachers. This may

---

137 *Sheaf,* Spring 1924, p. 3.
138 1997/23. Figures upon which the following conclusions are based can be found in the Appendix.
139 See Chapter Nine.
140 For details, see Chapter Nine.
141 There were girls from south Bedfordshire and some from Hertfordshire.
142 See Chapter Six.
143 Figures from attendance registers and *Sheaf* magazines at LMAG.

mean that the headmaster was not interested in the other girls or, as seems more likely, he only recorded facts which would add to the status of the school. There were, however, records of boys who went on to higher education or white collar jobs. By 1907, a few girls were going to colleges or universities.

Edward John Stafford, the manager of the cocoa factory, had two daughters, both of whom are recorded in the admission registers. Lucy was born in 1894 and went to the private Luton High School before being admitted to the Luton Modern School in 1906. She did very well and left in 1912 to go to University College, Reading.[144] Later she returned as a member of staff.[145] Her sister, Pamela, was admitted in 1907 and was mentioned as being 'at home' after she left in 1914. However, the entry adds 'now working at Munitions Office'. As this family was of a relatively high social standing in the town, this suggests that working for the war effort was acceptable. Another interesting entry concerns the daughter of Sanderson, the head of the school. Una Sanderson was born in 1902 and had a governess before being admitted in 1912 to her father's school where she stayed for four years. She then transferred to Wyggeston Girls' Grammar School, Leicester.[146] As Wyggeston School taught classics it may be that Sanderson wanted his daughter to follow that curriculum. Miss Edith Webb also remembers that Sanderson's two daughters had a teashop on Park Square for some time so that must also have been considered a respectable occupation.

The earliest admission register available for the girls' school is from 1930, which is strictly speaking beyond the scope of this study. However, details have been considered in order to see if any employment patterns can be determined.[147] Teaching is represented and a small minority of girls went into higher education, but millinery still had its attractions. However, interest in commerce was strong and figures demonstrate that occupations taken up by girls who were admitted to the school in 1930 bear a strong similarity to those which were open to boys in the early years of the century.[148]

Conclusion

Luton Modern School sat happily against a background of progress from a national point of view, but the way it was seen by the rest of the town can be judged by the attitude of Vigor.[149] He saw that the girls were being groomed for the middle classes and noted that any friendship with them was 'against all the odds'. It has been demonstrated that, during the years looked at in this study, Luton was not a town which sought high standards of academic success for its children because its first consideration had always been towards fitting boys for local industries. Prosperity was based on a commercial life and that set the boundaries of its aspirations. Girls could choose to continue their education as part of teacher training, which was acceptable as it was directly linked to the continuation of the status quo. Girls from

[144] Earlier in this chapter statistics given by Sanderson (1918) noted the successes of several boys. It has to be asked why he did not mention Lucy Stafford.

[145] Magazine of LMS 1916–1917.

[146] H. Whitbread and K. Zanker, ed., *Wyggeston Girls Centenary 1878–1978* (Stanley Hunt, 1978).

[147] The *Sheaf* magazines regularly mention occupations of former pupils.

[148] See Appendix.

[149] P.C. Vigor, *Memories Are Made of This*, p. 58.

the professional and commercial classes experienced a different kind of schooling in private 'respectable' schools.

Bedford, on the other hand, was a town where prosperity was, to a large extent, based on the excellence of its schools. When the 1902 Education Act required the county council to establish secondary schooling it had the inclination, the expertise and the experience to fulfil that obligation and no time was lost. Luton, on its own, would have had considerable difficulty in reacting so promptly. The headteachers of the secondary schools had no connection with the town. T.A.E. Sanderson was cast in the public school mould, which was reflected in the training of cadets and in the house system. He set high standards, but his inclinations were always towards the boys and he admitted his relief at losing the girls. It seems likely that Helen K. Sheldon had been educated according to the principles of Frances Mary Buss and she brought a completely new dimension to the education of girls in Luton.

The provision of free places gave excellent opportunities to a limited number of intelligent girls from the elementary schools to benefit from a secondary education with high academic standards. They subsequently enjoyed wider employment prospects, but opportunities were still limited on account of the expense involved in buying uniforms and the difficulties involved with the financial obligations of extra-curricular activities.[150] Parents in Luton had no experience of secondary education and had to be educated themselves to understand that their children would have to stay at school until they were sixteen in order to reap the full benefit of the curriculum. A considerable amount of pressure was needed to press this point home; signed agreements and fines had to be introduced. Even in 1931 it was acknowledged that, as there were 'a good many openings in employment' open for young people under sixteen, 'there was a certain leakage' of girls who did not stay to complete the first part of the secondary school course.[151] It is fitting here to acknowledge the contribution of so many parents who had the vision to support their children through years of secondary education even though this was undoubtedly a considerable financial sacrifice.

Although the schools catered for a minority who were middle class or who were being groomed to become middle class, they were respected and former students were valued in the employment market. However, it appears that they remained detached from the town and pupils preferred each other's company to that of children from other Luton schools.[152] If the Luton Modern School was regarded as élitist, then there was also a type of hierarchy within the school[153] where high achievers were the main focus of attention. Generations of girls who went there held it in high regard, usually with gratitude and often with affection, for they recognized that they were the recipients of opportunities which had never before been available to the girls of Luton. Not until the 1944 Butler Education Act would all the children in Luton be able to share the same aspirations.

---

[150] Ibid., p. 4.
[151] *Sheaf*, Spring 1931, p. 17.
[152] P.C. Vigor, *Memories Are Made of This*, p. 5.
[153] This refers to the girls' school in particular; this book has not focused on the boys' school.

Conclusion

This book has looked at the changes in education and employment prospects for girls in Luton and has tried to demonstrate how these two aspects of their lives were inter-related.

Increased opportunities

The date chosen for the commencement of this study (1874) was an important one for girls in Luton because it marked both the establishment of the School Board and the introduction of compulsory education. Whereas girls' time had once been dominated by the demands of the hat industry and their educational prospects had been at the mercy of parents' ability to pay fees and forgo their children's income, regular attendance at school was now obligatory.

Women in Luton had traditionally received education in less formal organizations and this kind of initiative was still alive, for example private commercial courses were available. Organizations such as the Sunday and adult schools no longer needed to teach basic literacy but continued to receive loyal support in classes which extended interests and stimulated discussions. Lectures given under the auspices of groups such as the Workers' Education Association (WEA) were also supported by Luton women. Middle-class families who were conscious of their status and who wished to have their daughters educated as young ladies, supported private establishments throughout the years covered in this book.

However, the fee-paying day secondary school which had been set up by Bedfordshire County Council (BCC) was open to all and became increasingly popular. Children whose parents were unable to pay could earn a free place, but there were other financial constraints such as purchasing uniforms and supporting charities. It was therefore inevitable that this school was seen to be for the privileged few. It also seems likely that some kind of selection existed within the girls' school itself when the emphasis became decidedly academic. However, by 1924 there was, for a small minority, the very real possibility of a university education.

There were also increased opportunities for girls in the employment market. Changes in the hat industry had required local businessmen to welcome other industries into the town, with the result that women had wider choices. Census figures show that, while the hat industry dominated the scene, many women were taking advantage of opportunities to work in local factories and offices. By the 1920s, a Juvenile Advisory Committee had been set up to offer advice to boys and girls who were leaving school. This would hardly have been necessary when one industry dominated women's lives, but times were changing.

Lost opportunities

Opportunities which were being lost were mainly connected with the traditional freedoms in the town. It had been possible for women to combine a domestic role with that of a working woman with economic power. These two roles were socially acceptable. Women were not subordinate; rather it was often the men who lacked economic status. The nature of the hat industry meant that women could work at home, sometimes earning more than their husbands, and at the same time run their homes and care for their children. There was no stigma as there might have been in other towns and no pressure to conform to the ideal of a working father with a dependent wife. However, the changing employment scene which came with the arrival of the new industries set in place patterns of changing attitudes.

Children also used to have economic power and could, from an early age, work long hours during the busy season. Compulsory schooling was a considerable challenge to this way of life. Compromises were made in the form of half-time working and Labour Certificates, but the education authorities continually had to assert control in the matter of absenteeism and punctuality; there was a continuing battle between the demands of school and work.

It might be considered simplistic to say that women had freedom over how they used their time and, admittedly, there must have been periods when the hat industry made excessive demands on them, but women in Luton did have significant freedoms compared with the lives of women in other parts of the country. Compulsion was not something which came easily to an independently minded population. Compulsory schooling threatened these freedoms, as did changes in the economic structure of the town. The people of Luton were having to accept a more structured way of life.

Institutions also lost some of their influence in the town. Before 1874, denominational schools had been dominant but, although several good schools remained, the influence of the Church was weakening in the face of schools set up by the Board and the Education Committee. Sunday and adult schools changed their emphasis, but the culture of the Sunday schools remained strong and even challenged the Local Education Authority (LEA) in the matter of holidays for annual treats. Many fee-paying schools closed their doors and it is probably true to say that in the later years of this study the choice of schools became more limited.

Opportunities were also closing for children to enter the teaching profession through the elementary school system. Student teachers were recruited from the secondary schools and were becoming a part of a more selective system. An interesting change in perspective involved the marriage bar. Copelman[1] has shown that teachers in London were different from women in other occupations because it was acceptable for them to marry and continue working. In Luton, hat workers enjoyed the same freedoms as the teachers: married women who worked did not pose a threat to the respectability of the family. Nationally the situation changed for married women teachers when stringent economies were introduced after the First World War. At the same time, married women in the hat industry were still free to be wives, mothers and workers.

---

[1]   D.M. Copelman, *London's Women Teachers: Gender, Class and Feminism 1870–1930* (Routledge, 1996).

Changes and continuities

The identity and character of the town does not appear to have changed to any great extent throughout the period under discussion. The small group of businessmen who dominated the town in 1874 were succeeded by similar groups of men who were conscientious, practical, mainly Nonconformist and Liberal. However, the influence of the BCC became stronger and Luton had to defer to the Bedfordshire Education Committee (BEC) in many respects, particularly with regard to the education of children over the age of fourteen. In 1903, the BEC also assumed responsibility over the schools in the hamlets. Luton saw education as utilitarian, but Bedford had wider horizons. It has been said that Luton, a town which appreciated individual initiative but did not aspire to high academic ideals, resented the secondary schools which were set up by the BCC Education Committee. This may be true in some respects, but many of those who were educated in these schools still owe them a debt of gratitude.

Attitudes had to change and to some extent they did. In the 1870s many parents and children saw education as less important than employment and, when loyalties were divided, it was often the demands of the local industry which took precedence. There was no history or tradition of schooling and families needed the money. The Board, and later the LEAs, set about changing these attitudes by using all the penalties and, later, rewards available to them and prided themselves on maintaining a high level of attendance. But, when children who had grown up within the compulsory system themselves became parents, they frequently had a problem in allowing their own children to stay on at the secondary schools until the age of sixteen. This became a continuing battle which had not been resolved by the 1920s.

The Board, the LEAs and the schools accepted that it was their duty to be agents of social control. Most importantly this was seen in the emphasis placed on domestic subjects in the curriculum. Although girls in Luton were recognized contributors to the prosperity of the local economy, the schools continued to hold before them the ideal of a wife and mother. Standards of behaviour were set before the girls; in the early days these would have been cleanliness, neatness and punctuality, for example, but, by the twentieth century, the emphasis was changing. Citizenship was being taught and standards of duty and service became part of an imperialist culture.

Instigators of change

Probably the most important factors in the provision of schooling for girls in Luton were the Education Acts. Luton resisted the imposition of a Board, but the government looked at the inadequate provision and insisted that an election should take place. Once established, the School Board worked conscientiously. There was a similar reaction when boards were about to be abolished; the Luton Board congratulated itself on the good work which had been done and petitioned the government to allow the continuation of the status quo. However, it was a different matter when economic matters were under consideration. While the patriarchy of Luton were reluctant to initiate any measures which would have provided schooling for all, it was more than willing to set up schemes to improve employment prospects as, for example, when the Town Council and the Chamber of Commerce succeeded in attracting new industries into the town. The town was happy to use its initiatives to work towards utilitarian ends, but education, especially for girls, was not seen to be as important.

Another major factor in the changes which were made in the schools of Luton was the influence of Bedfordshire Education Committee (BEC). Government initiatives required the BCC to provide technical education throughout the county, to supervise teacher training and provide education for children over fourteen years of age. After the Balfour Act, no time was lost in providing a secondary school for the south of the county. The Kindergarten and Physical Training Colleges in Bedford were led by women with vision and enthusiasm and their pioneering spirit influenced the curricula in the schools of Luton. However, probably the main contributor to higher ideals of education for girls was Miss H.K. Sheldon who was appointed by the BEC as the first headmistress of the girls' day secondary school. She provided a vision which had never before been presented to the girls of Luton.

Wars were also an influence for change. Early in the twentieth century the Boer War drew the attention of the country to the need to care for the health of the nation. Consequently, Education Acts were passed which made provision for medical examinations and school meals. The First World War brought fundamental changes to all aspects of life, especially in the employment of women who frequently took the place of men from local factories who had been called up for active service. The opportunity to earn higher wages tempted women from the hat factories, which were suffering from shrinking markets. Also, teachers left the schools, at least temporarily, for better remuneration and perhaps fewer responsibilities. Most significantly, there were many women who went to support the war effort in the munitions factories.

Although the hat industry was generally prosperous, it was seasonal and was also affected by market forces such as competition from abroad. Businessmen recognized the threat to their prosperity and invited other industries to the town. When these became established, the role of women in the town began to change. They had been major contributors to the family income, but gradually the balance was turning and men were beginning to earn more substantial wages in the factories. The changes did not happen overnight but continued well past the time covered in this book. Attitudes, too, were changing. Employers and employees had different expectations and a woman's role was beginning to evolve into a more subordinate one. This is by no means the whole story for some women still earned good money in the hat trade while others chose a domestic role.

It is probably true to say that compulsory schooling, opportunities for employment outside the hat industry, the widening of the curriculum, the influence of the war and the awareness of Empire helped to change the expectations and attitudes of women in Luton. There was scope for them to use their individuality and independence of spirit in other directions.

While changes in education affected employment, there is less evidence to suggest that employment affected girls' education. The only direct evidence which has been found is the BCC Technical Instruction Committee's attempt to introduce plaiting techniques into schools at the end of the nineteenth century. Needlework in schools does not appear to have been directed at the hat trade but at the family. Nor does it seem likely that domestic instruction was focused on training girls for employment in domestic service as this was not a large employer in the town.[2] For boys the case was different: the Technical Instruction Committee offered classes in the maintenance of machinery for the hat trade and, in the twentieth century, links between industry, especially Vauxhall Motors, and the classes taught at the Luton Technical Institution's evening classes were very strong. It is interesting to note that, as recently as 2001, it was stated that the University of Luton concentrates on a vocational rather than an academic education and courses are 'often set up in collaboration with industry'.[3]

A last word

The relationship between education and employment is a complex one. In the early days of this study Luton women had freedom over their lives. They were able to spend their time as they wished and they had economic power. This was important to the whole community because their work brought prosperity to the town. At the same time they had little interest in schooling because it was not seen to be necessary. External forces, in the form of national and local government, took away much of that freedom in the belief that something better was being offered. Women resented this control over their time and their capacity to earn but were obliged to conform. Market forces introduced new dimensions to the employment situation and meant that, in many cases, an educated work force would be more appropriate. This brought changing ideologies, wider opportunities and an alternative kind of freedom. Changing times bring changing needs. It would not be possible to go back to the freedoms of the past.

---

[2]   9.5% in 1911 and 14.5% in 1921. See census figures in Chapter One.

[3]   Report on Luton University in the *Sunday Times Good University Guide*, 16 September 2001: 'Some of the more traditional subjects, such as politics and history, were ditched in favour of vocational subjects.'

Appendix

Figures taken from LMS and LHS Admission Registers and relating to Chapter Ten

Occupations: fathers of girls admitted to the secondary school

	1904	1905 and 1907	1912
Schoolmaster	5	3	2
Straw/hat industry	4	6	12
Laundry		1	2
Commercial traveller	1		
Railway	1		
Farmer	2	1	1
Sanitary Inspector	1		
Corn dealer	1		
Manufacturer	1		
Printing	2	1	
Pawnbroker	1		
Hotel proprietor	1		
Furniture dealer	2		1
Dyer	1	1	
Post Office	1		1
Merchant	1		
Engineer	1	1	
Clerk	1	4	
Moulder	1		
Baker	1	1	
Builder	2	1	
Tailor/outfitter	1	1	
Draper		1	2
Grocer		2	1
Coal agent		1	
Editor		1	
Gamekeeper		1	
Manager of cocoa factory		1	
Minister		1	1
Fruiterer		1	
Boots and shoes		1	
Physician			1
Bleach			1
Butcher			2
RN*			1
Yeast			1
Painter			1
Prudential			1
Club steward			1
Stud groom			1

* presumably Royal Navy

Girls whose fees were remitted

	1904	1905 and 1907	1912
By the governors	9	3	2
Charities:			
Coppins		3	
Bigland, Gillingham & Long		5	
Chews			1
Bursars	8	1	3

Years of attendance

	1904	1905 and 1907	1912
Under a year	1	1	
1 year	7	1	5
2 years	10	4	6
3 years	0	5	8
4 years	9		4
5 years	7	1	3
6 years	1	2	3
7 years		1	4

Employment of girls leaving LMS

	1904	1905 and 1907	1912
Student teachers	8	1	
University		3	
Millinery		2	5
Costumier's		1	1
Chemist's		1	
Telephone clerk (Clark's College)		3	
Stationers		1	
At home		2	
Cookery school		1	
Munitions		1	1
Book-keeper		1	2
Monitor		1	
Drapers		2	1
Typist		1	2
Clerk		2	3
Bakery		1	
Printers		1	
Calibrating and testing			1
Tracer			1
Governess overseas			1
Chemist's apprentice			1

Employment of boys leaving LMS 1904–1907

These indicate the different expectations of boys and girls.

Imperial College of Science	1
King's College	1
Trinity College	1

Training College	1
Straw/hats	7
Customs	1
Clerks	4
PO/tel.	3
Clark's College	1
Retail	2
Accounts office	1
Coal merchants	1
Journalism	1
Office	1
Drawing office	1
Mining Co. NSW	1
Apprentice to draper	1
Vauxhall	1

Occupations taken up by girls who entered the school in 1930

These demonstrate that girls' horizons were widening.

Domestic College	1
Training College	3
University	2
Apprenticed to hairdresser's	2
Nursing	2
Commercial College	5
Clerk	14
Chemist's assistant	1
Shorthand/book-keeping	10
Millinery	1
Shop assistant	3
GPO and telephone	3
Tax office	1
School of Arts and Crafts	1
Drawing Office	1
Academy of Dressmaking	1
French conversation	1
Civil service exams	1
Observing in school	1
Apprentice Bright & Bourne?	1
Oaklands College St Albans	1
Home	1
Florists	1

Commercial colleges attended:
    Pitman's
    House and Williams

Shops where girls became assistants:
    Chemists
    Hannibal Bonds (drapers)
    Co-op
    Grocers
    Florists
    'Mother's'

Firms where girls became typists:
Skefko
Laporte's
Dale
Barclays
Adamant
Vauxhall
W.H. Perks

Firms where girls became clerks or clerical assistants:
Skefko
Electrolux
Paris House
GPO
Tax office
Davis Gas Stove
Walter, Webb & Baker
Town Clerk
Ribbon merchant
Farmers (music)
Adamant
Laporte's
Borough Electricity Co.
Waterlow

Bibliography

Primary Sources

Manuscripts and other collections held at Bedfordshire and Luton Archive and Record Service (BLARS)

Bedfordshire County Council Education Committee Minutes:
    EM1–EM9 (1903–1923)
Bedfordshire County Council Elementary Education Sub-Committee Minutes:
    E/Sub M 0/4/1–10 (1903–1925)
Bedfordshire County Council Higher Education Sub-Committee Minutes:
    E/Sub M 0/6/1–2 (1903–1927)
Bedfordshire County Council Minute Books of the Luton Secondary School (known after 1908 as Luton Modern School):
    SGM 31/1–4 (1904–1920)
Bedfordshire County Council Minutes of the Technical Instruction Committee:
    E/Sub M 0/11/1–4 (1891–1903)
Bedfordshire County Council Minutes of the Technical Committee:
    E/Sub 0/11 Technical Instruction and Farm Schools
    E/Sub 2 Further Education

School Logbooks:
    SD Hyde 1–2 Logbooks of Hyde School (1898–1912)

Miscellaneous:
EV 76   Luton Modern School and Technical Institution Governors' meetings
X 136/2/1   Minutes of the Joint Committee of the Bedfordshire Agricultural Society and the BCC Technical Instruction Committee 1896–1900
X 551/36 and X 563/1–66   Friends' Adult School Luton, Miscellaneous Papers
Z 209/73   *The Sunday School Teachers' Magazine and Journal of Education* Series 4, Vol. 6 (1855)
Z 210   *Souvenir of the Luton Gelatine Works* (Luton: 13 July 1906)
130 1953   Luton School Logbooks General History and Logbooks of Individual Schools
130 BED   Bedford Training College Archives
130 BED   Girls' Modern School Registers (1882–1894)
139 BED   Registers of the Girls' Modern School Bedford (1882–1884)
Bedfordshire c. 1890 Illustrated Bedfordshire Its History and Commerce Nottingham 1895 (Class 160)

Documents that were held at Denbigh High School Luton, formerly Luton High School for Girls, and are now at LMAG

Logbooks:
Beech Hill JM School, later Girls' School, from 1913

Denbigh Road Girls' School from 1921
BCC Education Minutes for the Luton Modern Schools from 1919
Various school magazines (*Sheaf*) from Luton High School for Girls
Visitors' Book (1930)

Manuscripts and other collections held at Luton Museum and Art Gallery

Education Boxes 1–4
M/216–224 Minute books of the LSB (until 1879) and the USD Luton (from 1879)
M/225–9 Minutes of the Preliminary Education Committee (1903) and Minutes of the
  Luton Education Committee (1903–1924)
M/235 Minute Book School Health and Attendance (1912–1932)
M/239–41 Letterbooks of the Luton School Board

Luton School Logbooks:
L/4/2/54 Hitchin Road Girls' and Infants' (1874–1901). This logbook contains material
  from both the Infants' and the Girls' School
L/4/2/54 Hitchin Road Infants' (1901–1924)
75/67–1 Hitchin Road Girls' (1900–1924)
L/13/5/54(3) Waller St Boys'
M/211 New Town St (St Paul's) Girls' and Infants' (1867–1915)
1997/35/2 Norton Road School (1913–1924)
L/1/2/54 St Matthew's Girls' (1874–1902)
L/5/5/54 The Chapel Street Continuation School (1896–1900)
1997/23/1–3 Admission Registers of Luton Modern Schools 1905, 1905–7, 1912 and 1930

Maps:
Map of the Borough of Luton 1876 by E.A. Cumberland, Luton (1876) Accession No. 262/65
Map of Luton presented as a supplement to the Luton and District Year Book and Almanack
  (1904) *The Luton Reporter*
Map of Luton based on the Ordnance Survey Map with the sanction of HM Stationery Office,
  Franklin and Deacon, Luton (1915)

Miscellaneous:
LM/BI/65 Labour Certificate (1897)
LM 1319 Dony, J.G., Notes on the Labour Conditions in the Luton Hat Industry
M/828/1 Luton School Board Certificate of Merit (1878)
M/840 Austin, T.G., *The Straw Plaiting and Hat and Bonnet Trade with a Digest of the
  Recent Census* (*1871*)
M/863 School song of Luton High School
M/958 1978 Rules and Regulations: Luton Free Library
M/1069/1–3 Magazines of the Luton Modern School
Z171/12–14 Three exercise books that belonged to Annie Welch (1907–1908)
5/98/36 Letter to Chairman of the School Board from HMI Mr C.F. Johnstone
6a/11/63 Advertisement for Dancing and Deportment Classes, York House School (1898)
219/52 Rules of the Luton School Board
6406 Marshall, M.A., 'Elementary Education in Luton 1809–1874' Typescript thesis (1960)
7865 Evans, V., 'Education in Luton' Typescript Essay (1963)
1979 F564 School Attendance Medals (1894–1895)
1996/44 Programme, *SKF*, *40 Years of Progress* (1910–1950)

1997/23/1–5   Admissions register Luton Modern School (1904–1919)
1997/23/11–12   Luton Secondary School admission forms (1904–1921)
1986/70   Luton Adult School Jubilee Celebrations (1862–1912) and Visit of the National Council of Adult School Unions, January 1912
103426   'The Story of George Kent Ltd' Part 1
103427   'The Story of George Kent Ltd' Part 2
   Typed no details 1955
5702   Inner Ring Skefko 'The First Fifty Years' Special Issue (1960)
7443   75th Birthday Souvenir of the Luton Industrial Co-operative Society Ltd (1883–1958) 1958
2261 and 7443   Luton Industrial Co-operative Society Ltd
103759/380 and 103759/6   *The Wheatsheaf*
A Souvenir of a Century of Wesleyan Methodism in the Town of Luton 1808–1908
103759/5   *The Co-operative News* 11 April 1903 and 18 October 1902
Luton Museum Oral History Archive

Documents held at Luton Central Library

L.LUT 371.01   Roberts, J., 'The Luton School Board (1874–1902) ' (Dissertation)
L.LUT 378   Prospectus of the Luton Technical College 1937–38
L.LUT 650   'Pride and Partnership: the early years and later influence of the Bedfordshire Chamber of Commerce on its Community 1877–1993' The Chamber of Commerce (1993)
L.LUT 914.2565   Sexton, Mrs, & Adam, Mrs, 'Luton Streets at the end of the First World War' (1982)
L.LUT 942.565   Kent, G., 'Luton from the Wings: Childhood Memories of Edwardian Luton' (Luton Libraries, 1979)
L.LUT 942.565   Kennett, D.H., 'Luton: A Centenary History' Typed (1976)
L.LUT 942.565   Luton Chamber of Commerce Register, Vol. III
L.LUT 942.565   Mears, J.A., 'History of Waller Street' Putteridge Bury College of Education (1971)

Newspapers and censuses on microfilm and microfiche

Printed sources

Parliamentary papers:
Digest of Returns to Circular Letter from the Select Committee on Education of the Poor (1818)
Abstract of Education Returns: (1833) County of Bedford
National Society Church-School Inquiry (1846–7)
Report on Straw Plait and Bonnet Manufacturers (1864)
Census of England and Wales (1871) Bedfordshire
Report of the Inspector of Factories for the Six Months ending 30 April 1874
Committee of Council on Education Report (1873–74) England and Wales (HMSO, 1874)
Committee of Council on Education Report (1874–75) England and Wales (HMSO, 1875)
Committee of Council on Education Report (1876–77) England and Wales (HMSO, 1877)
Committee of Council on Education Report (1877–78) England and Wales (HMSO, 1878)
Census of England and Wales (1881) Bedfordshire
Census of England and Wales (1891) Bedfordshire

Report of the Royal Commission on the Elementary Education Act [The Cross Report] 1888

Report of the Factory Inspectors for 1890 (1890–1891)

Royal Commission on Labour, The Employment of Women (February 1893)

Committee of Council on Education Report (1898–99) England and Wales (HMSO, 1899)

Census of England and Wales (1901) Bedfordshire

Census of England and Wales (1911) Bedfordshire

Census of England and Wales (1921) Bedfordshire

Board of Education Report of the Consultative Committee on Infant and Nursery Schools (HMSO, 1933)

Great Britain Department of Employment British Labour Statistics: Historical Abstract *(1886–1968)* (HMSO, 1971)

Trade directories:

Harrod's Royal County Directory of Bedfordshire Buckinghamshire Berkshire Oxfordshire Huntingdonshire and Northamptonshire (1876)

The Bedfordshire Almanack and County Handbook (1877) Bedfordshire Times and Independent

Kelly's *Bedfordshire Directory (1885)*

Kelly's Directory of Bedfordshire, Huntingdonshire and Northamptonshire (1890)

Kelly's Bedfordshire Directory (1894)

The Luton Year Book and Almanack (1900)

The Luton and District Year Book and Almanack (1902)

The Luton and District Year Book and Almanack (1904)

The Luton and District Year Book and Almanack (1905)

The Luton and District Year Book and Almanack (1906)

The Luton and District Year Book and Directory (1908)

The Bedfordshire Who's Who and Year Book (1909) Bedford Daily Circular

Kelly's Directory of Bedfordshire (1910)

Luton Year Book and Directory (1911)

Luton News Almanac (1912)

Luton Year Book and Directory (1912)

Luton News Almanac (1913)

Luton Year Book and Directory (1913)

Luton News Almanac (1916)

Luton Year Book and Directory (1918)

Kelly's Directory for Bedfordshire (1920)

Luton Year Book and Directory (1923)

Luton News Directory and Year Book (1925)

Newspapers and journals:

Daily Express, Daily News, Drapers' Record, Dunstable Gazette, Hatters' Gazette, Luton Advertiser, Luton Reporter, Luton News, Luton News and Bedfordshire Advertiser, Luton News and Dunstable Gazette Supplement, Millennium Memories, 200, *The Quiver, The Times, The Sunday Times,* Good University Guide

Books published before 1900:

Austin, T.G., *The Straw Trade* (Patrick O'Doherty, 1871)

Davis, F., *The History of Luton with its Hamlets* (Luton L Wiseman, 1855)

Davis, F., *Luton, Past and Present: Its History and Antiquities* (Luton: Stalker, 1874)

Gadsby's Educational Books for Sunday Schools, Families and First Book (1867)

Gouin, F., *The Art of Teaching and Studying Languages* translated by Swan, H., & Bétis, V., (Philip & Son, 1892)

Greenup, W.T., *Friendly Advice for Pupil Teachers* (London & Edinburgh: Chambers c.1877)

Hawkes, J., *The Rise and Progress of the Luton Wesleyan Sunday Schools* (A.J. Giles, 1885)

Hughes, Mrs, *The Sunday Scholar's First Book* (David Eaton, 1828)

Illustrated Bedfordshire Its History and Commerce (Thomas Forman & Sons, 1895)

Lamborn, C., *The Dunstaplelogia* (Dunstable: James Tibbett, 1859)

Luton Illustrated: A Descriptive Account of Luton (W.T. Pike, n.d. but c.1899)

Norman Commander F.M., RN, *Schoolmaster's Drill Assistant for Boys, Girls & Mixed* (Bemrose & Sons, 1875)

Piper, T.W., *Mental Arithmetic for Pupil Teachers and Students in Training Colleges* (Philip & Son, 1887)

Pride, S., *History of the Union Chapel, Luton* (Jubilee Celebration, 1887)

The First Class Book for Reading, Spelling and Catechizing (Sunday School Union, n.d. but almost certainly before 1900)

The Sunday School Teachers' Magazine and Journal of Education 4th Series Vol. the 6th (1855)

Trimmer, Mrs, *An Abridgment of Scripture History* (A. Wilson, 1811)

Wood, Revd J.G., *Natural History* (Routledge & Sons, 1894)

Wyatt, J., ed., *Bedfordshire Schools and Charities of Sir William Harpur* (Timaeus, 1856)

Secondary Sources

Articles

Aldrich, R., 'Educating Our Mistresses', *History of Education* Vol. 12, No. 2 (1983)

Aldrich, R., 'Elementary Education, Literacy and Child Employment in Mid-Nineteenth Century Bedfordshire: A Statistical Study', *History of Elementary School Teaching and Curriculum* Giovanni Genovesi ed. (Bildung und Wissenschaft; 1990)

Allen, A.B., 'The Schoolmaster' Part 1, *Bedfordshire Magazine* Vol. 12, No. 96 (Spring 1971); 'The Schoolmaster' Part 2, *Bedfordshire Magazine* Vol. 13, No. 97, (Summer 1971)

'Amongst the Bonnet-Sewers', *The Quiver* (1884)

Benson, B., and Dyer J., 'Luton's Hat King', *Bedfordshire Magazine* Vol. 26, No. 204 (Spring 1998)

Bergen, B.H., 'Only a Schoolmaster: Gender, Class, and the Effort to Professionalize Elementary Teaching in England 1870–1910', *History of Education Quarterly* (Spring 1982)

Betts, R., Review: Penn A.'Targeting Schools: Drill, Militarism and Imperialism', *History of Education Society Bulletin* No. 67 (May 2001)

Boon, C., and Dyer, J., 'Dr John Dony – An Appreciation', *Bedfordshire Magazine* Vol. 23, No. 177 (Summer 1991)

Bowlby, E., 'Ruth's Diary, A Luton Vicarage in Edwardian Times', *Bedfordshire Family History Society Journal* Vol. 13, No. 7 (September 2002)

Bushby, D., 'Half-timers at Marston', *Bedfordshire Magazine* Vol. 14, No. 112 (Spring 1975)

Bushby, D., 'Lace, Straw-Plait, and Child Employment', *Bedfordshire Magazine* Vol. 17, No. 131 (Winter 1979)

Cunningham, P., et al., 'McNair's Lost Opportunity: The Student-teacher Scheme and the Student-teacher's Experience', *History of Education* Vol. 24, No. 3 (1995)

Davis, J.E., 'Luton in Focus: T.G. Hobbs and His Times' Part 1: 'Trade, Trains and Temperance', *Bedfordshire Magazine* Vol. 15, No. 117 (Summer 1976)

Part 2: 'Trips, Tours and Timetables', *Bedfordshire Magazine* Vol. 15, No. 118 (Autumn 1976)

Davin, A., ' "Mind That You Do As You Are Told" Reading books for Board School Girls 1870–1902', *Feminist Review* 3 (1979)

Day, V., 'A Child's World of Two Dunstable Schools', *Bedfordshire Magazine* Vol. 14, No. 110 (Autumn 1974)

Day, V., 'Moretonia', *Bedfordshire Magazine* Vol. 25, No. 196 (Spring 1996)

Dony, J.G., 'How Luton became a Borough', *Bedfordshire Magazine* Vol. 15, No. 116 (Spring 1976)

Fletcher, S., 'Co-education and the Victorian Grammar School', *History of Education* Vol. 11, No. 2 (1982)

Goodman, J., 'Social Investigation and Economic Empowerment: The Women's Industrial Council and the LCC Trade Schools for Girls 1892–1914', *History of Education* Vol. 27, No. 3 (1998)

Horn, P., 'Child Workers in the Pillow Lace and Straw Plait Trades of Victorian Buckinghamshire and Bedfordshire', *Historical Journal* XVII 4 (1974)

Horn, P., 'The Recruitment, Role and Status of the Victorian Country Teacher', *History of Education* Vol. 9, No. 2 (1980)

Janes, Sir H., 'I Remember, I Remember Memories of Luton 80 Years Ago':
Part 1 *Bedfordshire Magazine* Vol. 12, No. 93 (Summer 1970);
Part 2 *Bedfordshire Magazine* Vol. 12, No. 94 (Autumn 1970)

Lea, J., 'E.V. Lucas and Luton', *Bedfordshire Magazine* Vol. 15, No. 37 (Summer 1956)

'Luton Straw Hat Workers', *Hatter's Gazette* (April 1st 1911)

Martin, J., 'Entering the Public Arena: The Female Members of the London School Board, 1870–1904', *History of Education* Vol. 22, No. 3 (1993)

Martin, J., 'Reflections on Writing a Biographical Account of a Woman Educator Activist', *History of Education* Vol. 30, No. 2 (2001)

Meadows, E., 'A Family Home and Business in Luton', *Bedfordshire Magazine* Vol. 26, No. 207 (Winter 1998)

Nichols, M., 'Straw Plaiting and the Straw Hat Industry in Britain', *Costume: The Journal of the Costume Society* No. 30 (1996)

Pederson, J.S., 'Schoolmistresses and Headmistresses: Elites and Education in Nineteenth-Century England', *The Journal of British Studies* Vol. XV, No. 1, (1975)

'Plait and Plaiters', *Cassell's Family Magazine* (1882)

Purvis, J., 'Working-class Women and Adult Education in Nineteenth-century Britain', *History of Education* Vol. 9, No. 3 (1980)

Robinson, W., 'In Search of a "Plain Tale": Rediscovering the Champions of the Pupil-teacher Centres 1900–1910', *History of Education* Vol. 28, No. 1 (1999)

Robinson, W., 'Pupil Teacher: Constructions, Conflict and Control 1860–1910', *Cambridge Journal of Education* Vol. 27, No. 3 (November 1997)

Robinson, W., 'Pupil Teachers: The Achilles Heel of Higher Grade Girls' Schools 1882–1904', *History of Education* Vol. 22, No. 3 (1993)

Sanderson, T.A.E., 'Founding a Grammar School', *Bedfordshire Magazine* Vol. 4, No. 30 (Autumn 1954)

Sparks, H.J., 'The Brown Family of Luton, Bedfordshire', *Bedfordshire Magazine* Vol. 4, No. 27 (Winter 1953–1954)

Storr, K., 'Belgian Children's Education in Britain in the Great War: Language, Identity and Race Relations', *History of Education Researcher* No. 72 (November 2003), pp. 84–93

Street, K., 'Stanny's Stues: Bedford Physical Training College 1903–1918', *Bedfordshire Magazine* Vol. 25, No. 190 (Autumn 1994)

Summerfield, P., ed., 'Women, Education and the Professional Labour Market 1900–1950: The Case of the Secondary Schoolmistress', *History of Education Society* Occasional Publication No. 8 (1987)

Testimonial, *Bedfordshire Magazine* Vol. 9, No. 71 (Winter 1964–1965)

Leading Export Industries IV, 'Luton and the Straw Trade', *The British Trade Journal* (1 March 1891)

Thody, A.M., 'School Management in the Nineteenth-century Elementary Schools: A Day in the Life of a Headteacher', *History of Education* Vol. 23 No. 4 (1994)

'Victorian Education', Occasional Publication No. 2, *History of Education Society* (Summer 1976)

Watson, D., 'Relations Between the Education and Employment Departments, 1921–45: An Anti-industry Culture Versus Industrial Efficiency?', *History of Education* Vol. 27, No. 3 (1998)

Books

Ainley, P., and Rainbird, H., ed., *Apprenticeship, Towards a New Paradigm of Learning* (London: Kogan Page, 1999)

Aldrich, R., *A Century of Education* (London: Routledge/Falmer, 2002)

Aldrich, R., *School and Society in Victorian Britain, Joseph Payne and the New World of Education* (London: Garland, 1995)

Aldrich, R., Crook, D., and Watson, D., *Education and Employment: the DfEE and Its Place in History* (London: Bedford Way Papers Institute of Education University of London, 2000)

Aldrich, R., and Gordon, P., *Dictionary of British Educationists* (London: Woburn Press, 1989)

Allsopp, A., *Crimson and Gold*: *Luton Modern School for Girls and Boys* Vol. 2 (Dunstable: The Book Castle, 2004)

Andrews, L., *The Education Act 1918* (London: RKP, 1976)

Aries, P., *Centuries of Childhood* (London: Pimlico, 1996)

Attar, D., *Wasting Girls' Time, The History and Politics of Home Economics* (London: Virago, 1990)

Austin, W., *The History of Luton and Its Hamlets*: *Being a History of the old Parish and Manor of Luton in Bedfordshire* Vols.1 & 2 (Isle of Wight, The County Press Newport, 1928)

Barnard, H.C., *A History of English Education from 1760* (London: University of London Press, 1969)

Bedfordshire County Council, *Report of County Surveyor of Schools. Part I Council Schools, Part II Voluntary Schools* (Timaeus, 1904)

Bedfordshire Education Committee, *Schools' Progress 1870–1970*

Bedfordshire Federation of Women's Institutes, *Bedfordshire Within Living Memory* (Bedford: Countryside Books, 1992)

Bell P.L., *Belief in Bedfordshire* (Bedford: Belfry Press, 1986)

Bentley, L., *Educating Women: A Pictorial History of Bedford College University of London 1849–1985* (Alma, Royal Holloway and Bedford College, 1991)

Best, G., *Mid-Victorian Britain 1851–1870* (Glasgow: Fontana, 1971)

Bingham, C., *The History of the Royal Holloway College* (Constable, 1987)

Bird, P., and Carrington, B., *Dunstable in Camera* (Whittlebury: Quotes Ltd, 1992)

Blakey, M., *The Story of Bedfordshire Railways* (Bedford: Bedfordshire Education Service, 1983)

Booth, F., *Robert Raikes of Gloucester* (Redhill: National Christian Education Council, 1980)

Boris, E., and Daniels, C.R., ed., *Homework, Historical and Contemporary Perspectives on Paid Labour at Home* (Urban: University of Illinois Press, 1988)

Boyd, W., and King, E.J., *The History of Western Education* (London: A. & C. Black, 1980)

Briggs, A., *Victorian People* (Harmondsworth: Penguin, 1955)

Broadway, C., and Buss, E.I., *The History of the School 1882–1982* (Luton: White Crescent Press, 1982)

Brown, C., *Luton Trams: The Story of a Small System 1908–1932* (Clophill: Irwell Press, 1999)

Bryant, M., *The London Experience of Secondary Education* (London: The Athlone Press, 1986)

Bryant, M., *The Unexpected Revolution: A History of the Education of Women and Girls in the Nineteenth Century* (London: University of London Institute of Education, 1979)

Bunker, S., Holgate, R., and Nichols, M., *The Changing Face of Luton* (Dunstable: The Book Castle, 1993)

Bunker, S., *Strawopolis: Luton Transformed 1840–1876* (Bedford: BHRS Vol. 78, 1999)

Burnett, J., ed., *Useful Toil: Autobiographies of Working People from the 1820s to the 1920s* (Allen Lane, 1976)

Burstall, S., *Frances Mary Buss, an educational pioneer* (London: SPCK, 1938)

Burstall, S., *English High Schools for Girls: Their Aims, Organisation and Management* (London: Longman, Green & Co., 1907)

Burstyn, J.N., *Victorian Education and the Ideal of Womanhood* (London: Croom Helm, 1980)

Bushby, D.W., *Elementary Education in Bedford 1868–1903; The Ecclesiastical Census Bedfordshire March 1851* (Bedford: BHRS Vol. 54, 1975)

Bushby, D., *The Bedfordshire Schoolchild Before 1902* (Bedford: BHRS Vol. 67, 1988)

Chamber of Commerce, *Pride and Partnership 1877–1993* (Luton, 1993)

Chapman, H., *Village Schooldays and Beyond, From Pupil to Teacher 1906–1923,* (Dunstable: The Book Castle, 1996)

Chapman, J.V., *Professional Roots, The College of Preceptors in British Society* (Epping: Theydon Bois Publications Ltd, 1985)

Chinn, C., *They worked all their lives: Women of the Urban Poor in England 1880–1939* (Manchester University Press, 1988)

Cockman, F.G., *The Railway Age in Bedfordshire* (Bedford: BHRS Vol. 53, 1974)

Collett-White, J., *Bedfordshire in the 1880s* Background Papers No.1 (Bedfordshire Record Office, County Hall Bedford, 1986)

Conisbee, L.R.A., *Bedfordshire Bibliography* (Bedford: BHRS, 1962)

Cooper, K., *Luton Scene Again* (Guildford: Phillimore, 1990)

Copeland, I., *The Making of the Backward Pupil in Education in England 1870–1914* (London: Woburn Press, 1999)

Copelman, D.M., *London's Women Teachers: Gender, Class and Feminism 1870–1930* (London: Routledge, 1996)

Craddock, D., *Where They Burnt the Town Hall Down: Luton, the First World War and the Peace Day Riots of July 1919* (Dunstable: The Book Castle, 1999)

Cruikshank, M., *Church and State in English Education 1870 to the Present Day* (London: Macmillan, 1963)

Currie, M.R., *Hospitals in Luton and Dunstable: An Illustrated History* (Advance Offset (Hitchin) Ltd, 1982)

Daglish, N., *Education Policy-Making in England and Wales: The Crucible Years 1895–1911* (London: Woburn Press, 1996)

Darby, A., *A View from the Alley* (Luton Museum and Art Gallery, 1974)

Davidoff, L., and Westover B., ed., *Our Work, Our Lives, Our Words: Women's History and Women's Work* (Basingstoke: Macmillan Education, 1986)

Dent, H.C., *The Training of Teachers in England and Wales 1800–1975* (London: Hodder and Stoughton, 1977)

Derbyshire, L.C., *The Story of Vauxhall 1857–1946* (Luton: Vauxhall Motors Ltd, 1946)

D'Erceville, S.M., *De Port-Royal à Rome Histoire des Soeurs de Sainte-Marie* (Paris: La Colombe Editions du Vieux Colombier, 1956)

Devonshire, A., and Wood, B., ed., *Women in Industry and Technology from Prehistory to the Present Day: Current Research and the Museum Experience* (Museum of London, 1996)

Dodwell, F., *Schooldays 1810–1900* Booklet No 2, Hitchin British Schools (North Hertfordshire District Council, 1993)

Dony, J.G., *A History of Education in Luton* (Luton Museum and Art Gallery, 1970)

Dony, J.G., *A History of the Straw Hat Industry* (Luton: Gibbs, Bamforth & Co., 1942)

Dony, J.G., on behalf of the WEA, *The Story of High Town* (Bedfordshire County Council, 1984)

Dony, J.G., 'The 1919 Peace Riots in Luton' in Bell P. ed., *Worthington George Smith and Other Studies* (Bedford: BHRS Vol. 57, 1978)

Drake, B., *Women in Trade Unions* (London: Virago, 1984)

Dyer, J., *The Stopsley Book* (Dunstable: The Book Castle, 1998)

Dyer, J., *The Stopsley Picture Book* (Dunstable: The Book Castle, 1999)

Dyer, J., and Dony, J.G., *The Story of Luton* 3rd edn (Luton: White Crescent Press, 1975)

Dyer, J., *The Story of the Stopsley Schools* (Luton: Luton Museum and Art Gallery, 1989)

Dyhouse, C., *Feminism and the Family in England 1880–1939* (Oxford: Basil Blackwell, 1989)

Dyhouse, C., *Girls Growing Up in Late Victorian and Edwardian England* (London: RKP, 1981)

Dyhouse, C., *No Distinction of Sex? Women in British Universities 1870–1939* (London: UCL Press, 1995)

Eaglesham, E.J.R., *From School Board to Local Authority* (London: RKP, 1956)

Eaglesham, E.J.R., *The Foundations of 20th Century Education in England* (London: RKP, 1972)

Ellis, A., *Educating our Masters: Influences on the Growth of Literacy in Victorian Working-class Children* (Aldershot: Gower, 1985)

Escott, B.E., *Twentieth-Century Women of Courage* (Stroud: Sutton, 1999)

Evans, K., *The Development and Structure of the English Education System* (London: Hodder & Stoughton, 1975)

Fifty Years' Work of the Bedfordshire County Council (Bedfordshire County Council, 1938)

Fletcher, S., *Women First: The Female Tradition in English Physical Education 1880–1980* (London: The Athlone Press, 1984)

Fraser-Newstead, B., *Bedfordshire's Yesteryears.*
  Volume 1 *The Family, Childhood and Schooldays* (Dunstable: The Book Castle, 1993)
  Volume 2 *The Rural Scene* (Dunstable: The Book Castle, 1994)
  Volume 3 *Craftsmen and Trades People* (Dunstable: The Book Castle, 1995)
  Volume 4 *War Times & Civil Matters* (Dunstable: The Book Castle, 1996)

Freeman, C., *Luton and the Hat Industry* (Luton: LMAG, 1953)

Freeman, C., *The Romance of the Straw Hat* (Luton Museum and Art Gallery, 1953)

Gardner, P., *The Lost Elementary Schools of Victorian England: The People's Education* (London: Croom Helm, 1984)

Gilbert, A.D., *Religion and Society in Industrial England, Church, Chapel and Social Change 1740–1914* (London: Longman, 1976)

Godber, J., *History of Bedfordshire* (Bedfordshire County Council, 1970)

Godber, J., *The Harpur Trust 1552–1973* (The Harpur Trust, 1973)

Godber, J., *The Story of Bedford* (Luton: White Crescent Press, 1978)

Godber, J., and Hutchins, I., ed., *A Century of Challenge, Bedford High School 1882–1982*, (Bedford: Bedford High School, 1982)

Godfrey, A., *Old Ordnance Survey Maps Luton 1922* The Godfrey Reprinted Edition of 1924 (Gateshead, 1990)

Gomersall, M., *Working-Class Girls in Nineteenth-Century England*: *Life, Work and Schooling* (Basingstoke & London: Macmillan, 1997)

Gordon, E., *Women and the Labour Movement in Scotland 1850–1914* (Oxford: Clarendon Press, 1991)

Gordon, P., Aldrich, R., and Dean, D., *Education and Policy in England in the Twentieth Century* (London: The Woburn Press, 1991)

Gosden, P., *How They Were Taught*: *An Anthology of Contemporary Accounts of Learning and Teaching in England 1800–1950* (Oxford: Blackwell, 1969)

Graff, H.J., *Literacy and Social Development in the West*: *Cambridge Studies in Oral and Literate Culture* (Cambridge: Cambridge University Press, 1981)

Gróf, L.L., *Children of Straw* (Buckingham: Barracuda, 1988)

Grundy, F., and Titmuss, R.M., *Report on Luton* (Luton: Gibbs, Bamforth & Co. Ltd, 1945)

Hackett, F., *Luton in Old Picture Postcards* (European Library, 1996)

Hall, A., *The Adult Movement in the Twentieth Century* Nottingham Studies in the Theory and Practice of Education of Adults, Department of Adult Education (Nottingham: University of Nottingham, 1985)

Hall, E., *Canary Girls and Stockpots* (Luton: Barnfield College, 1977)

Handbook of Suggestions for Teachers (HMSO, 1946)

Harris, B., *The Health of the Schoolchild*: *A History of the School Medical Service in England and Wales* (Buckingham: Open University Press, 1995)

Harrison, J.F.C., *Learning and Living 1790–1960*: *A Study in the History of the English Adult School Movement* (London: RKP, 1963)

Hart, R., *The Vauxhall and Bedford Story* (Leighton Buzzard: Farnon Books, 1996)

Hobbs, T.G., 'Recollections of Early Luton' (Reprinted from *The Luton News* 1933)

Holcombe, L., *Victorian Ladies at Work* (Hamden: Archon Books, 1973)

Holden, L., *Vauxhall Motors and the Luton Economy, 1900–2002* BHRS Vol. 82 (Woodbridge: The Boydell Press, 2003)

Horn, P., *Ladies of the Manor: Wives and Children in Country-house Society 1830–1918* (Stroud: Alan Sutton, 1991)

Horn, P., *The Victorian Country Child* (Stroud: Alan Sutton, 1985)

Horn, P., *The Victorian and Edwardian Schoolchild* (Stroud: Alan Sutton, 1989)

Horn, P., *Labouring Life in the Victorian Countryside* (Abingdon: Fraser Stewart, 1995)

Hughes, M., *A Victorian Family 1870–1900* (Aylesbury: Albion, 1990)

Hurt, J.S., *Elementary Schooling and the Working Classes, 1860–1918* (London: RKP, 1979)

Inwards, H., *Straw Hats: Their History and Manufacture* (London: Isaac Pitman and Sons, 1922)

John, A.V., ed., *Unequal Opportunities: Women's Employment in England 1800–1918* (Oxford: Basil Blackwell, 1986)

Jones, L., *The Training of Teachers in England and Wales* (London: Oxford University Press, 1924)

Kamm, J., *Hope Deferred* (London: Methuen, 1965)

Kamm, J., *How Different From Us* (London: Bodley Head, 1959)

Kaye, E., *A History of Queen's College London* (London: Chatto & Windus, 1972)

Lane, J., *Apprenticeship in England* (London: UCL Press, 1996)

Laqueur, T.W., *Religion and Respectability: Sunday Schools and Working Class Culture 1780–1850* (New Haven: Yale University Press, 1976)

Laslett, P., *The World We Have Lost – Further Explored* (London: Methuen, 1983)

Lawrence, B., *The Administration of Education in Britain* (London: Batsford, 1972)

Lawson, J., and Silver, H., *A Social History of Education in England* (London: Methuen, 1978)

Leese, J., *Personalities and Power in English Education* (Leeds: Arnold, 1950)

Letouzey et Ané, ed., *La Congrégation des Soeurs de Sainte-Marie. Les Ordres Religieux* (Paris: Librairie Letouzey et Ané, 1925)

Lewis, J., ed., *Labour and Love: Women's Experience of Home and Family 1850–1940* (Oxford: Basil Blackwell, 1986)

Lutt, N., *Bedfordshire at Work in Old Photographs* Bedfordshire County Record Office (Alan Sutton Publishing, 1994)

Mabey, R., *Flora Britannica* (London: Sinclair-Stevenson, 1996)

Maclure, J.S., *Educational Documents England and Wales 1816 to the Present Day* (London: Methuen, 1979)

Mangan, J.A., *'Benefits Bestowed'? Education and British Imperialism* (Manchester: Manchester University Press, 1988)

Mangan, J.A., ed., *Education and Imperialism: Four Case Studies* Aspects of Education: 40 (Hull: University of Hull, 1989)

Marsden, W.E., *An Anglo-Welsh Teaching Dynasty: The Adams Family from the 1840s to the 1930s* (London: Woburn Press, 1997)

Mate's Illustrated Guide to Luton 1907 (Reprinted Chantry Press, 1986)

McCann, P., ed., *Popular Education and Socialization in the Nineteenth Century* (London: Methuen & Co. Ltd, 1977)

McIntosh, P.C., *Physical Education in England Since 1800* (London: Bell & Hyman, 1968)

McIntosh, P.C., et al., *Landmarks in the History of Physical Education* (London: RKP, 1981)

McNair, D., and Parry, N.A., ed., *Readings in the History of Physical Education* Study Group in the History of Physical Education 1 Aufl. – Ahrensburg bei Hamburg: Czwalina (Hamburg, 1981)

Memories of Luton: Memories Series. University of Luton (Elland: True North Books Ltd, 1999)

Merry, E.J., and Irven, I.D., *District Nursing* (London: Baillière, Tindall & Cox, 1960)

Miller, J., *School for Women* (London: Virago, 1996)

Mitchell, B.R., and Deane, P., *Abstract of British Historical Statistics* (C.U.P., 1962)

Morrish, I., *Education Since 1800* (London: Allen & Unwin, 1970)

Morton, A., *Education and the State from 1833* Readers' Guide No.18 (Kew: Public Record Office Publications, 1997)

New Industries Committee, Keens T., Joint Secretary to the Chamber of Commerce & Sell G., Town Clerk, *Luton as An Industrial Centre* (Borough of Luton and Luton Chamber of Commerce, 1905)

North London Collegiate School 1850–1950: A Hundred Years of Girls' Education (Oxford University Press, 1950)

North London Collegiate School, *Sophie Bryant D.Sc. Litt.D. 1850–1922* (For Private Circulation, 1922)

Peaple, C.J., *The Blockers' Seaside: A Selective History of Leagrave* (Luton: Challney Community College, 1980)

Peers, R., *Adult Education: A Comparative Study* (London: RKP, 1958)

Penn, A., *Targeting Schools: Drill, Militarism and Imperialism* (London: Woburn Press, 1999)

Pennington, S., and Westover, B., *A Hidden Workforce: Homeworkers in England 1850–1985* (Hampshire: Macmillan Education Ltd, 1989)

Pickford, C., *Bedfordshire Population Figures 1801–1891* (Bedfordshire County Record Office, 1994)

Purvis, J., *Hard Lessons: The Lives and Education of Working-Class Women in Nine-teenth-Century England* (Cambridge: Polity Press, 1989)

Purvis, J., *A History of Women's Education in England* (Milton Keynes: Open University Press, 1991)

Reader, D., ed., *Urban Education in the Nineteenth Century* (London: Taylor & Francis, 1977)

Rich, R.W., *The Training of Teachers in England & Wales during the Nineteenth Century* (Cambridge: Chivers, 1933)

Roberts, E., *New Studies in economic and Social History: Women's Work 1840–1940* (Cambridge University Press, 1988)

Rogers, K., *The Stories and Secrets of Luton's Medieval Jewel* St Mary's Parochial Church Council (Luton, 2000)

Rowntree, J.W., and Binns, H.B., *A History of the Adult School Movement* Nottingham Studies in the Theory and Practice of Education of Adults, Department of Adult Education (University of Nottingham, 1985). This is a facsimile of an earlier edition. (London: Headley Brothers, 1903)

Sadler, M.E., *Continuation Schools in England and Elsewhere* (Manchester University Press, 1908)

Salmon, D., and Hindshaw, W., *Infant Schools: Their History and Theory* (London: Longman Green & Co., 1904)

Scholes, P.A., *The Oxford Companion to Music* (Oxford University Press, 1972

Scrimgeour, R.M., ed., *The North London Collegiate School 1850–1950: A Hundred Years of Girls' Education, Essays in Honour of the Centenary of the Frances Mary Buss Foundation* (Oxford University Press, 1950)

Searby, P., ed., *Educating the Victorian Middle Class* Annual Conference of the History of Education Society (Leicester: History of Education Society, 1982)

Schmid, C. von, *The Basket of Flowers* (Blackie & Son, n.d.)

Shorney, D., *Teachers in Training 1906–1985: A History of Avery Hill College* (London: Thames Polytechnic, 1989)

Simon, B., Studies in the History of Education: *The Two Nations and the Educational Struc-ture 1780–1870* (London: Lawrence & Wishart, 1960); *Education & the Labour Move-ment 1870–1920* (London: Lawrence & Wishart, 1965); *The Politics of Educational Reform 1920–1940* (London: Lawrence & Wishart, 1978)

Smart, R., *Bedford Training College 1882–1982: A History of a Froebel College and its Schools* (Bedford College of Higher Education, 1982)

Smart, R., *On Others' Shoulders: An Illustrated History of the Polhill & Lansdowne Colleges now De Montfort University Bedford* (Bedford: De Montfort University, 1994)

Smith, F.W., *Life and Works of James Kay-Shuttleworth* (Chivers, 1974)

Spedding, R.K., *The Hill of the Lord: High Town Primitive Methodist Church 1838–1932* (Luton, 1933)

Stannard, M., *The Way to School: A History of the Schools of Leighton Buzzard and Linslade* (Leighton Buzzard: Leighton-Linslade & District Museum Project, 1990)

Stephens, W.B., *Education, Literacy and Society 1830–1870: The Geography of Diversity in Provincial England* (Manchester University Press, 1987)

Stephens, W.B., *Regional Variations in Education During the Industrial Revolution 1780–1870: The Task of the Local Historian* (University of Leeds, 1973)

Stone, D., *The National: The Story of the National Training College of Domestic Subjects* (Brighton Polytechnic Press, 1973)

Sutton, F., *A History of Caddington and Its People* (Friends of All Saints Caddington, 1994)

Taylor, J., *Joseph Lancaster and His Lancasterian Monitorial Schools* (The Friends of the Hitchin British Schools, 1998)

Taylor, J., *Joseph Lancaster: The Poor Man's Friend* (The Campanile Press, 1996)

Thompson, E.P., *The Making of the English Working Class* (Harmondsworth: Penguin, 1981)

Thompson, F., *Lark Rise to Candleford* (London: Penguin, 1988)

Tilly, L.A., and Scott, J.W., *Women, Work and Family* (New York: Holt, Rinehart and Winston, 1978)

Tropp, A., *The School Teachers* (London: Heinemann, 1957)

Tuke, M., *A History of Bedford College for Women 1849–1937* (London: Oxford University Press, 1939)

Upstairs Downstairs: Wardown House Life in a Victorian Home, An Information Pack (Luton Museum Education Service, 1999)

Victoria County History: Bedfordshire Institute of Historical Research (University of London, 1908)

Vigor, P.C., *Memories Are Made of This* (Luton Museum and Art Gallery, 1983)

Vowles, G., *A Century of Achievement: A History of Local Education Authorities in Bedfordshire 1903–2003* (Bedfordshire County Council, 2003)

Walford, G., *The Private Schooling of Girls Past and Present* (London: Woburn Press, 1993)

Walvin, J., *A Child's World: A Social History of English Childhood 1800–1914* (Harmondsworth: Penguin, 1982)

Waterfall, E.A., *The Day Continuation School in England* (London: Allen & Unwin, 1923)

Weatherley P., *A History of St George's School, Harpenden* (Harpenden: St George's School, 1982)

Webster's Biographical Dictionary (G. & C. Merriam Co., 1972)

Whitbread, H., and Zanker, K., ed., *Wyggeston Girls' Centenary 1878–1978, Leicester* Printed by Stanley L. Hunt

Who's Who in Luton (London: Pullman Press Ltd, 1959)

Widdowson, F., *Going up into the Next Class: Women and Elementary Teacher Training 1840–1914.* Women's Research and Resources Centre Publications (London, 1980)

Wightman, C., *More than Munitions: Women, Work and the Engineering Industries 1900–1950* (London: Longman, 1999)

Wildman, R., *Victorian and Edwardian Bedfordshire* (London: B.T. Batsford Ltd, 1978)

Williams, V., and White, G.J., *Adult Education and Social Purpose: A History of the WEA Eastern District 1913–1988* (WEA Eastern District, 1988)

Wood, T., and Bunker, S., *A Hatful of Talent: The Founding of the University of Luton* (University of Luton Press, 1994)

Woodward, G. and S., *The Hatfield, Luton and Dunstable Railway* (Oakwood Press, 1977)

1834 Edition of Ordnance Survey Map (First Edition) of South Bedfordshire, Central Buckinghamshire and North Hertfordshire Ordnance Survey Map Bedfordshire, 1892

Dissertations and theses

Allinson, F.J., 'The Coventry School Board 1870–1903: The First Local Education Authority' (MA Dissertation, Institute of Education, University of London, 1994)

Allsopp, A., 'The Education and Employment of Girls in Luton 1874–1924 Widening Opportunities and Lost Freedoms' (Ph.D. Thesis, Institute of Education, University of London 2001)

Allsopp, A., 'The Provision, Development and Effects of Sunday Schools in Bedfordshire 1780–1870' (MA Dissertation, Institute of Education, University of London, 1984)

Axton, C., 'Aspects of the Development of Luton 1901–1914' (Dissertation, Trent Park College, 1977)

Bruce, N., 'Gender and Class: Langley Street Girls' Elementary School, Luton 1890–1922' (MA Dissertation, Institute of Education, University of London, 1990)

Bunker, S., ' "Strawopolis" The Transformation of Luton 1840–1876' (Ph.D. Thesis, University College, London, 1991)

Currie, M.R., 'Social Policy and Public Health Measures in Bedfordshire within the National Context 1904–1938' (Ph.D. Thesis, University of Luton, 1998)

Day, J., 'The School Board of the United School District of Luton 1874–1903' (4th Year B.Ed. Dissertation, 1978)

Dony, J.G., 'History of the Straw Hat and Straw Plait Industry of Great Britain to 1914 with Special Reference to the Social Conditions of the Workers Engaged in Them' (Ph.D. Thesis, London, 1941)

Draycott, B., 'The Story of Hyde' (Dissertation, Putteridge Bury College, Luton, 1969)

Gomersall, M., 'The Elementary Education of Females in England 1800–1870 with Particular Reference to the Lives and Work of Girls and Women in Industrial Lancashire and Rural Norfolk and Suffolk' (Ph.D. Thesis, Institute of Education, University of London, 1991)

Holden, L.T., 'A History of Vauxhall Motors to 1950: Industry, Development and Local Impact on the Luton Economy' (M.Phil. Thesis, Open University, 1983)

Hunt, M.F., 'Secondary Education for the Middle Class Girl: A Study of Ideology and Educational Practice 1870–1940 with Special Reference to the Harpur Trust Girls' Schools, Bedford' (Ph.D. Thesis, Newnham College, University of Cambridge, 1984)

Moore, V.J., 'The Families of the Browns and Greens of Luton 1700–1950' (Putteridge Bury College, 1970)

O'Flynn, K.L., 'Post-primary Education in West Ham 1918–1939' (Ph.D. Thesis, Institute of Education, University of London, 1996)

Pinder, D.A., 'The Luton Hat Industry' (Ph.D. Thesis, University of Southampton, 1970)

Parish, B., 'School Attendance in Rural Bedfordshire and Luton 1870–1903' (Dissertation, Hertfordshire College of Higher Education, 1977)

Phillips, T.R., 'The National Union of Elementary Teachers 1870–1882' (M.Phil. Thesis, Institute of Education, University of London, 1991)

Sammons, L.T., 'Adult Mutual Improvement in Leighton Buzzard 1866–1904' (M.Ed. Dissertation, University of Nottingham, 1992)

St John, D., 'The Guidance and Influencing of Girls Leaving School at Fourteen. A Study in the Content, Methods and Contradictions in the Process Based on the Girls' Departments of the London County Council Maintained Elementary Schools 1904–1924' (Ph.D. Thesis, Institute of Education, University of London, 1989)

Smithies, E.D., 'The Contrast between North and South in England 1918–1939: A Study of Economic, Social and Political Problems with Particular Reference to the Experience of Burnley, Halifax, Ipswich and Luton' (Ph.D. Thesis, Leeds, 1974)

Vyse, M.G., 'Elementary Schooling and Working Class Life in Kent 1862–1902' (MA Dissertation, Institute of Education, University of London, 1989)

Unpublished printed sources

Denbigh High School, 70th Anniversary booklet (2000)

George Kent Ltd, *The George Kent Centenary 1838–1938* (Kent's 1938)

Heathfield Lower School, *Across the Green Caddington School 1885–1952* (2000)

SKF, *Inner Ring, The First Fifty Years* Special Issue (1960)

Index

Page numbers in **bold** type refer to illustrations